"After frequently trying and failing to break the bondage of addiction, too many lose hope. Soon 'failure' becomes their identity. June deals with the roots of addiction and reveals the right route to freedom."

—FRANK MINIRTH, MD
President, The Minirth Clinic
Best-selling author/coauthor of more than 80 books or booklets

"Well aware that answers for overcoming addictions aren't 'one-size-fits-all,' June lays out a multilayered solution addressing the emotional, physical and spiritual dimensions. This comprehensive, practical handbook provides hope for those struggling with *any* form of addiction."

—MARIAN C. EBERLY, MSW﹍﹍﹍﹍﹍ D/CAND
Coauthor, *Eating Disorders:* ﹍﹍﹍﹍﹍﹍ *atment*

"For those struggling with an addiction, ﹍﹍﹍﹍﹍﹍﹍﹍ ut not for June Hunt, who, for 25-plus years, h ﹍﹍﹍﹍﹍﹍ sh past their debilitating strongholds. Here is your hop﹍﹍﹍﹍﹍ help!"

—TODD M CLEMENTS, MD
Founder, The Clements Clinic
Coauthor, *Blue Genes*

"After decades of counseling men and women from all walks of life, June knows how to lead readers to truth—truth that liberates because is it truth from God. In these pages, discover the precepts of life June masterfully presents...and the freedom that follows."

—KAY ARTHUR
CEO, Precept Ministries International
Author, *When the Hurt Runs Deep—Healing and Hope for Life's Desperate Moments*

"As an Addiction Specialist, I can assure you: June knows how to speak into the stronghold of addiction...and provide God's way out. Read this landmark book for yourself or a loved one—it could save a life."

—GREGORY JANTZ, PhD
Founder, The Center for Counseling and Health Resources (aplaceofhope.com)
Author, *Turning the Tables on Gambling*

HOW TO DEFEAT HARMFUL HABITS

JUNE HUNT

HARVEST HOUSE PUBLISHERS

EUGENE, OREGON

Cover by Garborg Design Works, Savage, Minnesota

Cover photo © iStockphoto / ImagineGolf

HOW TO DEFEAT HARMFUL HABITS
Copyright © 2011 by Hope for the Heart, Inc.
Published by Harvest House Publishers
Eugene, Oregon 97402
www.harvesthousepublishers.com

Library of Congress Cataloging-in-Publication Data
    Hunt, June.
    How to defeat harmful habits / June Hunt.
        p. cm.
    Includes bibliographical references.
    ISBN 978-0-7369-2329-3 (pbk.)
    ISBN 978-0-7369-4148-8 (eBook)
    1. Habit breaking—Religious aspects—Christianity. I. Title.
    BV4598.7.H86 2011
    248.8'62—dc23

                                           2011024631

With genuine delight I dedicate this book to my dear friend and dedicated partner in ministry, Jim Cress. Initially an announcer for our teaching program, *Hope For The Heart*, Jim also began cohosting my live two-hour call-in counseling program, *Hope In The Night* on opening night, 1996. Since then he has contributed immeasurably to its success on hundreds of stations.

Jim's deep, warm voice opens our program each weeknight, welcoming listeners and inviting their calls. Because he himself is a wise, seasoned counselor, I've relied on Jim countless times to help me think past a caller's *presenting problem* to get to the *real problem*. His insights have proven invaluable—especially helping me help strugglers caught in various addictions. And no one has been more used by God to help me understand the world of *dual addictions*.

With two master's degrees, Jim adroitly addresses these issues based on his specialized training as a Certified Sexual Addiction Therapist. But he also speaks from personal experience. As you can see on pages 328-30, Jim was a struggler-turned-overcomer who had an addiction that impacted every aspect of his life. And, instead of hiding his painful past, he has been willing to share how God has taken his "mess" and turned it into a ministry!

Having made the arduous climb to *the top of the mountain*, Jim maintains a thriving, private counseling practice in Charlotte, North Carolina. (That's right—thanks to the wonders of technology, he is the call screener and cohosts the broadcast "virtually"!) He also leads intensive workshops on a bimonthly basis for men seeking freedom from sexual addiction.

Jim's personality is disarmingly fun and winsome—the perfect balance to his bright, razor-sharp intellect. (Little-known factoid you won't hear from him: Jim aced New Testament Greek in seminary—coming in at the very top of his class!) Many times during a difficult call, I've asked Jim (off mic), "What do you think?"…and sure enough, Jim's insights were just what I needed.

Jim and his talented wife, Jessica, have three children—Jonathan, Joseph, and Julianna.

⌣

So, my dear friend Jim, thank you for the many years you have stayed up with me into the wee hours, offering help, healing, and hope in the night. And because of the spiritual growth I've seen in you over the years, I also *thank you for being an authentic man of God whom I genuinely respect.*

Acknowledgments

It's easy for me to understand the exhilaration of the mountain climber pictured on the cover of this book: He has just climbed a huge *mountain*—and I have just completed a huge *manuscript*! Both feats are cause for great celebration.

I feel sure the climber didn't make his journey without the help of others going before...marking the way...blazing the trail.

Giving credit where credit is due, this book would not exist were it not for the inexhaustible efforts of my very own "trekking team"—researchers and writers, editors and proofreaders—who helped me take six of my topical biblical counseling manuals (called *Biblical Counseling Keys*) and elevate their quality until they were ready for release in the volume you now hold in your hands.

It is, therefore, with the height of gratitude that I acknowledge:

Angie White for overseeing another mountainous publishing project—from our first steps at base camp to our long climb up to the summit. Your project management skills kept us on course, moving continually upward.

Barbara Spruill, Jill Prohaska, and **Elizabeth Cunningham** for your research, writing, and editing. You took our *Keys* to new heights, adding the accounts of real strugglers to help other climbers find a "toehold" for their own arduous ascent. And...to **Carolyn White** for finding 24,000 words to cut so we could make it to the top!

Titus O'Bryant, Phillip Bleecker, Karen Williams, Bea Garner, and **Trudie Jackson** for your impeccable research and citations, your detailed editing and proofreading. Without your sure-footed accuracy, we'd have been lost in a landslide. And...to **Kelley Basatneh**, who keyed in the very last words at the very last minute, getting us to the top of the peak.

Frank Billman, Karen Billman, Jim Cress, and **Ellen Teall** for sharing your riveting testimonies. Your perseverance through personal pain proves that addiction doesn't have to be a life-sapping sentence, but can become a life-changing testimony that profoundly inspires people—like me!

Todd Clements, MD, and **Cheryl LaMastra, LPC,** The Clements Clinic; **Adam Myers, MD,** Methodist Health System; **John Boop,** Betty Ford Center; **Sharon Seagraves,** The Elisa Project; and **Shannon McGowan Markle** for your subject-matter expertise, content review, and numerous contributions. Your insights served as seasoned trail guides.

Kay Deakins for your whatever-the-need service throughout the writing of the *Biblical Counseling Keys,* upon which this book is based. For 25 years you've been my intrepid climbing partner—going before me, clearing the way, helping me scale the next slope.

Steve Miller from Harvest House for your patience and thought-filled input…your patience and gentle prompting…your patience and prevailing grace. Never unnerved by my slower-than-usual progress, you encouraged me at every turn…then applied your meticulously-honed editorial skills to ensure a super-practical travel guide for all who want and need success for their climb.

I readily acknowledge that the Lord has been my personal Guide on my journey through life…and certainly, on my ascent up this mammoth mountain. Most gratefully I say to Him, "Your Word is a lamp for my feet and a light on my path."[1] Unquestionably, He has been my security, "He makes me as surefooted as a deer, able to tread upon the heights!"[2]

Indeed, He has led our team up heights we had never planned, heights we had not thought possible—heights full of hope. So now, if you need help, if you need healing, I offer you my hand of hope. Come join us on the journey!

CONTENTS

Part 1:

WELCOME TO THE WORLD OF ADDICTIONS

WELCOME TO THE
WORLD OF ADDICTIONS

O n the surface I realize the title above sounds somewhat absurd. Normally we welcome friends into a warm, inviting home or to a delicious dinner or to a positive experience. In fact, welcomes are most always positive, almost always pleasant.

Why, then, would I welcome you to the dark world of addictions, where sorrow, suffering, and shame permeate the atmosphere? Because I *want* you here—I *need* you here! I want to deepen your understanding of this debilitating world to help free you—or someone you love—from its gravitational grip.

And so I welcome you. I want you to learn about the isolated inner world of the addicted—the devastating, self-destructive struggles that characterize every day of their lives. I also welcome you to explore what has brought help to countless millions—the "crisis interventions," the various rehabilitation programs, the Christian 12-step world of recovery, and so much more. What better way to develop a compassionate heart for strugglers?

I further welcome you to learn about the ways to connect with, pray for, and reach out to a struggler. What better way to be used by God than to help meet a struggler's needs?

If you worked for a disaster relief organization and you were assigned to a country on the opposite side of the globe, you would surely take time to learn about its people and language, its currency and customs. You would want to educate yourself so you could be of greater help to those you are about to meet. The same is true when stepping into the world of addictions. The more you *enter* into an understanding of this world, the more you can help others *exit* this world.

Uncle Billy's World

I wish you had known my Uncle Billy. He was quite bright. His teachers said he was a stellar student who could make straight As without even coming to class. He had thick brown hair, deep-set dimples, and a winsome smile. Everyone wanted to be around Uncle Billy, yet he kept his distance. He seemed to keep an impenetrable wall between himself and others.

I always felt sorry for my uncle because he was somewhat the black sheep of the family. By the time I was a teenager, he had experienced many losses because of his heavy drinking. The worst, by far, was the day he discovered his business partner had run off with all of their company's money—and with his wife.

Uncle Billy was devastated. He not only lost his work and his wife, but he also lost *control of his life*—something else had control of him. He was an alcoholic, and he literally lost his life—he died as a result of suicide. We all loved Uncle Billy, but in the end, we lost him.

I've often wondered, *What might have helped my Uncle Billy? What would have delivered him from his addiction? What would have saved him from his own self-destruction?* Like my uncle, countless others have been destroyed by debilitating addictions, leaving family and friends grappling with the haunting "if onlys": *If only I'd grasped the gravity...If only I'd learned...If only I'd understood...*

The Hope of Freedom

With addictive habits affecting so many millions who continually relapse, some wonder, *Can those who struggle with addictions be set free—permanently?* The answer is *yes!* There is genuine hope—guaranteed hope—rooted in the promises of God. He can give the supernatural help so desperately needed—not only to *be* set free, but also to *stay* free. It all begins with the admission that there is a problem. Then there must be a willingness to face the problem so healing can begin.

And for every struggler who is reading this: Remember, *you are not alone.* God is ready to provide all the strength, power, and discipline you need. According to the prophet Isaiah, He is reaching out to you, saying, "I am the LORD, your God, who takes hold of your right hand and says to you, do not fear; I will help you" (Isaiah 41:13).

Do you need His help? Do you need His strong hand to get you on the road to recovery? If so, grab hold...start now. Keep in mind that every journey begins with a single step. So start walking. And if you stumble, that's okay. Don't give up! Get back up and keep going.

You *can* leave the world of addictions. You *can* live in the world of freedom. It's not impossible! The Bible gives you this absolute assurance: "Nothing is impossible with God" (Luke 1:37).

THE INNER WORLD OF THE ADDICT:

A Tale of Two Siblings

While putting the finishing touches on this book, I asked my dear friend Karen if she would review a certain chapter. More than willing, she also suggested I contact her brother Frank because of his firsthand knowledge of addiction. During ensuing conversations, Frank expressed concern that most people who haven't grappled with addictions don't grasp their overwhelming power.

For those with addictions (I call them *strugglers*), their physical bodies have found a "new norm." For example, the alcoholic's drinking can actually *stop* the shakes, *calm* the nerves, *relieve* the hangover. It can seemingly *create confidence* when, instead, the addiction has actually created chaos. Therefore, when dealing with addictions, there's so much more to resolving them than saying, "Just say no," or "Just don't drink." For the alcoholic, the body feels "normal" *only with the next drink*!

Most nonaddicts assume recovery is a tidy process in which strugglers decide they want to quit, acknowledge their need for God, do the steps, then—presto!—healing happens. How I wish this were true...but it simply isn't. Therefore I implore nonaddicts to avoid oversimplifying the road to recovery.

I also appeal to recovering sufferers to not lose hope when you find yourself farther back on the road than you'd hoped to be. One day, consistent success is entirely possible. The Lord can literally restore your life. "Though you have made me see troubles, many and bitter, you will restore my life again; from the depths of the earth you will again bring me up. You will increase my honor and comfort me once again" (Psalm 71:20-21).

A Frank Letter from Frank

The timing couldn't have been more perfect. Two days before my manuscript was due, Frank sent me the following letter. After reading his candid, unvarnished words, I now feel *I must share his letter with you.*

Dear June,

I wish more people understood the depth of despair and desperation that addicts live with daily. It would help them understand why the recovery process is long and hard. My battle with alcoholism lasted for about 25 years and nearly consumed me.

In the early and middle stages of my addiction, I was sure that I could quit *any time I wanted.* I even had a list of "motivators" that would provide me with the desire to quit: better job, better relationship, better life, better *whatever.* Occasionally I would manage to quit or cut back my usage—for a while—just to prove to myself or to others I could do it.

The problem was, I was so unconscionably miserable when I wasn't drinking, I couldn't stand life without my "relief medicine." Then I became a *dry drunk*—I wasn't drinking, but I had done nothing to quiet the desperation inside my head. I always ended up going back to the bottle, often with an increased dosage. I just "needed it" to make the pain go away.

In the later stages, I came to admit—*I didn't want to quit* (not necessarily that I couldn't). Alcohol provided the only peace/joy/happiness/relief that I could get in life, so why would I want to give all that up? I still tried to quit or cut back occasionally because I knew my dependency was the source of my problems (but those were halfhearted attempts at best).

My addiction had become *my life.* Every waking moment was spent planning my use: *Do I have enough to make it through the night? When can I sneak the next drink? What excuse can I use today for my behavior? How can I get away so I can drink the way I want to?*

My dependence was the most desolate place imaginable. It was both the root of my problem and my answer. It was my hell and my salvation. It was my curse and my blessing. It made life intolerable and was the only thing that made life tolerable.

This place was destroying me and everyone I loved, yet I still couldn't give it up. The guilt and despair were overpowering, but the fear of having to face even one day without it kept me going back for more. I absolutely couldn't stand the thought of living one more day "under the influence," but I also couldn't bear the thought of giving up "my only solution" to the way I felt.

This was my only prayer: I begged God, "Take my obsession or take my life." Either was acceptable.

As a Christian, my relationship with God was severely diminished. My feelings toward Him ranged from anger to fear to, at best, an overwhelming sense of guilt about my lifestyle. At this point, I was pretty much unreachable through Scripture and reason.

My drinking had progressed to the point where I felt certain it had a stronger hold on me than my faith, or my God. I had spent countless mornings promising Him, "Today is the day I'll quit." And countless evenings praying for God to remove the desire or the need to drink.

I had tried and failed so many times, eventually I could get no traction to try again. I knew that, through God and with God, I had the power to quit...but deep inside I knew I could never let go. People would tell me, "God is bigger and stronger than your addiction," and I knew that was true. But those words just served to increase my guilt a hundredfold. I was awash with resentment, fear, and guilt.

The good news is...I have been sober for three years. I never could have achieved this without the help of God, family, and the recovery community. Through God, I received the grace, clarity of mind, and strength *to ask for help*.

I would encourage anyone who is battling addiction to know that a fun, sober life is possible! Seek help from family, friends, and others who have traveled the same path. Don't give up hope—a new life awaits you!

Your friend, Frank

P.S. Let me add—"I was shown mercy so that in me, the worst of sinners, Christ Jesus might display his unlimited patience as an example for those who would believe on him and receive eternal life" (1 Timothy 1:16). This is me.

The Rest of the Story

Amazing! Immediately after reading Frank's letter, I shared it with Karen—who'd had her own ten-year battle with addiction—and told her how impressed I was with his candor and insights. Still...I was curious: After decades of defeat, what finally enabled Frank to find freedom? Was there a defining moment?

That's when Karen began to share with me "the rest of the story," showing how their stories intertwined and giving a glimpse of how the Lord used two siblings at *the critical time* to touch each other's lives. These are Karen's words, from her heart.

I was raised in church with godly, nondrinking parents, but during my first semester in college, I met a guy and began running with an entirely new group of friends. A habit of drinking began and grew—from just a drink or two when we went out, to getting drunk each time I drank. The semester before graduation, this man and I broke off our relationship. At that point I began drinking daily. I stopped going to classes and started hanging out with a really rough crowd.

My grades dropped so low that I was dismissed from the university. I stayed in the college town and went through several jobs before finally moving back to my hometown. I took a job that fit my drinking lifestyle and settled into a very embarrassing, demeaning way of living. For the next eight years I was drunk every night—except two that I remember, when I was too sick to get up and go to the store.

My feelings of worthlessness and hopelessness were overwhelming. I made hundreds of promises to God to quit…and by early afternoon, all was "forgotten" and I'd begun planning my drinking for the evening. I lied to family, bosses, and myself so many times it was impossible to feel any sense of self-worth at all.

I couldn't imagine myself sober and really didn't have the energy to try. I didn't want the heartbreak of working up a desire to quit—knowing I would fail. I often prayed to die. Afterward, the sick feeling of impending doom was terrifying.

I believed I couldn't make promises to God and fail to keep them without something horrible happening. I felt something even worse than this sick, worthless, disgraceful lifestyle was on the horizon. Still, I wouldn't do what was necessary to quit.

After leaving a party one night, I became so disoriented I couldn't find my way home. A patrol car pulled me over, and I ended up in jail for driving while intoxicated. My one and only phone call that night was to Frank, who posted my bail and picked me up the following morning.

When I got home, I locked myself in my apartment for two days, trying to determine how to take my life. I felt totally defeated with a desperate desire to resign from life. I don't know why God allowed me one more day, but He did. I stayed alive, praying and crying.

I never felt any determination to change—I didn't think I could. Nevertheless, I gave up all detrimental friendships, which honestly left me with none. Nothing in my life was clean or good or healthy.

Over time I became sick of everything that was "me" and wanted nothing to do with any part of who I'd been. I needed to make new choices: I needed to *choose* to go back to church, *choose* to build healthy relationships with the right people, *choose* to walk closely with the Lord, *choose* to make binding commitments.

During my coming-back days, however, Frank was going further away into his dependency and isolation. We had little communication and even less in common. Over the years, my walk with the Lord became more and more consistent. My relationship with Him was meaningful, and my prayers for my brother were constant.

Meanwhile, Frank began losing jobs, then taking jobs far beneath his ability. Obviously he was hurting and in trouble. My heart broke for him. I knew how utterly lost and hopeless he must be feeling, and I felt I could do nothing for him—except pray.

And so I did. Using Frank's name, I prayed the Psalms. I sang praise songs, interjecting his name in them. Whatever I lifted up to the Lord had Frank all over it.

We visited often by phone, but our communication had little depth. Then I passionately began praying for a way to relate—some way *to connect*, something for us *to share*.

Frank had owned a motorcycle for as long as I can remember. (I, basically, grew up on the back of his bike.) The Lord used this love for bikes to allow us time together. While we were visiting one day, I told him I was tired of riding on the back and wanted to learn to ride for myself. He was all over this. He hooked me up with a training course and even came out to watch me the last day when I tested for my license. Afterward we went online to find the "beater bike"— meaning it will *beat you up* and you will *beat it up* learning to ride!

My big brother was incredibly patient (for Frank), teaching me how to ride—first in parking lots and then on the streets. But the most fun was shopping for the *real* bike—the pretty one you don't intend to "lay down." He found the perfect one, I wrote the check, and most weekends we would ride together. It was fabulous!

At the end of one ride, he asked me to come inside his place. He seemed in total despair, beyond hope. His eyes looked dead, lifeless. He sat behind his desk, holding a sheet of paper. As he began reading, tears started flowing down his cheeks—I couldn't believe it! He was reading a plea for help—*asking me* to find him a place to get sober.

My heart nearly broke seeing him like this, but, at the same time, I was thrilled this was actually happening. I may not know much, but this I know: When strugglers ask for help, *jump—move!* Go full throttle and get them the help they know they need!

Today Frank's walk and ministry are amazing, and he is deeply dependent on the Lord. Truly, I could never have imagined him living the life he now lives. Be assured, my experience of addiction and my brother's are real-life stories of victory—victory made possible only through the grace of God and the unfailing love of Christ.

Karen

The Best of the Story

Words are totally inadequate for expressing the admiration I have for this brother-sister "dynamic duo" and how they are allowing God to use their lives to help others. Today, Karen is a gifted, licensed counselor who supervises social workers and counselors in seven children's homes throughout Texas, and her work extends to "at-risk" families. Because of this, when Frank made his plea for help, she immediately knew where to turn to find help (and she knows she was a part of God's plan for helping Frank).

Likewise, Frank has a huge heart for helping others to walk in victory. He works as a recovery pastor and 12-step sponsor, where he has many opportunities to come alongside those who are struggling with addictions.

My desire is that Frank and Karen's candor will help put a face on the desolation, the distortion, the disillusion of addicted strugglers—of those living in this painful world. I believe this previously untold "tale of two siblings" offers hope to the heart of any struggler caught in the web of addiction. As I think about these two special friends, I actually "see them" in this wonderful Scripture passage:

> *"If one of you [Frank] should wander from the truth*
> *and someone [Karen] should bring him back, remember this:*
> *Whoever turns a sinner from the error of his way will save*
> *him from death and cover over a multitude of sins"*
> (JAMES 5:19-20).

THE WORLD OF HABITS AND ADDICTIONS
Success in Self-control

THE WORLD OF
HABITS AND ADDICTIONS:
Success in Self-control

T he thrill of victory…and the agony of defeat!"[1] This is the universal experience of the athlete—the heart-racing thrill of finishing first, the gut-wrenching
angst of finishing last. But before athletes can even enter competition, they must
first train the mind…tighten the muscles…toughen the body.

However, even athletes—considered models of self-control—can allow
harmful habits to slip into their lives and sabotage their valiant efforts for victory. Self-control must not only be mastered, but also sustained. And as it is with
athletes, so it is with us: If we are going to win in the game of life, we must have
strict discipline. The apostle Paul made that point clear:

> *"Everyone who competes in the games*
> *goes into strict training"*
> (1 CORINTHIANS 9:25).

I. DEFINITIONS OF HABITS AND ADDICTIONS

Have you ever watched athletes competing in the Olympics and thought
almost in disbelief, *How on earth can they do that? It seems impossible!* Whether
it's a figure skater performing a leap with four 360-degree revolutions or a gym-
nast doing a series of backflips atop a narrow balance beam, one after another, we
ask with amazement, "How is that possible?"

The answer isn't rocket science. It's practice, practice, practice. Developing
the habit of doing a simple half turn again and again and again until it feels natural, until it can be done, in essence, without thinking.

Consider, for example, the biathlon. (In Greek, *bi* means "two" and *athlon*
means "contest.")[2] It's a curious combination of events—cross-country skiing

and rifle sharpshooting. One is aerobic, requiring speed, strength, and stamina. The other is stationary, requiring stillness, sight, and steady hands. These carefully honed skills developed by the Scandinavians in hunting and winter warfare led to the inauguration of this skiing/shooting sport in the 1960 Winter Olympics.

Training for the biathlon can be treacherous, particularly because of the hazardous effects of staying outdoors in continuously cold weather. Therefore, specialized physical conditioning is absolutely mandatory. A 31-year-old policeman from Norway developed highly productive habits to prepare himself for the 1968 Winter Olympics. And his disciplined fitness regimen got the world's attention.

Those who tenaciously train in this way can identify with these figurative words spoken by the apostle Paul:

> *"I beat my body and make it my slave"*
> (1 CORINTHIANS 9:27).

A. What Are Habits and Addictions?

He was a dark horse on the glistening white snow...

Magnar Solberg was far from being a favorite to win a medal at the Olympics in Grenoble, France. In fact, he wasn't even considered a serious competitor in the winter biathlon.[3] But he developed all the necessary habits that would enable him to train and qualify for the event—habits that included building leg and upper body strength, exercising in high-altitude environments, and sharpening precision skills in shooting.

But there was one habit that set Solberg apart from all the other skiers and shooters, and this particular exercise was conducted in blistering heat rather than blustery cold. Whether training for an athletic event or facing any other major challenge that requires us to shed old habits and adopt new ones, these words are most appropriate: "Let us discern for ourselves what is right; let us learn together what is good" (Job 34:4).

- **Habits** are learned patterns of behavior or attitudes repeated so often they become typical of a person. In the New Testament, the Greek word *manthano* means "to learn" (in any way) or to "get into the habit."[4]

> *"Our people must learn to devote*
> *themselves to doing what is good"*
> (TITUS 3:14).

— **Habits** are based on thinking, and reflect the heart. The Greek word *hodos*, meaning a "natural path or way," is used metaphorically in Scripture to mean "a course of conduct or way of thinking."[5] "Their hearts are always going astray, and they have not known my ways" (Hebrews 3:10).

— **Habits**, when based on trusting God, result in being consistently on the right path. The Hebrew word *derek*, usually translated as "way" or "road," means "habit or habitual way of behavior."[6] "Trust in the LORD with all your heart and lean not on your own understanding; in all your ways acknowledge him, and he will make your paths straight" (Proverbs 3:5-6).

• **Addictions** are a compulsive, enslaving dependence on something, resulting in detrimental patterns of thinking and behaving. There are *substance addictions* (e.g., alcohol, tobacco, heroin, inhalants) and *process addictions* (e.g., gambling, eating, shopping, sex).

> *"A man is a slave to whatever has mastered him"*
> (2 PETER 2:19).

— **Addictive habits**, when based on deceitful desires, result in a corrupt way of life. The Greek noun *anastrophe*, usually translated "life" or "way of life," means "one's conduct or behavior."[7] "You were taught, with regard to your former way of life, to put off your old self, which is being corrupted by its deceitful desires" (Ephesians 4:22).

— **Dual** or **poly addiction** refers to dependence on two or more addictions at the same time. The Greek word *poly*, translated "many," when used with addictions, means being dependent on multiple behaviors or substances. "God gave them over in the sinful desires of their hearts to sexual impurity...to shameful lusts...to a depraved mind, to do what ought not to be done" (Romans 1:24,26,28).

Typically strugglers have multiple addictions because one addictive "high" firing in the brain makes them highly susceptible to another addiction. Each addiction impacts the brain, training it to want the same chemical effect again and again. For example, when sexually acting out, dopamine (the "feel good" chemical) is released in the brain, then soon after, the body craves more. Both alcohol and crack cocaine can increase dopamine release. When the high of one addiction begins wearing off, the high of another replaces the craved chemical effect in the brain.

The rationale is often this: *If one addiction feels good, two will feel better. If two are better, three will feel great. Do anything to keep the highs coming!* Thus goes the logic of those who have given control of themselves to mood-altering addictions.

> *"They have become filled with every kind of wickedness,*
> *evil, greed and depravity…they invent ways of doing*
> *evil…they are senseless, faithless, heartless, ruthless"*
> (ROMANS 1:29-31).

B. What Is the Progression from Inclination…to Habit…to Addiction?

Solberg's coach for the biathlon used a bizarre training technique to prepare his student. In Solberg's own words: "On purpose, my coach placed the shooting stand right in the middle of an anthill. When I shot from this stand on hot summer days, my legs were immediately covered with ants. This was very disturbing, especially when they reached my face."[8]

Solberg's coach wasn't trying to *torture* the initially befuddled biathlete; he was trying to *toughen* him. He reasoned that if Solberg could learn to shoot precisely with hundreds of ants crawling all over him, "distractions" would be the least of their worries during the Olympic sharpshooting event.

And if we need to cultivate a new habit in life, we too are called to not be distracted: "Let us fix our eyes on Jesus, the author and perfecter of our faith" (Hebrews 12:2).

The natural inclination of the average person lying in an anthill would be to quickly get up and feverishly brush off the tiny, troublesome insects. But Solberg overcame this inclination, first in his mind and then in his behavior. He ignored the sting and focused on the target. He trained his mind to check his natural inclination so he might develop the habit of mentally blocking anything that might distract him from his goal.

An unchecked natural inclination generally follows this progression:

- **Inclination**—A natural desire that compels a person to act a certain way under a given set of circumstances. The Bible says everyone comes into this world with the natural inclination to sin.

> *"Even from birth the wicked go astray; from the*
> *womb they are wayward and speak lies"*
> (PSALM 58:3).

- **Impulse**—A sudden, spontaneous inclination to act impetuously[9]

  "Do not be quick with your mouth, do not be hasty in your heart"
  (ECCLESIASTES 5:2).

- **Habit**—A pattern of behavior acquired by frequent repetition[10]

  "They would not listen, however,
  but persisted in their former practices [habits]"
  (2 KINGS 17:40).

- **Obsession**—A persistent, disturbing preoccupation with an unreasonable idea[11]

  "In my obsession against them [Christians],
  I [Paul] even went to foreign cities to persecute them"
  (ACTS 26:11).

- **Compulsion**—An irresistible, irrational impulse to act against one's own will[12]

  "The man who has settled the matter in his own mind,
  who is under no compulsion but has control over his own will…
  this man also does the right thing"
  (1 CORINTHIANS 7:37).

- **Addiction**—A compulsive, overpowering dependence on an object, an action, or a feeling, resulting in major life problems[13]

  "Teach the older women to be reverent in the way they live,
  not to be slanderers or addicted to much
  wine, but to teach what is good"
  (TITUS 2:3).

C. What Is God's Heart on Habits?

With their eye on the gold medal, winter biathletes like Magnar Solberg cover a predetermined distance on skis, carrying bolt-action .22 rifles with nonoptical sights. Then they stop at a target range and lie down in the prone position while firing five shots. Shots that miss the target are penalized by adding time to an athlete's overall performance or by adding extra ski laps. The skiers then race around another lap and return to the range to shoot five more rounds, this time standing up. The pattern is then repeated, depending on the format of the race and whether the competition is for individuals or a team.

Obviously, those who have disciplined habits that enable them to sharpen their skills are more likely to win. The apostle Paul, who frequently used sports analogies, says this about believers who go into strict training:

> *"They do it to get a crown that will not last;*
> *but we do it to get a crown that will last forever"*
> (1 CORINTHIANS 9:25).

Now, habits can be like seesaws—they can either push you up or pull you down. To determine the degree to which your habits are good or bad, helpful or harmful, look at Scripture and see what conclusions you come to.

GOD'S HEART ON HABITS

- **Habits can be beneficial** and profitable.

> *"Blessed are those who keep my ways"*
> (PROVERBS 8:32).

- **Habits can be evil** and destructive.

> *"They get into the habit of being idle and going about from*
> *house to house. And not only do they become idlers, but also*
> *gossips and busybodies, saying things they ought not to"*
> (1 TIMOTHY 5:13).

- **Habits can be passed down** from generation to generation.

> *"The LORD was with Jehoshaphat because in his early years*
> *he walked in the ways his father David had followed"*
> (2 CHRONICLES 17:3).

- **Habits can reflect devotion** to God and God's character.

> *"His heart was devoted to the ways of the LORD;*
> *furthermore, he removed the high places*
> *and the Asherah poles from Judah"*
> (2 CHRONICLES 17:6).

- **Habits can increase consistency** and strengthen character.

  "The righteous will hold to their ways,
  and those with clean hands will grow stronger"
  (Job 17:9).

- **Habits are a choice**, a function of the will, but they can also be influenced by the emotions.

  "What you decide on will be done, and light will shine on your ways"
  (Job 22:28).

- **Habits can lead hearts astray** and hurt the cause of Christ.

  "Many will follow their shameful ways and will
  bring the way of truth into disrepute"
  (2 Peter 2:2).

- **Habits can be overcome through Christ.**

  "You, dear children, are from God and have overcome them,
  because the one [Jesus] who is in you is greater
  than the one [Satan] who is in the world"
  (1 John 4:4).

- **Habits can be a positive witness to others.**

  "Let your light shine before men, that they may see your
  good deeds and praise your Father in heaven"
  (Matthew 5:16).

D. What Are the Signs that a Habit Has Become an Addiction?

Although Magnar Solberg's practice of standing in an anthill while shooting initially appeared to be a *destructive* habit, it ultimately proved to be a *constructive* habit. At the Grenoble Olympics, the Norwegian hit all 20 targets in his event and his stringent training habits paid off with a gold medal. He competed again four years later at the Olympics in Sapporo, Japan, and at age 35, won another gold medal.

Solberg made a place for himself in the record books as the only Olympic biathlete to defend and keep his title in an individual event. And he's the oldest athlete to win a gold medal in an individual event at the winter Olympics.[14]

Typically, those who train and exercise regularly receive compliments and admiration. But what about those who overtrain, overexercise? What about those struggling with anorexia athletica or those who are obsessed with their body shape? Their training has gone from being a positive productive habit to a compulsive addiction. They are controlled not by God, but by their addiction. The Bible says, "Physical training is of some value, but godliness has value for all things, holding promise for both the present life and the life to come" (1 Timothy 4:8).

And what about you? Is it possible that you have developed an addiction in some area? If you suspect so, ask yourself these six questions:

- ☐ "Have I stopped the habit in the past, only to consistently relapse?"
- ☐ "Have I become abnormally preoccupied with the habit?"
- ☐ "Have I continued the habit in spite of suffering negative consequences?"
- ☐ "Have I engaged in the habit more and more often over time in order to achieve the same mood-altering experience I had in the beginning?"
- ☐ "Have I practiced this habit primarily because it changes my mood or comforts me?"
- ☐ "Have I persisted in this habit even though it is harmful to me?"

If the answer to any one of these questions is *yes*, you are on the way to forming an addiction. If the answer to all of them is *yes,* you are already wrapped up in the web of addiction and are powerless to free yourself. Your only recourse is to seek help in order to regain control of your life. When you do so, you can walk in the freedom Christ died to provide for you.

> *"You see, at just the right time, when we were still powerless,*
> *Christ died for the ungodly"*
> (ROMANS 5:6).

II. CHARACTERISTICS OF HABITS AND ADDICTIONS

"Lazy"…complacent…settle for mediocrity…"last guy in the building [for practic, team meetings, and games]…first guy out."[15]

You'd hardly expect an athlete with these self-described habits to succeed in a game of flag football, much less catapult to the pinnacle of the National Football League. But Michael Vick's career has been full of sad surprises.

Endowed with spectacular innate athleticism, Vick discovered as a boy—playing pick-up football in the gang-infested housing projects of Newport News, Virginia—that athletic achievement came easy for him. Sadly, so did a later life of habitual bad choices, moral shortcuts, and eventually, serious crime.

But the shocking truth about Vick's character was carefully concealed from his fans. During his ensuing glory years, the NFL's number one draft pick in 2001 earned a reputation as the most electrifying player in professional sports. And he became one of the highest paid, with a record $130 million contract.[16] As quarterback of the Atlanta Falcons, Vick led his team to the playoffs twice, ranking second among quarterbacks of all time in career rushing yards.[17]

Vick's meteoric rise to stardom led him to believe he could live life on his own terms—immune from the baggage of bad habits and destructive choices, and unwilling to embrace the biblical instruction to

> *"be very careful, then, how you live—not as unwise but as wise,*
> *making the most of every opportunity, because the days are evil"*
> (EPHESIANS 5:15-16).

A. What Is Characteristic of All Habits?

In 2007, the hidden habits of Michael Vick exploded into public view. A police raid on Vick's Bad Newz Kennels in rural Virginia turned up gruesome evidence of a savage dog-fighting operation. Investigators alleged that for six years, Vick and friends from his childhood bought, bred, and sold pit bulls, which fought to the death in kennel matches with gambling purses as high as $26,000.[18]

Ghastly reports of barbaric cruelty began to emerge. Dogs that lost fights or didn't perform well had been tortured mercilessly—beaten, shot, drowned, electrocuted. International media pounced on the news with the ferocity of Vick's own vicious pit bulls. The public outcry was deafening, the revulsion palpable.

In truth, pit bulls simply behave as they are trained. They develop learned behaviors and, consequently, can become brutal killers, or beloved pets, or brilliant service dogs for law enforcement, search and rescue teams, and therapy.[19] In the same way, a habit is a *learned behavior* that becomes a powerful force in your life, whether for good or bad, for virtue or vice. And, in the end, all wrong habits—whether perceived as good or bad—lead to death.

> *"There is a way that seems right to a man,*
> *but in the end it leads to death"*
> (PROVERBS 16:25).

ALL HABITS ARE...

H HABITUAL—They occur with regularity.

A AUTOMATIC—They happen without thinking.

B BEHAVIORAL—They outwardly reflect inner morals and character.

I INTENSE—They grow stronger and more ingrained with repetition.

T TENACIOUS—They persist and become hard to change over time.

S SATISFYING—They are purposeful and provide a degree of pleasure.

Your habits reflect your heart and communicate your devotion either to God or to the things of this world.

> *"No servant can serve two masters.*
> *Either he will hate the one and love the other,*
> *or he will be devoted to the one and despise the other"*
> (LUKE 16:13).

B. What Constitutes Four Categories of Habits?

Upon being indicted by a federal grand jury for dogfighting and other charges, Michael Vick's impulse was to...lie. Habitually. He lied to the media, the public, teammates, team owners, and eventually to a federal grand jury and judge.[20] Especially heartbroken by the immense betrayal was Atlanta Falcons' owner Arthur Blank, who had "bet the future of the franchise on the young quarterback, awarding him the largest contract in the history of the NFL...and stood by him as the charges piled up and Vick fell from grace."[21]

Still, Vick had no intention of halting his harmful habits, daringly defiant of the lifelong consequence that lay in wait. Michael was like those described in Romans 1:21:

> *"Although they knew God, they neither glorified him as*
> *God nor gave thanks to him, but their thinking became*
> *futile and their foolish hearts were darkened."*

Scripture uses words like "strongholds," "slavery," and "bondage" to paint a picture of being a prisoner to sin. Although you may not be enslaved to the more visible vices (e.g., drunkenness, gambling, or gluttony), you may be held captive to a seemingly "acceptable activity." Even behavior that appears "good," such as volunteer work, can be wrongly motivated and overindulged to the degree that it goes beyond God's will and thus becomes sin.

No behavior, whether viewed as harmless or helpful, is to have mastery over us. If it does, then it has enslaved us. The Bible clearly states, "A man is a slave to whatever has mastered him" (2 Peter 2:19).

Harmless Habits

Some habits are common to many but cause injury to none. They are at best innocuous and at worst irritants (e.g., nail biting and hair twirling, cracking knuckles and popping gum, belching and bellowing). The Bible offers this insight: "A fool shows his annoyance at once, but a prudent man overlooks an insult" (Proverbs 12:16).

Heart Habits

The heart that is not right in God's sight produces wrong attitudes and emotions that result in ungodly "heart habits" (e.g., envy and jealousy, prejudice and pride, ungratefulness and unforgiveness). The Bible directly states this truth: "Out of the heart come evil thoughts" (Matthew 15:19; see Jeremiah 17:9).

Hidden Habits

Some habitual actions are often not recognized as harmful addictions because they are not recognized as being habitual or regarded as being negative. They are viewed as "good behaviors" done to excess, which turns them into "bad" behaviors and "hidden habits" (e.g., *excessively* helping and rescuing others, working and cleaning, apologizing and procrastinating, shopping and spending). The Bible cautions against such excess: "The man who fears God will avoid all extremes" (Ecclesiastes 7:18).

Hard Habits/Addictions

Destructive habits create a damaging climate for everyone, making them "hard habits" (e.g., verbal and emotional abuse, drunkenness and divisiveness, vulgarity and violence, stealing). The Bible explains, "There is a way that seems right to a man, but in the end it leads to death" (Proverbs 14:12; see also Galatians 5:19-21).

Imelda—Compulsive Spending and Her Shoes, Shoes, and More Shoes

It was a compulsive shopping spree that lasted 20 years, and millions of Filipino people believe they footed the tab.

At the side of the corrupt President Ferdinand Marcos, his wife, Imelda Marcos, believed she was "a symbol of pride of the Philippines" and that her impoverished people expected her to wear expensive jewelry, clothing, and shoes—*lots* of shoes.[22] The photos released in the late 1980s stunned the world—Imelda posing beside her shoe collection, a casual "Exhibit A" that supported allegations of gross corruption. The grand total tallied…2,700 pairs of shoes!

That's when the calculations began: If Imelda wore a different pair of shoes every day, it would take over seven years to "see her store" of shoes. And if she changed shoes three times a day and never wore the same pair twice, it would take almost two-and-a-half years for her to stroll through her colossal collection. And because of her compulsive spending, Imelda most assuredly would continue to make many more additional purchases. Obviously, hundreds, if not thousands, of shoes would have never actually been worn.[23]

Following the ouster and exile of Ferdinand Marcos in 1986, subsequent Filipino governments accused the notorious pair of stealing $10 billion.[24] These governments tried to recover their losses, but to little avail. Despite hundreds upon hundreds of lawsuits and court cases, neither Ferdinand nor Imelda ever saw prison time. Ferdinand died in exile in Hawaii in 1989. Imelda—nicknamed the "Iron Butterfly"—was indicted and convicted, but her cases were either overturned or dismissed due to technicalities.

The alleged $10 billion theft by Ferdinand and Imelda bought a lot more than just shoes: two palaces, dozens of country homes, private and commercial real estate in New York, crates of gold and pesos, and plenty of reserves in bank accounts around the world. In 1978 at a price tag of $10 million, Imelda began building the Coconut Palace, a presidential guesthouse on Manila Bay that was constructed with chemically treated coconut lumber. All elements of the coconut tree were used to create the tropical palace, which was completed in 1981.

Imelda had hoped her first guest would be Pope John Paul II, for whom the Coconut Palace was actually commissioned. But the pope declined. Given the backdrop of a poverty-stricken nation, he perceived the idea of such a stay as ostentatious.[25]

The spending habits of both Ferdinand and Imelda Marcos stand in stark contrast to the life of Christ and couldn't be more contrary to the call of Scripture. Instead of compulsive buying, Jesus says, "Sell your possessions and give to the poor. Provide purses for yourselves that will not wear out, a treasure in heaven that will not be exhausted, where no thief comes near and no moth destroys. For where your treasure is, there your heart will be also" (Luke 12:33-34).

C. What Characterizes Those Controlled by Addictions?

Alone in prison, Michael Vick began considering the vast weight of his wrongdoings…and the gracious God of his youth. He contemplated his high school years, when he'd given his life to Christ and first begun reading the Bible. Finally, his future became clear: "The only thing I could do in prison was fall back on God," he said. "I wanted to do things right."[26]

As Vick yielded to Christ, his life began a remarkable transformation. Tony Dungy, retired coach of the Indianapolis Colts, began mentoring the imprisoned athlete. After his release, Vick began working with The Humane Society, traveling the country, speaking at churches, schools, and community events, imploring would-be dog fighters and gamblers to shun the gruesome sport that ravaged his life.

In 2009, Vick was reinstated into the NFL and went on to play for the Philadelphia Eagles. The following year, he became the Eagles' starting quarterback. In 2010, he played in his fourth career Pro Bowl, was named the Associated Press Comeback Player of the Year, and received the prestigious Ed Block Courage Award for steadfast commitment to sportsmanship and courage.[27]

Bad choices replaced by good ones led Vick to finally achieve what God had in mind for him all along—a yielded life—a life not controlled by addictive behaviors but by God. Certain characteristics are common among those who, like Vick, repeatedly practice addictive behaviors. These characteristics become so automatic that those who have them are often oblivious to their destructive damage.

Those controlled by addictive habits…[28]

- **Become mastered by multiple bad habits**

    Even though the Bible says, "'Everything is permissible for me'—but not everything is beneficial. 'Everything is permissible for me'—but I will not be mastered by anything" (1 Corinthians 6:12).

- **Don't obey the law or those in authority**

    Even though the Bible says, "Everyone must submit himself to the governing authorities" (Romans 13:1).

- **Think their addictions resolve their problems and give them peace**

    Even though the Bible says, "If only you had paid attention to my commands, your peace would have been like a river" (Isaiah 48:18).

- **Don't keep their bodies pure or treat them with respect**

    Even though the Bible says, "Let us purify ourselves from everything that contaminates body and spirit" (2 Corinthians 7:1).

- **Do not practice self-denial, self-discipline, or self-control**

    Even though the Bible says, "The grace of God that brings salvation has appeared to all men. It teaches us to say 'No' to ungodliness and worldly passions, and to live self-controlled, upright and godly lives in this present age" (Titus 2:11-12).

D. What Is a Harmful Habit Checklist?

During the course of Michael Vick's fall from football fame—and his reinstatement to the game—he lost many of his previous fans, but then gained many new ones. Still others remain in a wait-and-see mode, skeptical that his conversion may be one merely of convenience. Neither fans, detractors, nor skeptics, however, are nearly as important to Vick as the peace he says he has made with his Lord. "The main thing is, I don't want to disappoint God."[29]

Though the details of your life will differ from Michael Vick's, like him, most of us become adept at justifying our negative habits. So proficient are we at rationalizing that undesirable habits can remain hidden—even from ourselves!

So, consider this probing question: Is there a habit that has mastery over you? According to God's Word, "Sin shall not be your master, because you are not under law, but under grace" (Romans 6:14).

How can you know whether you have a destructive habit or a hidden addiction controlling you?

Desire to be accountable before God and take an honest look at your thoughts and actions. Ask yourself whether you have any habits or desires that would cause you to answer *yes* to the following questions:

THE HARMFUL HABIT CHECKLIST

- ☐ "Are my thoughts consumed with it?"
- ☐ "Is my time scheduled around it?"

- ☐ "Could my health be harmed by it?"
- ☐ "Does my guilt increase because of it?"
- ☐ "Are my finances affected by it?"
- ☐ "Am I defensive when asked about it?"
- ☐ "Are my relationships hurt by it?"
- ☐ "Am I upset when I can't do it?"
- ☐ "Is my spiritual growth hindered by it?"
- ☐ "Have I been asked to stop it?"
- ☐ "Would I discourage my children from doing it?"
- ☐ "Do I hide it from others?"
- ☐ "Would Jesus avoid doing it?"
- ☐ "Does it diminish my witness for Christ?"

Let David's prayer be your own personal prayer:

> *"Search me, O God, and know my heart;*
> *test me and know my anxious thoughts.*
> *See if there is any offensive way in me,*
> *and lead me in the way everlasting"*
> (PSALM 139:23-24).

III. Causes of Destructive Habits

At the 2000 Olympics in Sydney, Australia, Marion Jones won three gold medals in the 100-meter, 200-meter, and 1600-meter relay, as well as two bronze medals in the long jump and 400-meter relay. Her strong, athletic build and speed, along with her sweet smile, charmed the world and challenged young women to pursue their Olympic dreams.

But seven years later, those medallions of achievement no longer hung from the track and field queen's neck. They were taken away by the International Olympic Committee, leading to Jones' painful admission: "Making the wrong choices and bad decisions can be disastrous."[30]

> *"No discipline seems pleasant at the time, but painful.*
> *Later on, however, it produces a harvest of righteousness*
> *and peace for those who have been trained by it"*
> (HEBREWS 12:11).

From September 2000 to July 2001, Marion Jones trained more intensely than ever and had improved her running times and recovery periods. But the peak performances weren't due to modifications in diet and exercise. Jones had gotten swallowed up in the performance-enhancing promises of steroids, and they were paying off.

Her former coach originally told her he was giving her flaxseed oil, but she later realized it was an illegal substance, something Jones emphatically denied publicly for years. In 2004 she made the following statement: "I have never, ever used performance-enhancing drugs."[31] However, misguided choices marred her reputation.

> *"If anyone competes as an athlete, he does not receive the*
> *victor's crown unless he competes according to the rules"*
> (2 Timothy 2:5).

A. What Are Misplaced Dependencies?

Marion Jones' misplaced dependency on performance-enhancing drugs led to catastrophic consequences for her. The need to excel, to maintain an edge over her competitors, to retain her five Olympic medals drove Jones not only to lie to the public for years about her habitual steroid use but also to federal investigators. In 2008 she served a six-month federal prison sentence for those lies as well as for her involvement in a check fraud scam.[32] The Bible says, "There are six things the LORD hates, seven that are detestable to him: haughty eyes, a lying tongue, hands that shed innocent blood, a heart that devises wicked schemes, feet that are quick to rush into evil, a false witness who pours out lies and a man who stirs up dissension among brothers" (Proverbs 6:16-19).

The deepest longing of the human heart is to have intimacy with God through a loving, personal relationship with Him. God created each of us with this desire to seek Him. He knows He alone can fulfill us, and anything less will ultimately fail us! Everything and everyone except God is subject to death or decay, destruction or dissipation.

> *"You, O LORD, sit enthroned forever;*
> *your renown endures through all generations...*
> *In the beginning you laid the foundations of the earth,*
> *and the heavens are the work of your hands.*
> *They will perish, but you remain;*
> *they will all wear out like a garment.*
> *Like clothing you will change them and they will be discarded.*
> *But you remain the same, and your years will never end"*
> (Psalm 102:12,25-27).

Uncontrolled habits often represent our own attempt to meet our God-given inner needs for love, significance, and security through unhealthy dependencies on people, things, or activities.[33]

As you examine your habits, give honest answers to the following questions:

- **Are you seeking to meet your inner need** for unconditional love through sensual pleasure?

  - Sexual activity
  - Pornography
  - Drug use
  - Overeating

The Bible says,

> *"Among you there must not be even a hint of sexual immorality,
> or of any kind of impurity...Nor should there
> be obscenity, foolish talk or coarse joking, which
> are out of place, but rather thanksgiving"*
> (EPHESIANS 5:3-4).

God created you to have a loving, personal relationship with Him:

> *"The LORD appeared to us in the past, saying: 'I have loved you
> with an everlasting love; I have drawn you with loving-kindness'"*
> (JEREMIAH 31:3).

- **Are you seeking to meet your inner need** for significance through achievement?

  - Performance
  - Popularity
  - Position
  - Power

The Bible says,

> *"Whatever you do, whether in word or deed,
> do it all in the name of the Lord Jesus, giving
> thanks to God the Father through him"*
> (COLOSSIANS 3:17).

God created you to find your significance in His relationship with you:

> *"'For I know the plans I have for you,' declares
> the LORD, 'plans to prosper you and not to harm
> you, plans to give you hope and a future'"*
> (JEREMIAH 29:11).

- **Are you seeking to meet your inner need** for security through acquisitions?
  - Possessions
  - Property
  - Money
  - People

The Bible says,

> *"He who fears the LORD has a secure fortress,*
> *and for his children it will be a refuge"*
> (PROVERBS 14:26).

God created you to be secure in His relationship with you:

> *"You also were included in Christ when you heard the word of*
> *truth, the gospel of your salvation. Having believed, you were*
> *marked in him with a seal, the promised Holy Spirit, who is*
> *a deposit guaranteeing our inheritance until the redemption*
> *of those who are God's possession—to the praise of his glory"*
> (EPHESIANS 1:13-14).

Unfortunately, many of our efforts to meet these three inner needs have little or no connection to the provisions and promises of God. If you have developed behavioral patterns that make you *dependent* on anything or anyone other than your heavenly Father, you can find freedom by *seeking Him* now!

> *"'You will seek me*
> *and find me when you seek me with all your heart.*
> *I will be found by you,' declares the LORD,*
> *'and will bring you back from captivity'"*
> (JEREMIAH 29:13-14).

B. What Is Negative Self-talk?

Before the sober-faced judge, Marion Jones called herself what she believed was her new identity: *a liar and a cheat.* But what she felt she had become didn't have to be permanent. Change is always possible; forgiveness is always available. Following her court appearance, Marion read,

> It's with a great amount of shame that I stand before you and tell you that I have betrayed your trust. I have been dishonest and you have the right to be angry with me. I have let them [her family] down, I have let my country down, and I have let myself down. I recognize

that by saying I'm deeply sorry, it might not be enough and sufficient to address the pain and hurt that I've caused you. Therefore, I
want to ask for your forgiveness for my actions, and I hope you can
find it in your heart to forgive me.[34]

What "music" to God's ears!

> *"The sacrifices of God are a broken spirit; a broken*
> *and contrite heart, O God, you will not despise"*
> (PSALM 51:17).

As happened with Marion Jones, behavior springs from beliefs, and what you
tell yourself greatly influences your actions. If you are struggling with trying to
overcome a bad habit but having little success, it may be that you are entertain-
ing self-defeating thoughts. You need to be aware that

> *"the word of God is living and active.*
> *Sharper than any double-edged sword,*
> *it penetrates even to dividing soul and spirit, joints and marrow;*
> *it judges the thoughts and attitudes of the heart"*
> (HEBREWS 4:12).

Check the list of wrong beliefs below to see whether your thoughts are helping or hurting your efforts to rid yourself of an un-Christlike habit.

- ☐ "I cannot control this habit. It's simply too strong for me."
- ☐ "It shouldn't be this difficult to change; something must be wrong with me."
- ☐ "I don't have what it takes to overcome this habit."
- ☐ "It's unfair that I have to deny myself the enjoyment of this activity."
- ☐ "My desires are too strong for me to ever deny them."
- ☐ "I can't stand going without the pleasure this habit gives me."
- ☐ "I'm not worth all this trouble, effort, and pain anyway, so why try to change?"
- ☐ "God knows I am too weak to overcome this habit."
- ☐ "I'm just a loser anyway."
- ☐ "God won't help someone like me."

☐ "I've been doing this far too long to try to change now."

☐ "This has just become a part of who I am."

Self-defeating habits will continue to keep you in bondage if you fail to change your faulty thinking:

> *"Stop thinking like children.*
> *In regard to evil be infants, but in your thinking be adults"*
> (1 CORINTHIANS 14:20).

C. What Excuses Keep You Hooked?

Steroids seemingly surrounded Marion Jones. *Everybody else seemed to be doing it...*

Marion's ex-husband, C.J. Hunter, was busted for using performance-enhancing drugs. Tim Montgomery, the father of her son, was stripped of his world record in the 100 meters. But she ultimately realized that there were no excuses to be made. "I am responsible fully for my actions. I have no one to blame but myself for what I've done."[35] Her words reflect what is said in God's Word:

> *"Since we are surrounded by such a great cloud of witnesses,*
> *let us throw off everything that hinders and the sin that so easily*
> *entangles, and let us run with perseverance the race marked out*
> *for us. Let us fix our eyes on Jesus, the author and perfecter of our*
> *faith, who for the joy set before him endured the cross, scorning*
> *its shame, and sat down at the right hand of the throne of God"*
> (HEBREWS 12:1-2).

Just as behavior comes from beliefs, so do the excuses we make to justify our behavior, habits, and addictions. It logically follows that the lies we believe also generate the excuses we give for not breaking bad behaviors.

WHAT EXCUSES ARE YOU GIVING?

☐ "This makes me feel better; and besides, I deserve it."

☐ "A lot of people do this; after all, no one is perfect."

☐ "This habit is caused by my past. I really can't help it."

☐ "It's useless to try to change or quit."

☐ "I can control this anytime. I'll change when I'm ready."

☐ "I don't want to try to quit and risk finding out I can't."

- ☐ "Doing it one last time won't make any difference."
- ☐ "What I'm doing is not really that bad. A lot of people do worse things."
- ☐ "I've not been able to change before, so why try now?"
- ☐ "Everyone needs at least one vice."
- ☐ "If I give this up, something worse will just take its place."
- ☐ "This is not a good time for me to try to change."
- ☐ "I don't have time to focus on this right now."
- ☐ "As soon as I have a sign from God, I'll change."

Ultimately you will lose the war with wrong habits if you continue to make excuses for prioritizing yourself or others over pleasing the Lord. Take heed lest you become like those the prophet Jeremiah describes:

> *"They followed the stubborn inclinations of their evil hearts.*
> *They went backward and not forward"*
> (Jeremiah 7:24).

Habit vs. Addiction

QUESTION: "What is the difference between a common habit and a compulsive addiction?"

ANSWER: With any behavior, repetition leads to the forming of a habit that then develops into an addiction. The difference between a repeated habit and an enslaving addiction is the amount of time it takes from your everyday life and the power it has over you.

If the behavior has mastery over your life, then it is an addiction. But if you are determined to do what is right, God will give you the power to either gain and maintain mastery over the behavior or stop it.

> *"Sin shall not be your master,*
> *because you are not under law, but under grace"*
> (Romans 6:14).

=== *Addictive Personality* ===

QUESTION: "What does it mean when someone is said to have an addictive personality?"

ANSWER: The term *addictive personality* is generally applied to individuals who are prone to form multiple addictions. They are believed to possess certain genetic and psychological influences that make them vulnerable to developing substance and/or behavioral addictions. The apostle Peter's instruction to first-century Christians is pertinent to all of us today, and especially to those suffering with addictions:

> *"Be self-controlled and alert.*
> *Your enemy the devil prowls around like a roaring lion*
> *looking for someone to devour"*
> (1 PETER 5:8).

D. What Is the Root Cause?

Marion Jones recognized her need for change, and others recognized her need for a second chance. Marion eventually became one of the most popular basketball players in the Women's National Basketball Association, signing a multiyear deal as a point guard with the Tulsa Shock in February 2011.

More importantly, Marion maintained a spirit of humility and repentance. Once her thinking changed, her life changed. Why do others not change? Because they never change their wrong beliefs.

WRONG BELIEF—THE REBEL:

"I really don't want to change. What I'm doing is not that bad!"

RIGHT BELIEF—THE REBEL:

"I really need to change and take responsibility for my behavior. Instead of choosing to please myself, my deepest desire needs to be to please the Lord, yielding my life to Christ's supernatural control."

> *"Do not let sin reign in your mortal body so that you obey*
> *its evil desires. Do not offer the parts of your body to sin, as*
> *instruments of wickedness, but rather offer yourselves to God, as*
> *those who have been brought from death to life; and offer the*
> *parts of your body to him as instruments of righteousness"*
> (ROMANS 6:12-13).

WRONG BELIEF—THE REPENTANT:
"I really want to change and I've tried, but I can't. There is no hope for me."

RIGHT BELIEF—THE REPENTANT:
"I can have success by yielding my bad habit to Christ's supernatural control. My new habit is this: With Christ living in me, I will submit to His leadership so that His character can be clearly seen through my life."

> *"I can do everything through him who gives me strength"*
> (PHILIPPIANS 4:13).

IV. STEPS TO SOLUTION

> *911 Operator:* "911, do you have an emergency?"
> *Caller:* "Yeah, we have a shark attack."
> *911 Operator:* "And the person is still in the water?"
> *Caller:* "They're still in the water, yes. I think her arm might be gone."[36]

By age 13, Hawaiian surfing prodigy Bethany Hamilton had quickly risen through the ranks of amateur surfing in pursuit of her lifelong dream of turning pro. She had sponsors interested in endorsing her and a tight-knit family of surfing enthusiasts who staunchly supported her. But, in a matter of seconds—while paddling to catch the next wave off Kauai's North Shore—she had an arm savagely severed from her tiny frame by a 14-foot tiger shark.[37]

Emergency responders rushed Bethany to the hospital, radioing ahead to alert the staff. Bethany's father, Tom—prepped to undergo knee surgery that same morning—was quickly removed from the same operating-room table his daughter would occupy minutes later as doctors raced to save her life.[38]

After surgery, Bethany awoke to find more than her left arm missing. Gone, too, were her dreams and her identity as a surfing phenomenon. But not for long. Within days, an undeniable desire to surf the world's wildest waves came flooding back. *Was such a feat physically possible?* she wondered. *And, if so, how? What new habits and skills would be needed?* Bethany had more questions than answers. But of one thing she was certain: As soon as her stitches were removed, she would head straight back to the water with a surfboard under her right arm... her only arm.

A. Key Verse to Memorize

For as long as Bethany could remember, her parents emphasized having true faith in Christ and, indeed, she received Jesus as her personal Lord and Savior, entrusting her life to Him. Never in the ensuing years, however, had her growing faith been tested so severely as on October 31, 2003—the day of the attack—and in the grueling months to come.

Uncertainty over how to live life as an amputee—and a surfer—was a constant companion. How could she tie on her swimsuit top, much less tunnel through world-class waves balanced atop a bobbing board? Since the *Handbook of Habits for One-armed Surfers* didn't exist, Bethany turned to the only book she could trust to guide her—the Bible.

She had learned from it in church and at home, committing many Scripture verses to memory. Now they came flooding back, reassuring her that...

> *"I can do everything through him who gives me strength"*
> (PHILIPPIANS 4:13).

B. Key Passage to Read and Reread

"My mom and I were praying for God to show me His will," said Bethany. "I wanted to be a light for Him in everything I was doing. And then, a couple of weeks later, the shark attack happened."[39] At that point, had Bethany questioned God's plan for her life, few would have blamed her. To be sure, she grappled with at least two more critical questions: Would she spend her life in fear of whether God could be trusted, or would she *choose a life of faith*?

Of all the questions that crowded into her mind, "Why?" became the one she asked herself the most—but with a faith-filled twist. "I have this thought every second of my life," she said. "'Why me?' Not necessarily in a negative way—like, 'Why did this horrible thing have to happen to me?' But more, 'Why did God choose me and what does He have in mind for me?'"[40]

By habitually training her mind to focus on the *promise* of God's plan rather than fearing the possibility of future peril, Bethany discovered the freedom to pursue her dream.

YOUR TRUE FREEDOM
GALATIANS 5:13-17

Freedom! People live for it and die for it...cherish it and curse it. But what does it mean? How do you get it? How do you keep it? Some say freedom is being able to do and say whatever they want. Others are more restrictive, adding, "As long as no one else's freedom is violated." But freedom, from God's perspective, is not being able to do whatever we want but being able to do whatever is right. For those controlled by harmful habits, freedom means having the ability to choose how they will think and behave, which involves breaking the power of the habits controlling them.

According to God's Word, the solution to a bad habit is not just replacing it with a good habit, but also examining what first made us susceptible to developing that bad habit. The Bible says our natural inclination is to sin, which means doing things our own way rather than God's way. It's a struggle we all have in common, a struggle we all can win—as long as we are empowered by the Spirit of God to say *no* to our will and *yes* to God's will. Truly, there is no real freedom apart from Him.

> *"It is for freedom that Christ has set us free. Stand firm, then,*
> *and do not let yourselves be burdened again by a yoke of slavery"*
> (GALATIANS 5:1).

- You are called to be free, so don't use your freedom to be self-indulgent (verse 13).

- You are commanded to love, so don't fight one another (verses 14-15).

- You are to live empowered by the Spirit, so don't live to gratify your natural desires (verse 16).

- Your natural inclinations conflict with the Spirit's inclinations, so don't allow yourself to be enslaved (verse 17).

C. How to Have Success in Self-control

Just three weeks after the attack, Bethany Hamilton waded into the Pacific Ocean—her parents and brothers verbally encouraging her, though inwardly unsure of what to expect. Rather than the long board she was accustomed to using, Bethany started over with a beginner board. Never would she forget what happened next.

"In some ways it was like learning to surf all over again. I had to learn how to paddle evenly with one arm." Her initial tries didn't work. Discouraged, she thought returning to surfing would be easier. "Then it happened...It's hard for me to describe the joy I felt after I stood up and rode a wave for the first time after the attack. Even though I was all wet, I felt tears of happiness trickling down my face."[41]

Bethany had taken the first step toward her dream. Determination helped lift her atop her surfboard that November day...but another power was also at work. "It was what God had taught me growing up that helped me overcome my fear and get back on the board," she said. "Be strong and courageous. Do not be terrified; do not be discouraged, for the LORD your God will be with you wherever you go."[42]

To have self-control you must first know what self-control is *not*. It is *not* "pulling yourself up by your own bootstraps." It is *not* overcoming one bad habit only to replace it with another bad habit. It is saying *no* to a negative habit so that you can say *yes* to a positive habit. Self-control is a gift from God that empowers you to fulfill the will of God. It is what the Holy Spirit does in you when you yield your will to His will.

STEPS TO SELF-CONTROL

- **Start with a commitment to truth, admitting the habit God wants you to change.**
  - Believe: God wants only what is best for you.
  - Believe: God has the desire and power to help you.
  - Believe: God doesn't punish you, but disciplines you.
  - Believe: God is faithful, perfect, good, and just.

  Personalize: *"[My God] is [my] Rock, his works are perfect, and all his ways are just. A faithful God who does no wrong, upright and just is he"* (Deuteronomy 32:4).

- **Separate yourself from your sinful habit, writing out what it is costing you.**
  - Repent (change your thinking) and confess your habit as sinful.
  - Realize that yielding to your habit makes you a slave to sin.
  - Review the negative consequences of your habit regularly.
  - Read and memorize Psalm 1.

  Personalize: *"What shall [I] say, then? Shall [I] go on sinning so that grace may increase? By no means! [I] died to sin; how can [I] live in it any longer?"* (Romans 6:1-2).

- **Set a new goal, picturing yourself establishing the new habit.**
  - Make it your goal to be empowered by God.
  - Make it your goal to please God.

- Make it your goal to depend on God.
- Make it your goal to do the will of God.

Personalize: *"[I] make it [my] goal to please him, whether [I am] at home in the body or away from it. For [I] must...appear before the judgment seat of Christ, that [I] may receive what is due [me] for the things done while in the body, whether good or bad"* (2 Corinthians 5:9-10).

- **Stand on the truth, setting a time to begin.** [43]
  - Know: In Christ you are set free from the penalty of sin.
  - Know: In Christ you are set free from the power of sin.
  - Know: In Christ you are "dead to sin."
  - Know: In Christ you no longer have to be a slave to sin.

Read Romans chapters 6, 7, and 8. Write down every verse in which Paul mentions your freedom from sin.

Personalize: *"[I] know that [my] old self was crucified with him so that the body of sin might be done away with, that [I] should no longer be [a slave] to sin"* (Romans 6:6).

- **Substitute God's thoughts for your thoughts, identifying your weak points.** [44]
  - When you are tempted by a habit, remember:

    "No temptation has seized you except what is common to man. And God is faithful; he will not let you be tempted beyond what you can bear. But when you are tempted, he will also provide a way out so that you can stand up under it" (1 Corinthians 10:13).

  - When you think you are powerless over a habit, say,

    "He gives strength to the weary and increases the power of the weak" (Isaiah 40:29).

  - When you think you've had the habit too long to change, claim this promise:

    "If anyone is in Christ, he is a new creation; the old has gone, the new has come!" (2 Corinthians 5:17).

  - When you begin to rationalize that a habit is okay, remember this:

"Since Christ suffered in his body, arm yourselves also with the same attitude, because he who has suffered in his body is done with sin. As a result, he does not live the rest of his earthly life for evil human desires, but rather for the will of God" (1 Peter 4:1-2).

– When you think no one will know about the habit, remind yourself of this truth:

   "Nothing in all creation is hidden from God's sight. Everything is uncovered and laid bare before the eyes of him to whom we must give account" (Hebrews 4:13).

– When you have given in to a habit, remember:

   "The LORD upholds all those who fall and lifts up all who are bowed down" (Psalm 145:14).

Personalize: *"In view of God's mercy, [I]...offer [my body] as [a] living [sacrifice], holy and pleasing to God—this is [my] spiritual act of worship. [I will not] conform any longer to the pattern of this world, but [will] be transformed by the renewing of [my] mind. Then [I] will be able to test and approve what God's will is—his good, pleasing and perfect will"* (Romans 12:1-2).

• **Surrender your will to God and share your decision with an accountability partner.**

   – Acknowledge that you belong to God.

   – Acknowledge that God has authority over all your thoughts, words, desires, time, money, actions, relationships, and possessions.

   – Acknowledge that the decision to change is yours. You are making a choice!

   – Acknowledge that you have God's Spirit present within you to help you make the right choice!

Personalize: *"Just as [I] used to offer the parts of [my] body in slavery to impurity and to ever-increasing wickedness, so now [I] offer them in slavery to righteousness leading to holiness"* (Romans 6:19).

• **Stay on track, practicing your new habit daily for three months.**[45]

   – Avoid taking pride in gaining victory over your habit.

- Avoid thinking you have control over what caused your habit.
- Avoid thinking it will be okay to occasionally indulge the habit.
- Avoid moving out from under God's grace into self-sufficiency.

Personalize: *"Since [I] have been justified through faith, [I] have peace with God through [my] Lord Jesus Christ, through whom [I] have gained access by faith into this grace in which [I] now stand"* (Romans 5:1-2).

Sandra: The Tale of Two Women

This is the tale of two women whom I personally have known. One was athletic and energetic, the other was an alcoholic and a compulsive eater. One became Miss Vermont and entered the Miss America pageant, the other weighed well over 200 pounds and eventually attempted suicide.

One became actively involved in Broadway and television, the other became actively involved in psychics and the occult. One was married to a doctor and had the "perfect home," the other was twice divorced and a prescription-drug addict. One was a charity organizer who became an activist for social causes, the other was a chain smoker who became a compulsive spender. One became an artist who ended up with the American dream, the other became an anorexic who ended up in a hospital for the mentally ill.

The name of the beautiful woman in the first list is Sandra Simpson LeSourd. And the name of the bewildered woman in the second list is none other than Sandra Simpson LeSourd.

Sandy seemingly had it all. In fact, two years after the Miss America pageant, she became the coordinator of a Miss America foundation, managing the public appearance schedule of that year's Miss America winner. Later, Sandy landed a prominent public relations position with Pepsi Cola and was swept up into the world of celebrity.

But while Sandy seemed cool and collected on the outside...inside, her emotional circuitry was becoming increasingly a mangled mass of fear, shame, guilt, and *pain*. One or two alcoholic drinks soon became three or four. And during one stop to a boutique, she bought 22 pairs of shoes and five matching handbags. An entire month's salary—gone in an hour.

Sandy momentarily panicked about how to pay the rent, but then lost herself in the exhilaration of her spontaneous purchases. "I floated back to the hotel in a euphoric trance. From then on, shopping would give me what almost amounted to a chemical high."[46]

After living in her isolated, frightening world of multiple addictions, Sandy finally realized it really wasn't alcohol or shopping or drugs that she needed to battle, but the *compulsive personality* behind it all.

People with compulsive personalities fool themselves into thinking they'll have just one cookie or one beer, and before long, paper wrappings and bottles are strewn throughout the house. "For the compulsive personality, moderation is the hardest achievement of all," Sandy explains.[47]

The compulsions and the cross-addictions led to self-hatred, self-pity, and ultimately a suicide attempt. "I had everything to live for and yet something inside me was pushing me straight into a dark pit,"[48] Sandy remembers. Following a botched sixteenth birthday party for her daughter, Lisa, she fell headfirst into the pit after deeply wounding her daughter on Mother's Day.

Lisa prepared a surprise Mother's Day dinner, but Sandy and her husband chose to spend most of the day with friends—*drinking*. When they returned home at 11:30 p.m., Sandy, stumbling past pots of dried up broccoli and ribs, headed for Lisa's bedroom, where her anguished daughter had been crying. "Where were you, Mom? I've been so worried."[49]

Sandy responded with a hollow promise: "Please forgive me, honey. It will never happen again."[50] When she bent down to kiss Lisa goodnight, her worn-out daughter turned her face into the pillow.

That was it! The taunting voices inside Sandy's head had been urging her to take her own life, accusing her of making Lisa's life miserable as well as everyone else's. Sandy grabbed a stash of sleeping pills and a nearly full bottle of vodka. The deadly concoction also included two hot cups of vodka-laced coffee that Sandra reasoned would melt the capsules faster.

Waiting for death, Sandy found herself singing a song that she had sung alongside her Aunt Ethel as a child, a sweet melody about unconditional love. "Jesus loves me, this I know, for the Bible tells me so…" Sandy became baffled as to why she would recall the song, but it was all she could think about.

Drowsiness soon swept over Sandy, so she lay down and anticipated a finality of all pain, a sudden stop of all addictions. "My eyes rested on a framed watercolor of a red barn…a Vermont barn…then inky blackness…a howling wind. Nothingness."[51]

But next came the smell of ether, surgical tape, and a blinding light above her, and Sandy realized death had eluded her. Then something filled her with self-loathing: The very person she didn't want to hurt *found her*—the daughter she so desperately wanted to protect from pain. Flailing at the bottom of the pit, finally Sandy recognized she needed help to be pulled out.

While at a hospital for mental disorders, Sandy encountered a young woman who talked often about Jesus. Every mention of the name *Jesus* was grating—Sandy hated that name. Then one morning at 3:00 a.m., this woman suddenly appeared in Sandy's room, crying, pleading to have one question answered: "Does Jesus *really* love me?"[52]

In that moment of despair, Sandy awkwardly assured her, "Yes, Karen, Jesus loves you."[53] Suddenly the woman's sobbing stopped and something extraordinary happened: The moment Sandy spoke the name *Jesus*, a breaking of her bondage occurred—and Sandy received a spirit of lightness and peace.

Later, after leaving the hospital, Sandy attended a church service where she encountered the One who broke the bondage, and she began a relationship with Him. As a result, Sandy gained new insight, recognizing the root of her lifelong compulsive behavior—*shame*. It started at age five, when she was sexually abused by an uncle. Somehow, she thought the abuse was all her fault. Years later, when her parents divorced, Sandy again believed she was to blame, resulting in even more self-loathing.

Sandy desperately needed reassurance that she was lovable. But when relationships didn't work, she turned to food, alcohol, cigarettes…whatever she could find to dull the pain. Her occult involvement—fueled by a desperate search for self-worth—filled her, instead, with seething self-hate. "Soon all my compulsive behaviors and dependencies became woven together in a spider web trap. I'd break through one area only to be strangled in another," she said.[54]

Finally Sandy saw firsthand that she could be freed forever! She experienced the overwhelming love of Jesus and began calling upon Him for help to overcome her compulsive behaviors. "I was the object of a love greater than any I had ever known. My compulsive lifestyle was reordered by a power outside myself, which I continue to experience and call Jesus Christ."[55]

Addictions and the Tendency to Sin

QUESTION: "When I became a Christian, shouldn't that have changed my addictions and my tendency to sin?"

ANSWER: When you put your trust in Christ, you did indeed receive a new life! God's Spirit lives within you and enables you to overcome sin. While you have been saved from the penalty of sin (eternal separation from God) and while the power of sin over you has been broken, you must *still choose* to not sin when you are tempted. You must choose daily to put off your *old self* with all its bad habits and inclinations and not be controlled by it. Instead, you must put on your *new self* and be controlled by it—your new self, which was created to be like Christ.

> *"You were taught, with regard to your former way of life, to put off*
> *your old self, which is being corrupted by its deceitful desires; to be*
> *made new in the attitude of your minds; and to put on the new*
> *self, created to be like God in true righteousness and holiness"*
> (EPHESIANS 4:22-24).

D. How to Break a Bad Habit

Before releasing her from the hospital, Bethany Hamilton's doctor summarized her prognosis this way: "The list of what Bethany will have to do *differently* is long; the list of what she will be *unable* to do is short."[56]

Prior to the attack, her training routine was simple: Surf…and watch videos of herself surfing so she could improve her technique. Those habits would hardly suffice now, for she had to train to compete against elite athletes possessing endurance, strong core muscles, tremendous upper-body strength, and…two arms.[57]

To compensate, Bethany added workouts to her regime of grueling physical therapy that were nearly twice as hard as before. Because her spine began curving toward her stronger right side, she incorporated spinal realignment exercises into her routine. Instead of swimming (it's too hard on her arm), she runs, does push-ups (one-armed!), hikes, lifts weights, and, of course, surfs—between two to eight hours a day when the waves allow.

When Bethany found it too hard to duck underwater while paddling out to catch a wave, she formed a new habit—riding a custom-made board with a handle she could hold on to. She also learned to use her legs more efficiently to help compensate for her slower paddling.

"She's working at a huge deficit with only one arm," Bethany's trainer said. "Yet the things she is able to do…like competing in paddle battles, out-maneuvering two-armed surfers for waves, or getting whipped around in 25-foot surf…it's just amazing. She copes incredibly well with her disadvantage and makes it seem like it doesn't exist."[58]

Breaking free of an old habit is not a quick or easy task. Just as it takes time to develop a habit, it takes even more time to break it and establish a new habit. If it is true that we are creatures of habit, as the familiar saying goes, then we are establishing new or practicing old habits on a continuous basis—and sadly do so, often on a subconscious level. No wonder the psalmist beseeched God to examine him—something we all need God to do on a daily basis so we do not unwittingly develop dangerous addictions.

> *"Search me, O God, and know my heart;*
> *test me and know my anxious thoughts.*
> *See if there is any offensive way in me,*
> *and lead me in the way everlasting"*
> (PSALM 139:23-24).

As you seek to replace the old way with the new way, remember to…

- **Will to do God's will.**
    - Commit your will to God.
    - Regularly remind yourself of your heart's desire to do God's will.

    > *"I desire to do your will, O my God;*
    > *your law is within my heart"*
    > (PSALM 40:8).

- **Ask God for wisdom** to know and accomplish His will.
    - Discern God's priorities and plans for breaking the bad habits in your life.
    - Seek God's will regarding the best strategy for breaking each identified habit.

    > *"If any of you lacks wisdom, he should ask God, who gives*
    > *generously to all without finding fault, and it will be given to him"*
    > (JAMES 1:5).

- **Accept by faith** that God has already given you the wisdom you need.
    - Reject any thoughts that you may not be able to break your habit.

— Believe that God is guiding and enabling you to succeed.

> *"This is the confidence we have in approaching God:*
> *that if we ask anything according to his will, he hears us"*
> (1 JOHN 5:14).

- **Lay out in writing** the strategy God has placed on your heart.
  - Write down the first particular habit you plan to change and make a list of the reasons you want to change it.
  - Detail the steps you will take and the various strategies you will employ.

> *"I know that you can do all things;*
> *no plan of yours can be thwarted"*
> (JOB 42:2).

- **Identity the wrong beliefs** supporting your habit.
  - Recall the time, circumstances, and your internal dialogue surrounding the starting of this habit.
  - Replace each wrong belief with a biblically accurate belief.

> *"A simple man believes anything, but a prudent*
> *man gives thought to his steps"*
> (PROVERBS 14:15).

- **Plan ways to remove possible reinforcements** of your bad habit.
  - Make a list of the physical, emotional, and mental rewards reinforcing your habit.
  - Negate rewards for the bad behavior by replacing them with negative repercussions. Institute rewards for engaging in a desired behavior.

> *"The faithless will be fully repaid for their ways,*
> *and the good man rewarded for his"*
> (PROVERBS 14:14).

- **Share your plan** with an accountability partner.
  - Enlist a mature Christian to help strengthen and support you in your efforts and to correct you when you get off course.

- Commit to being completely honest and forthright about your successes and failures.

"Plans fail for lack of counsel, but with many advisers they succeed"
(PROVERBS 15:22).

- **Resolve to stay the course.**
  - Have no expectation that your fleshly desires will die or will accept defeat quietly, quickly, or easily.
  - Put on the full armor of God on a daily basis as you wage war against the world, the flesh, and the devil.

  "Put on the full armor of God so that you can take
  your stand against the devil's schemes"
  (EPHESIANS 6:11).

E. How to Hit the Bull's-eye

Despite her strong faith, determination, and courage, the possibility of another shark attack is not lost on Bethany Hamilton. She answers the inevitable question, "What about sharks?"

> To constantly dwell on what might happen would totally suck the joy out of the sport. Besides, it's like asking, "What if the roller coaster comes off the track?" (It has happened.) What if the horse throws you?...Life is full of what-ifs. You can't let it hold you back. If you do, you're not really living at all...just kind of going through the motions with no meaning.[59]

Rather than dwelling on all the reasons she shouldn't don a swimsuit, shouldn't get back in the water, shouldn't surf, Bethany has focused on her purpose, priorities, and plans—with great reward. In January 2004, just over a year after the attack, Bethany won the first national title of her career. In 2008, she began competing full-time, placing third in a contest against many of the world's best female surfers.

The key was learning what to focus on and what not to.

Have you ever said to yourself, *I'm not going to eat that chocolate pie*...and then all you can think about is chocolate pie? In the battle with temptation, you will shoot the arrow through your own foot if your thoughts are aimed downward. Understand that you hit what you aim at! Don't dwell on the negative.

Rather, focus on the positive. Realize that training and disciplining the mind to think victoriously and to reject even the possibility of failure is critical to winning in both the Olympics and in developing godly character. Set your thoughts high on God's character-building truths, then with Christ's strength, you can hit the target every time.[60]

> *"Whatever is true, whatever is noble, whatever is right, whatever is pure, whatever is lovely, whatever is admirable—if anything is excellent or praiseworthy—think about such things"*
> (Philippians 4:8).

Missing the Target

Check out your thoughts and self-talk to see if they are causing you to miss the target:

☐ "I must quit smoking!"

☐ "I'll never pick up a cigarette again."

☐ "Christians look down on smokers."

☐ "I will stop thinking about cigarettes."

☐ "God is ashamed of me for smoking."

☐ "God will punish me for smoking."

Living under the "law" never changes you. If you focus only on what you shouldn't do, you will be pulled more powerfully to do it.

> *"The power of sin is the law"*
> (1 Corinthians 15:56).

Hitting the Target with Positive Truth

• **Target #1: God's purpose** for me is to display Christ's character.

> *"Those God foreknew he also predestined to be conformed to the likeness of his Son"*
> (Romans 8:29).

– "Christ lives in me to conform my character into His character."

– "I will glorify Christ by accurately representing Him to everyone I encounter."

— "I will yield to His control and do what is best for my body and my spirit."

- **Target #2: God's priority** for me is to change my thinking.

    > *"Do not conform any longer to the pattern*
    > *of this world, but be transformed by*
    > *the renewing of your mind"*
    > (ROMANS 12:2).

    — "Christ lives in me to give me the strength to change my thought patterns."

    — "I will release my guilt to God and gain control over my thinking to line it up with God's thinking."

    — "I will replace my defeated thinking with positive promises of victory from God's Word."

- **Target #3: God's plan** for me is to rely on Christ's power to change me.

    > *"'My [Jesus'] grace is sufficient for you, for my power*
    > *is made perfect in weakness.' Therefore I [Paul] will*
    > *boast all the more gladly about my weaknesses,*
    > *so that Christ's power may rest on me"*
    > (2 CORINTHIANS 12:9).

    — "Christ lives in me to change me."

    — "I will give Christ increasing control of my life and my habit in order to taper off gradually."

    — "I will give Christ total control of my life and my habit in order to quit cold turkey."

EXAMPLE OF HITTING TARGET #3
BREAKING THE HABIT OF SMOKING

Those who break the habit of smoking either taper off or go cold turkey.

Tapering Off

"I will give Christ increasing control of my life and my smoking habit in order to taper off gradually."

- By carrying a limited number of cigarettes for each day along with a gradual cutback schedule
- By limiting buying cigarettes to only certain days of the month
- By buying only one pack at a time
- By entrusting my cigarettes to a friend so that I have to ask for one or by keeping them in an inconvenient place
- By setting restrictions on when, where, and around whom I will smoke (outside, when I take a walk around the block, not around loved ones, etc.)
- By breaking patterns of when I would normally smoke (not smoking while on the phone, immediately after a meal, in the car, before going to sleep)
- By making myself accountable to someone who is willing to help
- By memorizing and personalizing 1 Corinthians 6:19-20 and dwelling on it when I want a cigarette

> *"Do you not know that your [my] body is a temple of the Holy Spirit, who is in you [me], whom you [I] have received from God? You are [I am] not your [my] own; you were [I was] bought at a price. Therefore [I will] honor God with your [my] body"*
> (1 Corinthians 6:19-20).

Quitting Cold Turkey

"I will give Christ total control of my life and my smoking habit in order to quit cold turkey."

- By refusing to purchase cigarettes
- By not looking at cigarette ads
- By choosing not to dwell on the "comfort" of smoking
- By doing another preplanned activity when I desire a cigarette (especially doing something with my hands)
- By finding a substitute when I want something in my mouth (chewing gum, hard candy, ice, or a toothpick)
- By eliminating the unnecessary activities that cause me to want to smoke
- By memorizing Romans 14:21 and 1 Corinthians 6:12

*"It is better not to eat meat or drink wine or to do
anything else that will cause your brother to fall"*
(ROMANS 14:21).

Negative Reinforcement

QUESTION: "What is negative reinforcement?"

ANSWER: Negative reinforcement means presenting negative truths or reasonings to aid with decision making. For example, "What is the *truth* about tobacco?

Tobacco smoke contains more than 200 known poisons. Those who smoke two packs a day shorten their life expectancy by eight years. Tobacco...[61]

- Is the most common cause of lung cancer
- Is a major cause of hardening of the arteries, which in turn causes strokes and most heart attacks
- Is a major contributor in mouth and throat cancers, which can disfigure a person for life
- Causes emphysema, making breathing very taxing, which in turn causes death
- Produces chemicals that erode the lining of the stomach, which in turn causes gastric ulcers
- Increases the risk of bladder cancer
- Slows down physical healing
- Produces carbon monoxide and retards the growth of a fetus in a mother who smokes, which also increases the risk of premature birth and infant death
- Contributes to heart disease, the leading cause of death in men

*"'Everything is permissible'—but not everything is beneficial.
'Everything is permissible'—but everything is not constructive"*
(1 CORINTHIANS 10:23).

Chewing Tobacco

QUESTION: "Isn't chewing tobacco better than smoking tobacco?"

ANSWER: Absolutely not! Apart from the obvious yellow teeth stains and unpleasant taste (especially for the spouses of users), smokeless tobacco...[62]

- Causes cavities and tooth decay due to high quantities of sugar
- Possesses coarse particles that damage gums and erode tooth enamel
- Can lead to gum and tooth disease
- Is a common cause of mouth and throat cancer
- Can cause leukoplakia
- Contributes to increased heart rate and blood pressure
- Increases the incidents of heart disease and heart attack

The American Academy of Otolaryngology states that spit, chewing, and smokeless tobacco are "not a safe alternative to smoking. You just move health problems from your lungs to your mouth," providing a more potent nicotine rush to the blood.[63]

> *"The prudent see danger and take refuge*
> *but the simple keep going and suffer for it"*
> (PROVERBS 27:12).

Smoking

QUESTION: "What does God think about smoking?"

ANSWER: According to 1 Corinthians 6:19-20, smoking is a sin against the physical body because it causes sickness, disease, and possibly early death. But your salvation is not contingent upon it. Romans 10:9-10 says, "If you confess with your mouth, 'Jesus is Lord,' and believe in your heart that God raised him from the dead, you will be saved. For it is with your heart that you believe and are justified, and it is with your mouth that you confess and are saved." God's desire is for us to walk in freedom from any addiction or unhealthy habit. God's plan for our lives is good, and if we choose to shorten our lives due to this kind of vice, we may miss opportunities of ministry and the privilege of touching the lives of other people whom He had planned for us to influence.

> *"I urge you, brothers, in view of God's mercy,*
> *to offer your bodies as living sacrifices, holy and pleasing*
> *to God—this is your spiritual act of worship"*
> (ROMANS 12:1).

Compulsive Spending

QUESTION: "How can I stop my compulsive spending?"

ANSWER: You must first discover the need you are trying to meet through compulsive spending. What is the driving force behind it? Then you must commit to trusting God to meet your need and determine to please the Lord in the way you manage the financial resources He gives you.

Before you purchase anything, ask yourself:

- ☐ "Is this purchase a true *need* or just a *desire?*"
- ☐ "Do I have adequate funds to purchase this without using credit?"
- ☐ "Have I compared the cost of competitive products?"
- ☐ "Have I prayed about this purchase?"
- ☐ "Have I been patient in waiting on God's provision?"
- ☐ "Do I have God's peace regarding this purchase?"
- ☐ "Does this purchase conform to the purpose God has for me?"
- ☐ "Is there agreement with my spouse [if you are married] or accountability partner about this purchase?"

> *"Be on your guard against all kinds of greed;*
> *a man's life does not consist in the abundance of his possessions"*
> (LUKE 12:15).

In order not to be caught off guard or fall into deeper debt, make a plan that includes some of these practical steps that will enable you to develop healthy spending habits.

BREAKING THE HABIT OF OVERSPENDING[64]

- Avoid preferred shops and pick new stores to make your needed purchases.
- Check with stores before leaving home to ensure they have the things you need.

- Confine orders from catalogs, the Internet, and TV shopping channels to only those items already on your shopping list.

- When you feel the desire to go shopping divert your attention to another enjoyable activity.

- Keep only one credit card for emergencies.

- Limit your window shopping to after hours or when you have no means of making purchases.

- Never shop when you are tired, depressed, excited, or lonely.

- Plan your shopping trips to tempting locations late in the day so you will arrive with just enough time to limit yourself to purchasing necessities before the doors close.

- Put off buying anything you are hesitant about purchasing.

- Shop only when you have a shopping list, and purchase only items that are on the list.

- Tell your spouse, friend, or shopping buddy exactly what you plan to buy when you shop.

- Use cash, check, or debit card when you make your purchase.

- Use mail-order catalogs to purchase specific items only, not for browsing or compiling a list of items for purchase.

- When thinking about purchasing an item, ask yourself: *Do I really need this? Can I afford it?*

THE PLAN FOR FUTURE PURCHASES

- Formulate a realistic weekly, monthly, quarterly, and yearly budget with the help of a financially responsible person, and keep to it.

- Develop and implement a savings plan.

- Enter purchases in your checkbook and deduct them from your balance on the day they occur or within the next few days.

- Start a list of any expensive items you would like to purchase in the future, do three cost comparisons on each item, and then determine when you can realistically save the money to purchase each item.

- Disclose all of your purchases and the cost of each to your spouse, friend, or accountability partner.

- Purchase and wrap gifts early for loved ones you will be visiting throughout the year in order to avoid making superfluous or more expensive purchases during your visits.

Pray before walking into a store to purchase an item and ask, "Lord, is this a hasty decision or a well-planned one? Is this just my will or Your perfect will?" Remember…

"The plans of the diligent lead surely to plenty,
but those of everyone who is hasty, surely to poverty"
(PROVERBS 21:5 NKJV).

F. How to Help with Accountability Questions

Bethany Hamilton would be the first to say she has not made the journey from shark-attack victim to national surfing champ alone. It would be difficult to imagine a more supportive family than hers. Along with them, friends, fans, and a close-knit church community have cheered this surfer continuously.

Encouragement is important. But when it comes to shedding old habits, learning new ones, and achieving goals once thought unobtainable, nothing is more critical than accountability. For Bethany, that has come, first and foremost, in the form of her surfing coaches. She admits, "There are times when the last thing I feel like doing is running another mile…" And that is why she has a coach who pushes her "farther and harder than I ever think I (or any human!) can go."[65]

Through a caring, supportive network, God has shown Bethany that

"two are better than one, because they have a good return for
their work: If one falls down, his friend can help him up. But
pity the man who falls and has no one to help him up!"
(ECCLESIASTES 4:9-10).

Many who have struggled with and overcome temptation say, "I couldn't have made it without someone holding me accountable. God knew that's what I needed!"

But at times having an accountability partner isn't effective. Why? Because many strugglers hope no one will ask them *specifically* how they are doing in the area of their habits and addictions.

Asking specific questions is a key component of effective accountability. Strugglers need to know that they are going to be asked targeted questions. They also need to know they will have someone *trustworthy* to hold them accountable. The Bible says,

> *"If someone is caught in a sin,*
> *you who are spiritual should restore him gently.*
> *But watch yourself, or you also may be tempted"*
> (GALATIANS 6:1).

Accountability Questions

Since we last spoke:

1. Have you done anything that pricked your conscience?
2. Did you practice any undisciplined behavior?
3. Did you engage in any addictive behavior? Have you performed any other addictive behavior?
4. Have you done anything to violate any boundary? Have you set a boundary and kept it?
5. Has anything caused your thought life to stray? What steps will you take to avoid justifying the habit?
6. Did you find yourself in a compromising situation recently? How did you respond?
7. What beliefs about yourself and others have been conveyed through your recent habits (bad or good)?
8. What area of your life do you think God most wants you to change? What steps have you taken to make that change a reality?
9. What good habits do you believe God wants to develop in your life? What steps have you taken to see those habits become a reality?
10. Is there a part of your life that you've held back from God that you need to surrender?
11. Is there something you hope I won't ask about?
12. What is God telling you to do? What are you going to do about it?

> *"He who conceals his sins does not prosper,*
> *but whoever confesses and renounces them finds mercy"*
> (PROVERBS 28:13).

Additional Questions

- In what areas do you sense a need for change?
- Have you been pure in your thought life?

- Do you need to confess any sin?
- How has your spiritual life been? Have you been praying regularly?

Note to Mentors: Any of these questions can be deleted or exchanged for other questions. During the first session, ask the one who wants victory to select three or four questions most appropriate for their struggle.

- Ask, "Are there specific areas where you know you need to be held accountable?"
- After several sessions, ask, "How is this accountability working for you?"
- "If our positions were reversed, what would you do differently if you were me?"

Remember, Christ is shaping and maturing both of you through this time of accountability, and you want the struggler to be set free!

"As iron sharpens iron, so one man sharpens another"
(PROVERBS 27:17).

G. How to Develop and Demonstrate Good Habits

In 2010, Bethany Hamilton ranked twentieth on the Association of Surfing Professionals (ASP) Women's Tour. A legend in water-sports circles, her accomplishments may one day be eclipsed only by her efforts to minister internationally to the needs of those who, like her, have suffered a major setback in life.

On a ministry trip to Thailand, for example, she helped traumatized orphans regain their courage to enter the water which, years before, devastated their country through a deadly tsunami. Her foundation, Friends of Bethany, supports shark-attack survivors, traumatic amputees, and other charitable efforts.[66]

A movie about Bethany Hamilton's life, based on her book, was released in 2011, providing a platform for this star surfer to tell her story and share her faith around the world. To those struggling to understand and overcome, she says,

> I don't pretend to have all the answers to why bad things happen to good people. But I do know that God knows all those answers, and sometimes He lets you know in this life, and sometimes He asks you to wait so that you can have a face-to-face talk about it. What I do know is that I want to use what happened to me as an opportunity to tell people that God is worthy of our trust and to show them that you can go on and do wonderful things in spite of terrible events that happen.[67]

This habit will benefit Bethany for the rest of her days.

Many habits—good and bad—are the result of childhood experiences. Family and friends have a powerful influence on us. But as we grow older, like Bethany Hamilton we decide for ourselves the values and behaviors we want to incorporate into our lives. No longer a child, you do not have to be controlled by the attitudes and actions of others. You can choose to develop and demonstrate good habits that are desirable and pleasing to God.

> *"When I was a child, I talked like a child,*
> *I thought like a child, I reasoned like a child.*
> *When I became a man, I put childish ways behind me"*
> (1 CORINTHIANS 13:11).

Develop and demonstrate...

- **Moral Sensitivity**
  - Study the Scriptures daily so you will know God's standards.
  - Write out the Ten Commandments and apply each one to your life (Exodus 20:1-17).
  - Consider what it means to "have no other gods before me" (verse 3).
  - Memorize the Beatitudes and rehearse in your mind ways to apply them in your life (Matthew 5:3-12).
  - Measure all of your behavior with the yardstick of Scripture.

> *"I have hidden your word in my heart*
> *that I might not sin against you"*
> (PSALM 119:11).

- **Accountability**
  - Be open to the truth when others criticize you.
  - Say with appreciation, "It takes courage to point out where a person needs to change. Thank you for taking the risk."
  - Think about how your negative attitudes impact your life and the lives of others around you.
  - Confess your failures to God, and ask forgiveness from those you have offended.

— Daily or weekly, talk with a friend who will help you kick the habit that plagues you.

> *"Confess your sins to each other and pray for each other"*
> (JAMES 5:16).

- **Gratefulness**
  — Memorize Psalm 100, meditate on its message, and think of ways you can apply it to your life.
  — Acknowledge the gifts that God has given you, gifts for which you can be grateful.
  — Keep a prayer journal, and give thanks for answered prayer.
  — Always express gratitude to those who are helpful to you.
  — Thank God for what He is teaching you through each trial that He allows in your life.

> *"Be joyful always; pray continually; give thanks in all circumstances, for this is God's will for you in Christ Jesus"*
> (1 THESSALONIANS 5:16-18).

- **Forgiveness**
  — Know that forgiving others is required in order for you to receive the forgiveness of God.
  — Forgive by releasing that person into the hands of God.
  — Choose to forgive others even when you feel justified in your anger.
  — Remind yourself of the many times God has forgiven you.
  — Realize that forgiveness is often a process of forgiving again and again—not a one-time act. (See Genesis chapters 37–50. The key verse is Genesis 50:20.)

> *"If you forgive men when they sin against you, your heavenly Father will also forgive you. But if you do not forgive men their sins, your Father will not forgive your sins"*
> (MATTHEW 6:14-15).

- **Selflessness**
  - Set a high standard for yourself, but allow others to set their own.
  - Ask God to shine a spotlight on your acts of selfishness.
  - Avoid talking about yourself or bragging about your endeavors; rather, encourage others to talk about themselves and praise them for their godly qualities.
  - Resist the urge to criticize or to give unasked-for advice.
  - Perform an unsolicited act of kindness toward someone else each day.

> *"Do nothing out of selfish ambition or vain conceit,*
> *but in humility consider others better than yourselves"*
> (PHILIPPIANS 2:3).

- **Communion with God**
  - Spend time alone with God every day.
  - Eliminate preventable noise and remove other distractions.
  - Slowly say from your heart, "Lord, I do love You."
  - Close your mind to invading thoughts and focus on God's presence and character.
  - Be quiet in your spirit and wait on God to reveal Himself to you.

> *"May my meditation be pleasing to him, as I rejoice in the LORD"*
> (PSALM 104:34).

THE GAME OF LIFE

For each of us, the entry fee has been paid, and we are in the race—a race that must be run. How we develop our habits determines our personal outcome. When your life is yielded to the Lord—whether you finish first or simply achieve your personal best—you can echo the following words:

> *"I have fought the good fight, I have finished*
> *the race, I have kept the faith"*
> (2 TIMOTHY 4:7).

Even with the missteps and false starts that occasionally hinder you, imagine the joy of one day hearing the heavenly Father say, "Race well run...race well done."

Your habits will either make you or break you, depending
on your priorities. They will break the potential of
what God has planned or make it possible for you
to fulfill His plan. Be strong and you can't go wrong
when all your habits are right in God's sight!

—JUNE HUNT

Habits and Addictions: Answers in God's Word

QUESTION: "If we're totally forgiven by God's grace, can we go on sinning?"

ANSWER: *"What shall we say, then? Shall we go on sinning so that grace may increase? By no means! We died to sin; how can we live in it any longer?"* (Romans 6:1-2).

QUESTION: "Is it possible to serve two masters—to be devoted to God, yet be mastered by money?"

ANSWER: *"No servant can serve two masters. Either he will hate the one and love the other, or he will be devoted to the one and despise the other. You cannot serve both God and Money"* (Luke 16:13).

QUESTION: "I can do nothing about my habit—why try if I don't have the strength?"

ANSWER: *"I can do everything through him who gives me strength"* (Philippians 4:13).

QUESTION: "How do I avoid all extremes—especially all bad habits?"

ANSWER: *"It is good to grasp the one and not let go of the other. The man who fears God will avoid all extremes"* (Ecclesiastes 7:18).

QUESTION: "As a Christian, my body is my own responsibility. Why be obsessed with a lot of talk about honoring God with my body?"

ANSWER: *"Do you not know that your body is a temple of the Holy Spirit, who is in you, whom you have received from God? You are not your own; you were bought at a price. Therefore honor God with your body"* (1 Corinthians 6:19-20).

QUESTION: "Should I look at what society says is permissible for me or what is beneficial?"

ANSWER: *"'Everything is permissible for me'—but not everything is beneficial. 'Everything is permissible for me'—but I will not be mastered by anything"* (1 Corinthians 6:12).

QUESTION: "How can I not gratify the desires of my flesh and break the sinful habits that serve to meet those desires?"

ANSWER: *"Live by the Spirit, and you will not gratify the desires of the sinful nature"* (Galatians 5:16).

QUESTION: "What if I don't have the self-discipline to be faithful and to do what God calls me to do?"

ANSWER: *"The one who calls you is faithful and he will do it"* (1 Thessalonians 5:24).

QUESTION: "How should I pray in order to know if there is anything offensive in me?"

ANSWER: *"Search me, O God, and know my heart; test me and know my anxious thoughts. See if there is any offensive way in me, and lead me in the way everlasting"* (Psalm 139:23-24).

QUESTION: "Is there real hope that I can prepare my mind for a course of action and be self-controlled to conquer my habits?"

ANSWER: *"Prepare your minds for action; be self-controlled; set your hope fully on the grace to be given you when Jesus Christ is revealed"* (1 Peter 1:13).

THE WORLD OF ALCOHOL AND DRUG ABUSE
Breaking Free and Staying Free

THE WORLD OF ALCOHOL AND DRUG ABUSE:
Breaking Free and Staying Free

He was an all-American hero. Some say he was the greatest baseball player of all time.[1] Mickey Mantle had it all—fame, fortune, and millions of fans. On the day of his high school graduation, he signed with the world-renowned New York Yankees, a decision that began his road to stardom.

The statistics support his superstar status: 536 career home runs, three Most Valuable Player awards, career batting average of .298, seven world championships, and baseball's Triple Crown—leading the entire Major League one season by having the highest batting average, the most home runs, and the most runs batted in.

But during the years that Mickey achieved all his accomplishments, more than adrenaline was pumping through his veins. Too often dangerous quantities of alcohol also coursed through his body, poisoning what God had uniquely made, and ultimately causing his premature death.

For Mickey, the cry of his heart—and that of every addict—could easily echo that of the psalmist:

"The troubles of my heart have multiplied;
free me from my anguish"
(PSALM 25:17).

I. DEFINITIONS OF ALCOHOL AND DRUG ABUSE

They call it "the good life": the fun of swimming in a sea of booze, the fans always buying drinks for their heroes, the free wine bottles in all the hotel rooms. "The Mick" and his buddies considered it "the measure of being a man."[2]

How well they held their liquor, drink after drink—without physical or emotional collapse—was their symbol of "manliness."

Much later, however, Mickey recognized his warped view of life: "Baseball didn't turn me into a drunk. I drank because I thought we were having fun. It was part of the camaraderie, the male-bonding thing."[3] But what he called the *bonding thing* became more his *breaking* "thing"—breaking his health and causing his death, an unnecessary death solely due to alcoholism.

Although written centuries before, the Psalms reflect the sorrow in the life of this suffering hero:

> *"The cords of death entangled me,*
> *the anguish of the grave came upon me;*
> *I was overcome by trouble and sorrow"*
> (PSALM 116:3).

A. What Is a Drug?

For Mickey, it wasn't just *fun* that drove him to drink, but also *fear.*

Mickey's father died of Hodgkin's lymphoma at the young age of 40, and three other relatives succumbed to the disease before their fortieth birthdays. Afraid his life could also be cut short, Mickey decided to party hard because he might never see his sunset years. His drug of choice was alcohol.

A therapist commented, "Mickey is totally controlled by fear. He is filled with fear about everything."[4] His father's death was precisely what pushed Mickey over the edge—the critical turning point when his playful partying turned debilitating. Soon this baseball great slid into a self-made addiction, running from his fear instead of facing it.

With death all around, if Mickey had learned to yield his life to the Lord, he could have faced his fear and found comfort in knowing that God was with him, as the twenty-third Psalm says:

> *"Even though I walk through the valley of the shadow of death,*
> *I will fear no evil, for you are with me"*
> (VERSE 4).

- **Drugs** are chemical substances introduced into the body that produce physical, emotional, or mental changes. Some drugs are helpful, and other drugs are harmful.

- **Drugs** are used in three primary ways:
  - *Ingesting* (swallowing pills, powders, liquids)

- *Inhaling* (breathing in powders, smoke, fumes, and other inhalants)
- *Injecting* (inserting a substance directly into the muscle or veins for a faster effect or injecting the drug underneath the skin—called "skin popping"—which allows the drug to be absorbed more slowly into the bloodstream)

- **Drugs** are obtained in three ways:
  - *Over-the-counter drugs* (legal drugs acquired without a prescription)
  - *Prescription drugs* (legal drugs prescribed only by medical doctors)
  - *Illegal drugs* (drugs that are unlawful to purchase or even possess, although the legal status of certain drugs varies from state to state and from country to country)

One of the side effects of living in a world where evil abounds is that the very things God created for our good can be misused for our harm. Such is the case with drugs. Those who take what God intends for good but instead use for harm need to heed these words of warning:

> *"Woe to those who call evil good and good evil,*
> *who put darkness for light and light for darkness,*
> *who put bitter for sweet and sweet for bitter"*
> (ISAIAH 5:20).

B. What Are the Four Major Drug Classifications?

What Mickey hoped would help manage his life ultimately messed it up.

He turned to alcohol to both stimulate him and soothe him—to rev him up during the day, then settle him down at night. But what once went down smoothly later left him with a bitter aftertaste.

"I couldn't go on the way I was living, drunk and sick and depressed, covering up with lies, trying to remember where I was going or where I had been."[5] Then the greatest switch-hitter of all time gave this gut-wrenching statement: "Don't be like me."[6]

Mickey's words of warning parallel the words of protection found in the very first verse of the Psalms:

> *"Blessed is the man who does not walk in the counsel of the wicked*
> *or stand in the way of sinners or sit in the seat of mockers."*

Drugs are generally classified into four major groups, depending on their effect on the body.[7] (Note: Certain drugs can fit into more than one category.)

1. **Depressants** produce a calming effect and slow down the central nervous system.

   - *Prevalent types:* alcohol, sedatives (sleeping pills), tranquilizers (Valium), barbiturates ("downers"), and organic solvents (fast-drying glues and adhesives, gasoline, and aerosols)
   - *Psychological symptoms:* poor concentration, distorted thinking, lack of judgment, and aggressiveness
   - *Physical effects:* drowsiness, slurred speech, lack of coordination, tremors, decreased energy, coma, impaired vision, decreased pulse rate and blood pressure, respiratory depression, and even death

Interestingly, Isaiah 28:7 refers to those who

> *"stagger from wine and reel from beer...and are befuddled with wine; they reel from beer, they stagger when seeing visions, they stumble when rendering decisions."*

2. **Stimulants** excite bodily functions and speed up the central nervous system.

   - *Prevalent types:* cocaine, crack, meth, and amphetamines ("speed" or "uppers")
   - *Psychological symptoms:* excitability, increased energy, exaggerated self-confidence, heightened sexual drive, temporary exhilaration, irritability, apprehension, and intensified emotions
   - *Physical effects:* hyperactivity, restlessness, insomnia, loss of appetite, dry mouth, bad breath, itchy nose, dilated pupils, rapid and unclear speech, perspiration, headaches, dizziness, elevated blood pressure and heart rate, psychosis, and even death

The book of Proverbs describes those who walk outside of wisdom, those who are victims of sudden disaster—similar to those who die after taking stimulants:

> *"Disaster will overtake him in an instant;*
> *he will suddenly be destroyed—without remedy"*
> (PROVERBS 6:15).

3. **Hallucinogens** distort and alter a person's perception of reality.

   - *Prevalent types:* LSD, marijuana, PCP ("angel dust"), and mescaline

   - *Psychological symptoms:* hallucinations, heightened sensitivities, anxiety attacks, lowered inhibitions, and out-of-body experiences

   - *Physical effects:* vary with the drug—for example, LSD acts as a stimulant and marijuana acts as a depressant; reactions differ with each individual: sleeplessness, loss of appetite, increased energy, increased pulse rate and blood pressure, eyes fixed in a blank stare or rapid involuntary eye movements, slurred or blocked speech, higher rate of accidents and violence, disorientation, and even death

Although the Bible does not directly mention hallucinogens, it does address the hallucinogenic effect of alcohol, which can be disturbing and frightening.

> *"Your eyes will see strange sights and your mind imagine*
> *confusing things. You will be like one sleeping on the high*
> *seas, lying on top of the rigging. 'They hit me,' you will*
> *say, 'but I'm not hurt! They beat me, but I don't feel it!*
> *When will I wake up so I can find another drink?'"*
> (PROVERBS 23:33-35).

4. **Narcotics** reduce pain and elevate a person's mood.

   - *Prevalent types:* opium, morphine, codeine, heroin, methadone, and meperidine

   - *Psychological symptoms:* temporary euphoria, dulled senses, lethargy, and confusion

   - *Physical effects:* relief of pain, droopy eyelids, constricted pupils, slowed reaction and motor skills, drowsiness, lack of coordination, depressed reflexes, dry mouth, constipation, scars or abscesses at injection sites, and even death

When you are in pain, ask for the Lord's wisdom and direction for relief of your pain. Rather than abusing drugs, begin the journey toward freedom with dependence only on the Lord.

> *"I am in pain and distress;*
> *may your salvation, O God, protect me"*
> (PSALM 69:29).

=========== *Drug Abuse Without Addiction* ===========

QUESTION: "Is it possible to abuse drugs and alcohol without becoming addicted?"

ANSWER: Yes. Just as every drug is different, everyone's physical makeup is different.

- Some people become addicted with small amounts of a substance.
- Others consume greater quantities before becoming addicted.

Because of the destructive risk of addiction, using unnecessary drugs is dangerous. Substance abuse is like playing Russian roulette—it can cost you your life! Our bodies are not our own to abuse—they belong to God. First Corinthians 6:19-20 says,

> *"Do you not know that your body is a temple of the Holy Spirit,*
> *who is in you, whom you have received from God?*
> *You are not your own; you were bought at a price.*
> *Therefore honor God with your body."*

C. What Is Substance Abuse?

Mickey Mantle not only abused alcohol, he also abused the people around him.

His children spoke of his increasing inattention to the family while they were young. He became more depressed, more irritable. When the Yankees lost a game or when Mickey struck out, the children knew to leave Dad alone. The entire family walked on eggshells, hoping to prevent the inevitable verbal attack. Not only was Mickey in denial about his alcoholism, but his wife also minimized the problem.

Mickey made excuses for his absences (which often included time spent with other women). His increasing dependence on alcohol was a desperate attempt to boost his self-esteem. More and more, alcohol became necessary for him to function during the day. Then it became more and more necessary for him so he could fall asleep at night.

Mickey later reflected, "I am embarrassed by what I did when I drank: the foul language, the rudeness, having to face people the next day that I didn't remember insulting the night before."[8] The first verse of Proverbs chapter 20 confirms alcohol can prompt such behavior:

> *"Wine is a mocker and beer a brawler;*
> *whoever is led astray by them is not wise."*

- **Substance abuse** refers to the use of a chemical—legal or illegal—to the extent that the usage causes physical, mental, or emotional harm.[9]

- **Substance abusers** are identified in five ways:
  - *Experimental users* try drugs simply out of curiosity.
  - *Recreational users* get high on drugs on special occasions (parties, celebrations).
  - *Regular users* abuse drugs habitually while attempting to live a "normal life."
  - *Binge users* misuse drugs uncontrollably for a brief period of time and then abstain until the next binge.
  - *Dependent users* are emotionally, physically, and psychologically hooked on drugs. They are continually obsessed with getting drugs because of their all-consuming addiction.

While the following verse accurately describes everyone before they yield their lives to Christ, it especially illustrates the lifestyle of a substance abuser:

> *"All have turned away, they have together become worthless;*
> *there is no one who does good, not even one"*
> (ROMANS 3:12).

Recreational Drugs

QUESTION: "What's the harm in occasionally using recreational drugs with my friends in a safe environment—as long as I don't become addicted?"

ANSWER: The wrong use of any drug constitutes *drug abuse*. Likewise, there is no "right use" of illegal drugs or illegally acquired prescription drugs. And there is no "safe environment" for drug abuse because no situation exists where drug abuse doesn't cause physical, mental, emotional, or spiritual harm. By its very definition, *drug abuse* is harmful whether controlled or uncontrolled, chosen or compulsive, regulated or unregulated.

A true friend, a wise friend, does only what helps another friend. Ask God to give you genuinely wise friends and to help you become a wise friend yourself.

> *"He who walks with the wise grows wise,*
> *but a companion of fools suffers harm"*
> (PROVERBS 13:20).

D. What Is the Downward Spiral of Dependency?

If only the downward spiral of Mickey's dependency had been diagnosed sooner.

If only Mickey had acknowledged his alcoholism and received help earlier, his titles of *champion* and *hero* wouldn't have been marred by years of drinking.

If only he had processed the pain from his past—his childhood agony and his fear of death—then the downward spiral of dependency could have been deterred.

If only he had only found a meaningful way to spend his free time, rather than downing yet another drink. But because Mickey spent so much time waiting in airport lobbies and hotel rooms, boredom and binge drinking became his constant companions.

If only he had learned to live without alcohol, his four sons might not have also become alcoholics. If only he had learned to heed these words:

> *"Do not gaze at wine when it is red,*
> *when it sparkles in the cup, when it goes down smoothly!*
> *In the end it bites like a snake and poisons like a viper"*
> (PROVERBS 23:31-32).

LEVELS OF SUBSTANCE ABUSE[10]

- **Intoxication** occurs when the influence of a substance in your body causes changes in your behavior, including mood changes, faulty judgment, slurred speech, poor coordination, unsteady gait, sexual impropriety, aggressive actions, and impaired social functioning. Intoxication can result in a coma or even in death.

  - *Dorland's Illustrated Medical Dictionary* defines intoxication as "poisoning; the state of being poisoned" and "the condition produced by excessive use of alcoholic stimulants."[11]

  - How interesting that thousands of years before this writing, Moses said, "Their grapes are filled with poison...Their wine is the venom of serpents, the deadly poison of cobras" (Deuteronomy 32:32-33).

- **Abuse** occurs when your use of drugs causes you to:
    - Act irresponsibly
    - Fail to maintain healthy relationships
    - Put yourself or others at risk of harm
    - Break the law

- **Addiction** occurs when you experience these three leading indicators:
    - *Drug tolerance*—needing increasingly more of a substance to obtain the same effect
    - *Physical dependence*—suffering from chemical withdrawal symptoms such as nausea, sweating, shaking, and anxiety
    - *Intense craving*—developing a pattern of compulsive substance use

    Other common indicators include:

    - *Loss of control*—failing at attempts to decrease or stop the substance abuse
    - *Targeting activities*—choosing events only where alcohol or drugs are available
    - *Continual substance abuse*—continuing to use despite negative ramifications

- **Withdrawal** occurs when the distress caused by a lessening or lack of the drug:
    - Severely disrupts your daily life
    - Renders meaningless normally meaningful activities, such as work and relationships
    - Drains the emotions until all joy is gone

The prophet Isaiah describes such a time when

> *"no longer do they drink wine with a song…*
> *In the streets they cry out for wine;*
> *all joy turns to gloom, all gaiety is banished"*
> (Isaiah 24:9,11).

=============== *Responsibility for Drug Dependence* ===============

QUESTION: "How can I be held responsible for my drug dependence? After all, most drugs are addictive and cause the addiction."

ANSWER: Your drug dependence has been created both by your choice to use drugs and by the drugs themselves. Intoxication results from the makeup of the drug you choose to use and the way it is metabolized by your body. The only sure way to avoid addiction is to avoid addictive drugs altogether.

> *"How long will you keep on getting drunk?*
> *Get rid of your wine"*
> (1 SAMUEL 1:14).

II. CHARACTERISTICS OF ALCOHOL AND DRUG ABUSE

Now consider another all-American hero: In 2010 alone, he was selected as one of baseball's all-star players, voted the American League's Most Valuable Player (MVP), and Player of the Year.[12]

During his growing-up years, the star outfielder for the Texas Rangers couldn't have been more "squeaky clean." Josh Hamilton never neglected to give his grandmother a kiss before each high school game. And while his teammates partied after each game, he was home with mom and dad.

Through all four years of high school, neither drugs nor alcohol entered Josh's body, but that all changed in the spring of 2001.[13] Two major setbacks stalled his promising career in major league baseball, and the fallout almost proved fatal.

It's as though Josh had written these words:

> *"When I expected good, then evil came;*
> *When I waited for light, then darkness came"*
> (JOB 30:26 NASB).

A. What Checklist Helps Discover a Chemical Dependency?[14]

The changes in Josh Hamilton's lifestyle and behavior read like a checklist for discovering chemical dependency, with almost every box checked *yes*.

The new crowd of friends—found in a tattoo parlor—was a far cry from the fresh, innocent faces of his youth. In their company, Josh took his first drink of alcohol, which eventually culminated in drinking a bottle of whiskey every day. And in their company, he experimented with his first drug, which culminated in countless encounters with a crack pipe.[15]

Josh Hamilton, the schoolboy pitcher who could fire off balls to the plate at 96 mph and who once swung a bat clocked at an incredible 110 mph—Josh Hamilton, the first high school player to be the #1 draft pick since Alex Rodriguez in 1993—became tragically addicted to both alcohol and cocaine.

"I never used one without the other," Josh remembers. "When I'd get mad, I'd go use. When I'd get sad, I'd go use."[16] Josh abused drugs and alcohol to numb his painful feelings, but later realized "they'd always be there the next day."[17]

This checklist will help reveal whether a person is chemically dependent:

C   Do you ***conceal*** *your habit* from others?

H   Do you ***hope*** *to get help* for your habit?

E   Is your ***employment*** *affected* because of your habit?

M   Is your ***memory*** *impaired* because of your habit?

I   Are you ***intoxicated*** *periodically*?

C   Are you ***criticized*** *unfairly* (in your opinion) because of your habit?

A   Do you ***assume*** *you can avoid problems* by using the substance?

L   Do you ***lose*** *relationships* as a result of your habit?

L   Do you ***lower*** *your intake* but then return to your previous level of consumption?

Y   Are your ***young*** *ones neglected* because of your habit?

D   Are you ***defensive*** *or argumentative* about your use?

E   Are you ***emotionally*** *unavailable* because of your use?

P   Is your ***physical*** *health affected* by your use?

E   Do you ***enjoy*** *functions only* if the substance is available?

N   Is your ***need*** *draining* your finances?

D   Do you ***deny*** *repercussions* from your habit?

E   Are you ***exasperated*** *by fear* that your habit is abnormal?

N   Is your ***need*** *affecting your life* because of your habit?

T   Is your ***tolerance*** *level getting higher* for the substance?

If you answered *yes* to five or more of the above questions, you may have a serious dependency problem.

> *"Woe to those who are heroes at drinking wine*
> *and champions at mixing drinks"*
> (ISAIAH 5:22).

============= *Change Can Happen* =============

QUESTION: "If I am a habitual, compulsive drinker and drug user, can I really change and permanently stop?"

ANSWER: All habits, compulsions, and addictions are highly resistant and are therefore very difficult to change, yet not impossibly so.

- Repeating certain actions actually alters the brain, making it more difficult to bring about change.
- However, new patterns of behavior can be learned, which, in turn, will alter your brain.
- Replace bad habits and addictions with good, healthy habits and activities with supportive people.

If you are a true believer, you have *His Word* to change your way of thinking, *His church*—often with specialized community groups—to support your life change, and *His Spirit* to empower you from within to follow through and stop abusing alcohol and drugs.

> *"It is God who works in you to will
> and to act according to his good purpose"*
> (PHILIPPIANS 2:13).

B. What Are the Warning Signs of Substance Abuse?

On the day Josh Hamilton was drafted by a major league baseball team, the team's scout commented on why Josh was chosen. "I think character may have been the final determining factor. You read so many bad things about professional athletes, but I don't think you ever will about Josh."[18]

But then a dump truck sped through a red light and smashed Josh Hamilton's entire life. The devastating blow resulted in twisted metal and a twisted back. Josh had been on the smooth road to success—drafted by Tampa Bay with a record signing bonus of almost $4 million and dubbed the top major league prospect in the minors—when the accident sidelined the 19-year-old with lingering back problems.

His parents, also hurt in the crash, were forced to return to North Carolina to recover from their injuries, leaving Josh alone for the first time in his life.[19]

In the Bible, we read of another person whose life took an unexpected and dramatic turn for the worst. For Job, life was good. He had everything he could possibly want. Then, in the space of just a few traumatic hours, he lost everything.

"And now my soul is poured out within me; days of
affliction have seized me. At night it pierces my bones
within me, and my gnawing pains take no rest"
(JOB 30:16-17 NASB).

Even in the midst of stressful circumstances, it's possible to discern the warning signs that indicate a person has an addiction problem. For a substance abuser, a combination of many symptoms can be observed—symptoms that fall into five basic categories: *emotional, physical, behavioral, relational,* and *spiritual.*

Emotional Warning Signs

- Anger
- Anxiety
- Depression
- Fear of rejection
- Frustration over little things
- Guilt—"My choices are bad"
- Shame—"I am bad"
- Unpredictable mood swings

Because Jesus cares about our hearts, He gives us these words of warning:

"Be careful, or your hearts will be weighed down with
dissipation, drunkenness and the anxieties of life, and
that day will close on you unexpectedly like a trap"
(LUKE 21:34).

Physical Warning Signs

- Bloodshot eyes
- Loss of sexual desire
- Night sweats
- Poor general health
- Shaky hands
- Skin breakouts
- Tendency to look older
- Unhealthy looking complexion
- Weight gain or puffiness

The Bible describes those who are addicted as those who have sorrow in their hearts:

"Who has woe? Who has sorrow?... Who has bloodshot eyes?
Those who linger over wine, who go to sample bowls of mixed wine"
(PROVERBS 23:29-30).

Behavioral Warning Signs

- Compulsive drug use
- Defensive about the addiction
- Denial that there is a problem
- Dishonest about usage
- Obstinate about change

- Rebellious toward those in authority
- Reclusive from those wanting to help
- Secretive about time spent on the addiction

Many a person has made an alliance with an addiction. God issues this warning to those who make choices that are contrary to His will for their lives:

"'Woe to the obstinate children,' declares the LORD,
'to those who carry out plans that are not mine,
forming an alliance, but not by my Spirit, heaping sin upon sin'"
(ISAIAH 30:1).

Relational Warning Signs

- Associating primarily with other users
- Attempting to hide addictive behavior
- Being too weak to stop and too stubborn to get help
- Deceiving others about money spent on the addiction
- Lying to others about frequency of use
- Prioritizing the drug over people and profession
- Refusing to act responsibly in relationships
- Shifting blame to others for problems

All close relationships are harmed when anyone struggles with an addiction. The Bible describes the warning signs of an abuser:

"This son of ours is stubborn and rebellious.
He will not obey us. He is a profligate and a drunkard"
(DEUTERONOMY 21:20).

Spiritual Warning Signs

- Aversion to Scripture
- Conviction by the Spirit

- Diminished prayer life
- Fear of God's punishment

- Feel estranged from God
- Hardened heart toward God
- Lack of joy
- Withdrawal from church life

The Lord describes those who choose to turn away from Him and choose "new wine":

> *"They do not cry out to me from their hearts*
> *but wail upon their beds. They gather together for grain*
> *and new wine but turn away from me"*
> (HOSEA 7:14).

Josh Hamilton was placed on the team's disabled list for a month, and other sports-related injuries were quick to follow, keeping the star off the baseball diamond more than on it. Separated from his parents and hampered by injury, Josh said, "The two things that I really knew in life, baseball and my parents, were taken away from me at the same time." [20]

The one-two punch sent Josh reeling, and before long the warning signs of severe substance abuse surfaced—at least four failed drug tests and eight trips to rehab.

C. What Delineates Binge Drinking?

A growing number of people today engage in *binge drinking*—that is, drinking an excessive amount of alcohol in a short period of time. While some cases of "overdoing" may be harmless, when it comes to alcohol, binge drinking is not only dangerous but it can also be deadly. Long before it was faddish to binge drink, the biblical book on wisdom gave this warning:

> *"Do not join those who drink too much wine or gorge*
> *themselves on meat, for drunkards and gluttons*
> *become poor, and drowsiness clothes them in rags"*
> (PROVERBS 23:20-21).

According to surveys taken in the United States...

- **Binge drinkers...**
  - Are more likely to be male [21]
  - Are 14 times more likely to experience alcohol-impaired driving [22]
  - Are 3 times more likely to binge drink when they consume alcohol mixed with energy drinks [23]

- Are more likely to have unprotected sex, multiple sex partners, cause unintended pregnancies, and acquire sexually transmitted diseases[24]

- Typically have a blood alcohol concentration (BAC) of 0.08 grams percent or above, which generally occurs when a man consumes five or more drinks in a two-hour period and a woman consumes four or more drinks in a two-hour period[25]

- **Binge drinking** accounts for...
  - About 90 percent of the alcohol consumed by youth under the age of 21[26]
  - About 75 percent of the alcohol consumed by adults[27]
  - Over 50 percent of the deaths related to alcohol
  - About 66 percent of the YPLL (years of potential life lost)[28]

- **Binge drinking** contributes to numerous health and social problems, including...[29]

  - Alcohol poisoning
  - Uncontrolled diabetes
  - Liver disease
  - Neurological damage
  - Fetal Alcohol Spectrum Disorders
  - Sexual dysfunction
  - Unintentional injuries (car crashes, falls, burns, drowning)
  - High blood pressure, stroke, and other cardiovascular diseases
  - Intentional injuries (firearm injuries, sexual assault, domestic violence)

D. What Differentiates Men and Women Drinkers?

The differences in when and how men and women begin drinking and fall into substance abuse is known as the "telescoping phenomenon." Women generally begin drinking later in life than men, but they develop habitual patterns of drunkenness and dependence on alcohol at a faster rate than men. Women also tend to develop a drinking habit in an effort to manage stress, anxiety, or depression.[30]

Women and Alcohol: Health and Pregnancy[31]

- **Drinking alcohol excessively** increases the risk of...
  - A disrupted menstrual cycle
  - Infertility
  - Miscarriage
  - Stillbirth
  - Premature delivery
  - Cancer

- **Drinking alcohol while pregnant** increases the risk of having a baby with Fetal Alcohol Spectrum Disorders (FASD), whereas refraining from drinking while trying to become pregnant and while pregnant completely prevents FASD. There is absolutely no safe amount of alcohol consumption during pregnancy. The most severe result of drinking during pregnancy is Fetal Alcohol Syndrome (FAS), which causes...
  - Emotional problems
  - Mental retardation
  - Birth defects

- **Drinking alcohol while pregnant** increases the likelihood of having a baby die from Sudden Infant Death Syndrome (SIDS). This risk substantially increases when a woman binge drinks during her first trimester of pregnancy.

Men and Alcohol: Health and Sexual Function[32]

- **Drinking alcohol excessively** can interfere with testicular function and male hormone production, resulting in impotence and infertility.

- **Drinking alcohol excessively** can significantly increase risk of injury or death due to...
  - Driving recklessly while intoxicated
  - Blood poisoning

- **Drinking alcohol excessively** results in increased aggression and impaired judgment, which in turn increases the risk of committing sexual assault and engaging in risky sexual activity. Such excessive drinking can lead to...

- Participating in sex without protection and with multiple partners
- Mistaking a woman's friendship as sexual interest
- Misjudgments about one's own strength and forcefulness
- Acts of violence, including rape

Gender Differences for Drinkers[33]

MALES

- More drink excessively
- Almost two times as likely to be intoxicated prior to a fatal vehicle accident
- 62 percent of adults drink
- 17 percent develop alcohol dependence
- More seek treatment for abuse
- Most treatment programs are male-oriented
- Less initially impacted by alcohol
- Bodies carry more water, which dilutes alcohol absorption
- Effects of alcohol metabolize faster
- Less physically affected by alcohol/drugs (2 drinks for males = 1 for females)
- Have higher levels of the ADH[34] enzyme that breaks down alcohol
- Higher rates of alcohol-related deaths and hospitalizations due to risky behavior

FEMALES

- More get high or drunk
- Nearly half as likely to be intoxicated prior to a fatal vehicle accident
- 47 percent of adults drink
- 8 percent develop alcohol dependence
- More reluctant to receive treatment

- Most treatment programs fail to embrace women's needs
- More immediately impacted by alcohol
- Bodies carry less water and more fatty tissue, which increases alcohol absorption
- Effects of alcohol last longer
- More physically affected by alcohol/drugs (1 drink for females = 2 for males)
- Have lower levels of the ADH enzyme, thus become addicted to alcohol faster
- Higher risk for cirrhosis of liver, brain damage, and heart damage

Over and over, the Bible offers strong warnings about alcohol:

> *"Woe to those who rise early in the morning to run after their drinks, who stay up late at night till they are inflamed with wine"*
> (ISAIAH 5:11).

E. What Clues Are Characteristic of Children with an Addicted Parent?

Josh Hamilton's newborn daughter, Sierra, was only a few days old, and her daddy was drunk and high. The day Sierra left the hospital and went to her very own home—where her crib, stuffed animals, and toys awaited her—should have been a very happy one. Her mother, Katie, whom Josh married during a brief period of sobriety in 2004, sent him on an errand to pick up some prescription medicine. But a task that should have taken only ten minutes to do seemed to stretch into an eternity.

Katie called a local bar—yes, Josh was there. "That's when I knew we had the battle of our lives on our hands," Katie recalls.[35]

Fortunately, Sierra was too young to bear the clues characteristic of children with an addicted parent. Later, Josh became sober and drug free—yet Katie knew that if he hadn't changed, their children would have suffered. The Bible says,

> *"Fathers, do not exasperate your children; instead, bring them up in the training and instruction of the Lord"*
> (EPHESIANS 6:4).

Does the child struggle with...

- *Guilt* . . . . feeling responsible for a parent's chemical dependency?

- *Anxiety* . . . . worrying about the home situation?
- *Embarrassment* . . . . feeling too ashamed to invite friends home or too embarrassed to ask for help?
- *Lack of trust* . . . . having difficulty trusting others because of having an untrustworthy parent?
- *Confusion* . . . . feeling insecure because of a parent's inconsistent behaviors and unpredictable moods?
- *Anger* . . . . feeling angry at the addicted parent and the nonaddicted parent for enabling?
- *Depression* . . . . feeling lonely, fearful, and helpless to change the situation?
- *Hypervigilance* . . . . experiencing extreme sensitivity to the moods of others?
- *Excessive responsibility* . . assuming immediate, inordinate responsibility for others?
- *People pleasing* . . . . avoiding conflict by trying to please others—no matter the cost?

In order to "be loyal" and "take care" of their addicted parents, many children will lie, manipulate, and do simply anything—no matter how wrong—in order to keep the peace at home. Jesus had this to say about a person who causes a child to sin:

> *"It would be better for him to be thrown into the sea with a millstone tied around his neck than for him to cause one of these little ones to sin"*
> (LUKE 17:2).

III. CAUSES OF ALCOHOL AND DRUG ABUSE

Josh Hamilton's life was spinning out of control like a wildly thrown pitch. He was caught in a chaotic cycle of failed drug tests, baseball suspensions, trips to rehab, periods of sobriety, baseball reinstatement, and then...another relapse.

Following one reinstatement in May 2003, Josh hammered a home run over the center-field wall of the ballpark. Obviously he still had what it took to soar to the top. Some baseball buddies invited him to go drinking. Josh declined. Then he went out alone...and *got trashed.*

"I did it on purpose," Josh said. "I just couldn't come to grips with how to deal with life. I remember a couple days after that, I showed up for early hitting knowing I had failed a test. I sat in the dugout with hitting coach Steve Henderson. I looked at the pitcher's mound and the field and I just said, 'This might be it for me.' I started to cry."[36]

Josh's worst fear was realized—at least for a while. He was banned from baseball for three years. Decidedly, drugs dictated his life—indeed, sin (anything outside of God's will) had mastery over him. As the Bible clearly warns,

> *"A man is a slave to whatever has mastered him"*
> (2 PETER 2:19).

A. What Causes Chemical Dependency?

Josh's ban from baseball only heightened his dependency on drugs. He likened the drug highs to the adrenaline rush he got after throwing a runner out at base or hearing the crowd roar after he hit a home run. Yet now he was in exile, and he was in great emotional pain. No longer could he hit a homer and "earn" the adrenaline highs—so instead, he made the choice to chemically induce the highs. But all too soon he found himself in life-threatening situations—like the time he wrote a $2000 check to a menacing drug dealer, a bad check he knew would bounce.

Ultimately, Josh's father-in-law bailed him out on Josh's twenty-fourth birthday. Josh said he will forever remember this night as the "night from hell."[37]

As his heart became darker, his sin became deeper—like the sins of those trapped in a blindness of their own making.

> *"But the way of the wicked is like deep darkness;*
> *they do not know what makes them stumble"*
> (PROVERBS 4:19).

THE CYCLE OF ADDICTION

Most people don't start their lives being dependent on substances; rather, they *become* dependent through repetition—by repeatedly using a substance to satisfy some unmet need. Here's how the cycle typically progresses:

- **Past pain**—provocation for using drugs
  - "My heart is aching because of what happened in the past."

> *"Even in laughter the heart may ache, and joy may end in grief"*
> (PROVERBS 14:13).

- **Mood-altering drugs**—seeking temporary solutions to emotional pain
  - "I don't like these feelings; I just want to feel better."

    "How long must I wrestle with my thoughts and
    every day have sorrow in my heart?"
    (PSALM 13:2).

- **Addiction**—abusing mood-altering drugs on a regular basis
  - "I have to have more to help medicate my pain."

    "When you were slaves to sin, you were free from the control of
    righteousness. What benefit did you reap at that time from the
    things you are now ashamed of? Those things result in death!"
    (ROMANS 6:20-21).

- **Violating values**—breaking your internal moral code by using drugs
  - "I don't care what I have to do to get it—I need it!"

    "Our fathers were unfaithful; they did evil in the eyes of the LORD
    our God and forsook him. They turned their faces away from
    the LORD's dwelling place and turned their backs on him"
    (2 CHRONICLES 29:6).

- **Guilt**—being convicted about your wrong attitudes and actions
  - "I know what I did wasn't good—it was bad."

    "My guilt has overwhelmed me like a burden too heavy to bear"
    (PSALM 38:4).

- **Shame**—feeling you're no good, worthless, hopeless
  - "I know I'm no good—I'm just bad."

    "My disgrace is before me all day long,
    and my face is covered with shame"
    (PSALM 44:15).

The alcoholic then thinks, *I hate feeling this shame, so I need some drug to help me feel better*—and that only repeats the cycle. Once drug use is established, the user ends up in a vicious cycle that entraps and enslaves. But it's a cycle that *can* be broken!

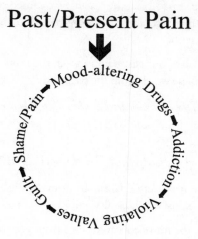

Past/Present Pain

Mood-altering Drugs → Addiction → Violating Values → Guilt → Shame/Pain →

=== *Escaping Emotional Pain* ===

QUESTION: "How can I stop using drugs in an attempt to escape the pain from my childhood?"

ANSWER: Face the facts of your past pain. Take the necessary steps to stop making decisions based on your emotional pain, including your desire to escape and feel differently. The drugs you turned to for help are now controlling you. Drugs, however, are not lasting solutions. They only mask your pain—they don't remove it. To break free of both drugs and the pain from your childhood, you need to take these action steps:

- Evaluate your painful thoughts (write each one down).
- Redirect them toward God (tell Him what was so painful, and release each pain to Him).
- Get help. Talk to a friend, counselor, pastor, coach, or other trusted person in your life.
- Get support. Meet with others who have similar issues or addictions and are seeking sobriety.

- Choose to forgive each person who has hurt you (release each one to God).
- Forgive even if you feel that the person who caused your pain doesn't deserve it. Remember, a refusal to forgive ends up hurting you, not the unforgiven one.

The more you release your past pain to God, the more He will bring about healing. Remember these words from the psalmist:

> *"He heals the brokenhearted and binds up their wounds"*
> (PSALM 147:3).

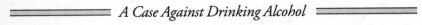

A Case Against Drinking Alcohol

QUESTION: "Is there any objective data apart from the Bible or cultural morality that supports a case against drinking alcohol?"

ANSWER: Yes. While the numbers can change from year to year, the following statistics from recent research within the United States prove to be quite sobering.

- Up to 57 percent of domestic violence incidents involved alcohol use.[38]
- The third-leading preventable cause of death is alcohol abuse.[39]
- Nearly 40 percent of all traffic fatalities are alcohol-related.[40]
- Up to 37 percent of convicted murderers abused alcohol at the time of their crime.[41]

If you are trying to quit drinking, consider reading the following passage every day to help strengthen your stand and to reinforce your resolve:

> *"Wine is a mocker and beer a brawler;*
> *whoever is led astray by them is not wise"*
> (PROVERBS 20:1).

Personal Conviction

QUESTION: "Why do some people have a personal conviction that leads them to abstain from alcohol?"

ANSWER: There are varying reasons for why some people choose not to drink.

Some choose to avoid alcohol and drugs because they have seen the havoc these substances can cause; others make such a choice based on a biblical perspective.

- While the Bible does not completely prohibit the consumption of alcohol, it does give us strong warnings, such as the one in Proverbs 20:1: "Wine is a mocker and beer a brawler; whoever is led astray by them is not wise."

- Second, the Bible warns that someone might stumble because of our example. Since people tend to be followers, if we drink alcohol or do drugs, those who follow our example could stumble, and their lives could be harmed on account of following in our footsteps. Even if some are able to control their own usage, what if others around them cannot? According to the apostle Paul,

> *"It is good not to...drink wine or do anything*
> *that causes your brother to stumble"*
> (ROMANS 14:21 ESV).

B. What Are the Influential Factors that Help Form an Addiction?

For the first time, Josh was hit by pain unlike any he had ever experienced—pain that proved almost lethal.

The absence of his moral parents, the presence of his immoral friends, the absence of baseball's adrenaline rush, and the presence of narcotics' chemical rush all factored together to create a toxic combination that almost destroyed Josh Hamilton's life. Then came the lowest point of his dark journey, which took place in the summer of 2005.

Josh was absolutely clueless. He was coming off a crack binge and had no idea where he was. He woke up in a stiflingly hot mobile home, surrounded by half a dozen stoned strangers. His first thought wasn't *Run for your life*, but *Run to the crack dealer*! Josh desperately wanted *more* crack, so he loaned his truck to a dealer. The dealer never returned. Soon Josh took off on foot and, although they were estranged at the time, he called his wife, Katie, and asked her to pick him up.[42]

According to Josh, that was the darkest season of his life. His sole focus at the time was to get more crack. He couldn't see past the darkness of his addiction.

> *"If your eyes are bad, your whole body will be full of darkness.*
> *If then the light within you is darkness, how great is that darkness!"*
> (MATTHEW 6:23).

No two people have exactly the same story about what contributed to the development of their drug dependency. But no matter how many different factors are involved in a person's journey to chemical dependency, ultimately, those factors fall into one of two categories: external or internal influences.

External Influences—Family and Social

Check all that apply to you:

FAMILY ENVIRONMENT

☐ Were you raised in a family that was fine with social drinking?

☐ Did any of your family members use drugs?

DYSFUNCTIONAL FAMILY

☐ While growing up, did you feel as if you did not "belong" or that one or both of your parents were physically or emotionally unavailable?

☐ Was there any abuse in the family?

PHYSICAL PROBLEMS

☐ Are you dependent on medication for pain relief, headaches, sleeplessness, or dieting?

☐ Do you suffer from a chronic condition or a physical disability?

SOCIAL ACCEPTANCE

☐ Are you offered alcohol or drugs at the social functions you attend?

☐ Do you feel out of place or uncomfortable in groups?

PEER PRESSURE

☐ Are you seeking social acceptance from those who drink or use drugs?

☐ Do you feel desperate for approval?

CULTURAL ENDORSEMENT

☐ Do you continually expose yourself to alcohol through the media—that is, movies, ads, and magazines?

☐ Does drinking fit who you see yourself to be?

The Bible gives this instruction for countering our secular culture:

> *"Do not conform any longer to the pattern of this world,*
> *but be transformed by the renewing of your mind.*
> *Then you will be able to test and approve what God's will is—*
> *his good, pleasing and perfect will"*
> (ROMANS 12:2).

Saying No to Friends

QUESTION: "Without offending them, how can I say *no* to my heavy-drinking friends who offer me drinks?"

ANSWER: A simple "No, thank you" or "Thank you; I'm not interested" should suffice. Most people don't like to drink or do drugs alone. However, most will also respect—if not envy—someone who is strong enough to not "follow the crowd." If they are offended, that is a reflection on their own insecurity, not on your convictions. Remember:

• You and you alone are accountable for the boundaries you set for your life.

• Anyone can give in to peer pressure.

• Only those who have strength of character will resist peer pressure.

Be aware that those who entice others to drink are walking on dangerous ground. The Bible says,

> *"Woe to him who gives drink to his neighbors,*
> *pouring it from the wineskin till they are drunk"*
> (HABAKKUK 2:15).

Internal Influences—Genetic and Psychological

INHERITED INCLINATION FROM FAMILY

☐ Were you born to an alcoholic parent?

☐ Do you have close relatives who are alcoholics?

The risk for alcohol dependence is three to four times higher for those who have close relatives with a dependence on alcohol.[43]

INHERITED VULNERABILITY FROM AN ETHNIC GROUP

☐ Were you born within an ethnic group that has a high rate of alcoholism within its population?

Scandinavians, northern Europeans, and the Irish are more susceptible, whereas Asians are less susceptible. "The low prevalence rates among Asians appear to relate to a deficiency, in perhaps 50% of Japanese, Chinese, and Korean individuals, of the form of aldehyde dehydrogenase that eliminates low levels of the first breakdown product of alcohol known as acetaldehyde."[44]

Alcoholics process alcohol in a way that reinforces their addiction. Acetaldehyde works within them to create addictive chemical compounds that interfere with the brain's processes and create an opiate-like addiction.[45]

PSYCHOLOGICAL MAKEUP

☐ Are you prone to seek drugs as a relief from anxiety and stress?

☐ Are you prone to struggle with excessive guilt and shame?

Alcohol soothes the underlying nerves, and thus calms intense responses to stress—that is, perspiring palms, flushed skin, and an increase in heart rate and blood pressure.

HABITS AND COMPULSIONS

☐ Do you have habits you feel are resistant to change?

☐ Do you compulsively fixate on activities that involve drinking or drugs?

Repetitive alcohol and drug use alters the brain itself. Eventually the connections between the brain neurons are slowly modified, thus making it more difficult for you to make different choices.

No matter what reason we give for becoming enslaved to a habit that has mastery over us, God says we can change masters:

> *"If you do what is right, will you not be accepted?*
> *But if you do not do what is right, sin is crouching at your door;*
> *it desires to have you, but you must master it"*
> (GENESIS 4:7).

═══════════════ *Inherited "Disease"* ═══════════════

QUESTION: "Is alcoholism an inherited disease over which I have no control? My father and grandfather are alcoholics."

ANSWER: Medical professionals continue to debate whether or not alcoholism is a disease. Because of the strong and lasting changes alcohol can have on the brain and other organs, many consider it a disease. Others, however, take the position that alcoholism is more of a behavioral problem.

A disease is defined as an "abnormal condition of the body" caused by... [46]

- Infections (catching the flu or smallpox from a germ or virus outside the body)
- Genetic defects (being born with diabetes or with a genetic makeup that causes alcohol to not be processed normally)
- Environmental factors (being exposed to toxins and pollutants, or developing cirrhosis of the liver, in which excessive alcohol caused so much stress on the liver that it no longer functions properly)

While alcoholism can be influenced by genetics and chemical alterations, the vital fact to remember is that *you have total control over whether or not you choose to drink*. Your family background can make you more susceptible, but such influences can be resisted. No matter what your family's alcoholic history, the Lord, in His mercy, will meet you at your point of need.

> *"Do not hold against us the sins of the fathers; may your mercy*
> *come quickly to meet us, for we are in desperate need"*
> (PSALM 79:8).

C. What Excuses Do People Give?

No one has to be taught the art of justifying wrong behavior. Somehow we seem to come by that skill very naturally. People who are chemically dependent become proficient at rattling off reason after reason for using their drug of choice, but, ultimately, there is no valid justification—only excuses. In the final analysis, they are persuaded that they genuinely need it, or they feel entitled just because they want it. [47]

> **"I need it**...to help pick me up."
> ...to help quiet me down."
> ...to help relieve my pain."
> ...to help me be more sociable."
> ...to help me forget my failures."
> ...to help me satisfy my cravings."

"I want it...to help me relax."
...to help me feel good."
...to help me have more fun."
...to help me relieve my stress."
...to help me be more accepted."
...to help me escape my situation."

As the Bible says,

> *"All a man's ways seem innocent to him,*
> *but motives are weighed by the LORD"*
> (PROVERBS 16:2).

=== *Disease or Sin?* ===

QUESTION: "If alcoholism can be both inherited and a disease, how can it be a sin? Isn't the fact I'm an alcoholic something that's beyond my control?"

ANSWER: Many identify themselves as alcoholics based on physiology, but they choose not to drink. In regard to sin: It's not a sin for you to be a *nondrinking alcoholic*. It is a sin to be a *drunk alcoholic*. In the Bible, drunkenness is listed among the sins that we are commanded to avoid. Even if alcoholism were a disease over which you have no control, *drunkenness* is clearly a sin over which you *do* have control. Choosing not to drink means setting a boundary for your life that will help you to break the power this sin has over you.

The Bible clearly describes drunkenness as sin.

> *"The acts of the sinful nature are obvious: sexual immorality,*
> *impurity and debauchery...and envy; drunkenness"*
> (GALATIANS 5:19,21).

D. What Is the Root Cause of Alcohol or Drug Abuse?

For too long, Josh Hamilton's craving was for drugs. But in October 2005, he finally realized what he really needed was the Lord. God used a rare rebuke from his beloved grandmother to get his attention: "I'm tired of you killing yourself. I'm tired of watching you hurt all the people who care about you."[48]

All of a sudden, something in Josh clicked.

He immediately recognized his need for supernatural help. It was the only way he could fight the demons of drugs and alcohol. So he offered up his broken spirit to God.

"I can't try anymore because I fail on my own," Josh humbly confessed to God. "You do with me what you want to do with me, but I surrender."[49]

And with that surrender came new strength and the power to live a godly life. Finally, Josh could proclaim along with the psalmist:

> *"I love you, O LORD, my strength. The LORD is my rock, my fortress*
> *and my deliverer; my God is my rock, in whom I take refuge. He*
> *is my shield and the horn of my salvation, my stronghold"*
> (PSALM 18:1-2).

Initially people take drugs for two reasons: either to treat a legitimate medical problem, or to feel a pleasurable sensation. Those who are trying to *feel differently* typically begin drinking or using drugs because of peer pressure or to satisfy their curiosity. But they continue their usage in order to satisfy their *perceived* needs. Substance abuse occurs when the substance moves from being a need-meeter to becoming the need itself. Instead of using a substance to *relieve* stress, they end up using a substance because its mere absence *causes* stress.

God designed every person with legitimate needs—physical, emotional, relational, and spiritual. And His design is for all people to come to Him and to be dependent on Him as their true Need-meeter.

> *"My God will meet all your needs*
> *according to his glorious riches in Christ Jesus"*
> (PHILIPPIANS 4:19).

WRONG BELIEF:

"I don't have a chemical dependency. I just enjoy the way it makes me feel. I could stop anytime, but it helps me cope with my difficult situations and eases my painful emotions."

RIGHT BELIEF:

"I realize that what I depend on in my life will have control of my life. I choose not to let any chemical have control over me. Instead, I choose to give Christ control of every area of my life and to depend on Him to satisfy my needs."

The Bible says,

> *"The LORD will guide you always; he will satisfy your needs in a*
> *sun-scorched land and will strengthen your frame. You will be*
> *like a well-watered garden, like a spring whose waters never fail"*
> (ISAIAH 58:11).

Norm—the Blustering Goliath

"God, help me! I can't handle it!"[50]

This desperate cry was born out of a sobering crisis, for at long last, Norm recognized that he had been following in his father's staggering footsteps. In fact, he had become just like his father: an alcoholic. For 20 years, Norm hit the hard stuff through countless drinking binges that didn't end until the bartender declared, "Last call!"

Norm's dad introduced him to alcohol. On Saturday afternoons at his service station, Norm's father would set up a little bar in a back room and invite regular customers in for a drink. He said he just wanted to have a little fun. But on many Saturdays, by around 8:00 p.m., the fun was over. Norm remembers watching men carry his father home and put him to bed.[51]

With his dad drowning in a sea of alcohol, Norm took his first dip in junior high and was quickly immersed. Partying rather than studying became Norm's priority, and he soon began hanging with the heavy-drinking crowd. At college, Norm drank even more but somehow managed to graduate, get married, and start working at the Interstate Batteries distributorship in Memphis with his dad and brothers.[52]

Later, Norm moved to Texas to work as a traveling salesman based at the company headquarters. In his first year, he spent more than eight months on the road—a lifestyle that revolved around "drinking, partying, and selling!"[53] On the Friday afternoon plane rides home he bought drink after drink after drink, so by the time the plane landed, he was already loaded. But for him, the partying had only just begun. He would then go to bars and stay until closing time, with blackouts often ending the bingeing.

After Norm was convicted twice of driving while intoxicated,[54] he was once again pulled over by a policeman, but he managed to talk his way out of being arrested. He continued on home that night and, the next morning, woke up with a hangover so bad that he called in sick to work. Norm recounts, "As I lay there in bed, the truth overwhelmed me." That's when a thought hit him like a bottle breaking across his head. "I was an alcoholic just like my father. I'd lost control of my life. That was a frightening realization!"[55]

In the next moment, Norm experienced a most miraculous transformation. As soon as he blurted out, "God, help me! I can't handle it!" his addiction to alcohol ended—suddenly and *immediately*. "I'll never forget those words, because He completely took away the compulsion to drink. It was over right then," Norm recalls with amazement.[56]

There is yet another intriguing twist to Norm's account of deliverance—a significant sign and reminder of God's amazing grace. At the time he cried out in desperation, he wasn't even sure if he even *believed* in God. Work and alcohol had been his gods. Norm hadn't given any thought to the prospect of a *personal*, all-powerful God—big G. "Religion meant nothing to me," Norm states.[57]

Around this time, a friend told Norm that the Bible is a guidebook for life. It reveals what life is really all about and how to live. Norm quickly dismissed his friend, declaring that unless he could *prove* that the Bible was the absolute truth, he wouldn't budge from his belief that the Bible was a book filled with outdated philosophies—and was altogether irrelevant.

Norm, like a blustering "Goliath," quickly discovered that his friend was indeed the "David" in his life. He provided Norm with a myriad of materials on archaeological finds, the authenticity of biblical manuscripts, and the fulfillment of hundreds of Old Testament prophecies in the New Testament. "The supporting evidence was so strong that I began reading the Bible and attending a Bible study," Norm remembers.[58] Then, just like the towering Philistine giant in the Bible, Norm's faulty assumptions about the Bible were knocked down in one fell swoop.

Ultimately, a diligent search of the Scriptures led Norm to an encounter with Christ and the beginning of a life-changing relationship with Him.

Norm Miller represents the epitome of the American dream. He worked his way up through the ranks of Interstate Batteries, from being a traveling salesman to the premier post he occupies now. As chairman of Interstate Battery System of America, Norm has molded the corporation to earn an unrivaled reputation for excellence and integrity, as well as sustained success in the marketplace. No longer a blustering Goliath, Norm is considered a giant of ethics and integrity in his field, a man committed to the call and commands of Christ. He stands tall as a mighty example to others of how the faith of an authentic Christian at the top of a corporation can powerfully impact all aspects of the workplace.

While Norm is now one of the most persuasive representatives of Christ in corporate America, he has never forgotten his past. His longing is for those who are enslaved to alcohol to be set free. Indeed Norm knows the truth, and he quotes Jesus, who is the Truth: "You will know the truth, and the truth will set you free" (John 8:32).

IV. Steps to Solution

What Josh Hamilton clearly stated, his wife, Katie, affirmed: "I put her through absolute hell for a long time."[59]

And on January 22, 2009, Katie thought she just might be taking a trip back to the dark side. Sober and drug-free for three years, a sobbing Josh called her from Arizona and said that upon encountering a bar at a pizza restaurant, he ended up having one drink, then another, then another. Then Josh and Katie's biggest fear as a celebrity couple came true. Seven months later, photographs of Josh carousing with three young women were made public.[60] The fact is all too true: "A man is a slave to whatever has mastered him" (2 Peter 2:19).

A. Key Verse to Memorize

The prayer that Josh and every struggler needs to pray often is this:

> *"Teach me to do your will, for you are my God;*
> *may your good Spirit lead me on level ground"*
> (Psalm 143:10).

Katie admitted that the boundary lines had become blurred. They had let their guards down, and Josh had relapsed. So then, in his desire to stay firmly grounded in Christ, Josh set for himself "double boundaries" to prevent another relapse. To minimize the possibility of succumbing to temptation, Josh stopped carrying money with him. The monetary allocations for his baseball road trips were carried by someone else.

Josh stopped going out alone at night, and he stopped going out with his teammates. And a certain someone was given the task of knowing Josh's whereabouts at all times. Johnny Narron, a former first baseman and batting coach who looms large in Josh's life, served as his mentor, confidante, chaperone, and stalwart brother in Christ. The two always have adjoining rooms on the road, and Johnny stays with Josh if Katie and their three daughters are away.

The boundaries must be firm, rigid, *immovable* for a recovering addict, and Josh's life is a testimony to that truth. "That's why I go to the ballpark, and I go home. Park. Home. Park. Home."[61] Josh takes the following Scripture literally:

> *"He who ignores discipline despises himself,*
> *but whoever heeds correction gains understanding"*
> (Proverbs 15:32).

B. Key Passage to Read and Reread

For evidence that Josh Hamilton has dabbled on the dark side, to see that he has indeed wrestled with his "inner demons" of chemical dependency, you can simply look at his arms.

His past so-called "friends" influenced Josh in yet another way besides substance abuse. Tattoos line both of Josh's arms—26 in all on his body—and they aren't images of butterflies and buttercups.[62] Staring at him from the crook of his left elbow is a personification of the face of Satan, a permanent reminder that as a recovering addict, evil is so very near. Blue flames shoot down both arms, and blank-eyed demons sprawl across his skin.

Josh deeply regrets having gotten the tattoos, but there is one on the back of his right leg that looms large—the radiant face of Jesus superimposed over a tall cross. This image is a powerful reminder that, despite the debilitating drugs and evil tattoos, he can experience freedom in Christ. He gives total credit to Christ for victory and knows that

> *"in all these things we are more than*
> *conquerors through him who loved us"*
> (ROMANS 8:37).

10 TRUTHS ABOUT TEMPTATION
1 CORINTHIANS 10

1. If you think you're fairly invulnerable to temptation, be vigilant and careful so that you won't fall.

   > *"So, if you think you are standing firm,*
   > *be careful that you don't fall!"*
   > (VERSE 12).

2. If you think your temptation is unique, clearly it's not.

   > *"No temptation has seized you*
   > *except what is common to man"*
   > (VERSE 13).

3. God won't let you be tempted beyond what you can bear.

   > *"And God is faithful; he will not let you be tempted*
   > *beyond what you can bear"*
   > (VERSE 13).

4. God will provide a way for you to withstand the test.

> *"But when you are tempted, he will also provide a*
> *way out so that you can stand up under it"*
> (VERSE 13).

5. Don't prioritize what is permissible—prioritize what is beneficial.

> *"'Everything is permissible'—but not everything is beneficial.*
> *'Everything is permissible'—but not everything is constructive"*
> (VERSE 23).

6. Don't focus on yourself—focus on the good of others.

> *"Nobody should seek his own good, but the good of others"*
> (VERSE 24).

7. Don't violate the conscience of others—curb your freedom for their sake.

> *"But if anyone says to you, 'This has been offered in sacrifice,' then*
> *do not eat it, both for the sake of the man who told you and for*
> *conscience' sake—the other man's conscience, I mean, not yours"*
> (VERSES 28-29).

8. Let your eating and drinking—and everything else you do— bring glory to God.

> *"So whether you eat or drink or whatever you*
> *do, do it all for the glory of God"*
> (VERSE 31).

9. Don't do things that cause others to stumble.

> *"Do not cause anyone to stumble,*
> *whether Jews, Greeks or the church of God"*
> (VERSE 32).

10. Seek the good of others so that they might be truly saved.

> *"For I am not seeking my own good but the good*
> *of many, so that they may be saved"*
> (VERSE 33).

C. How to Discover Deliverance from Dependency[63]

As happened with Josh, it took a crisis for Mickey Mantle finally to turn away from substance abuse. With his body deteriorating, his memory lapsing, and his family crumbling, Mickey did what everyone thought was unthinkable—he entered rehab.

But immediately after he finished treatment, Mickey felt enormous pressure to relapse back into drinking. His son Billy died of a heart attack and then his mother died. Just as there had been great expectations upon him to "drink with the guys," Mickey now knew there were great expectations upon him to stay sober.[64]

Son Mickey Jr. assessed the situation: "Out of all the things he did, the World Series teams he starred on, the home runs he hit, the records he broke, his induction into the Hall of Fame, what I admired him for the most was getting sober."[65] To face his fear, Mickey experienced on a very personal and profound level the transforming truth of these words:

> *"I am the LORD, your God, who takes hold of your right*
> *hand and says to you, Do not fear; I will help you"*
> (ISAIAH 41:13).

Just as a chemical dependency doesn't occur overnight, neither does deliverance from dependency. (See chapter 1, pages 15–20 for more on this.) And just as a sequence of events takes place when people are led into bondage, another sequence of events can help lead people into freedom. (One such sequence is presented in chapter 11, on pages 379-84.)

D. How to Recognize the Seven Don'ts for Deliverance[66]

Mickey made the call at 6:00 in the morning. "Betsy, let me talk to Bobby, I want him to pray for me."[67] The request was inconceivable—it seemed impossible that the raucous, rebellious slugger would ever solicit God's help. Yet Mickey phoned his Yankee teammate Bobby Richardson because he finally recognized that he needed God in his life.

For too many years, Mickey had succumbed to one temptation after another. But now he wanted to stand in the strength and grace of the God that his friend Bobby knew. Bobby prayed with Mickey, and afterward, the aged baseball buddies had several more conversations about spiritual matters.

> *"This is what we speak, not in words taught us by*
> *human wisdom but in words taught by the Spirit,*
> *expressing spiritual truths in spiritual words"*
> (1 CORINTHIANS 2:13).

"It's hard to look back. But you learn from it...I want to make a difference, not because I hit home runs, but because I changed my life. If I can, anyone can. It is never too late."[68]

Reading Mickey Mantle's words, there is no doubt they were uttered by a man whose life had experienced deliverance ultimately through the power of Christ. And the message Mickey sends to strugglers is a very important "don't": *Don't ever give up!*

Bobby Richardson's life modeled that same very important don't: Don't ever give up. Bobby never gave up on his former fellow Yankee. How blessed "the Mick" was to have a faithful friend who consistently shared the hope of Christ with him. Bobby's availability and willingness to show he cared represents the heart of this passage:

> *"My brothers, if one of you should wander from the truth*
> *and someone should bring him back, remember this:*
> *Whoever turns a sinner from the error of his way will save*
> *him from death and cover over a multitude of sins"*
> (JAMES 5:19-20).

As you go through the process of deliverance from dependency, knowing what *not* to do can be just as helpful as knowing what *to* do. So as you practice living in the truth of God's Word...

1. ***Don't*** fight addiction on your own. Participate in a legitimate recovery program.

   > *"Two are better than one, because they have a good return for*
   > *their work: If one falls down, his friend can help him up. But*
   > *pity the man who falls and has no one to help him up!"*
   > (ECCLESIASTES 4:9-10).

2. ***Don't*** be blind about your ability to lie to yourself and to others.

   > *"The heart is deceitful above all things and*
   > *beyond cure. Who can understand it?"*
   > (JEREMIAH 17:9).

3. ***Don't*** socialize with those who encourage your habit.

   > *"Do not be misled: 'Bad company corrupts good character'"*
   > (1 CORINTHIANS 15:33).

4. ***Don't*** worry about the future. Walk with God one day at a time.

> *"Do not worry about tomorrow, for tomorrow will worry*
> *about itself. Each day has enough trouble of its own"*
> (MATTHEW 6:34).

5. ***Don't*** give up if you relapse. It is never too late for you to get back on track.

> *"If we confess our sins, he is faithful and just and will forgive*
> *us our sins and purify us from all unrighteousness"*
> (1 JOHN 1:9).

6. ***Don't*** become prideful as you succeed in the recovery process.

> *"Pride goes before destruction, a haughty spirit before a fall"*
> (PROVERBS 16:18).

7. ***Don't*** be surprised when temptation strikes unexpectedly—especially after you've known success for a while.

> *"No temptation has seized you except what is common to*
> *man. And God is faithful; he will not let you be tempted*
> *beyond what you can bear. But when you are tempted, he will*
> *also provide a way out so that you can stand up under it"*
> (1 CORINTHIANS 10:13).

E. How to Recover Using Ten Spiritual Steps[69]

Bobby Richardson had agreed to officiate at Mickey Mantle's funeral when he was summoned to Dallas, Texas. Three days before the death of baseball's greatest athlete, Bobby visited Mickey in the hospital. Knowing this might be his very last opportunity to make an appeal that would direct the eternal destiny of the Mick, there was no time for small talk or hesitation.

"Mickey, I love you, and I want you to spend eternity in heaven with me."[70] Nothing more needed to be said, for Bobby had already clearly communicated before to Mickey that Jesus died on the cross for his sins and rose again, opening the door for full forgiveness and the free gift of eternal life. So how would his friend respond in these final moments? Would he accept or reject the amazing grace being extended to him?

Mickey smiled and serenely said, "Bobby, I've been wanting to tell you that I have trusted Jesus Christ as my Savior."[71] Baseball legend Mickey Mantle died *a healed man.* Physically, he no longer suffers the pain and anguish of a disease-ravaged body. And he was healed *spiritually*—every single sin Mickey Mantle had ever committed had been forgiven by Christ—never, ever to be brought up again.

> *"In him we have...the forgiveness of sins"*
> (EPHESIANS 1:7).

Your freedom must first be gained in the spiritual realm before it can be experienced in the physical, emotional, and relational realms. Take to heart the following steps as you walk down the road to recovery:

1. The time to begin your recovery is today.

> *"Today, if you hear his voice, do not harden your hearts"*
> (HEBREWS 3:15).

2. Realize that recovery is a lifelong process, not a one-time event.

> *"Not that I have already obtained all this, or have*
> *already been made perfect, but I press on to take hold*
> *of that for which Christ Jesus took hold of me"*
> (PHILIPPIANS 3:12).

3. Pray daily for victory! God protects you through prayer.

> *"Watch and pray so that you will not fall into temptation.*
> *The spirit is willing, but the body is weak"*
> (MATTHEW 26:41).

4. Read your Bible every day in order to get strength from God.

> *"My soul is weary with sorrow; strengthen*
> *me according to your word"*
> (PSALM 119:28).

5. Meditate on Scripture to fight against falling into sin.

> *"I have hidden your word in my heart*
> *that I might not sin against you"*
> (PSALM 119:11).

6. Attend church every week to worship God and to grow with others.

> *"Let us consider how we may spur one another on*
> *toward love and good deeds. Let us not give up meeting*
> *together…but let us encourage one another"*
> (HEBREWS 10:24-25).

7. Share your struggles with caring loved ones.

> *"Confess your sins to each other and pray for*
> *each other so that you may be healed"*
> (JAMES 5:16).

8. Have confidence in God! Prioritize deepening your relationship with Him.

> *"Seek first his kingdom and his righteousness,*
> *and all these things will be given to you as well"*
> (MATTHEW 6:33).

9. Depend on Christ's strength to stay drug-free.

> *"I can do everything through him who gives me strength"*
> (PHILIPPIANS 4:13).

10. Know that permanent change is possible.

> *"Jesus…said, 'With God all things are possible'"*
> (MATTHEW 19:26).

Epilogue: The Two Heroes

> *"Forget the former things; do not dwell on the past.*
> *See, I am doing a new thing!"*
> (ISAIAH 43:18-19).

Hero #1: Josh Hamilton

A new thing. That's the best way to describe the transformation God brought about in Josh Hamilton's life. Josh is not only back in the game, he's on top of his game.

In September 2010, the Texas Rangers clinched the American League West Championship, and their star outfielder racked up impressive stats for the year: .361 batting average, 31 home runs, and 97 runs batted in. And the years since his reinstatement to baseball marked stellar accomplishments for Josh, who has been nicknamed "the Hammer" for his powerful batting arm. Among Josh's honors since 2008 are his being named the Rangers' Most Valuable Player, making the all-star team, and hitting the second most home runs in history in the annual home run derby preceding the all-star game. What's more, "the Hammer" has been likened to "the Mick."

As the Texas Rangers celebrated their championship with champagne and beer showers in the locker room, Josh Hamilton stayed dry outside—and sober—choosing instead to be at the ballpark to speak at Faith Day.[72] And it's all because God had done a new thing.

> "See, I am doing a new thing! Now it springs up; do you not perceive it? I am making a way in the desert and streams in the wasteland"
> (ISAIAH 43:19).

Hero #2: Mickey Mantle

A new thing is also the best way to describe the transformation God brought about in Mickey Mantle's life—not when he was on top of his game, but in the final inning of his life.

> At Mickey's funeral, Bobby Richardson told 2,000 mourners and a national TV audience that there are only two groups of people: those who say "yes" to Christ and those who say "no." He added that, since none of us knows when he will face his own final inning, saying "maybe" is really saying "no."[73]

Bobby, Mickey's Yankee teammate, knew that in the final inning of his life, Mickey said *yes*, and crossed over from death to life. As Jesus said, "Whoever hears my word and believes him who sent me has eternal life and will not be condemned; he has crossed over from death to life."[74]

Our all-American hero became a new creation even as he approached death. Mickey died on August 13, 1995, at the age of 63, and his final months were not marred by his trademark foulmouthed, falling-down-drunk behavior. One writer described the "new" Mickey Mantle: "In those last days and weeks, even as his body was breaking down, Mickey Mantle had acquired, quietly and with almost an ethereal elegance, a strength and dignity he did not know he possessed. He faced his own death with that strength and became a new kind of hero."[75]

The Bible says, "If anyone is in Christ, he is a new creation; the old has gone, the new has come!" (2 Corinthians 5:17). This new strength and dignity did not come from Mickey Mantle, but from the Lord Jesus Christ Himself. Ultimately, at the end of his earthly life, he gained eternal life.

You may say, "I can't…I've tried…I just can't do it!"
Well, maybe it's true that you don't have the stamina to stop
and stay stopped. But understand, Christ hasn't called you
to stay sober alone. The Bible reveals this secret…

"He who calls you is faithful; he will surely do it"
(1 Thessalonians 5:24 esv).

—June Hunt

Drug Name (Classification)	Desired Effect (How Administered)	Dangers	What to Look For
Alcohol Beer, wine, liquor, booze, juice, sauce, brew, vino *(Depressant)*	Intoxication, sensory alteration, anxiety reduction (Swallowed)	Addiction, toxic overdose, toxic psychosis; nausea, headache/hangover, brain, stomach, and liver damage; fetal alcohol syndrome; dependency, blackouts, aggression; depression, withdrawal, accidents due to impaired motor control and judgment	Smell of alcohol on clothes or breath, relaxation, intoxication, drowsiness, slow reflexes, glazed eyes, uncoordinated movement, slurred speech, confused behavior, excessive sleep
Amphetamines *Adderall, Biphetamine, Dexedrine, Dextroamphetamine:* Black beauties, hearts, LA turnaround, truck drivers, uppers, ups, speed, crank, Strawberry Quick, white crosses, dexies, bennies, crystals, Rx diet pills *(Stimulant)*	Alertness, energy (Injected, swallowed, smoked, snorted)	Addiction, increased heart and blood pressure, elevated metabolism, impulsive behavior, uncontrolled movements/teeth grinding, verbal outbursts, rapid/irregular heartbeat, reduced appetite, weight loss, dry mouth, stomach upset/pain, nausea/vomiting, diarrhea, sleeplessness, dizziness, headache, malnutrition, stroke, delusions, hallucinations, irritability, agitation, aggression, paranoia, toxic psychosis, violence, depression, skin disorders, ulcers, tremors, loss of coordination, anxiety, restlessness, delirium, panic, tolerance, seizures, heart failure, death	Pills, capsules, talkativeness, wakefulness, weakness, slurred speech, loss of sleep and/or appetite, irritability, anxiety, weight loss, hyperactivity

Amyl and butyl nitrite Liquid incense, poppers, room odorizer, video head cleaner, leather cleaner, rush, locker room, snappers *(Stimulant, Vasodilator)*	Exhilaration (Inhaled)	Damage to heart and blood vessels, may aggravate heart problems	Sold in small brown bottles labeled as "video head cleaner," "room odorizer," "leather cleaner," or "liquid aroma"
Anabolic or Androgenic Steroids Arnolds, gym candy, pumpers, roids, stackers, weight trainers, juice *(Synthetic hormone)*	Increased muscle mass and strength (Injected, swallowed, applied to skin)	Acne, irritability, aggression, male breast development, cardiovascular disease, stroke, blood clots, liver damage, jaundice, fluid retention, high blood pressure, increased LDL cholesterol, decreased HDL cholesterol, renal failure, trembling	Pills, syringes, needles
Analogs of synthetic narcotics China White, synthetic heroin, MPTP, MPPP, PEPAP, ecstasy, MDA, MDMA, Eve, MMDA, MDEA, XTC, TMA, STP, PMA, DOB *(Narcotic-opiate, analgesic)*	Euphoria, exhilaration (Injected, smoked, snorted, swallowed)	Addiction, MPTP-induced Parkinson's disease, (uncontrollable tremors, drooling, impaired speech, paralysis), permanent brain damage, overdose, death	Lethargy, needle marks, needles, syringes, spoons, pipes, pinpoint pupils, cold and moist skin, fever

(NOTE: This chart is not exhaustive, but includes the most prevalent drugs today.)

Drug Name (Classification)	Desired Effect (How Administered)	Dangers	What to Look For
Barbiturates *Amytal, Nembutal, Seconal, Tuinal, Phenobarbital:* Downers, bluebirds, barbs, reds, red birds, red devils, goofballs, phennies, yellows, yellow jackets, blues, blue heavens, Christmas trees, rainbows *(Depressant, sedative, hypnotic)*	Anxiety reduction, euphoria (Swallowed, injected)	Severe withdrawal, dependency, possible convulsions, toxic psychosis, birth defects, lowered inhibitions, slowed pulse, lowered blood pressure, poor concentration/fatigue, confusion, impaired coordination/memory/judgment, respiratory depression and arrest, death	Capsules, tablets, needles/syringes
Benzodiazepine Class Other than flunitrazepam; *Ativan, Xanax, Valium, Librium, Halcion:* candy, downers, sleeping pills, tranks *(Depressant, sedative Rx drugs)*	Relaxation (Swallowed, injected)	Dependence, unusual excitement, euphoria, sedation, drowsiness, hallucinations, memory loss, hypotension, muscle twitching, tremor, aggression, mania, impaired motor function, life-threatening withdrawal, suicidal ideation, coma	Capsules, tablets, needles/syringes

Drug	Effects (Method)	Risks	Paraphernalia
Cocaine Coke, rock, crack, toot, blow, bump, C, candy, Charlie, snow, pearl flake, girl, doing a line, lady, base, baseball, crank *(Stimulant, local or topical anesthesia)*	Stimulation, excitation, euphoria (Injected, smoked, snorted)	Addiction, malnutrition, depression, violence, convulsions, nasal injury, chest pain, heart attack, seizure, psychosis, stroke, brain or lung damage, dependency; elevated heart rate, increased blood pressure/temperature, restlessness, delirium, panic, aggression, paranoia, death	Glass vials, glass pipe, white crystalline powder, crystalline rocks, razor blades, syringes, spoons, needle marks, straws, mirrors, rolled bills
Cocaine freebase Base, freebase, crack, rock, C, dynamite, snorting *(Stimulant, local or topical anesthesia)*	Shorter and more intense cocaine effects (Smoked)	Weight loss, depression, agitation, hypertension, hallucinations, psychosis, chronic cough, tremors	Glass vials, glass pipe, crystalline rocks, razor blades, syringes, spoons, needle marks
Codeine *Empirin with Codeine, Fiorinal with Codeine, Robitussin A-C, Tylenol with Codeine:* Captain Cody, schoolboy; with *glutehimide:* doors & fours, loads, pancakes and syrup *(Narcotic-opiate, analgesic)*	Euphoria (Injected, swallowed)	Addiction, constipation, loss of appetite, nausea, organ damage, overdose, death	Liquid cough syrup with codeine, pills, syringes, needle marks

(NOTE: This chart is not exhaustive, but includes the most prevalent drugs today.)

Drug Name (Classification)	Desired Effect (How Administered)	Dangers	What to Look For
Dextromethorphan Found in some cough and cold medicines, such as *Robitussin, Coricidin*: DXM, CCC, Triple C, Skittles, Robo, Poor Man's PCP *(Hallucinogen, high doses of over-the-counter antitussive cold medicines)*	Heightened perceptual awareness, altered time perception, visual hallucinations (Swallowed)	Hyperexcitability, dissociative effects, distorted visual perceptions to complete dissociative effects, lethargy, slurred speech, sweating, hypertension, increased blood pressure, liver damage, central nervous system toxicity, cardiovascular toxicity, sudden death	Liquid, pills, or capsule cough/cold medicine
Fentanyl/ Fentanyl Analogs *Actiq, Duragesic, Sublimaze:* Apache, China girl, China white, dance fever, friend, goodfella, jackpot, murder 8, TNT, Tango and Cash *(Narcotic)*	Euphoria (Injected, smoked, snorted)	Addiction, weight loss, constipation, loss of appetite, heart disease, congested lungs, abortion, birth defects, staggering gait, contamination from unsterile needles (hepatitis, AIDS), overdose, death	Tablet cancer pain medication, syringes, needle marks

Substance	Effect	(Method)	Potential Health Consequences	Appearance
Flunitrazepam *Rohypnol:* forget-me pill, Mexican Valium, R2, Roche, roofies, roofinol, rope, rophies, "date rape" drug *(Depressant)*	Memory loss (Swallowed, snorted)		Visual and gastrointestinal disturbances, urinary retention, blackouts, disorientation, vulnerability to sexual assault, memory loss during time under drug's effects, death	Small white tablet, can be crushed and snorted
GHB *Gamma-hydroxybutyrate:* Liquid Ecstasy, Liquid X, Georgia Home Boy, Grievous Body Harm, G, date rape drug, scoop, goop, soap, Easy Lay *(Depressant)*	Euphoria, intoxication (Swallowed)		Drowsiness, dizziness, nausea, amnesia, visual hallucination, reduced blood pressure, decreased heart rate, convulsions, severely depressed respiration, loss of consciousness, loss of reflexes, coma, and death; withdrawal: insomnia, tremors, anxiety, sweating, seizures	Tablet, capsule, white powder can be mixed with flavored drinks or alcohol
Heroin H, cheese, junk, dope, smack, black tar, harry, horse, brown, brown sugar *(Narcotic-opiate, analgesic)*	Euphoria (Injected, smoked, snorted)		Addiction, weight loss, constipation, loss of appetite, heart disease, kidney and liver disease, congested lungs, abortion, birth defects, staggering gait, contamination from unsterile needles (hepatitis, AIDS), overdose, death	Powder or brownish black tar substance, pipe, syringes, spoons, needle marks; "cheese" heroin mixture of heroin and Tylenol PM

(NOTE: This chart is not exhaustive, but includes the most prevalent drugs today.)

Drug Name (Classification)	Desired Effect (How Administered)	Dangers	What to Look For
Inhalants Paint, paint thinner, solvents, gasoline, glue, gases, transmission fluid, correction fluid, hair or deodorant aerosols, fabric protector sprays, vegetable oil sprays, laughing gas, poppers, snappers, whipped cream aerosols or dispensers, "whippets"; "huffing" *(Stimulant)*	Intoxication (Inhaled)	Suffocation, nausea, vomiting, damage to brain and central nervous system, dizziness, wheezing, lack of coordination, loss of appetite, intoxication, irritability, hearing loss, depression, unconsciousness, cramps, muscle weakness, damage to cardiovascular and nervous systems, dependency, heart failure, sudden death	Chemical odor on breath/cans/paper or plastic bags/clothing, paint stains on face/hands/clothes, redness/sores/rashes around nose/mouth, intoxication, slurred speech, drowsiness, poor muscle control, red/runny nose, flushed skin
Ketamine Special K, Vitamin K, New Ecstasy, Ketalar, Ketaject, Super K, Kit Kat, cat Valium *(Depressant, hallucinogen, dissociative anesthetic)*	Sensory alteration, relaxation (Injected, snorted, smoked)	Delirium, amnesia, nausea, vomiting, impaired motor function, high blood pressure, racing heart, depression, flashbacks, respiratory problems, paranoia, unconsciousness, death	White powder or liquid injectable, syringes, spoons, needle marks, twitching eyes

Drug	Possible effects	Dangers	Signs / Paraphernalia
LSD *Lysergic acid diethylamide*: acid, LSD-25, blotter acid, boomers, cubes, microdot, yellow sunshines, "windowpane" pictures on paper, mellow yellow *(Hallucinogen)*	Insight, distortion of senses, exhilaration, mystical/religious experience (Swallowed, absorbed through mouth tissues)	Intensifies existing psychosis, panic, confusion, suspiciousness, flashbacks, possible brain damage, strong psychological reaction, impaired judgment, persistent mental disorders	Capsules, tablets, micro-dots, paper blotter squares, unpredictable behavior, emotional instability, violent behavior
Marijuana (Cannabis) Pot, grass, dope, weed, homegrown, skunk, sinsemilla, Maui-wowie, reefer, J, Thai sticks, joint, blunt, herb, roaches, indica, smoke, mary jane, MJ, bugs, bag, dime, quarter, ganja, Acapulco Gold, THC, purple haze Concentrated resin called hash or hashish (boom, chronic, gangster, oil, hemp) *(Depressant, hallucinogen)*	Euphoria, relaxation, increased sensory perception (Swallowed, smoked)	Cancer, bronchitis, conjunctivitis, birth defects, brain cell destruction, gateway to other drugs, immune system damage, severely strains cardiovascular system, frequent respiratory infection, alters mood, inhibits motivation, impairs short-term memory, hampers concentration, dependency, altered perception, anxiety, slowed thinking/reactions, addiction	Rolling papers, cigar wrappers, pipes, water bong, green or gray dried plant material, seeds, plastic bags, odor of burnt hemp rope, cigarette holders ("roach clips"), dry mouth, unusual hunger, reduced concentration or coordination, disproportionate laughter

(NOTE: This chart is not exhaustive, but includes the most prevalent drugs today.)

Drug Name (Classification)	Desired Effect (How Administered)	Dangers	What to Look For
MDA, MDE, MDMA, MMDA *Methylenedioxy-methamphetamine:* love drug, E, ecstasy, STC, X, Adam, clarity, Eve, Lover's speed, peace, STP, Hug, Go, hug drug, beans *(Hallucinogen, Amphetamine-based neurotoxin)*	Same as LSD (Swallowed, injected, snorted, or used as a suppository)	Neurotoxic, same as LSD, time distortion, sense of distance and estrangement, anxiety, catatonic syndrome, paranoia, brain damage, confusion, depression, psychotic episodes, physical effects can last weeks, increased heart rate and blood pressure, acne-like rash, liver damage, loss of appetite, fatigue	Fever, variety of pills with different logos stamped on tablets (produced illegally)
Mescaline (peyote cactus) Mesc, peyote, peyote buttons, cactus *(Hallucinogen, milder than LSD)*	Same as LSD (Swallowed, smoked)	Same as LSD, and extreme mood swings, distortion of senses and perceptions, deep depression	Disk-shaped buttons chewed, soaked in water and drank or ground into powder and placed in a capsule
Methadone (dolly) *Dolophine, Methadose, Symoron, Physeptone, Heptadon:* fizzies, chocolate chip cookies *(Narcotic-opiate, analgesic)*	Euphoria, opiate withdrawal prevention (Swallowed)	Addiction, constipation, loss of appetite, nausea, increased sleep apnea, respiratory suppression, organ damage, overdose, sudden cardiac arrest, death	Capsules, tablets

Methamphetamine *Desoxyn:* Crystal, crystal meth, chalk, crank, fire, glass, go fast, ice, meth, tweak, speed, dope, raw, Strawberry Quick *(Stimulant)*	Euphoria, alertness, loss of appetite (Injected, swallowed, smoked, snorted)	Irritability due to sleeplessness, illness due to weakening of the immune system, tooth loss, sexual compulsion, seizures, stroke, narcolepsy, hyperthermia, cardiac toxicity, renal failure, liver toxicity	Tablets, powder, crystalline rocks, syringes, spoons, needle marks; meth mixed with strawberry flavoring to mask acidic taste; pseudoephedrine cold medicine and household products used to illegally produce methamphetamine
Methaqualone *Quaalude, Sopor, Parest:* Ludes, 714S, mandrex, quad, quay, sopors, blue/red devils, yellows, candy, rainbows, Q's, downs *(Depressant, sedative hypnotic)*	Euphoria, aphrodisiac (Injected, swallowed)	Coma, convulsions, insomnia, dependency, severe anxiety, increased sleep apnea, respiratory suppression, sudden cardiac arrest	Capsules, tablets, needles/syringes
Methylphenidate *Ritalin, Concerta, Metadate, Methylin, Focalin*—treatment for ADD/ADHD: Jif, MPH, R-ball, Skippy, the smart drug, vitamin R *(Stimulant)*	Euphoria, alertness, loss of appetite (Injected, swallowed, snorted)	Dependency, chest pain, heart attack, seizure, stroke, brain or lung damage, elevated heart rate, increased blood pressure/temperature, restlessness, delirium, panic, aggression, paranoia, death	Capsules, tablets, needles/syringes

(NOTE: This chart is not exhaustive, but includes the most prevalent drugs today.)

Drug Name (Classification)	Desired Effect (How administered)	Dangers	What to Look For
Morphine *Roxanol, Duramorph:* Miss Emma, monkey, white stuff, M, morf *(Narcotic-opiate, analgesic)*	**Euphoria** (Injected, swallowed, smoked)	Addiction, constipation, loss of appetite, nausea, organ damage, overdose, death	Capsules, tablets, liquid, needles/syringes
Nitrous Oxide (laughing gas) Gases, whippits, nitrous, blue bottle, hippy crack, cartridges *(Depressant, inhalation anesthetic)*	Euphoria, relaxation (Inhaled)	Kidney or liver damage, peripheral neuropathy, spontaneous abortion, violence, nausea, vomiting	Gas canister, balloon with valve
Nonprescription stimulants Speed, ups, uppers *(Stimulant, appetite suppressant, decongestant)*	Alertness, energy, weight loss (Injected, swallowed)	Same as amphetamines plus hypertension, heart problems, anxiety, headaches, increased blood pressure, fatigue leading to exhaustion	Capsules, tablets, needles/syringes

Drug	Effect / Method	Symptoms / Effects	Form
Opium *Laudanum, paregoric;* Big O, black stuff, block, gum, hop *(Narcotic-opiate)*	Euphoria (swallowed, smoked)	Addiction, constipation, dizziness, fainting, lethargy, nausea, vomiting, anxiety, euphoria, drowsiness, insensitivity to pain, confusion, severe allergic reaction (rash, hives, swelling), difficulty urinating, pupil constriction, watery eyes, runny nose, fast or slow heartbeat, seizures, tremor, respiratory arrest, overdose, death	Liquid, tablets, pipe
Opioid Class *OxyContin, Lortab, Oxycodone HCL, Vicodin, Percocet, Percodan, Hydrocodone:* Vike, Watson-387, O.C., killer, oxycotton, cotton *(Narcotic, analgesic, prescription pain killers)*	Relaxation (Swallowed, snorted, injected)	Addiction, lethargy, nausea, vomiting, anxiety, euphoria, drowsiness, insensitivity to pain, hypotension, pupil constriction, watery eyes, runny nose, respiratory arrest, overdose, death	Capsules, tablets, needles/syringes
PCP Crystal, tea, THC, angel dust, hog, peace pill, rocket fuel *(Hallucinogen, dissociative anesthetic)*	Distortion of senses, stimulant (Injected, swallowed, smoked)	Psychotic behavior, violence, coma, detachment, shallow breathing, numbness, nausea/vomiting, blurred vision, drooling, loss of balance, dizziness, terror, psychosis, convulsions, impaired judgment, dependency, confusion, seizures, excessive salivation, schizophrenic behavior, paranoia	White crystalline powder in metal foil or can be mixed in liquid, made into tablet or capsule form

(NOTE: This chart is not exhaustive, but includes the most prevalent drugs today.)

Drug Name (Classification)	Desired Effect (How Administered)	Dangers	What to Look For
Psilocybin Magic mushrooms, shrooms, purple passion *(Hallucinogen, milder than LSD)*	Same as LSD (Swallowed)	Same as LSD, and sleeplessness, tremors, heart and lung failure, nervousness, paranoia, flashbacks	Eaten raw, dried, cooked in food or stewed in tea
Tobacco/Nicotine Cigarettes, cigars, cigarillos, cigs, smokes, butts, cancer sticks, coffin nails, puff, chew, chaw, snuff, dip or spit tobacco, rub, bidis *(Stimulant, toxin)*	Relaxation (Smoked, snuffed into nostril, placed in cheek or between lip and gum, chewed)	Loss of appetite, addiction, cancer (lung, jaw, mouth), birth defects, chronic lung disease, cardiovascular disease, increased blood pressure and heart rate, stroke, second-hand smoke, death	Cigarettes, cigars, cigarillos, rolling papers, loose tobacco, snuff, chew, spittoon

(NOTE: This chart is not exhaustive, but includes the most prevalent drugs today.)

* For further information on drugs see U.S. Drug Enforcement Administration, "Drug Information" (Washington, D.C.: DEA, n.d.), http://www.justice.gov/dea/concern/concern.html and National Institute on Drug Abuse, "Commonly Abused Drugs" (Washington, D.C.: NIDA, n.d.), http://www.drugabuse.gov/DrugPages/DrugsofAbuse.html.

ALCOHOL AND DRUG ABUSE: ANSWERS IN GOD'S WORD

QUESTION: "Why is it important for me to talk about my drug problem when I feel embarrassed to ask for advice or accept instruction?"

ANSWER: *"Listen to advice and accept instruction, and in the end you will be wise"* (Proverbs 19:20).

QUESTION: "Is it unwise to think I can handle my drug problem alone? Am I being led astray?"

ANSWER: *"Wine is a mocker and beer a brawler; whoever is led astray by them is not wise"* (Proverbs 20:1).

QUESTION: "Is it possible for me to please God and still follow the pattern of the world?"

ANSWER: *"In view of God's mercy...offer your bodies as living sacrifices, holy and pleasing to God—this is your spiritual act of worship. Do not conform any longer to the pattern of this world, but be transformed by the renewing of your mind. Then you will be able to test and approve what God's will is—his good, pleasing and perfect will"* (Romans 12:1-2).

QUESTION: "What harm is there in drinking alcohol or using drugs in the presence of others when it is socially acceptable?"

ANSWER: *"It is better not to eat meat or drink wine or to do anything else that will cause your brother to fall"* (Romans 14:21).

QUESTION: "What can I do to be released from the snare of my addiction?"

ANSWER: *"My eyes are ever on the LORD, for only he will release my feet from the snare"* (Psalm 25:15).

QUESTION: "What should I do if my substance abuse is a danger?"

ANSWER: *"A prudent man sees danger and takes refuge, but the simple keep going and suffer for it"* (Proverbs 22:3).

QUESTION: "If I struggle with abusing alcohol, why shouldn't I gaze at and taste the sparkle of wine when it looks so appealing?"

ANSWER: *"Do not gaze at wine when it is red, when it sparkles in the cup, when it* *goes down smoothly! In the end it bites like a snake and poisons like a viper"* (Proverbs 23:31-32).

QUESTION: "I know my body is God's temple, but don't I have the right to do with it as I please without fearing that God will destroy me?"

ANSWER: *"Don't you know that you yourselves are God's temple and that God's Spirit lives in you? If anyone destroys God's temple, God will destroy him; for God's temple is sacred, and you are that temple"* (1 Corinthians 3:16-17).

QUESTION: "How is it possible to break the hold of my addiction when it has controlled my life for years?"

ANSWER: *"All things are possible with God"* (Mark 10:27).

QUESTION: "Can I ever hope to find a way out of a temptation that is beyond what I can bear and stand up under?"

ANSWER: *"No temptation has seized you except what is common to man. And God is faithful; he will not let you be tempted beyond what you can bear. But when you are tempted, he will also provide a way out so that you can stand up under it"* (1 Corinthians 10:13).

THE WORLD OF ANOREXIA AND BULIMIA
Control that Is Out of Control

4

THE WORLD OF ANOREXIA AND BULIMIA:
Control that Is Out of Control

"I miss Ana,"[1] an anonymous blogger laments in a candid Internet post. Her dear friend is gone.

And with that departure, her world turned upside down.

But now she wants everything back to the way it used to be. That's when she had control over her life…that's when Ana was crucial in her life. Yet others objected—those who pushed Ana away.

Today, however, the bereft blogger has asked Ana to return, and she's determined to get Ana back. Her familiar friend, her best friend, her only friend called Ana—short for *Anorexia*.

It's startling! Around the globe, growing numbers characterize themselves as "pro-ana," namely, *pro-anorexic* or prone to self-starvation. They wear the label with pride, fastening it to their slowly withering figures. They claim, "Anorexia is not an eating disorder but rather a *lifestyle choice*." And now hundreds of "pro-ana" Web sites dispense their dark, distorted message of death.

Web sites and blogs alike help these individuals to link forces internationally to share tragic tips on everything from how to become anorexic to how to hide their noneating habits. And for the "Mias" (short for *bulimia*), who binge and purge food, there are "pro-mia" sites as well.

An unmistakable cloud of darkness hovers over these deadly eating disorders. Meanwhile, too many *anas* and *mias* in the world proudly declare that they're simply *dying to be thin*.[2]

For those who are painfully deluded, God's plan differs dramatically from the one destroying their lives. For God wants them to eat and enjoy the *daily* bread He provides, and He wants to be their "bread of life" for all their tomorrows. For it was Jesus who said,

"I am the bread of life"
(John 6:48).

I. Definitions of Anorexia and Bulimia

Karen Carpenter—the internationally acclaimed vocalist—could never have imagined being at center stage for anything other than her music.

She was the sister in the sibling duo The Carpenters—a sound sensation in the 1970s and early 80s that repeatedly rose to the top of the pop music charts. Songs like "We've Only Just Begun" and "Close to You" contributed to this Grammy award-winning pair's achieving worldwide sales of albums and singles exceeding 100 million.[3] Karen was known for her vibrant glow and velvety voice, a combination that ignited invitations for stage performances all around the world.

But February 4, 1983 marked her final curtain call. She was found unconscious at her parents' home and rushed to the hospital, where, a short time later, she was pronounced dead. Karen died of a heart attack at the tender age of 32. And it was her medical diagnosis that once again catapulted her back to center stage.

Proverbs, the biblical book of wisdom, presents this painful truth:

*"There is a way that seems right...
but in the end it leads to death"*
(Proverbs 16:25).

A. What Is Anorexia?

Before Karen Carpenter's death, the word *anorexia*—unknown to the average person—was only occasionally uttered in doctors' offices, hospitals, and rehab facilities. But all that changed in the early 1980s when a stunned public learned that the gifted "girl next door"—America's singing sweetheart—had literally starved herself to death. From that day forward, the word *anorexia* became more and more a part of everyday language.

The obvious question both then and now is this: Why would anyone enter into self-starvation, especially if they, like Karen, had it all—fame, family, fortune? In truth, Karen's battle with anorexia began as a desperate and deliberate attempt to eliminate her curves because she loathed her "hourglass figure."[4]

At age 17, the 5'4" brunette began focusing on her figure when she reached 145 pounds. At that point she went on a diet, and in 6 months lost 25 pounds. She then maintained an average weight of 120 pounds for the next 6 years.[5] But in August 1973, Karen was appalled at pictures of herself in a concert. An unflattering dress revealed what Karen perceived to be a bloated belly—and then her painful journey began.[6]

Those in the throes of this debilitating eating disorder continually struggle with a warped sense of beauty and a distorted self-image, and if asked, they would be the first to admit the accuracy of these words from the Bible:

> *"Charm is deceptive, and beauty is fleeting"*
> (Proverbs 31:30).

- **Anorexia** is an eating disorder characterized by compulsive, chronic self-starvation with a refusal to maintain a body weight within 15 percent of a person's normal weight.[7] The word *disorder* indicates that the normal function of the mind and/or body is impaired.

- **Anorexia** is derived from a Greek word that means "without appetite,"[8] which is actually "a misnomer because loss of appetite is rare."[9] However, after the body goes without nourishment for three days, natural hunger subsides—at least for a period of time.

- **Anorexics** weigh far less than what should be their normal body weight, which is different for every person, based on age, height, bone structure, and muscle mass. Body weight that is 15 percent below normal poses a serious threat to a person's physical health.[10] (Sometimes the word *manorexia* is used for males.)

- **Anorexics** may experience a different cause for this life-threatening eating disorder than the irrational fear of weight gain or distorted body image. (For example, if you believed that God told you to eat and drink nothing indefinitely—and that to consume anything would be a clear act of rebellion against His supreme deity—then out of "obedience" you could become anorexic and literally starve yourself to death. Someone like this may be suffering from a type of obsessive-compulsive disorder known as *scrupulosity*.)

Regardless of the reason for the lack of eating, the Bible says,

> *"My knees give way from fasting; my body is thin and gaunt"*
> (Psalm 109:24).

B. What Is Anorexia Nervosa?

When it came to consuming food, Karen Carpenter displayed willpower—to a fault.

Unlike bulimics, who binge on food and then purge it, Karen was never found raiding the fridge for favorites like ice cream or hoarding hidden candy. Her world revolved around weight *loss*—every potential calorie was a threat. Karen's spiral downward into a full-fledged eating disorder began in November 1973, following an appearance on a Bob Hope TV special.

After viewing the videotape, Karen was distressed by how she looked, and Richard, her brother and singing partner, agreed that she looked heavier than before.

Richard passed off the conversation as insignificant, yet Karen vowed "to do something about it."[11] In the process, she abandoned logical, adult reasoning and embraced irrational, deceptive thoughts, seeing herself through the distorted lenses of her flawed perceptions.

Sadly, she shared the distressing thoughts of the psalmist: "How long must I wrestle with my thoughts and every day have sorrow in my heart? How long will my enemy triumph over me?" (Psalm 13:2). Being deceived, Karen did not heed the words of God:

> *"This is what the Lord Almighty says:*
> *'Give careful thought to your ways.'…*
> *The wisdom of the prudent is to give thought to their ways,*
> *but the folly of fools is deception"*
> (Haggai 1:5; Proverbs 14:8).

Describing the Affliction

Those afflicted with anorexia are assaulted by a barrage of obsessive thoughts about body image and food and are consumed with irrational fear and anxiety.

- **Anorexia nervosa** is an intense fear of gaining weight or becoming fat, even though a person is dangerously underweight (at least 15 percent below normal).[12]

- **Anorexia nervosa** is psychological in that the *mind* pictures a distorted image of what the body looks like and produces an abnormal fear of weight gain.[13]

- **Anorexia nervosa** is seen in two subtypes:[14]

    - *Restricting anorexics* maintain their dangerously low weight by

excessively restricting their eating and possibly excessively exercising their bodies.

— *Binge/purge anorexics* restrict their eating but also purge by self-
induced vomiting, laxatives, diuretics, or enemas; they may also
engage in binge eating.

Many who have anorexia nervosa move back and forth between these two
subtypes. Sadly, it's as though they are living out the words from the book of Job:

> *"A man may be chastened on a bed of pain with constant*
> *distress in his bones, so that his very being finds food repulsive*
> *and his soul loathes the choicest meal. His flesh wastes away*
> *to nothing, and his bones, once hidden, now stick out"*
> (Job 33:19-21).

C. What Is Anorexia Athletica?

Many people caught in the cruel web of compulsive weight loss are also
caught in the snare of compulsive exercise. The two compulsions work hand
in hand for those seeking to control their weight not only by controlling their
caloric intake, but also by controlling the amount of calories their bodies burn
through excessive exercise. They abuse their bodies through both starvation and
severe workouts. These desperate souls create their own excruciating experience
by starving their bodies while working them to death.

While the Israelites worked under the whip of the Egyptians, those who are
enslaved to anorexia athletica all too often whip themselves into early graves.
Unlike the Israelites, who cried out to God for a deliverer, these slaves suffer in
silence. But God hears their unvoiced cry and yearns to deliver them from their
cruel taskmaster just as He delivered the children of Israel:

> *"The LORD said, 'I have indeed seen the misery of my people*
> *in Egypt. I have heard them crying out because of their slave*
> *drivers, and I am concerned about their suffering. So I have*
> *come down to rescue them from the hand of the Egyptians*
> *and to bring them up out of that land into a good and*
> *spacious land, a land flowing with milk and honey'"*
> (Exodus 3:7-8).

- **Anorexia athletica** is also called "Compulsive Exercise," "Obliga-
tory Exercise," "Exercise Addiction," and "Activity Disorder," and

refers to those who no longer exercise for pure enjoyment, but feel compelled to exercise more and more excessively over time.[15]

- **Anorexia athletica** sufferers live to do physical workouts.

  – They experience severe guilt and anxiety after missing a workout, and not even exhaustion, depression, anxiety, sickness, or injury can stop them from fulfilling their perceived need for exercise.[16]

  – With excessive stress on the heart, an unhealthy diet, and a refusal to allow their damaged body the time it needs for healing, the end result can be severe depression and even death.

Although exercise, in and of itself, is not wrong, the Bible presents exercise in its proper perspective.

> *"Physical training is of some value,*
> *but godliness has value for all things, holding promise for*
> *both the present life and the life to come"*
> (1 TIMOTHY 4:8).

Self-destruction

QUESTION: "Why do anorexics seem so determined to destroy themselves?"

ANSWER: The negative thinking patterns of anorexics have convinced them that…

- They don't deserve to live.
- Their natural longing for love is not realistic.
- They have made too many mistakes.

Often the self-pity, negative thinking, and anger of anorexics cause the breakup of marriages and withdrawal of friends. In the acute stages of the disease, some try to burn themselves in hot showers, cut themselves, or jump out of buildings.[17] Others become so exhausted from fighting the mental battles that they see no hope and give up on life. As the Bible says,

> *"Hope deferred makes the heart sick"*
> (PROVERBS 13:12).

D. What Is Bulimia?

In the period of history known as the Greco-Roman era, lifestyles of the opulent included lavish feasts and banquets, unabashed indulgences, and sometimes orgies. One common practice was vomiting after overindulging in food and alcohol to make room for more. Today the practice of "bingeing and purging" still occurs—a pattern characteristic of bulimia. In comparison to anorexia, bulimia is more frequent, harder to diagnose, more secretive, and often coexists with anorexia.

While the Bible instructs us to purge ourselves of impure evil thoughts and actions, it never even suggests that we are to purge ourselves of the food our bodies require for sustenance.

"Jesus declared all foods 'clean'"
(MARK 7:19).

- **Bulimia** comes from a Greek word meaning "great hunger."[18]
  - Bulimics are those whose continual abnormal appetite is actually an emotional hunger that no amount of food can fill.
  - The hunger that bulimics have is not necessarily a physical hunger.
  - Bulimics binge in an attempt to fill their three God-given inner needs for love, significance, and security.
  - They then purge to maintain or lose weight, and especially to get rid of the guilt that comes from eating too much.[19]

- **Bulimia** is a psychological eating disorder characterized by repeated or sporadic "binge and purge" episodes. Over time, bulimics ruminate their food.

  - *Bingeing* is an unrestrained consumption of large amounts of food in a short amount of time.
  - *Purging* may be done by the intentional vomiting of food or by the use of laxatives and diuretics.
  - *Rumination* is the unforced regurgitation, chewing, and reswallowing of food—much like the way a cow chews its cud.[20]

The Bible states a clear position on the misuse of the stomach:

"Their destiny is destruction, their god is their stomach, and their glory is in their shame. Their mind is on earthly things"
(PHILIPPIANS 3:19).

Overeating vs. Bulimia

QUESTION: "What's the difference between overeaters and bulimics?"

ANSWER: While both eat food to excess, an overeater may have little concern about being overweight, while the bulimic is consumed with body image and self-loathing.

Just as Job began to despise himself, bulimics despise their bodies and are frequently filled with bitterness.

> *"I loathe my very life; therefore I will give free rein to my*
> *complaint and speak out in the bitterness of my soul"*
> (JOB 10:1).

E. What Is Orthorexia?

Before manifesting obvious symptoms of anorexia, Karen Carpenter bore the trademarks of a different eating disorder. After her initial concern about her appearance, Karen got caught up in the trendy health food craze sweeping through California at the time. She cut junk food out of her diet, hired a personal trainer, and purchased exercise equipment to use at home and on tour.

But obsessing over healthy foods (orthorexia) and obsessing over exercise didn't bring Karen the results she wanted. She became distressed when she realized that all the exercising was actually making her bulk up rather than thin down. Finally, Karen stopped most of her exercising and eventually stopped eating. [21]

These words from the book of Job reflect a soul in anguish:

> *"Sighing comes to me instead of food;*
> *my groans pour out like water"*
> (JOB 3:24).

- **Orthorexia** (or orthorexia nervosa) refers to a fixation on eating only the "right" food—an obsession with eating only healthy food.
  - What a health-conscious person perceives to be healthy can later lead to severe malnutrition or even death. [22]
  - An anorexic wants to avoid food in order to lose weight.
  - An orthorexic wants to restrict food intake in order to feel pure, righteous, healthy, and natural.

Both obsessively fixate on food—the anorexic on calories and the orthorexic on purities. Both have similar character traits—they are both perfectionists, overly self-critical, obsessive-compulsive, and controlling.

- **Orthorexia** comes from a Greek word, *orth*, meaning "correct" or "right," and another Greek word, *orexis*, meaning "appetite."
  - Foods considered unhealthy usually contain fats, preservatives, man-made food additives, animal products, or other ingredients considered by the person to be unhealthy.[23]
  - Fruits and most vegetables are considered healthy.

Sadly, many who suffer from orthorexia set themselves up as a higher judge of foods than God Himself by declaring unclean many of the foods He has declared to be clean. The Lord gave Peter this vision:

> *"I saw something like a large sheet being let down from heaven by its four corners...and saw four-footed animals of the earth, wild beasts, reptiles, and birds of the air. Then I heard a voice telling me, 'Get up, Peter. Kill and eat.' I replied, 'Surely not, Lord! Nothing impure or unclean has ever entered my mouth.' The voice spoke from heaven a second time, 'Do not call anything impure that God has made clean'"*
> (ACTS 11:5-9).

=========== *Orthorexia* ===========

QUESTION: "Is there an easy way to determine whether I am orthorexic?"

ANSWER: Yes, there is a simple way to assess whether you might be having a problem with orthorexia. Honestly answer the following questions:

- Are you increasingly confining yourself to rigid rules for eating healthy foods?
- Are you concerned only about benefiting from food, and not enjoying it?
- Are you socially isolating yourself because of your special diet of "healthy" food?

If you answered *yes* to these questions, you are either presently suffering from orthorexia or well on your way. You would benefit from learning to develop a healthy, *balanced* view of food.

In the process, you will need to abandon your desire for control and relinquish the reins of your life to God—the only One who can truly grant you freedom and meet your every need.

> *"His divine power has given us everything we need for life*
> *and godliness through our knowledge of him who called us*
> *by his own glory and goodness. Through these he has given*
> *us his very great and precious promises, so that through*
> *them you may participate in the divine nature and escape*
> *the corruption in the world caused by evil desires"*
> (2 PETER 1:3-4).

F. What Is EDNOS?

One day, 14-year-old Sally saw *Babe*, an adorable movie about an endearing talking pig who saved the lives of numerous talking animals. Babe's heart went out to all the vulnerable farm animals (who were somewhat humanized in the film). So did Sally's heart.

As a result, young Sally felt sorry for any turkey that could be roasted, for any goose that could be cooked, for any pig that could be barbecued.

Sally felt so sorry for any and all animals that could be killed for food that soon after, she became a vegetarian. After she eliminated all meat—a significant source of protein—from her diet, she reasoned that she could meet her body's need for protein through eating beans.

But then Sally became avidly against eating the beans she needed to eat to get protein into her system. Soon Sally became skin and bones, and her parents feared for her life.

If only Sally—and all those who struggle with any kind of eating disorder—would accept the truth that God values us so much that He gives us everything we need to sustain us:

> *"Everything that lives and moves will be food for you. Just as*
> *I gave you the green plants, I now give you everything...All*
> *flocks and herds, and the beasts of the field, the birds of the*
> *air, and the fish of the sea, all that swim the paths of the seas"*
> (GENESIS 9:3; PSALM 8:7-8).

- **EDNOS**—some eating disorders have this psychological classification, which stands for Eating Disorders Not Otherwise Specified.[24] These eating disorders can be as dangerous as specified eating disorders.

- **EDNOS** is the category for eating disorders that do not match *all* the characteristics for either anorexia or bulimia.[25] For example:

  ☐ Meeting the anorexic criteria except not being underweight

  ☐ Meeting the anorexic criteria except still having regular menses

  ☐ Bingeing and purging or using laxatives (for weight control) only a few times a month (that is, far less regularity than bulimia)

  ☐ Purging only small amounts of food (such as three crackers)

  ☐ "Chewing and spitting" (the addictive disorder of chewing a large amount of food and then spitting it out to avoid swallowing it and to avoid the guilt of eating "bad food")

All those with an eating disorder are guilt-ridden because they have made for themselves unreasonable rules and unattainable goals regarding food and weight. Their guilt is not true guilt but rather false guilt. It is a guilt of their own making. They could fully identify with this heart cry from the Bible:

> *"If I am guilty—woe to me! Even if I am innocent, I cannot lift my head, for I am full of shame and drowned in my affliction"*
> (JOB 10:15).

Body Dysmorphic Disorder

QUESTION: "What exactly is body dysmorphia disorder, and how does it relate to eating disorders?"

ANSWER: *Body dysmorphic disorder* is a psychiatric disorder in which a person is excessively concerned about an imagined or minor defect in their physical features.[26]

- This disorder may result in a person's complaining of several specific features, a single feature, a vague feature, or their general appearance, causing a psychological distress that impairs the person's occupational and/or social functioning, sometimes to the point of complete social isolation.

- For example, Karen Carpenter appeared to single out her stomach as the target of concern. Over time, this concern evolved into full-blown anorexia. The end result was that she starved herself to death in an attempt to get rid of a perceived bulge in her stomach.

- Those who suffer from body dysmorphia have a perception disorder that prevents them from perceiving truth rather than error.

Whenever we live with deception, we cannot walk in freedom. That is why we need to be willing to hear the truth about ourselves:

> *"'You live in the midst of deception'…declares the LORD"*
> (JEREMIAH 9:6).

G. What Are Compulsions and Obsessions?

The compulsion not to eat proved catastrophic.

In January 1982, Karen Carpenter began seeing a therapist five times a week for 11 months, which met with problematic, not positive, results. By the end of the year, Karen weighed 80 pounds. She was hospitalized and underwent a medical procedure that increased her weight by 25 pounds, but Richard still felt quite unsettled about her condition. [27]

Although Karen's body appeared healthier, her energy had been sapped from her years of physical and emotional struggle. Most disturbing of all, according to Richard, the "life had gone out of her eyes." [28] Tragically, about three months later, the life had gone out of her body.

Karen's untimely death left many questions unanswered for her family and fans. One question begs to be answered by all who put their lives at risk over food:

> *"Why do I put myself in jeopardy*
> *and take my life in my hands?"*
> (JOB 13:14).

- **Obsessions** are intrusive, anxiety-producing thoughts that preoccupy the struggler's mind. "God says I must fast. If I eat food, I am guilty of disobeying Him. Eating food is bad and sinful."
- **Compulsions** are persistent drives or irresistible impulses to behave in ways that tend to make a person become irrational. [29] "I must fast, walk, and pray, but I must not eat. I will not eat!"
- **Compulsions** drive those with an eating disorder to eliminate food or fat by a variety of means: strict dieting and fasting, emetics and self-induced vomiting, multiple laxatives and diuretics, strenuous physical exercise and smoking, ADD medications and diet pills, and drinking large amounts of caffeinated coffee and tea.
  - An *emetic* is a drug that causes vomiting.

– A *laxative* is a drug that causes bowel elimination.

– A *diuretic* is a drug that causes an increase in the flow of urine.

The struggler who is controlled by these obsessions and compulsions is severely out of control.

> *"Like a city whose walls are broken down*
> *is a man who lacks self-control"*
> (PROVERBS 25:28).

In the midst of all her struggles, did Karen Carpenter ever get a glimpse of God's unconditional love? Was she aware that He loved her whether she was overweight, underweight, no matter her weight? She mattered to Him, not the numbers on her scales.

Such is the love of God—boundless and beautiful, deep and abiding. Once they experience the extraordinary unconditional love of God, many strugglers discover the light of hope on the path toward healing.

> *"The LORD your God is with you, he is mighty to save.*
> *He will take great delight in you, he will quiet you with his love,*
> *he will rejoice over you with singing"*
> (ZEPHANIAH 3:17).

II. CHARACTERISTICS OF ANOREXIA AND BULIMIA

"It really was Elvis Presley time again."[30]

That's how world-renowned Elton John described his wake-up call to not only seek help for his drug addiction, but also for his bulimia. Elvis Presley—a childhood musical icon for Elton—also suffered from bulimia and was also consumed by other compulsive behaviors. When Elton finally got the chance to meet Elvis in the 1970s, he walked away in tears, aghast at the bloated, visibly troubled figure that had just stood before him.

Not wanting to end up like Elvis, the five-time Grammy award winner sought help for his addictions. "I had to change because I was frightened. I didn't want to die angry and bitter and sad, and that's what I had become, physically ugly, spiritually ugly, a slob, a pig."[31]

As the saying goes, appearances can be deceiving. So much so that often they hide an anguishing heart.

> *"The troubles of my heart have multiplied;*
> *free me from my anguish"*
> (PSALM 25:17).

A. What Are the Warning Signs of Bulimia Nervosa?

"Despite all the success, I think I just wanted to be loved. I wanted someone to love me."[32]

A low sense of self-worth, loneliness, and depression marked Elton John's days as he battled bulimia. He turned to food for comfort to meet his hunger for love. But even an international rock superstar can't escape what those with eating disorders experience.

Instead of being the source of love, Elton's bulimia became the source of self-loathing. His actions and appearance distressed him, and he remembers saying to himself, "Here you are, just sitting here, fat, [with] vomit all over your dressing gown."[33]

And Elton found out later that just as he had walked away from Elvis in tears back in the 1970s, in the 1980s people had walked away from Elton in tears, saddened by his spiraling, out-of-control state.

So in 1990, Elton John checked into a Chicago rehabilitation clinic and devoted a full year toward recovery—no touring, no recording commitments.

Those who suffer with bulimia engage in a recurring cyclical pattern of binge eating (uncontrollable bursts of overeating) followed by overcompensatory behaviors such as crash dieting, overexercising, and purging. Those caught in this cycle desperately need to access the power of God in their fight to gain freedom from these two addictions, these two enemies—bingeing and purging. Those who do can say with the prophet Samuel,

> *"He rescued me from my powerful enemy,*
> *from my foes, who were too strong for me"*
> (2 SAMUEL 22:18).

Binge episodes are often compared to...

- Feeling instantaneously comforted
- Experiencing a physical high
- Going on autopilot
- Losing control
- Numbing out

Overcompensatory behaviors are the means a bulimic uses to get rid of excess calories and regain control over mind, body, and food. But those who engage in such maladaptive behaviors only end up feeling famished and emotionally empty again, which then leads to another uncontrollable binge, and thus the cycle repeats itself.

Bulimics engage in extreme obsessive-compulsive eating and exercise habits, and these, in turn, often flow over into other destructive behaviors such as sexual promiscuity, pathological lying, and shoplifting.

They...

- Practice a strict diet with intervals of binge eating—consuming large amounts of food in a short period of time
- Communicate great guilt or severe shame due to eating so much
- Cope with emotional stress through overeating/bingeing
- Focus excessively on their body shape and weight even though they may have normal weight or be underweight

They...

- Practice self-induced vomiting after eating
- Suffer from general depression
- Lack self-control when it comes to food
- Experience possible fluctuations in weight

They...

- Exercise excessively and compulsively
- Base their self-worth on personal performance
- Abuse laxatives or diuretics
- Push their bodies way beyond normal healthy limits

Those who binge and purge cannot be at rest. Their obsession over food allows them no peace. They could have written these words spoken by Job himself:

> *"I have no peace, no quietness;*
> *I have no rest, but only turmoil"*
> (JOB 3:26).

Emotional or Binge Eater

QUESTION: "How can I tell if I am an emotional or binge eater?"

ANSWER: It's not out of the norm for all of us to occasionally turn to food for comfort—whether we are trying to wind down with a cola and fries after a long day or cool down with a pint of ice cream after an argument. But when eating becomes the main strategy for managing emotions and dealing with stress, it can develop into an unhealthy and uncontrollable food addiction.

The Emotional Eater: Do you use food to...

- ☐ Feel better about yourself?
- ☐ Calm down or soothe your nerves?
- ☐ Cope with stress or worries?
- ☐ Escape from problems?
- ☐ Fill a void in your life?
- ☐ Reward yourself?
- ☐ Cheer yourself up?

Emotional eating can be triggered by a depressed or anxious mood, but also when a person feels tense, lonely, or bored. Men who are suffering from what's been coined *manorexia,* or bulimia, can also struggle with shame because eating disorders are primarily associated with adolescent girls and young women.

Emotional eaters eat to fill their emotional emptiness rather than their physical emptiness. The problem is that emotional eating doesn't solve anything. It may offer momentary comfort, but eventually reality will set in, along with regret and self-loathing.

If you answer *yes* to more than half of the questions below, you likely have a binge-eating problem.

The Binge Eater: Do you...

- ☐ Eat in secret?
- ☐ Eat until you feel sick?
- ☐ Feel out of control when you eat?
- ☐ Feel disgusted or ashamed after you eat?
- ☐ Think about food most of the time?
- ☐ Eat to escape from worries or to comfort yourself?
- ☐ Feel powerless to stop eating, even though you want to?

Emotional eating is typically done in secret, as is the case with almost all other types of eating disorders. Those who practice these behaviors fail to focus on the always-abiding love and presence of the Lord, who is everywhere all the time and who never slumbers or sleeps.

> *"'Can anyone hide in secret places so that I cannot see him?' declares the Lord. 'Do not I fill heaven and earth?' declares the Lord"*
> (Jeremiah 23:24).

B. What Effect Does Bulimia Have on the Body?

Eating disorders are primarily associated with women, but in recent years an increasing number of men—such as musician Elton John and actors Dennis Quaid and Billy Bob Thornton—have been diagnosed as anorexic or bulimic. A 2007 Harvard University study determined that men comprised 25 percent of all people with anorexia or bulimia.[34]

Media images portraying the ideal male physique can wield tremendous pressure on men who are extremely fitness conscious, and homosexual men tend to be more prone to eating disorders than heterosexual men. Among gay men, 14 percent suffer from bulimia and more than 20 percent are anorexic.[35]

Don't be deceived. Not all anorexics or bulimics will appear greatly underweight. That is why it is important that you be alert to other warning signs of an eating disorder. And don't be misled about the danger of these disorders—both can be deadly. The Bible tells us that

"a prudent man sees danger and takes refuge,
but the simple keep going and suffer for it"
(PROVERBS 22:3).

HOW BULIMIA AFFECTS YOUR BODY

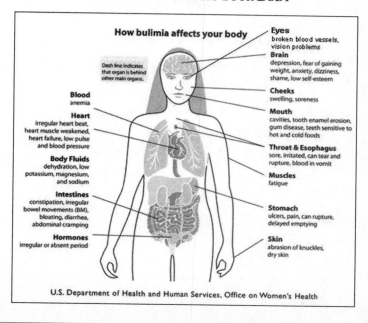

How bulimia affects your body

Dash line indicates that organ is behind other main organs.

Blood
anemia

Heart
irregular heart beat, heart muscle weakened, heart failure, low pulse and blood pressure

Body Fluids
dehydration, low potassium, magnesium, and sodium

Intestines
constipation, irregular bowel movements (BM), bloating, diarrhea, abdominal cramping

Hormones
irregular or absent period

Eyes
broken blood vessels, vision problems

Brain
depression, fear of gaining weight, anxiety, dizziness, shame, low self-esteem

Cheeks
swelling, soreness

Mouth
cavities, tooth enamel erosion, gum disease, teeth sensitive to hot and cold foods

Throat & Esophagus
sore, irritated, can tear and rupture, blood in vomit

Muscles
fatigue

Stomach
ulcers, pain, can rupture, delayed emptying

Skin
abrasion of knuckles, dry skin

U.S. Department of Health and Human Services, Office on Women's Health

- **Blood Problems**
  - Anemia
  - Poor circulation, low body temperature
  - High blood pressure, hypertension
  - Ketoacidosis (high levels of acid buildup in the blood)
  - Type II diabetes mellitus

- **Body Fluids**
  - Dehydration
  - Low potassium, magnesium, sodium (out-of-balance electrolytes can cause cardiac arrest)

- **Kidneys**
  - Problems from diuretic abuse
  - Infections from vitamin deficiencies, dehydration, and low blood pressure

- **Intestines**
  - Abdominal cramping and bloating
  - Chronic constipation and diarrhea
  - Irregular bowel movements, abnormal bowel functioning
  - Excessive use of laxatives, causing bowels to no longer function without total dependence on laxatives

- **Hormones**
  - Irregular or absent menstrual period
  - Imbalances causing multiple problems throughout the body
  - Imbalances can occur even after recovery when healthy eating habits are being practiced

- **Brain**
  - Distorted body image
  - Excessive fear of weight gain
  - Anxiety and depression
  - Dizziness

- Seizures
- Difficulty concentrating
- Low self-esteem and shame
- Neurological and mental deterioration

- **Cheeks/Jaw Area**
  - Swelling, soreness, TMJ (temporomandibular joint)
  - Swollen salivary glands in cheeks

- **Mouth**
  - Purging of food brings up hydrochloric acid from stomach that washes across the teeth
  - Teeth sensitive to hot and cold foods
  - Tooth enamel erosion and discoloration (teeth look clear)
  - Cavities and tooth loss
  - Gum disease and pain
  - Sores in the mouth, swollen salivary glands in the cheeks

- **Throat and Esophagus**
  - Sore and irritated
  - Tears and ruptures
  - Esophageal reflux, damage to larynx and lungs
  - Bleeding esophagus
  - Cancer of the esophagus, larynx, and throat

- **Muscles**
  - Fatigue and aching
  - Atrophy

- **Stomach**
  - Pain and soreness
  - Delayed emptying
  - Ulcers and ruptures
  - Deficiency in digestive enzymes
  - Pancreatitis caused by repeated stomach trauma

- **Skin**
  - Abrasions and calluses on knuckles
  - Dry flaky skin

- **Heart**
  - High cholesterol
  - Elevated triglyceride levels
  - Electrolyte imbalances
  - Irregular heartbeat
  - Heart muscle weakened, thickened
  - Heart failure with a mortality rate from 5 percent to 15 percent of bulimics due to cardiac arrest

- **Lungs**
  - Shortness of breath
  - Increased infections

- **Eyes**
  - Broken blood vessels in the eyes
  - Vision problems

- **Pregnancy**
  - Miscarriage
  - Difficulty getting pregnant
  - Baby stillborn (not born alive)
  - Baby born early and low birth weight
  - Birth defects, such as blindness or mental retardation

- **Weight Swings or Drops**
  - Chronic bingeing/purging causes extreme weight fluctuation within short periods of time

Tragically, those who believe the lies that produce and propagate this fatal eating disorder have failed to guard their hearts and their minds, thereby putting their lives in danger. No wonder Scripture strongly admonishes us to

> *"above all else, guard your heart,*
> *for it is the wellspring of life"*
> (Proverbs 4:23).

C. What Are Some Warning Signs of Anorexia Nervosa?

They're known as "thinspiration"—famous female celebrities idolized by anorexics and praised on pro-anorexia Web sites for their skeletal frames.

One of the most popular thinspiration figures is Victoria Beckham, formerly known as Posh Spice of the Spice Girls, a British pop music group with a string of hits in the 1990s. A posting on one Web site reads, "I envy her thin legs and chest. She has beautiful bones sticking out of her chest."[36]

The glamorization of anorexia is closely linked to a consistent message from all different types of media: *You can't be thin enough*.

Those who struggle with anorexia are hungry for love—they feel love-starved. Their deepest hunger for love can be satisfied only by the One who is love—God Himself.

Realize that people will let you down. People can provide only a temporary filling of love that will once again end in hunger for love. No one has demonstrated more love to you than God has—love that has tremendous potential impact both now and for all eternity. The Bible speaks of His continual love for you:

> *"Praise be to God, who has not rejected my prayer*
> *or withheld his love from me!"*
> (PSALM 66:20).

Those who suffer from anorexia nervosa have a "fat phobia," an intense fear of gaining weight. Their desired weight represents their self-worth, self-control, and status. They generally fall into the following two subgroups, with many crosses back and forth between the two during the course of their illness:

1. *Restricting food intake* and possibly exercising excessively (anorexia athletica)

2. *Bingeing and purging food*

They...

- Deny ever feeling hungry
- Postpone major events
- Refuse to maintain even minimal body weight
- Put their life on hold until they "get thin"

They...

- Exercise excessively
- Diet exceedingly

- Weigh repeatedly
- Lose hair frequently

They constantly...

- Obsess about food, calories, and nutrition
- Feel bloated, fat, or nauseated from eating even small amounts of food
- See themselves as fat when they are truly thin
- Believe they are overweight even while continuously losing weight

In addition, they necessarily...

- Feel cold even when the temperature is normal
- Set unobtainable performance goals for themselves
- Experience amenorrhea (the absence of at least three consecutive menstrual cycles)
- Avoid mirrors and photos and engage in constant self-criticism, thus sabotaging their self-esteem

For those in the midst of the struggle, no matter what they do, their hearts are not at peace. Their pain is ever-present. They can feel the hurt spoken by Job in his deep suffering:

> *"If I speak, my pain is not relieved; and*
> *if I refrain, it does not go away"*
> (Job 16:6).

Ellen—Counting Calorie After Calorie After Calorie

It's nighttime and Ellen was curled up in bed with her cookbooks—processing, calculating, obsessing.

"Hmmm...chicken marsala, one serving...232 calories." She turned the page. "Smoked salmon, one serving...159 calories." In another section of the cookbook, Ellen gasped at the number of calories in a savory slice of pecan pie—800 calories!

Ellen had no intention of cooking, *nor did she have any intention of eating.* She was simply swimming in a sea of numbers, compulsively calculating the calorie content of all kinds of food. She paused for a moment, reflecting on her day: *Just how many calories were in that piece of chewing gum?* But then Ellen got right back to her cookbooks and calculations, counting calorie after calorie after calorie.

At 78 pounds, Ellen was a *hungry* young woman—hungry not only for food, but also for love. Adopted and the youngest of eight children, Ellen was abused by her adoptive father. Apathy best characterized her mother, who turned a blind eye to many things, including her daughter's eating disorders. (Ellen struggled with both anorexia and bulimia.) Once, after hearing Ellen purging her food, her mother instructed, "Make sure you clean up the bathroom."

Neglect, abuse, and a desperate search for significance all drew Ellen into the competitive realm of chronic overachieving, where she felt compelled to be "the best." In high school, she was a cheerleader who shone on the sidelines and a runner who raced competitively around the track. She maintained an average weight of 110 pounds during her first three years, but as a senior, something snapped, and Ellen determined she wasn't *thin* enough.

From January to March Ellen lost 15 pounds, largely due to her new diet. Nothing for breakfast, an apple and Diet Coke for lunch, and as little as she could get away with for dinner. During lunch at school, Ellen had to sit on a heater because she was always cold—her *necessary* body fat was disappearing along with her necessary pounds.

Looking back, Ellen wondered how she even endured. Despite her rigid diet, she still participated actively in track and cheerleading. Following each evening meal—consisting of only 200 to 300 calories—she would go for an hour-long evening run. All the while, her body sustained yet another form of abuse—bruises from her father's hurtful hands.

After high school, Ellen started working in a restaurant, an irony for someone trying to avoid food. But soon her willpower weakened and bulimia dominated her life. She often purged during breaks at work and adopted two other hurtful habits as well: Looking for liquor to numb all the pain (Ellen became a heavy drinker) and looking for love in all the wrong places (Ellen became promiscuous).

Ellen's food binges continued, but because she didn't like throwing up, soon the unthinkable occurred—her pant size swelled and "fat comments" start coming her way. Ellen quickly figured out another way to get rid of the pounds—laxatives, building up to 60 a day. Laxative abuse took a tremendous toll on Ellen's body, and eventually purging made its way back into the picture. As a result, Ellen became extremely dehydrated and weak. Because she had to climb three flights of stairs when she arrived home from work, she was exhausted by the time she got to her room and needed a full hour to recuperate.

There she lay at 78 pounds…with excruciating pain coursing through her body. Ellen frequently woke up screaming in the middle of the night from agonizing muscle cramps in her legs. She suffered from other signs of starvation as well—brittle hair, much of which had fallen out, and she hadn't menstruated for three years. And her eyes had become dull and lifeless, signifying a soul barely surviving. "I wasn't living, only existing."[37]

Tender concern from siblings and a brother-in-law and new health benefits from her job finally prompted Ellen to see a doctor. Following some blood work, a shocking discovery was made. Ellen's sodium and potassium levels were the lowest the doctor had *ever* seen. He said if he hadn't known the levels came from Ellen, he would have thought they came from *a dead person*! Ellen realized, "I literally could have died any day with my heart giving out."[38]

After struggling with eating disorders for 12 years, Ellen finally received the medical attention she so desperately needed. She also found emotional and spiritual healing for her deep wounds. God provided an insightful Christian counselor who helped her "dig up and out"[39] a myriad of painful issues rooted in her childhood. And the counselor also helped draw Ellen to Christ. "Our relationship isn't one-sided anymore,"[40] Ellen beamed, because she now knows God never left her side.

The words *passionate* and *compassionate* describe Ellen—as well as *happily married, wife, mother*, and *personal trainer/nutritionist* who teaches moderation. No longer does she compulsively count calories, obsess over food, or gulp down laxatives—her focus now is on balanced nutrition for optimal health and energy. Once on the verge of death, Ellen is now completely healed and full of life—a life of moderation. And it's all because of the Giver of Life. "I thank God every day for…saving my life," Ellen gratefully shared. "I may have given up on myself, but He didn't give up on me!"[*41]

---

* **NOTE:** Today, Ellen Teall is available to speak about eating disorders, nutrition, and girls' self-esteem issues at schools, churches, and civic events.

D. What Effect Does Anorexia Have on the Body?

Victoria Beckham, in her autobiography, admits to having an eating disorder and being consumed with her appearance while singing with the Spice Girls. "It was awful," she recollects. "I was very obsessed. I could have told you the calorie and fat content in anything."[42] A picture published in a British newspaper was accompanied by the headline "Skeletal Spice."

HOW ANOREXIA AFFECTS YOUR BODY

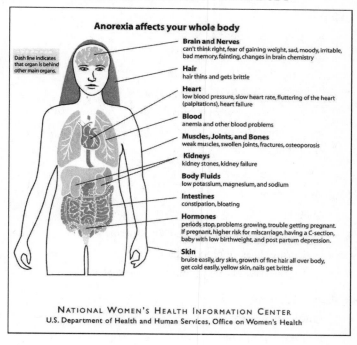

Anorexia affects your whole body

Dash line indicates that organ is behind other main organs.

Brain and Nerves
can't think right, fear of gaining weight, sad, moody, irritable, bad memory, fainting, changes in brain chemistry

Hair
hair thins and gets brittle

Heart
low blood pressure, slow heart rate, fluttering of the heart (palpitations), heart failure

Blood
anemia and other blood problems

Muscles, Joints, and Bones
weak muscles, swollen joints, fractures, osteoporosis

Kidneys
kidney stones, kidney failure

Body Fluids
low potassium, magnesium, and sodium

Intestines
constipation, bloating

Hormones
periods stop, problems growing, trouble getting pregnant. If pregnant, higher risk for miscarriage, having a C-section, baby with low birthweight, and post partum depression.

Skin
bruise easily, dry skin, growth of fine hair all over body, get cold easily, yellow skin, nails get brittle

NATIONAL WOMEN'S HEALTH INFORMATION CENTER
U.S. Department of Health and Human Services, Office on Women's Health

- **Brain and Nerves**
  - Cognitive impairment, disordered thinking, extreme forgetfulness, seizures due to malnutrition
  - Irrational fear of weight gain
  - Sadness, depression
  - Moodiness, irritability
  - Fainting, dizziness
  - Changes in brain chemistry

  – Numbness or sensations in hands or feet (neuropathy)
  – Structural changes (reduction in gray matter) and abnormal brain activity (sometimes permanent)

- **Hair**
  – Thinning hair gives a balding appearance
  – Brittle hair falls out, white fuzz (called *lanugo*) appears on the body to help keep it warm

- **Heart**
  – Reduced blood flow
  – Slow heart rate, irregular rhythms
  – Abnormally low blood pressure
  – Fluttering of the heart (palpitations)
  – Decreased size of heart—muscles shrink from starvation
  – Electrolyte imbalance/death
  – Heart failure
  – Heart attack

- **Blood**
  – Anemia
  – Low levels of vitamin B12, causing anemia
  – Low production of blood cells
  – Lack of red blood cells (at life-threatening levels)

- **Malnutrition**
  – Low body weight
  – Respiratory infections
  – Brittle nails
  – Blindness
  – Death

- **Psychological Problems**
  – Distorted view—seeing themselves as fat even though they are "skin and bones"
  – Anxiety, depression, suicidal
  – Insomnia

- **Pregnancy Problems**
  - Infertility
  - Miscarriage
  - C-section
  - Complicated deliveries
  - Baby with low birth weight
  - Birth defects
  - Postpartum depression

- **Muscles, Joints, and Bones**
  - Muscle atrophy (wasting away of muscle and decrease in muscle mass) resulting from the body feeding off of itself
  - Weak muscles, swollen joints, temporary paralysis
  - Chronic Fatigue Syndrome related to weakened immune system
  - Loss of bone minerals (osteopenia)
  - Loss of bone density (osteoporosis), fractures, brittle bones
  - Lack of hormones and vitamins (arthritis)
  - Failure to develop strong bones in children and teenage girls
  - Retarded growth in children and adolescents
  - Stunted growth in boys due to declining testosterone levels

- **Kidneys**
  - Kidney stones
  - Kidney failure

- **Body Fluids**
  - Dehydration leading to kidney failure, seizures, brain damage
  - Low potassium, magnesium, sodium, and electrolyte imbalance, causing heart failure

  Note:
  - Hyponatremia (insufficient sodium in the blood) can result from drinking too much water too quickly, causing the lungs to fill with fluid, the brain to swell, vomiting, confusion, and death.

– Edema (swelling of soft tissues) can result from excess water retention.

– Refeeding Syndrome (life-threatening fluid and electrolyte shifts) can result from aggressive nutritional support therapies—nutritional support needs to increase slowly.

- **Intestines/Gastrointestinal Problems**
  – Abdominal pain, cramps, and bloating
  – Constipation and diarrhea
  – Gastric rupture, stomach erosion, or perforation
  – Gastrointestinal bleeding, Crohn's disease

- **Hormones**
  – Cessation of menstrual cycle (amenorrhea)—when fat levels drop below 22 percent of normal weight, deficiency in fat (essential for good health), causing menstrual cycles to stop
  – Growth stunted
  – Lower reproductive hormones
  – Low thyroid levels
  – Higher stress hormone levels
  – Hypoglycemia—low blood sugar, causing fatigue, dizziness, headaches

- **Skin**
  – Bruises easily
  – Dry yellow skin
  – Growth of fine hair all over body (lanugo)
  – Low body temperatures
  – Brittle nails
  – Dark circles under the eyes

- **Dental Problems**
  – Decalcification of teeth
  – Erosion of tooth enamel
  – Severe staining and decay
  – Gum disease

- **Organ Problems**
  - Prolonged lack of calories lead to dangerously high blood levels of liver enzymes
  - Multiple organ failure results in death
  - Pancreatitis can result from digestive enzymes related to repeated stomach trauma

- **Weight Swings or Drops**
  - The self-starvation of the anorexic causes the body weight to get so low that kidneys and other organs start to shut down, leading to death.

Make no mistake—anorexia is life-threatening. Therefore, don't be in denial. Like this admission in the Psalms, admit your anguish and weakness. That's the first step toward healing.

> *"My life is consumed by anguish and my years by groaning;*
> *my strength fails because of my affliction,*
> *and my bones grow weak"*
> (PSALM 31:10).

NOTE: If you are experiencing any of these physical or emotional problems, be sure to consult your health care professional immediately.

E. What Effect Does Starvation/Anorexia Have on the Brain?

In the same way that the entire body is impacted by the presence of life-sustaining food, the body—including the brain—is also affected when there is an absence of food. Sufferers will find it increasingly more difficult to make sound decisions because their mind is not sharp and their thinking is murky. They are unable to know the peace of God because their minds are unable to trust completely in God. The Bible says this about God:

> *"You [God] will keep in perfect peace*
> *him whose mind is steadfast,*
> *because he trusts in you"*
> (ISAIAH 26:3).

A recent study has shown that brain function in those who suffered and recovered from anorexia is different from those who have never suffered from an eating disorder.[43] For example:

- Brain function in recovered anorexic women *showed little emotional response to winning or losing a simple game,* while brain function in nonanorexic women revealed a stronger emotional response to the same situations.

- Brain function in recovered anorexic women *showed little difference in distinguishing between positive and negative feedback,* while brain function in nonanorexic women revealed stronger degrees of activity when it came to discriminating between positive and negative responses.

- Brain function in recovered anorexic women *showed stronger emphasis on strategic methods of game play,* while brain function in nonanorexic women revealed greater enjoyment of game play.

- Brain function in recovered anorexic women *revealed undue worry over making mistakes and a desire to discover "rules" where none exist,* while brain function in nonanorexic women showed an aptitude for making choices and then moving on more easily.

In addition, the human brain needs sufficient nutrition and relaxation. Studies show that stress and starvation deprives the brain of necessary nutrients and slows down the thought processes, leaving starving people feeling...[44]

- Fearful and distraught
- Dull and mentally slow
- Moody and mentally foggy
- Agitated and without good judgment

In an experiment, a group showed some distinct characteristics after experiencing six months of reduced food intake.[45]
They...

- Obsessed about food
- Conversed constantly about food
- Expressed interest in nothing but food

Clearly, anyone who is starving becomes preoccupied with food, just like the anorexic. Interestingly, this food obsession can disappear when normal caloric intake resumes. Just as a well-oiled engine is able to run silently and smoothly, a well-fed brain is able to take thoughts captive and control unhealthy urges.

"We take captive every thought to make it obedient to Christ"
(2 Corinthians 10:5).

III. Causes of Anorexia and Bulimia

Hers should have been a storybook life—complete with the happiest ending. But even though she lived in a palace, the princess couldn't hide the pain.

Lady Diana Spencer walked the aisle and onto the world stage when she married Prince Charles on July 29, 1981, and became Princess Diana. The 20-year-old bride was beautiful, bashful, and immediately beloved.

She would go on to become arguably the most famous woman in the world, her every move recorded, photographed, adored. But what went on behind closed castle doors didn't fit with the regal, public façade.

Prince Charles' previous longtime romantic relationship with Camilla Parker Bowles interfered with Diana's marriage, as did the prince's ensuing adultery. Both Diana's marriage and her spirit were broken. Thus, the princess would seek consolation in food—large amounts of it. Yet it was only a fleeting fix for her pain, for she would always purge it back up.

"Rampant bulimia" was her recourse upon learning that Prince Charles had resumed his relationship with Camilla.[46] Her external out-of-control bingeing and purging merely reflected her internal depth of despair.

"So my heart began to despair over all
my toilsome labor under the sun"
(Ecclesiastes 2:20).

Diana described "a feeling of being no good at anything and being useless and hopeless and failed in every direction."[47]

Her husband's love for another woman also led to increased isolation. Diana recalled Charles' friends labeling her sick, unstable, and in need of being put in some sort of home to get better. "I was almost an embarrassment."[48]

The Princess of Wales was a princess in pain. She felt helpless over her husband's infidelity and inadequate around the royal family. "Anything good I ever did nobody ever said a thing, never said, 'well done,'" she shared. "But if I tripped up, which invariably I did, because I was new at the game, a ton of bricks came down on me."[49]

By her own admission, the rejection and loneliness led her into an illicit affair; her low self-worth was the setup for her eating disorder. And because of her husband's betrayal, her dignity was damaged and her security was destroyed. Any struggler in such emotional pain could identify with the suffering of Job:

> *"Terrors overwhelm me; my dignity is driven away*
> *as by the wind, my safety vanishes like a cloud"*
> (Job 30:15).

A. What Distortions Contribute to Anorexia or Bulimia?

In a 1995 interview, Princess Diana contemplated her marriage into the royal family and the adjustments she had to make to life in the limelight. Diana believed she had Charles' support, but it wouldn't take long for external pressures to put a strain on their marriage. *She*—not he—would become the media darling, a source of "phenomenal" pressure while trying to operate publicly as a couple. [50]

Diana's struggles with insecurity surfaced early on, even hinting at the deception and distortion over one's personal appearance that accompanies bulimia. She in no way saw herself as the world saw her: "It took a long time to understand why people were so interested in me...As far as I was concerned I was a fat, chubby, 20-year-old, 21-year-old, and I couldn't understand the level of interest." [51]

The eyes of the world were riveted on England as the death of Princess Diana stirred profound curiosity about the details of her life. Of paramount interest was her struggle with an eating disorder. Reports depicted the princess as having a monumental appetite, yet pictures portrayed a beautiful woman who was stylishly thin.

In public interviews, she had admitted she had struggled through bouts with bulimia. Both anorexia and bulimia are addictive behaviors, yet both are part of a syndrome of suffering that is never beyond God's healing hand.

> *"Heal me, O Lord, and I will be healed;*
> *save me and I will be saved"*
> (Jeremiah 17:14).

Denial, the mental process that leads sufferers to conclude they are okay and do not have a problem, is common among those who have various forms of eating disorders. Defiance is often the result when they are confronted with the possibility that something is wrong.

Initial steps for intervention include encouraging a loved one to mark on a checklist for anorexia or bulimia all emotions and behaviors pertaining to that person. Seeing something written, something tangible, might help raise red flags and initiate first steps toward the road to recovery. Taking the time to consult with a medical professional is also highly beneficial.

But more often than not, interventions are intense because people with anorexia and bulimia are driven by one solitary fear—the fear of getting fat.

While you might prefer to avoid facing a sufferer's irrational thinking and strong emotional displays, remember that the earlier the intervention, the greater the chance for recovery.[52]

Also, realize the responsibility you have to do everything within your power to rescue your loved one from the very real and ruthless jaws of death that await all who fail to escape the deadly grip of anorexia and bulimia.

> *"Rescue those being led away to death;*
> *hold back those staggering toward slaughter"*
> (PROVERBS 24:11).

ARE YOU PUZZLED OVER HAVING AN EATING DISORDER?

Puzzles are solved by carefully putting the pieces together so that they depict a complete picture. When you put the emotional clues of an eating disorder together, the picture emerges of a person in pain—one who feels love-starved, security-deprived, insignificant.

Learning the truth and resting in the Lord's unfailing love are the key to solving the problem, to beginning the healing process of returning the sufferer to wholeness.

The following words in Isaiah comforted the nation of Israel long ago, and they can offer comfort to an anorexic or bulimic today:

> *"'Though the mountains be shaken and the hills be removed,*
> *yet my unfailing love for you will not be shaken*
> *nor my covenant of peace be removed,' says the LORD,*
> *who has compassion on you"*
> (ISAIAH 54:10).

As you read through the following list, check each item that applies to you or your loved one:

- ☐ "I hate how I look."
- ☐ "I hate how I feel."
- ☐ "I don't like my body."
- ☐ "I feel fat and powerless."
- ☐ "I constantly compare my body to the bodies of those who are thin."
- ☐ "I would be happy if I could control how I look."

☐ "I obsessively weigh myself more than once a day."

☐ "I obsessively think about food."

☐ "I eat when I'm not hungry."

☐ "I eat when I'm stressed, anxious, or bored."

☐ "I count calories and fat grams every time I eat."

☐ "I hide how many meals I skip."

☐ "I hide how much I eat."

☐ "I hide how much I vomit."

☐ "I hide how much I exercise."

☐ "I hide how many laxatives and/or diuretics I take."

☐ "I hide my true feelings."

☐ "I avoid conflict at all costs."

☐ "I avoid being around people because I feel fat."

☐ "I have a hard time eating when other people are present."

☐ "I have a hard time asking for help."

☐ "I avoid letting people really know me."

☐ "I feel a lot of guilt over my past."

☐ "I feel a sense of shame about who I am."

☐ "I feel a sense of low self-worth."

☐ "I feel good because I'm a perfectionist."

☐ "I wish I could just disappear."

☐ "I wish I could stop my pain."

If this list accurately reflects your thoughts, feelings, and behaviors, you will quickly and completely identify with the words of Job:

> *"I cannot lift my head, for I am full of shame*
> *and drowned in my affliction"*
> (JOB 10:15).

B. What Is the Hunger for Love?

Princess Diana sought love and attention not from the world, but from those most closely around her.

And yet they didn't "get it," for she was constantly on the front pages of newspapers and magazines. The last thing she needed, they mistakenly presumed, was more *attention.*

But the princess continually cried out—to the point of injuring herself. "I didn't like myself; I was ashamed because I couldn't cope with the pressures."[53] She would cut herself on her thighs and arms, sometimes even in front of Prince Charles.

An adoring public helped Diana carry through with her official duties and provided some relief from her emotional pain.[54]

Princess Diana described her bulimia as a "secret disease," something you inflict upon yourself because "your self-esteem is at low ebb and you don't think you're worthy or valuable."[55] Stuffing her stomach with food created a false feeling of comfort, like "a pair of arms" around her. But the momentary solace always gave way to disgust as she peered down at her bloated stomach, and Diana would then vomit up all the food. Not once, not twice, but up to five times a day.[56]

Diana suffered from bulimia for "a number of years." The bingeing and purging occurring daily with alarming frequency during the most stressful periods of her life.[57]

But eating disorders can cover the gamut, with some people engaging in the practice of bingeing and purging only once or twice a week. Others habitually chew their food, savoring the flavor and texture, and then spit it out. And still others will induce vomiting not after two packages of cookies, but after just two cookies.[58]

Bingeing and purging was an escape mechanism for Diana, a distraction from her stress-filled marriage.

> *"I was overcome by trouble and sorrow…I have suffered much"*
> (PSALM 116:3; 119:107).

Eating disorders are merely the surface symptoms of an underlying problem. Those suffering from these eating disorders have believed lies and have lost sight of the truth. But God wants us to face the truth, as seen in this psalm:

> *"Surely you desire truth in the inner parts;*
> *you teach me wisdom in the inmost place"*
> (PSALM 51:6).

Those with eating disorders experience…

- **Confusion over values**—which is more important:
  - Appearance or achievement?
  - Thinness or intelligence?
  - Beauty or brains?

- **Deception of self and others**
  - Stealing food or laxatives
  - Cutting food into tiny bites to appear to be eating; secret rituals with food
  - Lying about eating; pretending to swallow food but spitting it out later
- **Depression over feeling "fat"** (even though their weight is normal or they look like skin and bones)
  - Processing information becomes utterly painful
  - Logical thinking becomes virtually impossible
  - Life becomes a subconscious—or a conscious and deliberate—attempt at suicide
- **Compulsion for some feeling of control**
  - "Eating is the one part of my life I can control."
  - "I can eat as much as I want and still not gain weight."
  - "This way I can make the pain go away."
- **Loneliness because of the desire to avoid discovery**
  - "I long for closeness, yet I'm scared of it."
  - "I feel claustrophobic if people get too close to me."
  - "I just cannot talk to anyone about this problem."
- **Low self-worth because personal value is based on appearance**
  - "I'm a fat pig."
  - "I don't deserve any help. I am a bad person."
  - "I don't deserve to live."
- **Perfectionism because they believe that everything must fit just right or it's horrible**
  - "I must have the perfect body like the models in the magazines."
  - "I must make a perfect appearance or I shouldn't appear at all."
  - "I must perform perfectly or no one will love me."
- **People-pleasing with an excessive desire for approval**
  - "If I'd just done better, my parents wouldn't have divorced."

— "If I'd just looked better, I wouldn't have been abandoned."

— "If I'd just weighed less, I might have been loved."

The Bible, instead, encourages us to evaluate our priorities:

> *"Am I now trying to win the approval of men, or of God?*
> *Or am I trying to please men? If I were still trying to*
> *please men, I would not be a servant of Christ"*
> (GALATIANS 1:10).

Common Cause

QUESTION: "What is the most common cause of someone's developing an eating disorder?"

ANSWER: All behaviors, including eating disorders, are a product of our minds, our thought processes, and the personal beliefs we form and then act upon. The reasons for a sufferer's thoughts, beliefs, and behaviors may vary, but the outcome is nonetheless the same—the sufferer engages in behaviors that are harmful, all the while rationalizing or justifying his or her actions. In other words, *disordered behavior* is the natural outgrowth of *disordered thinking* that leads to the forming of *disordered beliefs*.

People who develop a problem with eating disorders do so in an attempt to fix another problem. They feel a need to be in control because at some point they felt their life was chaotic and out of control. For example, they may have experienced...

- Overwhelming life events that leave them feeling vulnerable and powerless to take charge of their everyday circumstances and powerless to bring order out of chaos.

- Overbearing but boundaryless parents who leave them feeling the need to take control of at least one area of life to establish separateness. After all, nothing is more easily controlled than eating food. Even tiny babies are capable of refusing to eat.

- Disconnection from family or friends, which leads them to feel a need to draw attention to themselves or to fill the emptiness they feel inside with food.

Those who engage in the repeated unhealthy actions of a person who has an eating disorder can end up developing both behavioral and chemical addictions. As the body begins to deteriorate through starvation, powerful and addicting chemicals are released in the brain, which give a momentary sense of euphoria.

> *"They loathed all food and drew near the gates of death"*
> (PSALM 107:18).

C. What Are the Situational Causes?

Princess Diana battled bulimia for seven years, and she knew the eating disorders revealed a far deeper problem than "not being able to get into a size 10 dress."[59]

While Diana readily admitted that societal demands for physical perfection can trigger anorexia or bulimia, there are other causes at work as well, including a distorted relationship with something everyone needs for survival—food.

People with eating disorders "turn nourishment of the body into a painful attack on themselves," and what appears to be a surface environmental cause— vanity—actually goes much deeper.[60]

An eating disorder could become a "shameful friend," according to Diana. By focusing tremendous energy on controlling the body, a sufferer could find "refuge" from having to face the more painful issues at hand.[61]

Sadly, those who refuse to face the painful truths in their lives most often hate their very lives and reflect the heart of this verse:

> *"I loathe my very life; therefore I will give free rein to my*
> *complaint and speak out in the bitterness of my soul"*
> (JOB 10:1).

Here are some of the deeper issues that can trigger anorexic or bulimic behavior:

- **Feeling worthless** because of abuse in the home
    - Verbal assaults or emotional starvation
    - Physical or sexual abuse
    - Alcoholism or drug abuse

- **Feeling inadequate** because of unrealistic expectations of others
    - Critical, perfectionist, or extremely weight-conscious parents
    - Acceptance based on performance or appearance
    - Conditional love

- **Feeling driven** by exposure to a high-performance atmosphere
  - Dancers, musicians
  - Models, actors, actresses
  - Athletes, particularly wrestlers, gymnasts, jockeys
- **Feeling hopeless** as a result of depression from past behaviors
  - Denial of reality
  - Deep sadness
  - Guilt from personal actions
- **Feeling powerless** because of obesity or other eating problems in the family
  - One or both parents being overweight
  - A propensity for gaining weight
  - Fear of being fat
- **Feeling angry** because of past mistreatment
  - Teased or ridiculed by peers
  - Bullied because of size or weight
  - Rejected because of physical flaws or limitations
- **Feeling anxious** due to stressful life changes
  - Moved to another city, state, or country
  - Changed jobs
  - Experienced a traumatic event

Feelings rather than facts dominate the decisions of those dealing with an eating disorder. The result is increased internal and external chaos because their feelings are skewed; thus they lack a solid basis for making decisions. When distorted feelings rule, sufferers are unable to bring control into their lives because unpredictability reigns. Rather than being in control of situations, their feelings control them.

But God designed for our feelings to be the caboose and not the engine that drives our life choices. It is reason based on facts that enables us to make right decisions.

> *"'Come now, let us reason together,' says the LORD. 'Though*
> *your sins are like scarlet, they shall be as white as snow;*

> *though they are red as crimson, they shall be like wool. If*
> *you are willing and obedient, you will eat the best from*
> *the land; but if you resist and rebel, you will be devoured*
> *by the sword.' For the mouth of the LORD has spoken"*
>
> (ISAIAH 1:18-20).

D. What Is the Root Cause of an Eating Disorder?

Princess Diana believed a couple of the common root causes of an eating disorder were childhood pain and the self-doubt and uncertainty associated with adolescence.

The pressure of youth who feel the need to be perfect, coupled with their inability "to express their true feelings...of guilt, of self-revulsion, and low personal esteem" can lead them in adulthood to want to "dissolve like a disprin (aspirin) and disappear," she said, speaking from experience. [62]

By taking the time to understand the root causes of eating disorders, we can be proactive and help meet the emotional needs of children as a preventative. "As parents, teachers, family and friends, we have an obligation to care for our children. To encourage and guide, to nourish and nurture and to listen with love to their needs, in ways which clearly show our children that we value them. They in their turn will then learn how to value themselves." [63]

Until her untimely death from a car accident in 1997, Princess Diana was a public advocate for the diagnosis and treatment of eating disorders. She put an international spotlight on the troubling issue. Just as Diana longed for children to become adults who "value themselves," a biblical perspective assures that people recognize their God-given value.

Jesus wants us to recognize and always remember that we are unique creations, masterpieces, and that we are loved beyond measure. He longs for us to realize our value and significance to Him.

Jesus can fill the deepest longings of every person, and that includes those who suffer from anorexia and bulimia. No matter what your situation, He loves you with an everlasting love. He has paid for you and claimed you as His very own. He has a perfectly designed plan and purpose for your life. He can provide lasting sustenance for your emotional and spiritual hunger. And He wants you to nourish and take special care of your body because it was compassionately created with utmost precision. Value yourself, and know your God-given worth:

> *"Before I formed you in the womb I knew you,*
> *before you were born I set you apart"*
>
> (JEREMIAH 1:5).

Both the anorexic and the bulimic have *an obsessive focus on being thin.* The bulimic does not love food any more than the anorexic loves to starve.

In fact, the bulimic comes to hate the food just as much as the anorexic does. The bulimic uses food as a means to numb feelings and as a tool to lose weight. It provides something to purge, thereby eliminating calories and leading to weight loss.

WRONG BELIEF:

"I'm so fat no one could love me. I hate who I am. The only way I can be loved is to take control of my body and get it to the right size."

> *"There is a way that seems right to a man,*
> *but in the end it leads to death"*
> (PROVERBS 14:12).

RIGHT BELIEF:

"The issue in life is not my size but to see myself through God's eyes. The Lord loves me just as I am. Instead of being consumed by control, I'm choosing to release control of my life and trust the Lord Jesus with every part of my heart."

> *"Trust in the LORD with all your heart and lean not on*
> *your own understanding; in all your ways acknowledge*
> *him, and he will make your paths straight"*
> (PROVERBS 3:5-6).

THE PEOPLE'S PRINCESS

To the world, Diana appeared physically and emotionally healthy—a picture-perfect image that catapulted her to the top of fashion and "most admired" lists. But the hidden truth was that the Princess of Wales was suffering and starving...*for love.*

She often felt misunderstood or ignored by those she needed the most, and the deep hurt manifested itself in desperate acts: "you have so much pain inside yourself that you try and hurt yourself on the outside..."[64]

Because Diana's weight appeared normal—which isn't the case with anorexics—she believed she could "pretend the whole way through" her seemingly ceaseless bouts of bulimia.[65] But there were some who were watching...some whose eyes penetrated through the pretense. Diana would receive comments like, "I suppose you're going to waste that food later on?"[66] That placed yet more pressure on her, prompting her to relieve it the best way she knew—by vomiting.

For bulimics, their tumultuous struggle is not something to be discussed. Therefore Diana never sought help from the royal family. "When you have bulimia you're very ashamed of yourself and you hate yourself."[67]

Diana's eventual "going public" about her bulimia gave hope to others. In England, the number of sufferers who admitted their struggles doubled after Diana's public admission, with 60,000 cases reported in the mid-1990s. This was dubbed "the Diana effect," prompting people, primarily young women, to first acknowledge their problem and then to seek treatment.[68]

What's more, anorexia and bulimia affect far more people than just the sufferers. During the recovery process, those with eating disorders typically have fits of rage and depression, and their loved ones may find themselves strongly tempted to pull back emotionally, withdraw more and more from the sufferer, or "even throw in the towel."[69]

But don't. What recovering anorexics and bulimics need more than ever—what they've hungered for all along—*is love.* The Bible says we should

> *"be patient, bearing with one another in love"*
> (EPHESIANS 4:2).

IV. STEPS TO SOLUTION

She was a member of the "ideal American family," and it almost killed her.[70]

Her father, famed singer Pat Boone, achieved star status alongside Elvis Presley in the late 1950s, but with an entirely different image—he was wholesome, winsome.[71] Pat Boone's smooth sound landed him 38 Top-40 hits, and his record sales exceeded 45 million albums.

Cherry described the pressure she felt as her father's youngest daughter of four: "Being Pat Boone's daughter was very much like being a celebrity's kid and a preacher's kid all at the same time: maintaining the Boone image was like balancing on a tightrope."[72]

And at age 14, Cherry fell off.

Every person who is starved for love needs to know about and accept the love of the Lord so they can meet their deep-seated inner need for love. Our God of love says,

> *"I have loved you with an everlasting love;*
> *I have drawn you with loving-kindness"*
> (JEREMIAH 31:3).

A. Key Verse to Memorize

Young Cherry felt continual emotional pressure as a member of the touring musical group The Pat Boone Family. "Stared at on stage…scrutinized in fan magazines," seen as perfect, Cherry soon developed an *unhealthy* dose of self-consciousness along with an *unrealistic* perception of her physical image.[73]

"For a performer, physical appearance becomes of primary importance," Cherry recalled. "Suddenly, every imperfection, real or imagined, is a focal point for alteration and improvement."[74]

And at age 13, just one offhand comment by an 18-year-old guy about the virtues of being thin prompted Cherry to start dieting. A year later, she turned to anorexia to trim unwanted pounds, and she continued to struggle with this eating disorder for the next decade.

Those who know what it is like to struggle for years with an addiction or any kind of affliction know through personal experience the necessity of having faith in God our Savior, who offers hope—not only for the future but also for the present. They know the need to have a life-changing relationship with the Lord, who goes before you and will be with you, and who will never leave you nor forsake you. The Bible says,

> *"The LORD himself goes before you and will be with*
> *you; he will never leave you nor forsake you. Do*
> *not be afraid; do not be discouraged"*
> (DEUTERONOMY 31:8).

B. Key Passage to Read and Reread

Teenager Cherry Boone had a typical battle with her feelings, but her emotions were anything but skin-deep. Deep, deep down, she hated herself.

"Furious hatred of my fat translated into a furious hatred of myself,"[75] Cherry recalled. She completely rejected her God-given body. Along with not eating, she began a daily, two-hour exercise regimen that she practiced "religiously"—for years. At 5 feet 7 inches tall, Cherry should have weighed around 140 pounds. But over time, her obsession made her tip the scales at a scant 92 pounds—almost 50 pounds *under* her appropriate weight.[76]

Often Cherry wore baggy clothes to conceal her skeletal physique. But one day a loose garment slid off her back, revealing ribs protruding from an emaciated body. Cherry's mother was *horrified*.[77]

Cherry struggled with how her body looked. However, acceptance of her God-given body would be essential to achieving victory over anorexia and bulimia.

If, like Cherry, this is your struggle, even though you may have difficulty accepting your appearance, know that God sees you and loves you as His precious creation. You are valuable to Him. The more you realize that God is with you from the moment you are conceived until your final breath, the more you will be able to value both your body and your life.

Do you know that God designed you as a one-of-a-kind creation? Do you know that God considers you so special that He has a personalized plan for your life? Do you realize He knit your body together while you were still inside your mother's womb?

Realize the thoroughness of God's knowledge of you. He states you are "wonderfully made" (Psalm 139:14). And His thoughts are always with you. You are always on His mind. That should give you comfort.

Read Psalm 139 and say out loud the truths found in these verses. Then you will begin to see how precious you are to God.

Jena and Her Sinister "Sister"

The sinister "sister"...the taunting twin...she stood, stared, and glared.

"Cake?" she sneered as Jena undressed before the bathroom mirror, preparing to shower. "You ate cake last night? What were you thinking? I never gave you permission to eat cake. And now you'll pay for it, you greedy pig. Get on the scale. Now!"[78]

The words Jena heard were not audible; rather, they were thoughts blasting chaotically through her brain, drowning out the voice of reason. Her mind was in mayhem as she apologized and promised not to eat all day. But the sinister "sister," the evil twin inside her, wasn't finished.

For almost all of her life, Jena Morrow had been tormented by a three-letter word—*fat*. And she remembers precisely when the struggle began. She was riding in the family car when suddenly her eyes were drawn down to her thighs and she became alarmed at how they "squish themselves out wide" on the seat.[79] Jena's eyes then roamed a little higher to her pink windbreaker, which was puffed out at the moment, making it appear as though she had a baby in her belly. And all of a sudden—not at age 13 *but at age 3*—Jena concluded she was fat.[80]

And here's irony from Jena: "I have never actually *been* fat, and yet I cannot recall a time when I did not *feel* fat."[81] This false perception on her part triggered a terrible turn of events that almost took her life. The distorted image Jena had of her body drew her into the dark and dangerous world of anorexia, and to this day she still has to fight to stay in the light.

What surfaced at age 3 ran rampant at age 12 when a nightmare scenario emerged that would frighten anyone struggling with body image distortion—the dreaded gym class shower. Jena did *everything* she could to avoid gym class—continually feigning illness, hiding in bathroom stalls, even trying to rebreak a healed broken ankle. But eventually she was found out, and after informing a school social worker in no uncertain terms that there was no way she would take off her clothes to shower, the school official probed a little further and found out about Jena's perception of her own body.[82]

And just how did Jena perceive her body? "I told her I hated mine and would like to cut it up."[83] That's all the social worker needed to hear to send Jena to a child psychiatrist, who soon declared her "emotionally unstable."[84]

Through her middle and high school years, Jena continually struggled, but it wasn't until college that anorexia assaulted her body like never before and Jena found herself at death's door. Her desire to lose weight took her on a downward spiral toward a desire to literally shrink or disappear. And then yet another desire was spawned that came from no less than the pit of hell itself—*self-destruction.*

Once, after shoving three handfuls of cereal into her mouth Jena panicked and downed an entire bottle of ipecac, an antidote for accidental poisoning. The recommended dosage? One tablespoon, followed by eight ounces of water. Jena never made it to the water, for her stomach immediately began to lurch and churn violently. Vomiting ensued all throughout the night. The next morning, Jena was surprised she was still alive.[85]

Wanting nothing more to do with emetics, Jena turned to laxatives and worked her way up to taking about 25 pills a day. In early spring 1996, Jena weighed what she did at age 10—about 90 pounds. Although her family was appalled, the eating disorder would continue to dominate her life. Jena was hooked—she was a hardcore addict of anorexia.[86]

Jena described the "high" that initially accompanied her self-starvation—the euphoria that anorexics experience when they start seeing results such as looser and looser jeans and having to pull up plunging waistbands. This high is caused by chemical changes that occur in the brain that are similar to the releasing of endorphins following a jog in the park or sexual intimacy.[87] "An eating disorder, in the beginning, is like being in love," Jena explained. "Everything else takes a back seat to your new passion."[88]

But Jena's passion turned excruciatingly painful as her body began to writhe in agony from sustained abuse. Further down the path of self-destruction, Jena became "a gobbler of pills"[89]—any pills she could find, including her grandmother's Alzheimer's medication and her dog's thyroid tablets. Jena describes that as one of her darkest seasons, and soon her life turned almost totally black. It all began with a muffin.

Jena had never wanted anything more in her life. The buttery, sweet smell was wafting through her car. She wanted to devour the muffin she had just purchased. At this time, the signs of starvation were well evident—Jena's lips and fingernails were blue, her teeth were chattering, and the heater in her car was cranked up even though it was summer.[90] But then the sinister sister, the evil twin, made her presence known, and the accusations began to fly.

Jena took just one tiny bite of the muffin, and then tossed the rest out the window. While at a stoplight, she grabbed what comprised her usual diet and downed 15 laxative pills along with a handful of diuretic tablets and caffeine capsules. It proved to be a woeful wake-up call, as Jena later began shaking uncontrollably experiencing raging fever. It was then that she finally agreed to get help at a Christian treatment center for eating and anxiety disorders.[91]

Up to this time, Jena had struggled for many years with a distorted body image. Absolutely nothing had shaken her terrible misperception of herself. So it was remarkable that for one brief moment, *she came to see herself as she really was*. She tried on a bathing suit, and standing before a dressing room mirror, she couldn't believe what she saw.

> I stared at my reflection. My legs were milky white, webbed with blue veins, and my feet were a ridiculous shade of purple. My upper arm was precisely half the width of my elbow, and my thighs were no wider than my knees, all the way up. My face was scariest of all: gray with sunken eyes and cheeks, and a big, blue vein bulging and pulsing at the center of my forehead.
>
> In a flash of clarity, I caught a fleeting glimpse of the ugly truth, and I had an epiphany: *I had become a monster.*[92]

Drained physically, emotionally, and spiritually, Jena began feeding on truths from the Bible that related to her struggle. The Word of God became a healing balm to Jena's wounded soul, and she began eating nutritionally.

But then she suffered a setback. She suddenly became distraught over her increasing caloric intake and growing waistline—disappointed because thousands of dollars in treatment had not yet "cured" her. Soulful sobs swelled up and spilled out. Jena was outside in an arid desert environment, sitting on a bench with an unopened Bible by her side. After what seemed an eternity, she finally summoned the strength to open her Bible, which "happened" to open to Isaiah chapter 58. Jena's eyes were drawn like a magnet to verse 11: "The LORD will guide you always; he will satisfy your needs in a sun-scorched land and will strengthen your frame." Jena couldn't believe it. Joy began to sweep over her, for there she sat in the *sun-scorched* Arizona desert receiving a promise from her heavenly Father that He indeed would strengthen her frame.[93]

Hungering for more words of life, Jena turned to one of her favorite passages, Jeremiah 29:11: "'I know the plans I have for you,' declares the LORD, 'plans to prosper you and not to harm you, plans to give you hope and a future.'" Tremendous peace washed over Jena as she realized God's plans for her life superseded her own, that He was in control of *everything*, and that He had never intended for her to be the one controlling everything. There had been several times when Jena should have died, but that was not part of God's plans for her. Instead, He began using her to minister to other young women who struggled with anorexia.

"But what happens after I return home?" is a typical question. "Will I revert to past patterns?" is a serious concern. And indeed, the sinister sister, the taunting twin came charging back into Jena's life. "You ate cake—you greedy pig!"

"You're gonna pay for yesterday. Open the cabinet." Jena knew what was coming next. She saw the deadly stockpile of medicine in front of her. "Take the pills, any you can find. Do it! I don't care what—just take something. You've been bad, and you must be punished."[94]

Jena sensed herself weakening, the belittling and the bullying becoming too much for her to bear. But then she reached for the sharpest of "swords" contained in a stack of index cards strategically placed by the mirror.

"I am God's creation, made in His image. God takes pleasure in me," Jena read aloud.

There was an uneasy silence. Jena continued, "I am the righteousness of God in Christ. I have been chosen and set apart for God's holy purpose."[95]

The Bible had once again proven itself to be powerful: "The word of God is living and active. Sharper than any double-edged sword, it penetrates even to dividing soul and spirit, joints and marrow; it judges the thoughts and attitudes of the heart."[96]

The sinister sister had once again been rendered speechless.

C. How to First Acknowledge Seven Key Needs

People like Cherry, who suffer from anorexia or bulimia, need to be told *it's not about the food.*

They *need* to acknowledge that their true need is to have emotional wounds healed, and they *need* to understand that the starving and the bingeing and purging are actually distractions that cause them to avoid facing painful feelings deep within.

Anorexics and bulimics also *need* to be firmly told that society's constant message that "thinness is the way to happiness" is a lie. People with eating disorders tend to isolate themselves from friends and social activities, and experience self-loathing rather than self-acceptance. Healthy eating leads to heightened energy, as well as a more robust attitude toward life.[97]

The primary need of the person suffering from anorexia or bulimia is not the food they need to receive, but the Lord they need to believe. They need to know experientially the One who made them and loves them and longs to heal them and meet their deepest inner needs.

> *"My God will meet all your needs*
> *according to his glorious riches in Christ Jesus"*
> (PHILIPPIANS 4:19).

If you have concerns—or if others have expressed concern—about your weight or your eating and exercise patterns, take to heart these general principles:

1. **Agree to get a thorough medical checkup**. This condition is life threatening!

   > *"The prudent see danger and take refuge,*
   > *but the simple keep going and suffer for it"*
   > (PROVERBS 27:12).

2. **Acquire as much knowledge about eating disorders as possible—** for yourself and for those close to you.

> *"Plans fail for lack of counsel,*
> *but with many advisers they succeed"*
> (PROVERBS 15:22).

3. **Attend weekly (or regular) sessions** with a knowledgeable, professional Christian counselor.

> *"Apply your heart to instruction and your ears*
> *to words of knowledge"*
> (PROVERBS 23:12).

4. **Admit your inability to control your eating patterns.**

> *"I do not understand what I do. For what I want*
> *to do I do not do, but what I hate I do"*
> (ROMANS 7:15).

5. **Abandon the idea that you just need more willpower.** This is not a diet or willpower problem, but a battle that addresses strongholds.

> *"The weapons we fight with are not the weapons of the*
> *world. On the contrary, they have divine power to demolish*
> *strongholds. We demolish arguments and every pretension*
> *that sets itself up against the knowledge of God, and we*
> *take captive every thought to make it obedient to Christ"*
> (2 CORINTHIANS 10:4-5; read also 2 Corinthians 12:9-10).

6. **Allow yourself to forgive those who have hurt you.** And even forgive yourself.

> *"Bear with each other and forgive whatever grievances you may*
> *have against one another. Forgive as the Lord forgave you"*
> (COLOSSIANS 3:13).

7. **Act in total faith on God's power** to rescue you.

> *"In you, O LORD, I have taken refuge; let me never be put to shame.*
> *Rescue me and deliver me in your righteousness; turn your ear to*
> *me and save me. Be my rock of refuge, to which I can always go;*
> *give the command to save me, for you are my rock and my fortress"*
> (PSALM 71:1-3).

D. How Do You Therapeutically Treat Eating Disorders?

The false starts should have proven fatal for Cherry Boone O'Neill. The huge ingestion of food into an emaciated body…the wretched ritual of purging…the swallowing of 60 laxative tablets in one sitting.[98]

Make no mistake—Cherry had a death wish, and it looked like it was coming true.

However, a full family intervention motivated Cherry to seek medical and mental help. She desperately needed a comprehensive understanding of the emotional needs she was trying to meet through her eating disorder. "The need for acceptance and approval—the need to be perfect—had been a driving force that ultimately brought me to the brink of death…I expended every effort to be the best I could possibly be in any given area of endeavor, only to repeatedly fall short of my goals and risk losing value in the eyes of others.

"Trying even harder, only to miss the mark again and again, resulted in compounded guilt and self-hatred."[99]

This type of self-loathing guilt is seen in the Psalms:

> *"My guilt has overwhelmed me like a burden too heavy to bear"*
> (Psalm 38:4).

No single approach to breaking addictions is ever enough because bondage is multi-faceted, and thus deliverance must incorporate numerous approaches. All addictions involve not only the body, but also the heart and soul of those they hold captive. That being the case, it is understandable that the Bible instructs us to

> *"love the Lord your God with all your heart*
> *and with all your soul and with all your strength"*
> (Deuteronomy 6:5).

When we have the grace of God operating in our lives, we are both equipped and empowered to make good use of the following treatment approaches to gain inner healing and overcome eating disorders.

- **Care from a medical professional:** Anorexia and bulimia exact a tremendous toll from the body. Health consequences can remain years after harmful eating habits have been conquered. A doctor and dietician can often offer helpful advice and treatment for those who have suffered from an eating disorder.

- **Counsel from a mental health professional:** Deeper issues and insecurities that contribute to an eating disorder must be confronted for lasting change to occur. Often a professional counselor can help direct someone with destructive eating patterns to a healthier view of one's self and of food.

- **Connection with a community of believers:** Being part of a group of people who desire to follow Christ, are willing to reveal their vulnerabilities, and are available to offer and receive support is essential for permanent life-change in a believer. Become an active part of a group of Christians so you can receive spiritual direction and cultivate bonds that can support you when you need them most.

> *"Carry each other's burdens,*
> *and in this way you will fulfill the law of Christ"*
> (GALATIANS 6:2).

E. How to Know Your True Spiritual Worth

Once Cherry started to receive sound biblical counsel, sustained support from her new loving husband, and an awareness of her true worth in God's eyes, the humiliation of those tangled times of life began to lessen. "I likened myself to an intricately designed, fine gold chain that had become badly tangled in knots,"[100] Cherry recalled. And it became a refreshing revelation "that the chain had never lost its original value merely because it was tangled."[101]

At age 23, Cherry realized she needed to discover her own God-given identity—apart from her famous parents and apart from her husband. She began to gain a true understanding of her worth. After all her years of struggle, she was eager to answer a befitting question: "Who is this Cherry, anyway?"[102]

Not only Cherry, but women all around the world need to know their God-given worth because the images holding them are inescapable—the idols of thinness that typically trigger anorexia.

The media's message is this: "Beauty shines as the smallest number on the bathroom scales." That lie is literally destroying young women. Even women in other countries who at one time weren't exposed to Western media are now being snared by the *self-starvation syndrome*.

Decades ago, anorexia was primarily associated with young, affluent, white women. Now this eating disorder is being diagnosed within all demographics: all races, ages, and socioeconomic levels.[103]

South Pacific islanders in Fiji have traditionally held to a different concept of beauty than those in the West, but according to a study conducted by Dr. Anne

Becker of the Harvard Eating Disorders Center, that began to change in the late 1990s when television became more easily accessible. In just three years, the number of teenage girls at risk for an eating disorder more than doubled, and the number of girls who said they forced themselves to vomit in order to maintain a specific weight increased from 3 percent to 15 percent.[104]

When Cherry Boone O'Neill changed her focus, she was set free from anorexia—she looked to a different standard, an eternal standard, God's standard of truth. Based on the Bible, your true worth isn't based on your outward appearance, but on who you are in Christ. In Him, you are infinitely loved and valued:

> *"Neither height nor depth, nor anything else in all creation,*
> *will be able to separate us from the love of God*
> *that is in Christ Jesus our Lord"*
> (ROMANS 8:39).

According to the Bible, you can...

- **Know that if you have come into a personal relationship with the Lord Jesus**, your *true identity* is in *Christ* Himself.
  - You are a new creation in Christ. You are no longer what you were.
  - If you allow Jesus to become the focus of your life—not food, not compulsion, but Christ—you will increasingly find freedom.

> *"If anyone is in Christ, he is a new creation; the*
> *old has gone, the new has come!"*
> (2 CORINTHIANS 5:17).

- **Know that the old "you" died.**
  - When you trusted in Christ alone as your Savior, the old "you" died, and He gave you a new nature, a new life, a new identity—in Him.
  - Your thinking and behavior patterns may still compel you to crave food and obsess over thinness. These patterns, however, no longer need to control you because Christ has broken the power of your sin.
  - As you learn to renew your mind with the help of God's truth, the Lord will continue to break those compulsive patterns and set you free.

> *"I have been crucified with Christ, and I no longer live,*
> *but Christ lives in me. The life I live in the body, I live by faith*
> *in the Son of God, who loved me and gave himself for me"*
> (GALATIANS 2:20).

- **Know that even in the midst of your trials**, you are totally accepted by the Father.

  – Regardless of how you've been treated by family members and friends, your heavenly Father loves and accepts you unconditionally.

  – God loves you just the way you are, and *because* He loves you, *He will change you.* He will take your hand, as a father takes the hand of a little child, and will walk you toward freedom.

  > *"Fear not, for I have redeemed you;*
  > *I have summoned you by name; you are mine...*
  > *You [God] give me your shield of victory, and your right*
  > *hand sustains me; you stoop down to make me great"*
  > (ISAIAH 43:1; PSALM 18:35).

- **Know that the Spirit of Christ will bring about His control in you.**

  – Producing positive change in your life is not a matter of more self-control on your part; it's a matter of yielding to the Spirit's *control* in you. When you are rooted in Christ, He will naturally produce the fruit of self-control in you.

  > *"The fruit of the Spirit is love, joy, peace, patience,*
  > *kindness, goodness, faithfulness, gentleness and self-*
  > *control. Against such things there is no law"*
  > (GALATIANS 5:22-23).

- **Know that your freedom comes through Christ.**

  – Family and friends will be used by God, but total freedom from bondage comes *only through Christ.*

  > *"Through Christ Jesus the law of the Spirit of life*
  > *set me free from the law of sin and death"*
  > (ROMANS 8:2).

What Is the Truth about You?

- The *world* tells you a lie . . . . *"You can't be too thin—thin is in!"*

- The *flesh* tells you to live a lie . . . . *"You've got to be thin to be accepted."*

- The father of lies, *Satan*, tells you . . . . . *"You will not surely die"* (Genesis 3:4).

But...

- The Truth, *Jesus*, tells you . . . . *"The truth will set you free"* (John 8:32).

  – Be free from being controlled by the opinion of others.
  – You are free to be the healthy size God created you to be.
  – The world's supermodels and movie stars are generally underweight and unhealthy.

> *"So if the Son sets you free, you will be free indeed"*
> (John 8:36).

People with eating disorders are love-starved. Express your love to them by keeping eye contact with them and spending time with them—lots of time. This is how they spell love: T-I-M-E. Those with eating disorders don't feel valued. So show that you value them.

You will confirm other people's value when you tangibly reach out to them and touch them. Even if they don't seem to respond at first, know that they are desperately seeking your acceptance. They desperately long for unconditional love—*your love, the Lord's love.*

> *"Come to me, all you who are weary and burdened, and I will give you rest. Take my yoke upon you and learn from me, for I am gentle and humble in heart, and you will find rest for your souls"*
> (Matthew 11:28-29).

F. How to Find Your Way to Freedom

Like a struggling swimmer, Cherry was trying to stay afloat in the sea of self-disdain, but she was barely surviving. She was caught in the undertow of self-hatred, and she couldn't break free.

Caught? Yes, caught and caught again! At the same time, her fiancé, Dan, caught her squatting on the floor, gorging on leftover lamb chops—in the Boone family's dog bowl.[105] Cherry was anything but free.

True freedom can be found by anyone who is trapped in any kind of bondage. But it means facing the facts, assuming responsibility, making choices, taking action, sticking it out. Finding freedom and living in it takes work. But this freedom is worth the labor. Freedom cuts the cords of perfectionism so that you can soar to become all that God created you to be.

It was for this purpose that Jesus was sent:

> "...to bind up the brokenhearted, to proclaim freedom for the
> captives and release from darkness for the prisoners...to comfort
> all who mourn, and provide for those who grieve...to bestow on
> them a crown of beauty instead of ashes, the oil of gladness instead
> of mourning, and a garment of praise instead of a spirit of despair"
> (ISAIAH 61:1-3).

THE WAY TO FREEDOM

If you have an eating disorder, here are your first steps to freedom:

- **Recognize you have an eating disorder.**
  - Face the truth of your unhealthy weight loss and obsession with fat and food.
  - Accept the fact that your life and health are seriously compromised.

- **Acknowledge your need.**
  - Admit your enslavement to an eating disorder and its power over your life.
  - Share your struggle with a trusted friend and break the power of the secret.

- **Get professional help.**
  - Seek out a therapist experienced in successfully treating those ensnared by an eating disorder.
  - Realize that it is vital to get help for understanding your illness and overcoming its hold on you.

- **Discover your past predispositions.**
  - Explore the family dynamics that "set you up" to have an eating disorder.
  - Evaluate past events that still impact your life today and influence your decision making.

- **Identify your present stressors.**
  - Examine your life (activities and relationships) and pinpoint areas of stress.
  - Reflect on any similarities between past life experiences and present-day situations.

- **Avoid your destructive patterns.**
  - Recognize activities where food is the focus and break those patterns.
  - Replace energy-draining behaviors involving food with enjoyable energy-producing activities not involving food.

- **Flee the triggers that entice unhealthy eating habits.**
  - Reflect on times and events that have entrenched you further in destructive eating behaviors.
  - Devise a plan of action to overcome unexpected temptations to skip a meal or to binge/purge.

- **Resist the urges that compel your wrong eating behaviors.**
  - Commit to distracting yourself whenever you suddenly feel compelled to "act out" with food.
  - Plan an activity you will do when you feel the urge to binge or purge.

You cannot hope to walk in freedom unless you walk in the truth. Tell yourself the truth: "Lord, You created my body. You know what is best for my body." Then pray every day…

> *"Teach me your way, O LORD,*
> *and I will walk in your truth;*
> *give me an undivided heart,*
> *that I may fear [honor] your name"*
> (PSALM 86:11).

THE WAY TO SUSTAINED FREEDOM

Here are the keys to achieving true and total freedom:

- **Yield yourself to God.**
  - Surrender your life, your heart, your mind, your will, and your emotions to Christ.
  - Submit to God's rule in your life over your relationships, your thoughts, and your actions.

  > *"Submit yourselves, then, to God.*
  > *Resist the devil, and he will flee from you"*
  > (JAMES 4:7).

- **Claim your victory in Christ.**
  - Accept by faith the fact that Christ has set you free from the power of sin and death.
  - Act on your faith by thinking, talking, and living in ways that reflect your position as an overcomer through Christ, as one who has moved from death to life.

  > *"Do not offer the parts of your body to sin, as instruments of*
  > *wickedness, but rather offer yourselves to God, as those who*
  > *have been brought from death to life; and offer the parts*
  > *of your body to him as instruments of righteousness"*
  > (ROMANS 6:13).

- **Picture your success.**
  - Count yourself dead to the call of temptation that would cause you to give in to sin.
  - Consider yourself a citizen of heaven—one who is submitted to Jesus Christ and walks in victory over worldly and fleshly desires.

  > *"Our citizenship is in heaven. And we eagerly await a Savior*
  > *from there, the Lord Jesus Christ, who, by the power that enables*
  > *him to bring everything under his control, will transform*
  > *our lowly bodies so that they will be like his glorious body"*
  > (PHILIPPIANS 3:20-21).

- **Replace lies with the truth.**
  - Reject negative thoughts about yourself and replace them with biblical truths that affirm your value and worth to God and the extent of His commitment to you as His child, His priceless possession.
  - Remember that feelings change and cannot be trusted, but God does not change. He is totally trustworthy, and His promises are utterly reliable in every circumstance and at all times.

  "Since we have these promises, dear friends, let us purify ourselves from everything that contaminates body and spirit, perfecting holiness out of reverence for God"
  (2 CORINTHIANS 7:1).

- **Devise a plan for daily success.**
  - Begin and end each day in prayer, praise, and worship, thanking God and seeking His continued guidance.
  - Be sure to lay out a detailed plan for each day that contains your daily activities, including balanced meals, Bible study, Scripture memorization, and other healthy practices.

  "As long as he sought the LORD, God gave him success"
  (2 CHRONICLES 26:5).

- **Enlist the support of others.**
  - Get involved in a group Bible study or prayer group where you can study God's Word and share prayer requests with other Christians on a regular basis.
  - Gather some friends who will help hold you accountable by checking with you on a daily basis, asking you questions about how you're doing, and praying for you to keep walking in freedom.

  "If one falls down, his friend can help him up.
  But pity the man who falls and has no
  one to help him up!...Perfume and incense
  bring joy to the heart, and the pleasantness of
  one's friend springs from his earnest counsel"
  (ECCLESIASTES 4:10; PROVERBS 27:9).

- **Throw away your bathroom scale.**
  - Make it your goal to eat healthily, not to lose or gain weight. Trust God to fulfill His promise to provide for your needs as you delight in Him and focus on His desires for you.
  - Manage your life well, maintain a good balance in all areas, make a plan, and then carry out that plan. Put away your bathroom scale, which will only hold you captive to human traditions.

  "See to it that no one takes you captive through hollow and deceptive philosophy, which depends on human tradition and the basic principles of this world rather than on Christ"
  (COLOSSIANS 2:8).

- **Journal your journey.**
  - Realize that it is important for you to remember your journey with Christ into the freedom He died to secure for you.
  - Record in a daily journal the ways the Lord is manifesting His power in your life. Then share them with your loved ones—both young and old—to encourage them and to bring glory to God.

  "Fix these words of mine in your hearts and minds; tie them as symbols on your hands and bind them on your foreheads. Teach them to your children, talking about them when you sit at home and when you walk along the road, when you lie down and when you get up. Write them on the doorframes of your houses and on your gates"
  (DEUTERONOMY 11:18-20).

Remember this biblical truth as you walk the road of freedom in Christ Jesus:

*"It is for freedom that Christ has set us free.
Stand firm, then, and do not let yourselves be burdened
again by a yoke of slavery"*
(GALATIANS 5:1).

G. How to Eat Your Way to Good Health

If a little is good, a lot is better. So goes the thinking of overeaters who struggle to find balance in their life—and in their diet. Much of the time, when a little is good, a lot is not! And at other times, especially for anorexic and bulimic strugglers—if a little is good, less is not!

In our pursuit of what we perceive to be best for ourselves, we sometimes throw out the good and end up with something worse. We can forget that when God saw all He had created, He said, "It is good."

Healthy is good. *Balance* is good. Healthy, balanced eating is good, and it is possible—even for the anorexic and bulimic. The questions you need to ask are these: Will you do it? How will you do it? When will you do it? Where will you do it? And what are the ramifications of not doing it?

> *"God saw all that he had made, and it was very good"*
> (Genesis 1:31).

- **Decide to try healthy, balanced eating:**
  - Keep unhealthy foods out of sight and in hard-to-reach places.
  - Learn how to eat healthy, not how to avoid eating or how to purge after eating.
  - Make a nutritional plan for each day, using a variety of foods and recording your calorie intake.
  - Make a shopping list, and don't shop when you are hungry.
  - Realize that strict diets lead to sure failure, whereas a lifestyle of healthy eating leads to sure success.
  - Reward yourself for eating healthily, but don't reward yourself with food.
  - Rid your residence of binge and trigger foods (usually sugary or starchy), and stock up on healthy snacks.
  - Stop focusing on weight loss. Instead, focus on healthy, balanced eating.
  - To determine whether a particular food is okay to eat, think about how it makes your body feel.

- **Practice following these guidelines:**
  - Eat three meals a day at scheduled times.
  - Eat small snacks between meals, and do so only at preplanned times.
  - Eat meals and snacks at the breakfast or dining table and never in a vehicle, bedroom, bathroom, or when in a hurry.

— Eat nothing before or during meal/snack preparation, or after the meal/snack is over.

— Determine to truly experience your food, noting its color, size, taste, shape, texture, and scent.

— Eat slowly, chewing each bite, enjoying the flavor.

— Take time to relax as you eat your meal. Think about things other than eating, such as a visit with someone or the scenery outside the window.

— Take just one or two bites of fattening foods. Such small amounts won't make a difference to your body.

— Remind yourself that everyone feels full and clothes feel tighter around the waist after eating. These feelings will go away as your body digests the food and puts it to use.

As you seek to gain God's perspective on food and to make God-honoring decisions regarding your food intake, remember what the Bible says:

> *"So I commend the enjoyment of life,*
> *because nothing is better for a man under the sun*
> *than to eat and drink and be glad.*
> *Then joy will accompany him in his work*
> *all the days of the life God has given him under the sun"*
> (ECCLESIASTES 8:15).

H. How to Know the Do's and Don'ts for Family and Friends

For Cherry Boone O'Neill, the most critical "do's" for family and friends include pouring out loving compassion upon the struggler and dispensing huge doses of hope. Cherry said, "Dan and I have found that hope is among the most positive motivators in achieving health that loved ones—and victims of eating disorders—can have. Maintaining hope for ourselves, and sharing hope with others, allows for the possibility—even the likelihood—that a distant light is glowing at the end of the dark tunnel."[106]

When all is said and done, people who are struggling with anorexia and bulimia truly need *hope for their hearts:*

> *"Now, Lord, what do I look for?*
> *My hope is in you"*
> (PSALM 39:7).

The female figure can be a fanatical issue. Tell a young woman her thighs are too big or tease her about a bulging belly, and she can immediately spiral downward into a dangerous world of dieting and self-starvation. One comment is often all it takes for a young woman's self-esteem to sink and her figure fixation to rise. Therefore, family and friends must be keenly sensitive to teasing and offhand comments, particularly in a society where eating disorders are rapidly enslaving more and more young women because of society's glorification of thinness. Be sure to

> *"be completely humble and gentle;*
> *be patient, bearing with one another in love"*
> (EPHESIANS 4:2).

As a loving support person, here are some good things you can do:

- *Deemphasize dieting* and emphasize healthy eating habits and fitness.
- *Arrange schedules* to eat more meals together.
- *Critically discuss* the unhealthy body images portrayed in the media.
- *Clearly expose* the massive amount of retouching done to published photos of models.
- *Create a scrapbook* of healthy body images.[107]

And here are some good truths to remember:

> *"Do you not know that your body is a temple of the Holy Spirit,*
> *who is in you, whom you have received from God?*
> *You are not your own; you were bought at a price.*
> *Therefore honor God with your body"*
> (1 CORINTHIANS 6:19-20).

Here Are the Do's[108]

- *Do* learn everything you can.

  Knowledge is your friend, and ignorance is your enemy. Find the best material you can at the library, on the Internet, or from competent professionals.

> *"Listen to advice and accept instruction,*
> *and in the end you will be wise"*
> (PROVERBS 19:20).

- ***Do*** confront in a loving way.

    Confrontation is not easy! But doing nothing is the opposite of truly loving someone.

    > *"Reckless words pierce like a sword,*
    > *but the tongue of the wise brings healing"*
    > (PROVERBS 12:18).

- ***Do*** seek professional help for the one in need.

    A mark of wisdom is acknowledging your need for advice. Locating a specialist in eating disorders may require asking a pastor, a physician, or a school counselor for help.

    > *"Pride only breeds quarrels, but wisdom is*
    > *found in those who take advice"*
    > (PROVERBS 13:10).

- ***Do*** talk about emotions, and strive to reach deeper levels of communication.

    Ask, "Why do you feel this way?" Seek to uncover the underlying causes behind this crisis.

    > *"The purposes of a man's heart are deep waters,*
    > *but a man of understanding draws them out"*
    > (PROVERBS 20:5).

- ***Do*** listen, listen, listen with your heart.

    The best conversationalist is someone who knows how to listen. People love to hear their words repeated: "So what you are saying is…" Listening and repeating what is said helps build trust and opens up communication, which in turn leads to healing.

    > *"[There is] a time to be silent and a time to speak"*
    > (ECCLESIASTES 3:7).

- ***Do*** verbalize your genuine, heartfelt love by using tender, endearing terms.

    Positive reinforcement is crucial. Using tender terms such as *precious* or *dear*, or saying a person's name in a tender way, will often help someone to feel nurtured. Make sure your concern sounds genuine and not contrived. A pet name can be especially endearing to both men and women.

> *"A word aptly spoken is like apples of gold in settings of silver"*
> (Proverbs 25:11).

- *Do* express love with physical affection.

  Looking someone in the eyes, reaching out to touch a hand, or a gentle touch on the shoulder can be helpful. In certain family relationships, hugging, holding, and kissing can be especially meaningful.

  > *"A friend loves at all times, and a brother is born for adversity"*
  > (Proverbs 17:17).

- *Do* be honest about the dangers.

  The debilitating effects of eating disorders wreak havoc on the body. Those in need of help need to learn to think about the very real long-term dangers of eating disorders.

  > *"Encourage the timid, help the weak, be patient with everyone"*
  > (1 Thessalonians 5:14).

- *Do* stay with your loved one around the clock.

  In high-risk situations, for a limited period of time during a health crisis, enlist other nurturing people to be present, if necessary. Frequently, being present with the sufferer means paying the high cost of commitment, but salvaging a life is worth the cost.

  > *"A man of many companions may come to ruin,*
  > *but there is a friend who sticks closer than a brother"*
  > (Proverbs 18:24).

- *Do* pray faithfully.

  Let your loved one know you are specifically praying for him or her by name. Pray with the person for the courage to overcome and to know healing.

  > *"The prayer of a righteous man is powerful and effective"*
  > (James 5:16).

And Here Are the Don'ts

Cherry Boone O'Neill states a definite "don't" for family and friends of strugglers—*don't expect a quick fix.*[109] Eating disorders are a complicated phenomenon, an intertwining of emotional, physical, and spiritual issues, and *time* is a necessary healer. It may take years for a sufferer to fully rebound and regain self-control, and even then, some people can relapse into old routines at any moment.

Another important "don't" from Cherry: *Don't fail to forgive.* Anorexics and bulimics are desperately in need of the "70 times 7" principle of forgiveness taught by Jesus, which tells us to *always* forgive.

- ***Don't*** be forceful or controlling.

  One mother succeeded in getting her daughter to eat by distracting her from negative thoughts with constant praise and unconditional love during all of her waking moments.

  > *"Pleasant words are a honeycomb,*
  > *sweet to the soul and healing to the bones"*
  > (PROVERBS 16:24).

- ***Don't*** be unrealistic about your expectations for change.

  It has taken nearly a lifetime of negative thinking to reach this point. It may take a long time for full healing to take place.

  > *"A man's wisdom gives him patience;*
  > *it is to his glory to overlook an offense"*
  > (PROVERBS 19:11).

- ***Don't*** naively assume that all well-meaning doctors who treat anorexics and bulimics are equally capable. Find a competent, compassionate specialist who ministers to the inner needs of patients and with whom the patient can develop a deep bond of trust. If necessary, seek a second or third opinion.

  > *"Plans fail for lack of counsel, but with many advisers they succeed"*
  > (PROVERBS 15:22).

- ***Don't*** let anorexics see the numbers on the scale when they are weighed. Tell them you will relieve them of the responsibility of knowing their weight. No matter what the number, their negative thinking will tell them it's too high. If they don't have a number to fight, that's one less negative they have to contend with.

> *"The wise in heart are called discerning,*
> *and pleasant words promote instruction"*
> (PROVERBS 16:21).

- ***Don't*** expect an anorexic struggler to rejoice at putting on needed weight. Strugglers have a well-developed mental and emotional aversion to gaining weight. Their spontaneous reaction to weight gain will naturally be negative until their thought patterns and beliefs have changed through the renewing of their minds.

> *"Do not conform any longer to the pattern of this*
> *world, but be transformed by the renewing of your*
> *mind. Then you will be able to test and approve what*
> *God's will is—his good, pleasing and perfect will"*
> (ROMANS 12:2).

- ***Don't*** fail to request help from a former anorexic. Former anorexics know all the tricks, such as poisoning their food, exercising under the sheets, and slipping food up their sleeves to discard later. Nothing is more reassuring to someone with an eating disorder than a helping hand from someone who's been there—someone now living in victory.

> *"As iron sharpens iron, so one man sharpens another"*
> (PROVERBS 27:17).

- ***Don't*** assume that you are helpless if anorexics won't eat. Offer to hand-feed the person as a short-term *emergency* response (not a pattern of behavior). Because anorexics possess a negative mind-set that tells them not to eat, hand-feeding can relieve their self-imposed pressure of guilt and fear of overeating.

> *"Carry each other's burdens, and in this way*
> *you will fulfill the law of Christ"*
> (GALATIANS 6:2).

- ***Don't*** stock or eat "trigger" or unhealthy foods in your home if an anorexic or bulimic lives with you. Just as you would not flaunt alcohol in the presence of a recovering alcoholic, realize the anorexic's great struggle to eat healthily and tremendous need to avoid temptation.

> *"Lead us not into temptation, but deliver us from the evil one"*
> (Matthew 6:13).

- **Don't** compliment positive changes in body weight by saying, "You look healthy."

The word *healthy,* to strugglers, means "fat." To say they look healthy translates into telling them they look fat. Don't mention any weight gain. Tell them their eyes look sparkly and alive again, their skin youthful, their hair shiny and silky, and their energy level high.

> *"Each of us should please his neighbor for his good, to build him up"*
> (Romans 15:2).

- **Don't** give up. Patience, persistence, and perseverance are essential for helping restore your loved one to wholeness.

> *"Love is patient, love is kind. It does not envy, it does not boast, it is not proud....It always protects, always trusts, always hopes, always perseveres. Love never fails"*
> (1 Corinthians 13:4,7-8).

Religious Obsessions and Disordered Eating

Question: "Why would some anorexics view *not* eating as an 'act of faith'?"

Answer: If they come from a highly structured or authoritarian religious background, their refusal to eat helps them feel a sense of control in the midst of a life that's gotten out of control.

Lovingly remind them of these biblical principles:

- Using Scripture to justify destructive choices does not honor God. Remember, Satan twisted Scripture to match his twisted thinking.

> *"'If you are the Son of God,' he [Satan] said, 'throw yourself down. For it is written: "He will command his angels concerning you, and they will lift you up in their hands, so that you will*

*not strike your foot against a stone." ' Jesus answered him, 'It is
also written: "Do not put the Lord your God to the test" ' "*
(MATTHEW 4:6-7).

Is it possible that the sufferer is misusing Scripture to justify his or
her flawed attitude toward food?

- While Christ calls us to lay down our lives for Him, He never calls
  anyone to murder themselves (suicide), but desires for us to be "living" sacrifices.

  *"Therefore, I urge you, brothers, in view of God's mercy, to
  offer your bodies as living sacrifices, holy and pleasing
  to God—this is your spiritual act of worship"*
  (ROMANS 12:1).

What does it mean to be a "living" sacrifice to God, and how could
suicide (by refusal to eat) ever qualify as a "living" sacrifice that is
"holy and pleasing to God"?

- Christ intends for us to demonstrate to the world the fullness of life
  that only He can make possible.

  *"I have come that they may have life, and have it to the
  full...Let your light shine before men, that they may see
  your good deeds and praise your Father in heaven"*
  (JOHN 10:10; MATTHEW 5:16).

How does one's attitude toward food demonstrate the fullness of life
that Jesus provides?

- A biblical perspective on life and caring for one's body assumes that
  proper nutritional needs are met.

  *"After all, no one ever hated his own body, but he feeds and cares for
  it, just as Christ does the church—for we are members of his body"*
  (EPHESIANS 5:29-30).

Jesus takes care of His spiritual body, the church. Doesn't He expect us to care
for the physical body that He gave us?

Help strugglers to understand their inestimable worth to God and know that by refusing to eat, they are challenging God's assessment of their value. God provides food for birds, but if the birds were to reject God's gift of food, they would die. Rejecting food is not an act of dependence on God, but a rejection of the good gifts that God has provided.

> *"Look at the birds of the air;*
> *they do not sow or reap or store away in barns,*
> *and yet your heavenly Father feeds them.*
> *Are you not much more valuable than they?"*
> (MATTHEW 6:26).

I. The Prayer for Healing (Psalm 31)

"O LORD, I have come to you for protection; don't let me be disgraced. Save me, for you do what is right."

> I am Your child—heal me, O Lord. I give myself to You.

"Turn your ear to listen to me; rescue me quickly. Be my rock of protection, a fortress where I will be safe."

> I am Your child—heal me, O Lord. I give my heart to You.

"You are my rock and my fortress. For the honor of your name, lead me out of this danger."

> I am Your child—heal me, O Lord. I give my will to You.

"Pull me from the trap my enemies set for me, for I find protection in you alone."

> I am Your child—heal me, O Lord. I give my soul to You.

"I will be glad and rejoice in your unfailing love, for you have seen my troubles, and you care about the anguish of my soul."

> I am Your child—heal me, O Lord. I give my life to You.

"Have mercy on me, LORD, for I am in distress. Tears blur my eyes. My body and soul are withering away...I am wasting away from within."

> I am Your child—heal me, O Lord. I give my all to You.

"I am trusting you, O LORD, saying, 'You are my God!'"

> I am Your child—heal me, O Lord.

(SEE PSALM 31:1-4,7,9-10,14 NLT)

If we struggle with an eating disorder, we feel we have
no control. We conclude, "Food is the only thing I can
control—how much or how little I consume." Yet our
deepest need is not *getting* control, but rather *giving* control
of our lives to Christ. He is the One who sets us free.

—JUNE HUNT

ANOREXIA & BULIMIA: ANSWERS IN GOD'S WORD

QUESTION: "Why would a person with an eating disorder despise himself?"

ANSWER: *"He who ignores discipline despises himself, but whoever heeds correction gains understanding"* (Proverbs 15:32).

QUESTION: "Why does my appetite work against me and my hunger drive me?"

ANSWER: *"The laborer's appetite works for him; his hunger drives him on"* (Proverbs 16:26).

QUESTION: "Don't I have the right to refuse to eat or drink and to do whatever I want to do?"

ANSWER: *"Whether you eat or drink or whatever you do, do it all for the glory of God"* (1 Corinthians 10:31).

QUESTION: "Why, if I put in my mouth one bite of certain foods, do I feel fat, undisciplined, and 'unclean'?"

ANSWER: *"What goes into a man's mouth does not make him 'unclean,' but what comes out of his mouth, that is what makes him 'unclean'"* (Matthew 15:11).

QUESTION: "What if I've hidden my food and hidden my fixation with food so that people know nothing about my problem?"

ANSWER: *"Nothing in all creation is hidden from God's sight. Everything is uncovered and laid bare before the eyes of him to whom we must give account"* (Hebrews 4:13).

QUESTION: "What would I gain if I trusted God and heeded instruction?"

ANSWER: *"Whoever gives heed to instruction prospers, and blessed is he who trusts in the LORD"* (Proverbs 16:20).

QUESTION: "Why shouldn't I have the right to do whatever I want with my own body?"

ANSWER: *"Do you not know that your body is a temple of the Holy Spirit, who is in you, whom you have received from God? You are not your own"* (1 Corinthians 6:19).

QUESTION: "Even though God created everything, isn't eating food bad for me?"

ANSWER: *"Everything God created is good, and nothing is to be rejected if it is received with thanksgiving"* (1 Timothy 4:4).

QUESTION: "Why would the heavenly Father care about my needs? After all, I'm of no value to Him."

ANSWER: *"Look at the birds of the air; they do not sow or reap or store away in barns, and yet your heavenly Father feeds them. Are you not much more valuable than they?"* (Matthew 6:26).

THE WORLD OF GAMBLING
Betting Your Life Away

THE WORLD OF GAMBLING:
Betting Your Life Away

Nicknamed "Charlie Hustle," he delighted baseball fans for decades by slamming balls past dazed outfielders and scoring runs that put him both at the top of his game and at the top of his league. He won the National League batting title three times and the Gold Glove Award twice. He was named the National League's Most Valuable Player in 1973 and won three World Series rings. His biggest baseball accomplishment came when the celebrated slugger broke Ty Cobb's all-time batting record with hit number 4193.[1]

In 1989, baseball great Pete Rose was tagged with another label—*gambler*—a dark cloud over his once-shining reputation. He should have heeded this biblical warning:

"A prudent man sees danger and takes refuge,
but the simple keep going and suffer for it"
(PROVERBS 22:3).

I. DEFINITIONS OF GAMBLING

Pete Rose grew up in Cincinnati, Ohio, a city with a reputation for conservatism, but the neighborhood where he lived gave a black eye to that reputation. Bars and nightclubs lined the streets, displaying an overabundance of roulette wheels, slot machines, and tables filled with poker, craps, and blackjack players. Resembling a mini Las Vegas, bookies were readily available to assist with wagers on horse races, and madams promoting prostitution brashly posted signs for all to see.

Pete first accompanied his father to the racetrack at age six, and countless trips back continually fueled his exhilaration for the thrill of the "big win."[2] For

30 years Pete was a "regular" at the racetrack, and the Pick-Six tickets he purchased won him more than a million dollars.

Pete expanded his gambling ventures to wagering on sports, with football and basketball being his favorites. He quickly discovered that the games became more exciting when he played the dual role of both spectator and gambler. But despite some big wins, Pete regretfully admitted there were many more big losses, "and not just in money."[3] Sadly, to gamble is to run the risk of one day saying,

> *"When I hoped for good, evil came;*
> *when I looked for light, then came darkness"*
> (Job 30:26).

A. What Is Gambling?

Athletes participate in a sporting event while spectators watch and speculate about who will win. Some spectators place bets on the outcome. The athlete hopes to achieve a reward by winning; the gambler hopes to gain a reward by picking the winner.

Both winning an athletic competition and winning the bet on a sports competition are accompanied by an emotional and chemical high that can be as addictive as any drug-induced high. Likewise, winning at gambling can create a compulsion within a person to place bet after bet—perhaps initially lining the pockets, but then ultimately emptying them.

In addition, whether it comes to beating the competitor or the odds, the urge to win can take precedence over every relationship, every responsibility, and every resolve of the will. Some are greedy for money, others for fame, and still others for power. But *all* are pursuing the exhilaration that comes from the high of winning.

In contrast, the biblical book of wisdom states, "Better a little with the fear of the Lord than great wealth with turmoil" (Proverbs 15:16).

- **Gambling** is betting or taking a calculated risk for monetary or personal gain when the outcome is uncertain. For example:
  - *Waging money* on games of chance (or *gaming*) in the hopes of winning more money (classic betting games such as poker, blackjack, dice, bingo, roulette, and slot machines)
  - *Laying bets* on the winner of a future competition (putting money on horse and dog races, boxing and wrestling matches, chicken and dog fights, sports car races, and other sporting events)
  - *Taking a chance* on a "long shot" (lotteries or speculating with financial investments based on incomplete information)

- *Risking the loss of something of value* (car, savings account, month's salary, house, college tuition, even gambling away an inheritance)
- *Endangering something or someone* because of risky behavior
- *"Staking your life"* on something dangerous or rash (from street racing to cheating on taxes to not repaying the Mafia)

- **Pari-mutuel Gambling** occurs when gamblers aren't making wagers against "the house" (the gaming establishment), but rather against fellow gamblers.[4]

  - *Includes* a percentage of total winnings that are fixed, but the amount a winner receives depends on the total amount bet by all gamblers
  - *Involves* a betting pool in which those who place bets on competitive races (horses, dogs) strive to finish somewhere in the first three places and share the total amount with the other winners minus a percentage for the management[5]
  - *Comprises* the most common type of racetrack gamblers

QUESTION: What is coveting?

ANSWER: Gamblers are typically triggered by covetousness.

- *Covet*, in the Old Testament Hebrew text, is the word *chamad*, meaning "to delight in, to desire," and is used both positively and negatively.[6]
- *Covet* means to earnestly wish for or to strongly desire what belongs to another. The last of the Ten Commandments says, "You shall not covet" (Exodus 20:17).

QUESTION: What is greed?

ANSWER: The struggle with greed can be the gambler's number one downfall.

- *Greed* means a selfish, excessive desire for more than what is needed.[7]
- *Greed*, in the New Testament Greek text, is the word *pleonexia*, which refers to "striving for material possessions," usually by taking advantage of another.[8] Notice this warning from Jesus:

"He said to them, 'Watch out! Be on your guard against all kinds of greed; a man's life does not consist in the abundance of his possessions'"
(LUKE 12:15).

Those who engage in gambling not only run the risk of losing their money, but also their freedom. Casinos are full of those first entrapped and then enslaved by this addiction. But gambling can also result in death—death of a personal relationship, death to a right relationship with God. The Bible says,

> *"There is a way that seems right to a man,*
> *but in the end it leads to death"*
> (PROVERBS 16:25).

B. What Are the Different Types of Gambling?

In Pete Rose's own words: "Ask any real gambler and he'll tell you: It ain't about the money—it's about the action!"[9] Pete admitted his gambling spiraled out of control after he broke Ty Cobb's batting record. After such a monumental accomplishment, the need for the next thrill consumed his life, and gambling fueled that needed exhilaration.

"The more I gambled, the more I needed to gamble," he confessed. "And the more I lost, the more I tried to double-up to win back what I had already lost. I kept pushing the limit until I was so mixed up."[10] Pete was on the wrong road, doing *anything* but what was right. The first book of the Bible warns,

> *"If you do not do what is right, sin is crouching at your door;*
> *it desires to have you, but you must master it"*
> (GENESIS 4:7).

Once the exhilarating ecstasy of winning has captured the mind, will, and emotions, all bets are off on the likelihood that gamblers will find freedom on their own. Only the transforming work of the Holy Spirit has the power to bring—and to sustain—freedom. Compulsive behaviors are always dangerous because they can become all-consuming to the point of taking control of people, altering their belief systems, and driving them to participate in risky activity. Choice is surrendered and self-control is stripped of its power as the compulsion to gamble rules and reigns.

> *"Like a city whose walls are broken down*
> *is a man who lacks self-control"*
> (PROVERBS 25:28).

For those in the throes of compulsive gambling, the initial excitement of risk-taking eventually turns to enslavement. And it's not only themselves they are hurting. Every compulsive gambler affects somewhere between 10 to 17 individuals around them, including family members and coworkers.[11]

DIFFERENT CATEGORIES OF GAMBLING

There are many ways to gamble and many different types of gamblers, but all gambling can be classified into one of four categories. Each of these categories possesses unique identifying characteristics:[12]

- *Social Gambling*
  - Gambling revolves around creating and maintaining friendships
  - Financial setbacks are tightly monitored and minimal
  - Wagering does not become habitual or addictive

- *Professional Gambling*
  - Gambling becomes a way of life and a means of income
  - Strong personal self-control is required to avoid financial ruin

- *Compulsive Gambling*[13] (often called pathological gambling)
  - The need to wager overshadows all other concerns and endeavors
  - The desire for gambling becomes stronger over time
  - Great personal loss may not inhibit the gambler's behavior
  - An addiction exists that can be curtailed if caught in time

- *Pathological Gambling* (often called compulsive gambling)
  - Increasingly larger wagers provide a high that becomes addictive
  - Gambling behavior is beyond personal control
  - Placing bets becomes a way to escape from life's pressures and disappointments
  - Engaging in criminal activity provides money for more gambling
  - An uncontrollable impulse emerges to recoup lost resources ("chasing one's losses")
  - Deception of others increases in order to "keep the secret" of the obsession with gambling
  - Destruction or significant damage to one's personal and professional life occurs due to gambling

  "A man is a slave to whatever has mastered him"
  (2 PETER 2:19).

C. What Are Two Types of Compulsive/Pathological Gamblers?

As Pete's compulsive gambling progressed, rumors of his addictive habit started going public, and baseball officials started asking questions. In March 1989, an official investigation was launched into gambling charges. At the time, Pete was manager of the Cincinnati Reds, the team for which he once was a star player.

Gambling accusations were initially brushed aside by Pete, who stated publicly, "I'd be willing to bet you, if I were a betting man, that I have never bet on baseball."[14] But a 225-page report released in June of that same year indicated otherwise, citing a debt of $400,000 accumulated over a three-month period[15] and much, much more. Scripture is not silent about lying: "The LORD detests lying lips, but he delights in men who are truthful" (Proverbs 12:22).

Compulsive gamblers can be divided into two similar yet distinct categories based on their differing personalities and gambling styles. Both are ultimately controlled by consuming thoughts of gambling and the overpowering desire to engage in gambling activities. Without intervention, both groups wreak havoc on their own lives as well as the lives of others and ultimately feel helpless and hopeless. They could easily say these words:

> *"Our days on earth are like a shadow, without hope"*
> (1 CHRONICLES 29:15).

- **Action Gamblers...**
  - Typically begin betting during adolescent or preadolescent years
  - Initially wager small amounts, playing "skill games" like poker or similar card games with family or peers, then expand their gambling to horse or dog races and sports events
  - Generally project an inflated sense of self-esteem while harboring a deflated sense of personal worth
  - Invariably experience the three stages of compulsive gambling—winning, losing, and bankruptcy—over a period of 10 to 30 years

- **Escape Gamblers...**
  - Experience problems from gambling when they are in their thirties or older, unlike action gamblers
  - Enjoy "luck games" like bingo, slot machines, and video poker
  - Conceal their deflated sense of personal worth by manipulating and deceiving people

- Bet to escape troubles and feel more powerful, and can appear to be in a dazed state while gaming

All compulsive gamblers—both those who *long for action* and who *long for escape*—are ensnared in the grip of an addiction. But as with any addiction, a key problem is not only their compulsion but also their blindness to it, which prevents them from getting the help they desperately need. They are led astray by their own self-deception and are oblivious to the swath of destruction they leave behind. As the biblical book on wisdom says:

> *"The evil deeds of a wicked man ensnare him; the*
> *cords of his sin hold him fast. He will die for lack*
> *of discipline, led astray by his own great folly"*
> (PROVERBS 5:22-23).

II. CHARACTERISTICS OF GAMBLING

Pete Rose's hidden habit was now fully disclosed to a disbelieving public who finally recognized his problem as an addiction. And just how often did Pete gamble? According to a *New York Times* investigative report, he gambled "almost constantly."[16]

It is illegal for major league baseball managers to place bets on Major League Baseball games because of their ability to influence all aspects of their team's performance, including the outcome. For example, putting less-talented players into a game at key times can result in intentionally losing that game or "throwing a game." In addition, a manager's knowledge and influence is extensive throughout the leagues, putting them in a position of having an unfair advantage over other bettors. Bottom line, wagering presents a huge conflict of interest for managers.

This report revealed that Pete had unlawfully bet on baseball games from 1985 through 1987, including 52 Reds games in 1987, at a minimum of $10,000 a day. (In a display of team loyalty, Rose always bet that his team would win.[17]) And in the never-ending hunt for money to pay off his mounting gambling debts, Pete borrowed from drug kingpins, wrote numerous checks to fictitious payees, and secured large bank loans.[18]

> *"The wealth of the wise is their crown,*
> *but the folly of fools yields folly"*
> (PROVERBS 14:24).

A. What Are the Three Stages of Compulsive Gambling?

The Dowd Report revealed that Pete Rose, the "action gambler," had been involved in numerous unlawful actions. To avoid paying taxes, he purposely disguised his shares in "big win" tickets. And many of his bets were brazenly placed right from his clubhouse office, where bookies and "runners" intersected while others were fully aware of Pete's gambling activities.

On any given day, Pete would take a flight to a baseball card show to earn from $8,000 to $12,000, which translated into quick cash for gambling and rarely made it into the bank as a deposit. But at one point, in a sworn deposition, *Pete denied ever making a single bet on baseball.*[19] His denials were later discovered to be lies—all lies. Interestingly, the book of Proverbs says, "A truthful witness does not deceive, but a false witness pours out lies" (Proverbs 14:5).

While some people can form addictions quickly, compulsive behavior generally is manifested over time as exposure to a certain emotional high increases and the excitement intensifies. Before a repeated behavior evolves into a habit or addiction, there is a window of opportunity for self-will to stop the harmful activity.

The same is true for gambling. If initial excitement and involvement aren't intentionally contained, compulsive behavior can eventually hijack a gambler's self-disciplined behavior. Failure to consciously commit to a right course of action results in an subconscious commitment to a wrong one.

"He commits himself to a sinful course
and does not reject what is wrong"
(PSALM 36:4).

The formulation of compulsive/pathological gambling generally consists of three stages.

THE THREE STAGES OF COMPULSIVE GAMBLING[20]

An addiction to gambling is developed over time. Many of those who have been caught in the vice of compulsive gambling can identify at least three stages to their addictive behavior.

Stage One: "I'm Winning!"

The first stage is the winning stage, which often begins with significant gambling winnings. The gambler feels exhilarated and is highly stimulated by the distraction or amusement of gambling. The gambler experiences:

- Amusement
- Exhilaration

- The thrill of winning
- Periodic sizeable wins
- Unrealistic confidence
- Daydreaming about "big money"

Stage Two: "I'm Losing!"

Losing marks the second stage. The gambler fixates on betting and makes more frequent and riskier bets in order to recover lost money. Often the gambler's professional, social, and family life become damaged from lack of attention and the stress caused by mounting debt. The gambler experiences:

- Persistent intrusive thoughts about gambling
- Absences from work or school
- Changes in character, attitudes, and actions
- More betting with more losses
- "Chasing the bet" (betting to recoup lost money)
- Growing financial debt and the trade or sale of private possessions

Stage Three: "I'm Bankrupt!"

In the third stage, the gambler becomes desperate. When gambling has consumed a life, it degrades or destroys professional aspirations, family relationships, and vital friendships, leaving behind a desperate individual filled with fear and depression. In this state the gambler may turn to criminal activity or even suicide to manage their pain. The gambler experiences:

- Depleted resources
- Fearful desperation
- Devastated self-respect
- Loss of job or failure in school
- Isolation from significant others
- Criminal activity to cover gambling debts
- Suicidal thoughts or attempts

As with any addictive behavior, the sooner intervention occurs, the better the prognosis for overcoming the addiction and the faster the recovery time. Sadly, many ignore the constrictive cords tightening around them until the freedom to choose to stop their compulsive behavior has long been stripped from them. They become prisoners without even knowing they've been in a battle—a war to control their will. They keep gambling whether they want to or not.

> *"For what I do is not the good I want to do;*
> *no, the evil I do not want to do—this I keep on doing"*
> (ROMANS 7:19).

B. What Are General Characteristics of a Problem Gambler?

For gambling addicts like Pete Rose, "the substance they abuse is money," according to Keith Whyte, executive director of the National Council on Problem Gambling. "There's never enough money for a problem gambler. There's not enough money in the world." And one of the main characteristics of problem gamblers is lying about the extent of their involvement.[21] Pete Rose lied for 14 years until his public admission in January 2004 about his serious gambling problem.

The lives of problem gamblers are also characterized by destructive life events, such as divorces, bankruptcies, substance abuse, and suicides.[22] The longer they gamble, the greater their trouble. Because they see no way of escape, many feel disillusioned about life and some even desire to die.

> *"He who is pregnant with evil and conceives*
> *trouble gives birth to disillusionment"*
> (PSALM 7:14).

The term *problem gambler* refers to those whose gambling patterns interfere with their physical, psychological, social, spiritual and vocational lives. It refers both to those who have experienced significant problems due to gambling but are *not addicted* and to those who are considered full-blown *compulsive gamblers*.

One major difference between these two groups of problem gamblers is that nonaddicted, nonpathological gamblers are more likely to acknowledge they spend too much time and money on gambling and seek help. The Bible says, "He who conceals his sins does not prosper, but whoever confesses and renounces them finds mercy" (Proverbs 28:13).

Problem gamblers...

> — *Cannot seem to muster the willpower* to stop gambling even if they
> realize it's consuming too much time, energy, and money
>
> — *Consider gambling a viable means* of adding to their income

- *Convince family and friends to gamble* even when they have no desire to do so
- *Consume hours* of their time gambling alone
- *Customarily visit casinos,* race tracks, betting shops, or amusement arcades with slot machines numerous times over the course of a week
- *Convince themselves* that their excessive use of Internet gambling is normal
- *Constantly purchase lottery tickets* they cannot afford
- *Commit crimes* to support their gambling habit or pay off gambling debts
- *Continuously make comments* that "others" have gambling problems
- *Commonly carry around betting slips,* scratch cards, or tokens for fruit machines (slot machines)

Problem gamblers, like problem drinkers, are oblivious to their problem of overindulgence. Moderation escapes them, and their need for a fix drives them beyond the bounds of healthy behavior. While those closest to them see their bondage, they say, "I'm free to gamble—it's not against the law!" However, they fail to realize that just because something is legal doesn't make it right. In fact, an activity made lawful on the basis of man-made laws can be unlawful from God's perspective. While we are all free to choose between doing right or wrong, the Bible says,

> *"You, my brothers, were called to be free.*
> *But do not use your freedom to indulge the sinful nature;*
> *rather, serve one another in love"*
> (GALATIANS 5:13).

Signs of Problem Gambling

QUESTION: "What are clear indicators that gambling is having a negative effect on someone?"

ANSWER: One early indicator of a gambling problem is experiencing an increasing emotional high when winning and feeling increasingly low when losing. Generally, a pattern begins to develop that is referred to as "chasing"—gambling to recoup losses. Often driven by the shame of suffering greater and greater losses and coupled with the anticipated shame of being found out, gamblers relentlessly and tirelessly chase their losses in the hope of winning them back. Yet the result is almost always deeper losses accompanied by deeper shame.

Other indicators that gambling is having a negative impact are...

- Decrease in weight
- Disinterest in usual activities
- Extreme emotional ups and downs
- Frequent requests for money
- Hocking/selling possessions
- Increasing debt
- Less motivation
- Neglect of loved ones
- Poor concentration
- Secretive activity with bills and bank statements
- Sleep difficulties
- Stealing or other criminal activity
- Unexplainable times of generosity
- Withdrawal emotionally and socially
- Worry, anxiety, and depression

> *"My disgrace is before me all day long,*
> *and my face is covered with shame"*
> (Psalm 44:15).

C. What Characteristics Are Common Among Pathological Gamblers?

Pathological gamblers take a lot of risks to conceal and continue their harmful addictions despite losses that are nothing short of devastating. Pete Rose experienced one such loss in August 1989: He was officially banned from baseball for life, declared "permanently ineligible," and was replaced as manager of the Cincinnati Reds.

Pete's stellar baseball achievements have been forever tainted by his gambling exploits, and he has been barred from ever being inducted into baseball's Hall of Fame.

One of the most common characteristics among those ensnared by Pathological Gambling Disorder is deeply buried denial. But sadly, their bondage is readily recognizable by those closest to them—those most severely impacted by their addiction. And unfortunately, self-diagnosis is rare among sufferers of this devastating disorder. Their blindness to their precarious position and to the inevitable loss of financial resources that awaits them is staggering. Anyone with this disorder can identify with these words from the book of Job:

> *"He lies down wealthy, but will do so no more;*
> *when he opens his eyes, all is gone"*
> (Job 27:19).

Pathological gamblers must have at least five of the following characteristics to meet the criteria for a diagnosis of this disorder.[23] These compulsive gamblers...

- **Attempt** to avoid emotional pain and personal problems by gambling
- **Become** irritable and temperamental when attempting to curtail gambling
- **Chase** losses by wagering more and more money in an attempt to recover losses
- **Deny**, connive, and lie regarding the degree to which they gamble
- **Experience** seemingly never-ending thoughts about gambling
- **Find** others to bail them out of financial binds created by gambling losses
- **Gamble** with increasingly greater and greater amounts of money
- **Have** various problems at work and/or home as a result of gambling
- **Initiate** illegal and/or immoral acts to get money they can use to gamble
- **Make** numerous failed attempts to stop gambling

Once addicts are in the losing or bankrupt stages, their loved ones look for ways to break through the blindness and set a course for sustained change. Much prayer and preparation is necessary to meet such a critical and necessary task.

> *"My brothers, if one of you should wander from the truth*
> *and someone should bring him back, remember this:*
> *Whoever turns a sinner from the error of his way will save*
> *him from death and cover over a multitude of sins"*
> (James 5:19-20).

Professional vs. Pathological Gamblers

QUESTION: "Are professional gamblers considered compulsive gamblers?"

ANSWER: No, professional gamblers differ in that they limit their risks, discipline their behavior, and control their emotions. Pathological gamblers become overly excited to the point of appearing to be manic (a mental disorder characterized by excessive excitability and hyperactivity). They don't have true manic episodes, however, because once they are no longer in a gambling atmosphere their manic-like behavior disappears.

Male vs. Female Differences

QUESTION: "Do differences exist between male and female compulsive gamblers?"

ANSWER: Yes. While more and more similarities are emerging, differences still remain:

- Males commonly begin gambling in their teen years, while women usually begin at an older age.[24]
- Men are more addicted to "skill games,"[25] whereas women gravitate toward video gambling and other venues that bring faster results.
- Women become addicted more quickly, experience more bouts with depression over their gambling, and gamble more to avoid problems.[26]
- Over 60 percent of lifetime problem gamblers are male.[27]
- Women have more guilt and shame attached to their gambling due to a greater awareness of the negative impact of gambling on their families.
- Considerably more men than women enter treatment programs because of the greater social stigma attached to gambling for women than for men.[28]

A positive note for both men and women is that compulsive gambling can be overcome through treatment programs incorporating the Gamblers Anonymous concept. All who pursue a lifestyle of gambling would do well to heed the following admonition:

> *"Do not wear yourself out to get rich;*
> *have the wisdom to show restraint.*

Cast but a glance at riches, and they are gone,
for they will surely sprout wings
and fly off to the sky like an eagle"
(PROVERBS 23:4-5).

III. CAUSES OF GAMBLING

What began as a roast ended with a public display of repentance. Hearty laughter was soon followed by heaving sobs.

About 500 people had gathered to honor the twenty-fifth anniversary of Pete Rose's breaking of Ty Cobb's batting record and to hear Pete's former Cincinnati Reds teammates poke a few jokes at his expense. When the laughter was over, however, Pete's actions revealed the tremendous toll his gambling addiction had taken on him.

"I disrespected the game of baseball," Pete confessed before the crowd. "When you do that, you disrespect your teammates, the game, and your family." [29] And with that, he broke down and began to sob.

Before addicts can experience a lasting change of behavior they must have a genuine change of heart. The Bible says,

"The sacrifices of God are a broken spirit;
a broken and contrite heart, O God, you will not despise"
(PSALM 51:17).

A. What Causes People to Become Compulsive Gamblers?

Pete Rose has been a man of many labels: husband, father, baseball great, manager, and gambler. In light of his gambing, we can add two more to the list: risk-craver and sensation-seeker.

Pete said his propensity to live life on the edge led to his addiction. The exhilaration of the "big win" always temporarily met his insatiable need to take risks in order to experience an emotional high.

"I didn't realize it at the time, but I was pushing toward disaster," Pete recalled. "A part of me was still looking for ways to recapture the high I got from winning batting titles and World Series championships. If I couldn't get the high from playing baseball, then I needed a substitute to keep from feeling depressed." [30]

Causes abound for the *why* of compulsive gambling. All behaviors have a point of origin. Behaviors that result in physical, emotional, or spiritual pleasure are often pursued repeatedly to the point they develop into behavioral patterns...

then habits...then addictions. Like muscles, the more a behavior is exercised, the stronger it becomes.

The Bible tells us to say *no* to all kinds of "worldly passions." God gives us the grace—the strength we don't have—to say *no*.

> *"For the grace of God that brings salvation has appeared to all men.*
> *It teaches us to say 'No' to ungodliness and worldly passions, and*
> *to live self-controlled, upright and godly lives in this present age"*
> (Titus 2:11-12).

Here are five reasons people are drawn into addictive gambling:

- *The Escape from a Normal Existence*
  - Gambling creates a unique atmosphere very different from a person's normal existence.
  - The excitement and entertainment generated by gambling serve as powerful distractions from daily problems.
  - Gamblers are exposed to diverse surroundings, sights, sounds, and smells that powerfully arouse the senses.

- *The Enchantment of the Atmosphere*
  - Eye-catching, posh settings create an engaging environment that pleases the senses.
  - An abundance of appetizing foods and drinks draws people and sustains the gambling experience.
  - Sounds of people talking, laughing, and gambling create an energized atmosphere.

- *The Exhilaration of the Bet*
  - Gambling arouses excitement due to risky bets on uncertain outcomes.
  - The fun and excitement of winning releases a flood of euphoric feelings.
  - The hope of winning a jackpot stimulates a steady stream of adrenaline that further fuels a sense of euphoria.

- *The Endorsement of Fellow Gamblers*
  - Gambling creates the illusion of camaraderie and connectedness.

- Being surrounded by so many other gamblers endorses the behavior.
- The growing number of people who gamble first within their families and then in public results in fewer stigmas attached to gambling and is aiding in the empowerment of gamblers.

- *The Elevation of Brain Chemistry*[31]
  - Recent studies reveal a relationship between compulsive gambling and deficiencies of the chemicals norepinephrine and serotonin.
  - Gambling causes the brain to produce enough norepinephrine to create a chemical high in those with normally lower levels of norepinephrine than what social gamblers possess.
  - Both winning and anticipating winning activates the brain of a gambling addict like cocaine activates the brain of a cocaine addict.

These recent findings further confirm the power addictive behaviors have over those who practice them. Clearly, addictions affect not just behavior but the whole person—body, soul, and spirit. To acknowledge only one aspect of an addiction is to leave the remaining two-thirds unaddressed and untreated. Exploring the causes of addictions—taking into account *the whole person*—is critical to discovering solutions for the addicted.

> *"May God himself, the God of peace, sanctify you through and through. May your whole spirit, soul and body be kept blameless at the coming of our Lord Jesus Christ"*
> (1 THESSALONIANS 5:23).

Gambling Myths

QUESTION: "What are some common myths about gambling that many people embrace as truth?"

ANSWER: Unfortunately, many myths give people false hope of winning a game of chance. These mistaken notions appear logical on the surface but they are based on erroneous thinking and lead many to take risks they might not otherwise take. Here are some of the most problematic myths:

Myth: There are strategies to increase your odds of picking winning numbers.

Fact: No such strategies exist for predicting winning lottery numbers because the odds of winning never change. Every number has an equal chance of being drawn each time a drawing occurs because each drawing contains the same numbers, every time, no matter what numbers were previously drawn. There is no basis for developing a strategy to win when winning is based solely on chance or luck. If you're lucky, you win, and if you're unlucky, you lose.

Myth: The odds of a color or a number winning are increased if they haven't won for a while.

Fact: It doesn't matter how many times a number or color is selected by chance; the odds of it coming up again as a winner are the same each time. For example, because a roulette wheel always has an equal number of red and black spaces, the odds of landing on either color remains constant at 50/50 with each new spin of the wheel.

Myth: People who experience a string of losses usually manage to recoup their money by putting together a winning streak.

Fact: The gambling industry could not exist if this were true. No casino or any other gambling establishment could stay in business if their customers "broke even." The startling truth is that not only do gamblers lose, they lose big—often to the tune of everything they own and hold.

> *"Have nothing to do with godless myths and old*
> *wives' tales; rather, train yourself to be godly"*
> (1 TIMOTHY 4:7).

B. What Sets Some People Up to Form a Gambling Addiction?

Besides being a risk-craver and sensation-seeker, Pete Rose cited two other factors that set him up to form a gambling addiction—Attention Deficit Hyperactivity Disorder (ADHD) and Oppositional Defiant Disorder (ODD).

ADHD is associated with inattentiveness, difficulty in focusing or concentrating, and hyperactivity. ODD is diagnosed from a pattern of hostile and defiant behavior toward authority figures. Dr. David E. Comings of the City of

Hope National Medical Center assessed Pete's childhood behavior and made the following observations:

> Pete's personality as described by his teachers is very telling: a bright kid but bored by classroom activities, sensitive to criticism or rejection, stubborn and strong-willed, will not comply with the rules, tests the limits with every adult, short-tempered, inattentive, and aggressive—textbook ADHD, which is genetically linked to gambling in adults.[32]

C. What Are Common Demographics Among Problem Gamblers?

What were "the odds" that Pete Rose would become a problem gambler?

He shares demographic traits that are common among problem gamblers, such as the presence of mood disorders and a parent who has a mood disorder. Pete has fought a lifelong battle with ADHD as well as a persistent struggle with ODD, which he claims he got from his mother.[33]

Pete's lower socioeconomic status during his growing-up years also links him with problem gamblers. He grew up in a clapboard house alongside railroad tracks, and once reflected, "The Roses might have been poor...but we were resourceful!"[34]

Specific personal situations can cause a greater possibility that someone could become addicted to gambling. But don't be deceived—individual choice still plays a big part in all behaviors. The Bible tells us that "the mocker seeks wisdom and finds none, but knowledge comes easily to the discerning" (Proverbs 14:6).

Some common denominators have been identified in studies conducted over the years:

- Family history of addictions
- Lower socioeconomic status
- Member of a minority group
- Presence of a mood disorder (e.g., ADHD)
- Parent who has a mood disorder (about 25 percent of compulsive gamblers)

QUESTION: "What causes certain youth to be vulnerable to addictive gambling?"

ANSWER: Apart from the common demographics, younger gamblers choose gambling to overcome typical problems of youth: low self-esteem (seeking attention from peers), yielding to peer pressure (low impulse control for risk taking), and a problematic home life. They can easily become hooked by an early "big win," but there are additional distinctive contributing factors unique to youth who gamble:

- Early age gambling (approximately 10 years of age)
- Parental approval of youth gambling
- Parents who overemphasize money and possessions
- Parents who are overly comparing and competitive
- Youth who pridefully identify themselves as "gamblers"
- Youth who believe they cannot become addicted

Younger gamblers who think they are invincible—that they are not vulnerable to the devastation of prolonged gambling—need to take this biblical advice:

> *"Flee the evil desires of youth, and pursue*
> *righteousness, faith, love and peace, along with those*
> *who call on the Lord out of a pure heart"*
> (2 Timothy 2:22).

D. What Is the Root Cause of Gambling Addictions?

For too many years, Pete Rose operated under multiple wrong beliefs about gambling that kept him in the world of addiction. The rush of exhilaration blinded Pete to the devastating addiction that ultimately characterized his life. Contrary to the wrong belief that "a little gaming never hurt anybody," Pete discovered that his huge gaming habit hurt a lot of people—family, friends, teammates, and an adoring public who considered him a role model.

> *"All a man's ways seem innocent to him,*
> *but motives are weighed by the Lord"*
> (Proverbs 16:2).

We are all created with three God-given inner needs for love, significance, and security.[35] Those who turn to God as their Need-meeter through faith in Jesus Christ look to Him to meet these legitimate needs. But those who fail to rely on Him instead look to themselves or to a myriad of other substitutes to meet these needs.

If your life is controlled by any addiction, you are not allowing God's loving strength to give you victory. You are controlled by the addiction instead of allowing Christ to have control of you. Yet you have the opportunity to accept this truth: When you turn away from relying on yourself and toward relying on Christ, He has the power to set you free.

> *"You will know the truth, and the truth will set you free"*
> (JOHN 8:32).

WRONG BELIEF:

"A little gambling never hurt anybody. After all, life itself is a gamble…so gambling is just taking a normal chance. Besides, everybody wants something for nothing, and gambling provides that opportunity. I'm not addicted—I just gamble for entertainment."

RIGHT BELIEF:

"I realize that what I depend on in my life will have control of my life. I'm choosing not to let any activity, including gambling, have control over me. Instead, I choose to give Christ control of every area of my life and to depend on Him to satisfy my needs."

> *"His divine power has given us everything we need*
> *for life and godliness through our knowledge of him*
> *who called us by his own glory and goodness"*
> (2 PETER 1:3).

IV. STEPS TO SOLUTION

Members of Gamblers Anonymous, an international self-help organization for gambling addicts, share a joke among themselves that rings with time-tested truth:

Question: *How do you know when a compulsive gambler is lying?*
Answer: *When you see his lips move!*[36]

After more than a decade of lying, Pete Rose finally owned up to his addiction and thrust himself into another battle: pursuing reinstatement back into the world of professional baseball along with induction into the Major League Baseball Hall of Fame.

Setting personal goals in life and pursuing them provides us with a sense of purpose. The key is to set and pursue God-ordained goals first, giving them priority in our lives.

> *"Pursue righteousness, godliness,*
> *faith, love, endurance and gentleness"*
> (1 TIMOTHY 6:11).

A. Key Verse to Memorize

After decades of being banned from baseball, Pete Rose's passion to be reinstated burns as strong as ever. He made an official attempt to be reinstated in September 1997, but the baseball commissioner refused to lift the ban. Talks and negotiations have continued through the years, but today Pete's name still remains on the blacklist.

Pete's money problems have also extended past gambling, with tax troubles having dogged him through the years as well. In April 1990, Pete pleaded guilty to two felony counts of filing false income tax returns, served five months in prison, and was fined $50,000.[37] Just looking at Pete's life, it could have been so different had he sought help and wisdom from above.

"First seek the counsel of the LORD"
(1 KINGS 22:5).

B. Key Passage to Read and Reread

When it comes to being barred from baseball and the Hall of Fame, Pete Rose has been anything but accepting or content with his punishment. He believes the punishment far outweighs the crime, complaining he is "sick and tired of the double standard."[38] Pete is frustrated that other people with addictions (alcoholics and drug abusers) have been allowed into the Hall of Fame, but he believes the charge of gambling carries too much notoriety. "I never raised a hand to either of my wives or any of my children. Yet there are wife beaters in the Hall of Fame."[39] Pete continually compares himself with others and isn't about to be content! As a result, he has anything but peace. There are many who have gained freedom from gambling, but only after getting the right perspective on what brings true contentment.

GIVE UP GAMBLING, AND GAIN CONTENTMENT
1 TIMOTHY 6:6-11

Six Facts and One Act

- **FACT #1:** If you desire great gain, pursue godly contentment, not monetary gain.

  "Godliness with contentment is great gain"
  (VERSE 6).

- **FACT #2:** You didn't bring anything into this world when you were born, and you won't take anything with you when you die.

"We brought nothing into the world, and
we can take nothing out of it"
(VERSE 7).

- **FACT #3:** You can find true contentment by trusting in God's provision for your life.

"If we have food and clothing, we will be content with that"
(VERSE 8).

- **FACT #4:** The pursuit of wealth leads to bitter bondage, deadly desires, and addictive actions that result in ruin and self-destruction.

"People who want to get rich fall into temptation and
a trap and into many foolish and harmful desires
that plunge men into ruin and destruction"
(VERSE 9).

- **FACT #5:** The love of money will lure you into committing many sins.

"The love of money is a root of all kinds of evil"
(VERSE 10).

- **FACT #6:** The craving for money will compromise your faith and cause you grief upon grief.

"Some people, eager for money, have wandered from the faith
and pierced themselves with many griefs"
(VERSE 10).

- **ONE ACT:** Don't let your highest priority be anything that can be taken away from you. Therefore, turn from pursuing perishable wealth and pursue imperishable wealth, which is found in the development of Christlike character.

"Man of God, flee from all this, and pursue righteousness,
godliness, faith, love, endurance and gentleness"
(VERSE 11).

C. How to Know If You're a Problem Gambler

Pete Rose acknowledged he was a problem gambler but remained as determined as ever to argue his case for reinstatement into professional baseball and induction into the Baseball Hall of Fame. "My actions…call the integrity of the game into question," Pete admitted. "And there's no excuse for that, but there's also no reason to punish me forever."[40] In November 1999, Pete launched an official online petition to garner signatures for his reinstatement.

Given the fact that denial is a defense mechanism frequently found in problem gamblers and has proven to be a formidable roadblock to recovery, self-evaluation is synonymous with self-delusion and can result in self-destruction. Problem gamblers can no more accurately assess the destructiveness of their behavior than teenagers can accurately determine the degree of their maturity. Insight and honesty are required if you are to learn the truth about the dangers of your own gambling experiences. As Jesus said,

> *"Whoever can be trusted with very little can also be trusted with much, and whoever is dishonest with very little will also be dishonest with much. So if you have not been trustworthy in handling worldly wealth, who will trust you with true riches?"*
> (LUKE 16:10-11).

COMPULSIVE GAMBLING QUIZ

Answer with complete honesty the following questions with either *yes* or *no*:

1. Do you think about gambling on and off throughout the day, planning your next gambling experience or figuring out ways to aquire money?
2. Do you usually gamble longer than the time you originally allotted?
3. Do you continuously spend more money in order to get excited or emotionally high?
4. Do you ever feel depressed or suicidal as a result of losing money?
5. Do you become agitated, uptight, or ill-tempered whenever you attempt to curtail gambling?
6. Do you sometimes experience regret or guilt afterward, vowing never to do it again?
7. Do you ever gamble to avoid problems or because you feel bored, frustrated, or sad?
8. Do you sometimes gamble in an attempt to win back money you previously lost?
9. Do you view gambling as a legitimate means of taking care of your responsibilities?

10. Do you ever lie about how much you gamble or conceal gambling-related problems?

11. Do you borrow money to cover your losses?

12. Do you ever gamble away money previously earmarked for necessities?

13. Do you ever let bills accumulate while you gamble your paycheck or savings?

14. Do you ever take or steal money from someone you know?

15. Do you ever steal money from nonfamily members, shoplift, or commit any other illegal acts in order to get money?

16. Do you have conflicts with family or friends as a result?

17. Do you jeopardize relationships or job opportunities?

18. Do you have difficulty falling asleep because you can't stop thinking about it?

19. Do you skip school, miss work, break commitments, or fail to show at special events?

20. Do you ever seek help with paying your bills or mortgage/rent payments?

21. Do others ever question or criticize your gambling activities?

22. Do you spend large amounts of time gambling by yourself?

23. Do you resist spending your "gambling money" on anything else?

24. Do you have diminished interest in family, friends, or pleasurable pastimes?

25. Do you feel stunned, disoriented, and desperate to gamble again when you've run out of money?

If you answered *yes* to four or more of these questions, you need to meet with an expert in gambling addictions and seek help to be set free. To turn a blind eye to compulsive attitudes, desires, and behaviors is to play into the hands of the chief of all charlatans, to fall prey to the deadliest of all deceivers, to be victimized by the devourer of all the deceived. The Bible gives this caution…

"Be self-controlled and alert.
Your enemy the devil prowls around like a roaring lion
looking for someone to devour"
(1 Peter 5:8).

===== *Developing Treatment Programs* =====

QUESTION: "What are the usual components of a treatment program for problem gamblers?"

ANSWER: The four components usually incorporated into treatment programs for gamblers are...

- **Counseling (individual and group)**
  - Offered by skilled professional psychologists, counselors, and/or social workers
  - Provided often without charge or through government subsidies

- **Step-based Programs**
  - Gamblers Anonymous (modeled after Alcoholics Anonymous) is the best known and most prevalent
  - In addition, 12-step programs (both nonprofit and for profit) are available for treating general and/or specific addictions

- **Peer Support**
  - Gamblers Anonymous and other step-based programs provide peer support groups
  - Online support groups are also available for those who desire anonymity or want to avoid personal disclosure

- **Self-help**
  - Workbooks, study guides, devotionals, Bible studies, and videos are available along with telephone support
  - Online self-help sites are also beneficial for those who do not want to disclose their identity but still desire help

When it comes to overcoming addictions, step-based programs have stood the test of time and have proved their effectiveness. The Bible reminds us, "Plans fail for lack of counsel, but with many advisers they succeed" (Proverbs 15:22).

D. How to Walk Your Way Out of Debt

Gambling addicts like Pete Rose incur great debt as a result of their gambling. But by taking one step at a time in the right direction, they can find financial freedom. Although debt can be discouraging, it shouldn't be devastating. Just don't tackle the debt all at one time. The best plan for climbing out of financial debt is to pay off accounts with the highest interest rate and smaller bills first and then put those payment amounts toward paying off the biggest bills.

If you keep your eyes on the next step rather than on the entire mountain, your anxiety will cease and your motivation will increase. The best mountain climbers take just one step at a time, recognizing the biggest challenge awaits them near the top. Keep your eyes on the goal by regaining control of your finances. Only then will you move forward toward peace and debt-free living. Acknowledge your need of the Lord, for He will be your provider.

> *"My God will meet all your needs*
> *according to his glorious riches in Christ Jesus"*
> (PHILIPPIANS 4:19).

As you begin your journey out of debt, take the following steps—again, one step at a time:

- **Acknowledge your gambling addiction** to God and to significant others.
    - Confess your hidden addiction to God and to at least two trustworthy people.
    - Be open and totally honest about all aspects of your gambling-related behavior.

- **Assume personal responsibility** for your debt.
    - Don't blame others for your choices.
    - Fully disclose the extent of your indebtedness.

- **Get the help and support** you need to stop gambling.
    - Join a support group for gamblers and attend meetings faithfully.
    - Enlist the support of dependable, self-disciplined loved ones to hold you accountable.

- **Do not worry about your debt.** Make a covenant with God, yourself, and a support person.
    - Realize worry can be a trigger that throws you back into gambling.
    - Place Scripture cards in several strategic places around you to remind you of God's provision.

- **Evaluate your total financial picture** with objectivity.
  - Get expert assistance in setting up a yearly budget and a long-term savings and payment plan.
  - Destroy all but one credit card and temporarily entrust it and your bank card to a trustworthy person as you operate on a cash-only basis.
- **Learn about boundaries** regarding people and places.
  - Avoid people and places that tempt you to gamble.
  - Find new travel routes to and from work and other places you would leave to go gambling.
- **Institute emotional boundaries** with an accountability partner.
  - Be aware of your triggers, feelings, and mood swings and what impacts them both positively and negatively.
  - Pray, journal, memorize Scripture passages, study God's Word, engage in a hobby, call a friend, or go somewhere safe when you are tempted to gamble.

Remember that your hope for victory lies in your relationship with Jesus Christ and your total dependence on the Spirit of God within you. Memorize, personalize, and repeatedly quote God's promise to you that

> *"no temptation has seized you except what is common to man.*
> *And God is faithful; he will not let you be tempted beyond*
> *what you can bear. But when you are tempted, he will also*
> *provide a way out so that you can stand up under it"*
> (1 CORINTHIANS 10:13).

E. How Objective Data Can Persuade People Not to Gamble

Statistics abound that reveal the negative impact of gambling—related incidents of addiction, bankruptcy, crime, corruption, domestic abuse, destruction of marriages and families, and suicide attempts are higher among gamblers than among those with any other addiction. The progressive nature of gambling often leaves onlookers with the following concern:

> *"Whoever loves money never has money enough; whoever loves*
> *wealth is never satisfied with his income. This too is meaningless"*
> (ECCLESIASTES 5:10).

The following data is just the tip of the iceberg.

Crime

1. The crime rate in gambling communities is nearly double that of the national average.[41]

2. *Legalized* gambling increases *illegal* gambling by 300 percent.[42]

3. Among those arrested, the percentage of compulsive gamblers is 3 to 5 times higher.[43]

4. Studies of Gamblers Anonymous (GA) members report that approximately 50 percent of the participants had stolen in order to gamble and over 33 percent had been arrested.[44]

5. Casino communities in the United States have crime rates 84 percent higher than the national average. Crime within 30 miles of Atlantic City rose by 107 percent in the nine years following the introduction of casinos to the area.[45] And, in Deadwood, South Dakota—just three years after casinos were legalized—felony crimes rose 40 percent.

Family Violence

1. Case studies of 10 casino communities revealed that the majority of these communities witnessed increases in domestic violence related to the opening of casinos.[46]

2. The National Research Council (1999) reported on studies indicating that 25 to 50 percent of spouses of pathological gamblers have been abused.

3. Three years after casinos became legal in Deadwood, South Dakota, domestic violence and assaults skyrocketed 80 percent.[47]

Child Neglect/Abuse

1. A review of Indiana's state gaming commission records showed that 72 children were found abandoned on casino premises during a span of 14 months.[48]

2. Children of problem gamblers have been shown to have higher levels of tobacco, alcohol, and drug use and more problems with overeating than do their classroom peers.[49]

3. Children of compulsive gamblers are often more prone to suffer

abuse as well as neglect."[50] In South Dakota, child abuse increased 42 percent in the first three years after casinos were legalized.

Suicide/Depression

1. "Suicide attempts among pathological gamblers are higher than for any of the addictions."[51] And 76 percent of pathological gamblers are likely to develop a major depressive disorder.[52]

2. Ultimately, 1 in 5 compulsive gamblers attempt suicide,[53] and 1 in 10 spouses of gamblers attempt suicide.[54]

3. Suicides increased by 213 percent (from 24 to 75) in the first two years after casinos arrived in Gulfport, Mississippi. In nearby Biloxi, suicide attempts jumped 1000 percent in the first year alone.[55]

Negative Social Impact

1. Gambling has been called "the single fastest-growing driver of bankruptcy."[56] Gambling-related bankruptcies in the Detroit metropolitan area increased by as much as "40-fold within a year and a half of the opening of Casino Windsor."[57]

2. Legalized gambling depresses businesses because it diverts money that could have been spent to energize the economy. Money that could be invested, loaned, and recycled through the economy is instead risked in a legalized gambling scheme.

3. Legalized gambling siphons money that could be spent on education. More money is wagered on gambling than is spent on both elementary and secondary education. For every dollar a state receives in gambling revenues, it costs the state at least three dollars in increased social costs (for criminal justice and social welfare).[58]

4. The less education people have, the more likely they are to play the lottery.[59] The poor bet a far larger portion of their income than the middle class, the rich, or the well-educated. Those in the lowest income bracket lost more than three times as much to gambling (as a percentage of total income) as those at the wealthiest end of the spectrum.[60]

5. Gambling breeds greed. Research has shown that the number of compulsive gamblers increases between 100 percent to 550 percent when legalized gambling is brought into an area. Within 50 miles

of a casino, the prevalence of multiple problems and compulsive gamblers roughly doubles (called the "50-2x Rule").[61]

Those who struggle with gambling can be ruined by real risks and wrong rewards. Although a struggler may try to justify—"I don't have a problem. I only gamble for fun"—the human heart can be deceived, and pursuing that heart's desire can result in monumental mistakes. And God is just—He promises to settle accounts based on our choices, based on what we choose to do. As the Bible says, "The heart is deceitful above all things and beyond cure. Who can understand it? 'I the LORD search the heart and examine the mind, to reward a man according to his conduct, according to what his deeds deserve'" (Jeremiah 17:9-10).

Jasmine—from Rejection to Redemption

It's a typical weekday for little Jasmine. After returning from school and completing her homework, she begins stringing together necklaces—*lots of necklaces*—to sell on the streets of Hong Kong to help financially support her family. There is no time to play Catch the Dragon's Tail or Blind Man, two popular Chinese children's games. Instead, Jasmine must keep stringing necklaces…bead after bead. Later she wanders through the nearby vegetable fields, hoping to discover discarded produce for dinner.

Jasmine's mother knits and sells cardigan sweaters. And although her father works as a policeman, a measly pittance is spent supporting his seven children, of which Jasmine is the youngest. Rather than feeding his family, he is consumed with feeding his habit, betting big money to play an immensely popular game of mythical origin—Mahjong.[62]

Seated at a gambling table for countless hours, Jasmine's father discards and claims tiles to form certain combinations in hopes of creating a winning "hand." In the 1950s, when Jasmine was a girl, there were about 150 registered Mahjong parlors in Hong Kong,[63] affording plenty of opportunity to participate in the high-stakes game characterized by strategy, skill, and that untamable variable—*chance*. For almost 15 years, Jasmine's father spends far more time at the parlors than at home, emptying his wallet to amass thousands and thousands of dollars of gambling debts.

Jasmine's mother repeatedly dispatches her oldest daughter to beg her father to send money home, where it is so desperately needed. But she always faces the humiliation of returning home…empty-handed.

When Jasmine's father is at home, he is often angry and abusive. Once Jasmine had to distract him from chasing her sister with a cleaver. Jasmine herself not only endures her father's abuse and neglect, but also a more subtle form of cruelty: She wasn't officially named until the age of five, sending an unspoken message that Jasmine now aptly perceives as an adult: "We don't need you—you're a burden to the family."[64]

But it would be Jasmine's brother who would suffer the most from gambling's catastrophic clutch on the impoverished family. Jasmine's father had borrowed for gambling—and lost—a large sum of money from Hong Kong mobsters. Eventually, it was time to "pay up." He was given two options: either pay with cash or pay with the *unthinkable*—a life—the life of the unborn baby boy in Jasmine's mother's womb.

Following the baby's birth, the mob took the boy. But the little baby died at two months of age as a result of diarrhea—a very preventable death. Later, Jasmine learned that she, too, was almost exchanged for gambling debts, but her mother refused to endure such brutal, emotional trauma a second time.

Throughout Jasmine's young life, her father, who died at age 56, brought her great pain. But Jasmine had another Father, *her heavenly Father*, who brought her great peace and assurances of unconditional love. After giving her life to Christ as a teenager, Jasmine encountered an emotional and spiritual crossroads that determined her destiny. Would she allow devastating family tragedy to shadow her life, darkening hopes of ever receiving help and healing? Or would she, with God's help, become an overcomer, finding victory over victimization?

Jasmine ultimately made the decision: She not only wanted to become an overcomer but also a "dispenser of comfort" through her Lord, as described in 1 Corinthians 2:3-4: "…the Father of compassion and the God of all comfort, who comforts us in all our troubles, so that we can comfort those in any trouble with the comfort we ourselves have received from God." She eventually married a pastor, and God provided her with numerous counseling opportunities.

Seeking further education and equipping, Jasmine earned a master's degree in counseling and initially dealt in family violence cases. In 2007 Jasmine became involved with the International Ministry Department at Hope For The Heart and now trains Chinese men and women in biblical counseling. For Jasmine, biblical counseling has helped her "sort out all those childhood traumas and learn skills to help people."[65]

Addictive gambling no longer mars Jasmine's emotions nor denigrates her family life. "It was unfortunate to have those experiences," she concludes, "but God has used them to make me strong." Jasmine asked God to make her an overcomer...and He did. Not only for her own sake, but for the thousands of other lives she has touched—and continues to touch—around the world.

"Do not be overcome by evil, but overcome evil with good"

(ROMANS 12:21).

F. How to Grasp What the Bible Says About Gambling

Without ever using the word *gambling*, the Bible communicates a great deal about gambling as it lays out the principles by which we are to live our lives. God's Word indirectly addresses many ungodly activities in this way. God has given us principles by which we can guide our decision-making, and these principles serve as a grid through which we can determine right from wrong. The apostle Paul put it this way:

*"All Scripture is God-breathed and is useful for teaching, rebuking,
correcting and training in righteousness, so that the man
of God may be thoroughly equipped for every good work"*
(2 TIMOTHY 3:16-17).

The following scriptures present 12 basic principles for living life in a way that both pleases and glorifies God.

TWELVE GAMBLING PROBLEMS AND
GODLY PRINCIPLES FOR SUCCESSFUL LIVING

1. **Gambling Problem:** Gambling violates the principle of faith because the gambler is trusting in chance rather than in God to supply what is needed.

   Godly Principle: Demonstrate Faith

   *"Without faith it is impossible to please God, because anyone who
   comes to him must believe that he exists and that he rewards
   those who earnestly seek him...And God is able to make all grace
   abound to you, so that in all things at all times, having all that
   you need, you will abound in every good work...And my God will
   meet all your needs according to his glorious riches in Christ Jesus"*
   (HEBREWS 11:6; 2 CORINTHIANS 9:8; PHILIPPIANS 4:19).

2. **Gambling Problem:** Gambling doesn't cause contentment but is rather driven by discontentment, and is both unpredictable and unreliable, often leading to further discontentment.

   Godly Principle: Experience Contentment

   > *"Godliness with contentment is great gain...I have learned to be content whatever the circumstances. I know what it is to be in need, and I know what it is to have plenty. I have learned the secret of being content in any and every situation, whether well fed or hungry, whether living in plenty or in want. I can do everything through him who gives me strength"*
   > (1 TIMOTHY 6:6; PHILIPPIANS 4:11-13).

3. **Gambling Problem:** Gambling leads to a lack of self-control because it is addictive. And because it is not God's method of supplying our needs, it makes us vulnerable to attacks from our enemy, the devil.

   Godly Principle: Practice Self-control

   > *"Do not wear yourself out to get rich; have the wisdom to show restraint...the fruit of the Spirit is love, joy, peace, patience, kindness, goodness, faithfulness, gentleness and self-control"*
   > (PROVERBS 23:4; GALATIANS 5:22-23).

4. **Gambling Problem:** Gambling is generally driven by greed or the desire to gain more, leading to a focus on material possessions rather than on God and what He desires for us.

   Godly Principle: Avoid Greed

   > *"A greedy man brings trouble to his family...among you there must not be even a hint of sexual immorality, or of any kind of impurity, or of greed, because these are improper for God's holy people...For of this you can be sure: No immoral, impure or greedy person—such a man is an idolater—has any inheritance in the kingdom of Christ and of God"*
   > (PROVERBS 15:27; EPHESIANS 5:3,5).

5. **Gambling Problem:** Gambling produces envy because its goal is getting goods. This inevitably leads to comparisons and results in envy and resentment.

Godly Principle: Banish Envy

> *"A heart at peace gives life to the body, but envy rots the bones...For where you have envy and selfish ambition, there you find disorder and every evil practice"*
> (Proverbs 14:30; James 3:16).

6. **Gambling Problem:** Gambling creates an atmosphere that breeds worry over inevitable financial losses.

Godly Principle: Don't Worry

> *"Therefore I tell you, do not worry about your life, what you will eat or drink; or about your body, what you will wear. Is not life more important than food, and the body more important than clothes?"*
> (Matthew 6:25).

7. **Gambling Problem:** Gambling is all about easy money, excitement, getting rich, and getting high at the prospect of a big win—all of which ignores the richness of a right relationship with God.

Godly Principle: Don't Overrate Riches

> *"A faithful man will be richly blessed, but one eager to get rich will not go unpunished...A stingy man is eager to get rich and is unaware that poverty awaits him"*
> (Proverbs 28:20,22).

8. **Gambling Problem:** Gambling always involves money and always has more money as its goal, making money the master of all who love it and pursue it.

Godly Principle: Minimize Money

> *"No one can serve two masters. Either he will hate the one and love the other, or he will be devoted to the one and despise the other. You cannot serve both God and Money...Keep your lives free from the love of money and be content with what you have"*
> (Matthew 6:24; Hebrews 13:5).

9. **Gambling Problem:** Gambling violates the work ethic God established with the creation of Adam and Eve. He gave them the responsibility of tending the Garden of Eden and then benefiting from the work of their hands.

Godly Principle: Value Work

> *"He who works his land will have abundant food, but he who chases fantasies lacks judgment...Even when we were with you, we gave you this rule: 'If a man will not work, he shall not eat.' We hear that some among you are idle. They are not busy; they are busybodies. Such people we command and urge in the Lord Jesus Christ to settle down and earn the bread they eat'"*
> (PROVERBS 12:11; 2 THESSALONIANS 3:10-12).

10. **Gambling Problem:** Gambling robs a person of freedom by taking him captive, stripping him of the power to say *no*, seducing him away from the privilege of walking in the freedom Christ died to procure for us all.

Godly Principle: Respect Freedom

> *"'Everything is permissible for me'—but not everything is beneficial. 'Everything is permissible for me'—but I will not be mastered by anything...for a man is a slave to whatever has mastered him...It is for freedom that Christ has set us free...Live as free men, but do not use your freedom as a cover-up for evil; live as servants of God"*
> (1 CORINTHIANS 6:12; 2 PETER 2:19; GALATIANS 5:1; 1 PETER 2:16).

11. **Gambling Problem:** Gambling is dependent on the losses of others for its existence and, more often than not, those losses come from the pockets of the poor, who cannot afford to lose.

Godly Principle: Love People

> *"Love does no harm to its neighbor. Therefore love is the fulfillment of the law...It is better not to eat meat or drink wine or to do anything else that will cause your brother to fall...If anyone does not provide for his relatives, and especially for his immediate family, he has denied the faith and is worse than an unbeliever...Do nothing out of selfish ambition or vain conceit, but in humility consider others better than yourselves. Each of you should look not only to your own interests, but also to the interests of others"*
> (ROMANS 13:10; 14:21; 1 TIMOTHY 5:8; PHILIPPIANS 2:3-4).

12. **Gambling Problem:** Gambling displaces God as our priority and provider, our source of peace and purpose. It replaces the One who

is our all-in-all with an empty pursuit of empty pockets and empty lives.

Godly Principle: Love God

"'Love the Lord your God with all your heart and with all your soul and with all your mind.' This is the first and greatest commandment. And the second is like it: 'Love your neighbor as yourself'...Love the LORD your God, listen to his voice, and hold fast to him. For the LORD is your life...Set your minds on things above, not on earthly things. For you died, and your life is now hidden with Christ in God...You are not your own; you were bought at a price. Therefore honor God with your body"

(MATTHEW 22:37-39; DEUTERONOMY 30:20;
COLOSSIANS 3:2-3; 1 CORINTHIANS 6:19-20).

GUARANTEED!

Everyone wants success in life...a sure
foundation...to come out ahead.
There's an old time-tested saying:
"The only sure way for a gambler to come
out ahead is to buy the casino!"
—JUNE HUNT

In stark contrast, the Bible affirms
that God Himself is our sure foundation:

"He will be the sure foundation for your times,
a rich store of salvation and wisdom and knowledge;
the fear of the LORD is the key to this treasure"

(ISAIAH 33:6).

THE WORLD OF OVEREATING
Freedom from Food Fixation

THE WORLD OF OVEREATING:

Freedom from Food Fixation

Television commercials can be tantalizing—and at the same time, reflect what we wish weren't true. One long-running ad featured a bag of potato chips with the tagline, "Bet you can't eat just one."

This fascinating commercial featured different people who, after tasting one chip, were prevented from having another. Oh, oh, oh, the agony! First, they would fidget and sweat. Then they would leap over obstacles, tackling grocers to get to the chips. Finally, when they got their hands on those tasty tidbits…oh, the ecstasy of finishing off the whole bag!

We all share one common characteristic: When we find something we especially like, we want more of it! But if our common desire becomes a compulsive demand—if our natural drive to eat becomes a relentless slave driver—then we are out of control. The fact that our God-given appetite can turn into an all-consuming fixation is an example of this principle:

> *"A man is a slave to whatever has mastered him"*
> (2 PETER 2:19).

I. DEFINITIONS OF OVEREATING

The potato chip commercials were memorable for the clever way they showed people losing self-control—specifically, losing all sense of *portion size.* They always ate the whole bag! For those caught in the cycle of compulsive eating, the craving is for quantity, not quality. Consider ice cream: If one scoop is good, two would be better. And if two are better, three are best! (Or why not the whole carton?)

This same compulsive mind-set applies to cake and candy…fondue and frosting…bacon, biscuits, and brownies…in spite of the common-sense caution that says,

> *"It is not good to eat too much honey"*
> (PROVERBS 25:27).

A. What Is Overeating?

It all began in the 1980s.

The collective waistlines of people throughout the world began to spread at an unprecedented pace. Literally millions of people packed on millions of extra pounds because of food saturated in fat, sugar, and salt—food that drove them to eat even more fat, sugar, and salt. Increasingly, country after country became inundated with compulsive overeaters.

Along with poor food choices, other factors contributed to this worldwide weight gain, including the exploding availability of fast food, larger menu portions, and eating on the go rather than at a leisurely pace around the dining table at home.[1]

No wonder weight gain has spiraled out of control. We are controlled by the fruit of overeating instead of the fruit of the Spirit. The Bible explains it this way:

> *"The fruit of the Spirit is…self-control"*
> (GALATIANS 5:22-23).

- **Overeating** means excessive eating.[2]
- **Overeating** often results in obesity, a condition characterized by body fat 20 percent or more above recommended body weight.[3]
- **Overeating**, in Scripture, is described by the word *gluttony*, which means consuming excess food to the point of losing control. The Bible states,

> *"He who keeps the law is a discerning son,*
> *but a companion of gluttons disgraces his father"*
> (PROVERBS 28:7).

=== *Overeating and Sin* ===

QUESTION: "Can overeating be considered a sin?"

ANSWER: Yes, overeating is a pattern of yielding to fleshly desires instead of yielding to God. Those who habitually eat to excess are controlled by their natural appetites rather than controlled by the Spirit of God. The Bible contrasts the wise man with the foolish man:

> *"In the house of the wise are stores of choice food and oil,*
> *but a foolish man devours all he has"*
> (PROVERBS 21:20).

B. What Is Compulsive Eating?

The fanaticism for fatty foods in the 1980s didn't just tip the scales—it set new world records. Manuel Uribe went on a saturated fat and sugar spree and earned a title that landed him in the *Guinness Book of World Records* as the "World's Fattest Man."[4] At 1230 pounds, Manuel was the embodiment of compulsive eating—a man *completely out of control.*

Compulsive eating triggered another catastrophic consequence for Manuel. He turned to liposuction to improve his appearance, but his damaged lymph nodes left giant tumors on his legs—so weighty that he couldn't walk. Manuel readily pointed to one source for his sorrows: "It is all because of the junk food."[5]

Eventually Manuel became determined to no longer be the world's heaviest man. With serious dietary changes, he dropped his weight to around 700 pounds, and then set his sights on a new title: "World's Greatest Loser of Weight." What a change of focus!

Those like Manuel who need serious help controlling their compulsive eating can find invaluable strength from our powerful God:

> *"He gives strength to the weary and increases the power of the weak"*
> (ISAIAH 40:29).

- **Compulsive eating** is uncontrolled overeating based on satisfying emotional hunger, not physical hunger.
- **Compulsive eating** is a seemingly irresistible impulse to eat.[6]
- **Compulsive eating** is a food addiction that can result in a physical disorder and even death.

> *"He will die for lack of discipline, led astray by his own great folly"*
> (PROVERBS 5:23).

Overeating and Addictions

QUESTION: "Spiritually, is there a difference between a food addiction and other addictions such as smoking, gambling, or drinking?"

ANSWER: No, the Bible places them in the same category, although the physical ramifications can be more serious with certain addictions. The biblical book on wisdom states,

> *"Do not join those who drink too much wine or gorge*
> *themselves on meat, for drunkards and gluttons*
> *become poor, and drowsiness clothes them in rags"*
> (PROVERBS 23:20-21).

C. What Is Binge Eating?

"It's like having a pair of arms around you."[7] That's how Diana, Princess of Wales, described the comfort she felt after consuming large amounts of food. Before dying in a car crash in 1997, Princess Diana struggled for years with bulimia and knew how quickly those "comforting arms" could constrict.

Although she was considered the most popular woman in the world, it was not unusual for Princess Diana to binge up to five times a day, gorging herself with food, and then purging. While this futile cycle consumed her life, her lack of self-control turned to self-loathing. At times, she surely could have identified with Job:

> *"I despise my life; I would not live forever.*
> *Let me alone; my days have no meaning"*
> (JOB 7:16).

- **Bingeing** is a period of unrestrained indulgence and most often refers to binge eating and drinking, but can also refer to binge shopping and gambling.[8]

- **Binge eating** can easily become an addictive behavior.

  - *Binge eaters* who don't purge typically experience great weight gain.
  - *Binge eaters* who do purge through vomiting or excessive laxative use are *bulimics,* who often experience severe health hazards, including death.

- **Bingeing**, in the Bible, comes with a warning against overindulgence.

> *"If you find honey, eat just enough—*
> *too much of it, and you will vomit"*
> (PROVERBS 25:16).

In addition to binge eating, Princess Diana suffered from bulimia. Oh, that

Princess Diana would have turned to the Lord's "everlasting arms," which would have forever embraced her in unconditional love, as described in the Bible:

> *"The eternal God is your refuge,*
> *and underneath are the everlasting arms"*
> (DEUTERONOMY 33:27).

=== *Overeating vs. Bulimia* ===

QUESTION: "What's the difference between overeating and bulimia?"

ANSWER: While both eat food to excess, an overeater may have little concern about being overweight, while the bulimic is consumed with body image and self-loathing.

Just as Job began to despise himself, bulimics despise their bodies and are frequently filled with bitterness.

> *"I loathe my very life; therefore I will give free rein to my*
> *complaint and speak out in the bitterness of my soul"*
> (JOB 10:1).

D. What Is Night Eating Disorder?

The clock strikes 8:00 p.m., and the feeding frenzy begins.

Multitudes of people around the globe, including six million Americans, struggle with Night Eating Disorder. Strugglers find themselves agitated, restless, bored—and before they know it, they've consumed massive amounts of high-carb, high-calorie "comfort food." And for many, when the clock strikes midnight, they're back at it again, raiding the refrigerator into the wee hours of the morning, craving their comfort food to fill the hole in their hearts. At times we all need comfort, but when no one is near to provide comfort, some people look to food to be that friend. However, God never intended for food to fill our hearts. We need the blessing of need-meeting friends. But when that relationship void remains empty, we can find ourselves lamenting,

> *"This is why I weep and my eyes overflow with tears.*
> *No one is near to comfort me, no one to restore my spirit"*
> (LAMENTATIONS 1:16).

- **Night Eating Disorder** (Night Eating Syndrome) is a condition characterized by huge caloric intake during the after-dinner hours.

- **Night Eating Syndrome** (NES) is a disorder that affects more than 33 percent of "morbidly obese" people—those 100 pounds or more overweight.[9]
- **Night Eating Syndrome** often involves insomnia, since feelings of guilt, anxiety, and disgust can also hinder sleep.

But what is one step in the recovery process? Rather than focusing at night on gorging, the Psalms speak of meditating on the promises of God.

> *"My eyes stay open through the watches of the night,*
> *that I may meditate on your promises"*
> (PSALM 119:148).

II. CHARACTERISTICS OF OVEREATING

It's considered a world health epidemic, and it can't be treated with a shot or quick-fix medication. Across the globe there are more than one billion adults who are overweight, creating a health hazard that ranks just behind HIV and tuberculosis.[10] The increased risks for diabetes, cardiovascular disease, cancer, hypertension, and stroke that accompany overeating are weighing down already heavily burdened health care systems.

And the statistics for children are equally alarming. An estimated 22 million children under the age of 5 are overweight, and in the United States alone the number of overweight adolescents has tripled since 1980.[11]

With global modernization and urbanization comes easier access to foods chock full of saturated fats and sugar, and it seems people from Chile to China are increasingly choosing greasy cheeseburgers over grilled chicken. As waistlines expand, societies all over the world are feeling the financial pinch from sprawling health care costs. The Bible warns,

> *"A man reaps what he sows"*
> (GALATIANS 6:7).

Stuck in His Self-made Prison

His nickname was Crassus, and not because he was crass. *Crassus* is a Latin word for *fat*, and Raynald[12] III was more than abundantly fat. Grossly overweight, the Duke of Guelders had developed quite the reputation for his regal rolls of flesh, and not even this not-so-nice nickname motivated him to curb his eating.

Eventually, Raynald found it necessary to turn his attention from feasting to fighting—laying down his fork and knife and picking up his sword and shield—because his dukedom was being ripped apart by civil war.

In what is now Belgium, two clans were vying for power—the Hekeren (the aristocrats) and the Bronckorsten (the merchants)—and they would stop at nothing to rule over the coveted dukedom. Raynald was doing all he could to quash the uprising, but his conspiring younger brother, Edward, pulled a power play. Resentful that his older brother had received the dukedom and a greater inheritance, Edward became the leader of the Bronckorsten clan and proclaimed that he was the new duke of Guelders. Raynald attempted to keep the peace, but was eventually forced to side with the Hekeren clan, setting the stage for a showdown.[13]

On May 25, 1361, in the midst of battle, Edward captured Raynald. He then constructed, within the castle walls, a prison for his obese brother. However, this was a most unique prison, for it had normal-sized windows and a door, none of which were ever locked. Edward even told Raynald he would reinstate his royal title and property as soon as he left the prison. But in order to walk out, Raynald's much larger body had to be able to go through the much smaller door.[14]

Then clever, conniving Edward twisted the knife even more. He ordered that large, delicious meals be delivered every day to Raynald in his "prison" so that ultimately, food would be his ball and chain.

Once, when accused of being cruel and heartless toward Raynald, Edward matter-of-factly replied, "My brother is not a prisoner. He may leave when he so wills."[15]

Ten years later, Raynald was finally rescued—but only after Edward died amongst other warring dukes. And when the double-wide former duke was freed from his castle confinement, *he was fatter than ever*—and still in bondage to his enormous appetite. Gluttony had a stranglehold on Raynald, and he died within a year of his release.

Raynald embodies the truth found in Ecclesiastes 6:7: "All man's efforts are for his mouth, yet his appetite is never satisfied." As was the case with Raynald, we can become consumed with filling our inner hunger, but then quickly discover that the filling is ever so fleeting.

When Jesus describes Himself as the Bread of Life, He is identifying Himself as the source of lasting spiritual sustenance. We can never find true satisfaction through food, but we can discover lasting fulfillment through the Bread of Life—Jesus Christ. Through a life-changing relationship with Him, He promises we will "never go hungry."[16]

A. What Is the Compulsive Overeater Checklist?

Many people sincerely ask a question to which the answer seems obvious to others: "How do I know whether or not I am a compulsive overeater?" The best way to determine the answer is to go through the following checklist. If you find that food has control over you, seek God's strength to help you shift your focus, and "set your minds on things above, not on earthly things" (Colossians 3:2).

Place a check mark (✓) beside each question that applies to you: [17]

- ☐ Do you spend a lot of time thinking about food?
- ☐ Do you look forward to an event because of the food that will be available there?
- ☐ Do you eat when you are sad, angry, lonely, or depressed?
- ☐ Do you eat when you are bored or under stress?
- ☐ Do you eat certain foods as a personal reward?
- ☐ Do you eat even when you are not hungry?
- ☐ Do you ever feel ashamed of how much you eat?
- ☐ Do you fear not being able to stop eating once you start?
- ☐ Do you ever feel embarrassed about your personal appearance?
- ☐ Do you ever eat secretly to prevent others from knowing what or how much you eat?
- ☐ Do you lose weight on diets, then gain the weight (and more) back again?
- ☐ Do you feel that you have to eat everything on your plate and that you're being wasteful if you don't?
- ☐ Do you think you could control your weight if you really wanted to?
- ☐ Do you resent it when family or friends express concern over your weight?
- ☐ Do you find that food consumes your thoughts, your actions, your very life?

If you answered *yes* to three or more of these questions, you could be a compulsive eater. If at times you feel frustrated over your eating extremes, let this Scripture motivate you:

> *"I do not understand what I do.*
> *For what I want to do I do not do, but what I hate I do...*
> *Who will rescue me from this body of death?*
> *Thanks be to God—through Jesus Christ our Lord!"*
> (ROMANS 7:15,24-25).

B. What Are the Characteristics of Compulsive Overeating?

- *Physical Symptoms of Compulsive Overeating*
  - Anorexia/bulimia
  - Chronic neck and joint pain
  - Cycles of excessive eating/dieting
  - Diabetes
  - Gall bladder problems
  - Heart disease
  - High blood pressure
  - Kidney disorder
  - Limited range of motion and activity
  - Shortness of breath after mild exertion

- *Emotional Symptoms of Compulsive Overeating*
  - Anger
  - Anxiety
  - Depression
  - Guilt
  - Hopelessness
  - Irritability
  - Low self-esteem
  - Passivity
  - Powerlessness
  - Shame

- *Relational Symptoms of Compulsive Overeating*
  - Feeling embarrassed
  - Feeling inhibited
  - Feeling unaccepted
  - Feeling rejected
  - Becoming introverted
  - Becoming secretive
  - Becoming isolated
  - Becoming withdrawn

- *Spiritual Symptoms of Compulsive Overeating*
  - Disobedience
  - Distance
  - Distrust
  - Doubt

- Guilt   - Shame
- Self-condemnation   - Unworthiness

God created you and has a plan for you. His plan does not include harming yourself with out-of-control eating habits. Consider these verses from the Word of God:

> *"Don't you know that you yourselves are God's temple*
> *and that God's Spirit lives in you?*
> *If anyone destroys God's temple, God will destroy him;*
> *for God's temple is sacred, and you are that temple"*
> (1 CORINTHIANS 3:16-17).

Note: If you are experiencing any of these physical symptoms listed above, be sure to consult your health care professional.

C. What Are the Basic Characteristics of Binge Eating?

While overeating is certainly a component of bingeing, not everyone who overeats on a regular basis is necessarily bingeing on food, just as it's true that not everyone who abuses alcohol is bingeing on alcohol. Being human, we all engage in sinful behavior. As the Bible says, not only have we all sinned, but we can all change because we have an all-powerful Lord who loves us and by whom we have been "fearfully and wonderfully made" (Psalm 139:14) .

Ask yourself these quantifying questions if you think you may be binge eating:

- Do you consume large amounts of food in secret?
- Do you eat and eat and eat until you make yourself sick?
- Do you feel that you are totally out of control when you are eating?
- Do you eat in an attempt to escape from problems or to comfort yourself?
- Do you eat to satisfy an emotional need or to feel better about yourself, but end up feeling even worse?
- Do you feel disgusted with your behavior or ashamed of yourself after eating?
- Do you live with feelings of deep disgust and depression?
- Do you reject yourself and expect others to reject you?
- Do you feel totally unable to stop eating, even though you earnestly want to stop?

- Do you spend around two hours binge eating, or do you binge "graze" throughout the day?

- Do you often eat even when you are not hungry, and do you eat long after you are full?

- Do you sometimes stuff food in your mouth so fast you barely even taste what you are eating?

Unfortunately, those who binge fail to turn their focus from food as a temporal refuge to the One who is an eternal refuge.

> *"Taste and see that the LORD is good; blessed*
> *is the man who takes refuge in him"*
> (PSALM 34:8).

D. What Elements Characterize Emotional Overeating?

The most prominent physical characteristic of a compulsive overeater is easily identifiable—obesity. The terms *compulsive overeating* and *binge eating* are often used interchangeably; they refer to the same ailment and identical patterns of behavior.[18] Eating large quantities of food, often in secret, is symptomatic of compulsive overeating, but some binge eaters engage in another harmful habit—purging food. Bulimics may appear to be healthy when in fact they ingest huge amounts of food and then rid themselves of it. (See pages 135-205.)

Compulsive overeaters often use food for comfort to cope with the pressures of life and may allow lengthy intervals of time to pass between episodes of eating massive amounts of food. Those struggling with food should heed the call of Scripture:

> *"The prudent see danger and take refuge,*
> *but the simple keep going and suffer for it"*
> (PROVERBS 27:12).

When eating becomes the primary means of easing emotions, soothing stress, and putting off problems, it has become an unhealthy and uncontrollable addiction.

Some simple signs of emotional binge eating or overeating include eating food to…

- Avoid dealing with seemingly insurmountable problems

- Calm anxiety and soothe frayed nerves

- Cope with daily concerns and lessen life's stressors
- Lighten mood and lift spirits in order to feel good
- Relax and feel rewarded
- Satisfy a relational or emotional emptiness in life—whether real or perceived

Sadly, such people eat to feed their emotional emptiness rather than their physical emptiness. The problem, of course, is that emotional eating can never satisfy emotional hunger because food is matter and was created by God to satisfy physical hunger alone.

- Food contains no emotional component, so it can never be food for the soul—the mind, the emotions, or the will.
- The only way to meet emotional needs is through relationships that have an emotional component.
- Eating may provide comfort for a brief moment, but when reality sets in, the illusion goes and is replaced by remorse, regret, and self-loathing.
- Rather than solving problems, compulsive, emotional overeating leads to problems such as weight gain and obesity, which then serve to reinforce compulsive eating.
- The worse binge eaters feel about themselves and their appearance, the more they turn to food to cope.
- Eating to satisfy the emotions can become a vicious cycle: eating to feel better, feeling worse instead, and then turning back to food for comfort and relief.

What emotional eaters need to do is turn to the Lord who created them and who alone can satisfy their emotional emptiness and set their spirits free.

"Devote your heart and soul to seeking the LORD your God...
You open your hand and satisfy the desires of every living thing"
(1 CHRONICLES 22:19; PSALM 145:16).

Laxative Abuse

QUESTION: "What is the danger of using laxatives to lose weight?"

ANSWER: Laxatives do not prevent food or calories from being absorbed by the body. Rather, they cause the loss of water, minerals, electrolytes, indigestible fiber, and wastes from the colon. The result can be dehydration unless fluids are consumed to rehydrate the body, thus negating the weight loss. Some of the consequences of laxative abuse include:[19]

- Electrolyte and mineral imbalances that result in the improper functioning of nerves and muscles, including impairment of the colon and heart

- Severe dehydration that can lead to tremors, weakness, blurry vision, fainting, kidney damage, and even death

- Laxative dependency, which happens when the colon fails to respond to normal laxative doses and requires larger amounts of laxatives in order to function

- Internal organ damage, including lazy colon, colon infection, Irritable Bowel Syndrome, and colon cancer

Clearly, laxative abuse is physically dangerous and can even become life-threatening. Tragically, some with eating disorders so despise their bodies that they come to prefer death over life.

III. Causes of Overeating

Food can function like a drug.

We can eat food in an attempt to numb us from pain, thereby turning necessary sustenance into a form of solace. The phrase "comfort food" identifies its role in our lives—*to console.*

But its pacifying ability isn't permanent—the fix is fleeting because only a short time after eating, we can find ourselves rummaging through cupboards and cabinets or raiding the refrigerator yet again. As with drugs, food can become an addiction, consuming our thoughts and preoccupying us with when and where we'll get the chance to eat again.

Jesus instead offers food for both the soul and the spirit that will deeply satisfy, thereby helping us to minimize any fixations on our physical appetites. He calls Himself "the bread of life," the only One who can provide lasting spiritual sustenance and can shift our focus from what's in the fridge to what's in His Word. To be totally filled—to have your thirst fully quenched—heed Jesus' words:

> *"I am the bread of life. He who comes to me will never go*
> *hungry, and he who believes in me will never be thirsty"*
> (John 6:35).

In reality, no snack food can create an obsession. (Manufacturers only wish they could make that claim.) The causes of compulsive overeating are much more complex and deep-rooted. For many people, compulsive eating is not based on physical hunger, but on emotional hunger—a craving for the love and gratification they missed during their childhood.

As you search for the truth about your past and see within your heart what is true about your present, honest answers can be the first step toward healing, as confirmed by Scripture.

"Surely you desire truth in the inner parts;
you teach me wisdom in the inmost place"
(PSALM 51:6).

A. What Are the Situational Setups for Overeating?

There are cultural trends in various countries that can lead to situational setups for overeating. For example, in Egypt, considered the fifth most overweight nation in the world, cultural taboos inhibit women from exercising or participating in sports. So rather than reaching for a tennis racket, Egyptian women are more prone to reach for another plate of food. Obesity among Egyptian women is particularly high.[20]

And a study in New Zealand concluded that the children who spent the greatest amount of time watching television were at a far higher risk for developing adult obesity than children who viewed little television.[21] A sedentary lifestyle can be a situational setup for overeating and can become your "master" when instead God wants to be your Master.

"If you do not do what is right, sin is crouching at your door;
it desires to have you, but you must master it"
(GENESIS 4:7).

Other setups include…

- **Childhood Circumstances**
    - Overweight parents (modeling poor eating patterns)
    - Rejection (using food to mask emotional pain)
    - Sexual abuse (gaining weight to appear unattractive and to insulate inner self)
    - Verbal/emotional abuse (eating to soothe poor self-image)
    - Deprivation (turning to food as a source of security)

- **Physical Dynamics**
  - Less active lifestyle (discontinuing student physical education classes, changing jobs, retirement, becoming physically disabled)
  - Childbirth (gaining weight during pregnancy)
  - Hormonal changes with aging (lessening of metabolism, which affects the rate at which the body burns fat)
  - Underactive thyroid gland (having a hypothyroid condition that decreases production of fat burning hormones)
  - Weight-gaining medications (taking steroids, certain antidepressants, or hormones)
  - Genetic factors or chemical imbalances in the brain
  - Abnormal functioning of hypothalamus region of the brain, which controls appetite

- **Emotional State**
  - Depression (eating for emotional comfort)
  - Grief (relying on food to replace feelings of emptiness)
  - Anxiety (focusing on food to calm the nerves)
  - Loneliness (looking to food to compensate for lack of companionship)
  - Current abuse (feeling out of control except when able to choose food to eat)

- **Relational Patterns**
  - Business engagements (conducting business meetings over a meal)
  - Social gatherings (fellowshipping around food)
  - Busy schedule (eating out on the go rather than cooking healthily at home)
  - Boredom (preparing and eating meals to help pass the time)
  - Celebrating (using food as a reward)

- **Decision Making**
  - Weak impulse control (not saying *no* to the enjoyment of excess food)
  - Poor judgment (not considering size of portions)

— Family, peer, and cultural pressure (not wanting to "hurt people's feelings")

— Consumption of too much alcohol (not limiting the high caloric content of alcohol)

— Celebrating the conclusion of a diet (not realizing healthy eating is a *way of life*)

— Substituting one bad habit for another (replacing smoking with overeating)

If there are situations from the past that have served to set you up to be an overeater, realize that you are no longer living in the past, and you have the power to break the hold those situations have on you today. Even if your circumstances haven't changed, you have. You are no longer a child but an adult. You are no longer powerless but powerful. You are no longer unable to choose for yourself but free to exercise your will. You can walk in freedom from overeating!

> *"It is for freedom that Christ has set us free.*
> *Stand firm, then, and do not let yourselves be*
> *burdened again by a yoke of slavery"*
> (GALATIANS 5:1).

B. What Fakes, Fads, and "Fast Fixes" Can Lead to Defeat?

Eat this…*don't eat that*. Drink this…*don't drink that*.

As waistlines have broadened over time, so has the information on shedding unwanted pounds. But not all is factual. A lot of what we hear about eating healthily is fallacious and downright phony. Often what's "in" concerning healthy eating one year is "out" the next.

The Bible addresses the seasonal, cyclical nature of things on earth:

> *"There is a time for everything, and a season for every activity*
> *under heaven…Whatever is has already been, and what will*
> *be has been before; and God will call the past to account"*
> (ECCLESIASTES 3:1,15).

Some fakes, fads, and "fast fixes" include…

• Acupuncture, hypnotism

• Reducing machines, special wraps to melt fat calories

• Diet pills, fad diets

- Shots, surgery
- Fasting, laxatives
- Starvation, vomiting

The Bible issues this admonition regarding adopting twisted behavior patterns:

> *"Do not conform any longer to the pattern of this world,*
> *but be transformed by the renewing of your mind.*
> *Then you will be able to test and approve what God's will is—*
> *his good, pleasing and perfect will"*
> (ROMANS 12:2).

C. How to Identify and Satisfy Your Unmet Inner Needs

Every human being is born with three God-given inner needs—the need for unconditional love, the need for significance, and the need for security.[22] God designed the family to be the avenue through which He would populate the world and through which He would initially provide us with these needs. The family was to reflect His everlasting love, give us a sense of purpose, and provide us with emotional security. The family was intended to point children to God as the eternal, ultimate Need-meeter. He alone is able to provide all that we need, not only for living life but for living a life pleasing to Him—a godly life.

> *"His divine power has given us everything we need for life*
> *and godliness through our knowledge of him*
> *who called us by his own glory and goodness"*
> (2 PETER 1:3).

Have you tried to fill the emptiness of your soul by filling yourself with food? You need to understand that your destructive behavior is a result of trying to meet legitimate needs in an illegitimate fashion. Ask yourself:

- Did my overeating begin in response to a childhood experience or situation?
  - Was I loved unconditionally or accepted only on the basis of my performance?
  - Was my family a "safe place" for me to express myself?
  - Was I truly valued for myself and treated with respect?
- Am I continuing to overeat as a way to escape?
  - Am I trying to mute the pain of my past?

- – Am I trying to flee responsibility?
- – Am I trying to break away from another's control over me?

- What inner needs am I trying to satisfy on my own rather than relying on God to meet them?
  - – Do I understand the depth of God's love for me?
  - – Do I believe that I am valuable to God?
  - – Do I trust that God can and will take care of me?

The Bible answers us:

> *"If God is for us, who can be against us?...For I am convinced that neither death nor life, neither angels nor demons, neither the present nor the future, nor any powers, neither height nor depth, nor anything else in all creation, will be able to separate us from the love of God that is in Christ Jesus our Lord"*
> (Romans 8:31,38-39).

Abby's Tragedy and Triumph

It was a personal tragedy experienced not once, not twice, but three times over.

The news was inconceivable. Abby's heart was shattered like the shards of broken glass sprayed across the highway. Abby's husband, Rick, was driving with their infant son, Caleb, to take five-year-old Macy to a gymnastics class. Suddenly a vehicle speeding at more than 100 miles per hour smashed head-on into Rick's car, crumpling it like an empty soda can. Beneath a pile of mangled metal lay those most precious to Abby.

On October 13, 2006, Abby lost her entire family. All three loved ones were killed in a horrific accident by a reckless driver who himself died in the crash.[23] "Nobody in the world loved their family more than I loved mine," Abby reflects. "Nobody. They were everything I wanted in life."[24]

Following the accident, Abby was submerged in grief. Every bit of her energy was siphoned away by painfully raw emotions. The 5'4" teacher found herself turning to food for solace, and her weight spiked to 247 pounds. "My only real socialization was going out to eat," Abby recalls. "I had zero energy. I just felt like I had sludge in my veins. I was so lethargic."[25]

But one day Abby's life became energized by what she calls a divine appointment, changing the trajectory of her life. Abby had a gym membership that she rarely used, but she mustered enough energy to go for a workout. There, she met two contestants who had appeared on the popular television program *The Biggest Loser*. Brady and Vicky Vilcan had appeared during the sixth season of the show, which rewards contestants for losing weight, both individually and collectively as a team, and they inspired her to audition. "God has a way of putting the right people in your life at the right time,"[26] Abby observes. And she hoped that, if chosen to go onto the show, it would serve as a distraction from all of her pain.

The interview process turned out to be a time of intense soul-searching, with numerous questions forcing Abby to dig deeply into her painful emotions. "I shed a lot of tears answering those questions…that I spent a lot of time and prayer on," Abby remembers. "If it was supposed to happen, I reasoned, it would, and I'd be one hundred percent true to myself throughout the journey. I'd do everything I could to make me the best me I could be."[27]

Abby won the opportunity to achieve her absolute personal best when she was selected as a contestant for season eight. The environment proved to be both physically and emotionally beneficial. While shedding pounds, it was as if she were also shedding pain. Though she did not become the biggest loser, her participation on the show changed the course of her life and ushered in a needed season of healing.

Today, Abby could easily be called The Biggest Winner as she embraces a second shot at life. She knows that God has a purpose for her life—a truth that propels her to travel the country speaking at schools, churches, and community events to inspire others to have hope in their darkest of hours. And when Abby stands before crowds, there's 100 pounds *less* of her than when she made her national debut.

Abby feels compelled to communicate a key message that changed her life: *Although we can't always control what happens to us, we can control how we respond to what happens to us.* "Happiness is a choice. You choose how you respond in your life."[28]

Instead of looking to food for comfort, Christ is her comfort. And no matter where she travels, Abby can say, "I have learned in whatever state I am, to be content…I can do all things through Christ who strengthens me."[29]

D. What Is the Root Cause of Overeating?

As stated earlier, we all have three God-given inner needs for unconditional love, significance, and security.[30] Compulsive overeating is typically an attempt to meet one or more of these needs through consuming food. If you believe you don't have the willpower to resist foods that give you pleasure, be assured you *can* devise a successful plan that includes relying on God's promise to meet all of your needs. He can and will provide the power to resist temptations to overeat. The Bible guarantees this:

"The LORD will guide you always;
he will satisfy your needs in a sun-scorched land
and will strengthen your frame.
You will be like a well-watered garden,
like a spring whose waters never fail"
(ISAIAH 58:11).

Overeating is an attempt to meet one or more inner needs for...[31]

- **Unconditional love**—eating food in order to feel *nurtured*
- **Significance**—eating food in order to feel a sense of *control*
- **Security**—eating and hoarding food in order to feel *secure* because of fear of deprivation

The problem with using food to meet any of these inner needs is simple—it can't be done! Nothing physical—no human being and no food—can meet your inner needs and satisfy the longings of your heart. Only God can do that. When you yield your will to God's will, His supernatural power can give you the victory over overeating and provide joy in your life. Getting your habits under control will take a while, but today you can take the first step. You can embrace the hope and freedom that God is offering you.

WRONG BELIEF:

"I can't sustain enough willpower to resist the foods that give me pleasure."

RIGHT BELIEF:

"The issue is not the power of *my will*, but the power of *my God*—He *will* fulfill my deepest inner needs. When I have Christ living in me, He is able to change my fixation—from food...to faith."

"You will know the truth, and the truth will set you free"
(JOHN 8:32).

IV. Steps to Solution

Although she has forgiven him, she will never forget the judge's cruel comment as she prepared to perform on *American Idol* before millions of television viewers—"We're going to have to get a bigger stage."[32]

Mandisa initially got Simon Cowell's attention for her out-of-control curves instead of her polished "pipes," but later all that changed. After losing more than 80 pounds, even the acerbic judge was singing her praises.

Mandisa, a finalist on the fifth season of *American Idol*, has been set free from what she describes as a food addiction, and she is forever grateful for the dramatic change that now has become apparent in her life. The most difficult part eventually became the most empowering part—learning to retrain her brain not to be preoccupied with food, *but with God*.[33] And Scripture tells us the benefit of having a Spirit-controlled mind:

> *"Those who live according to the sinful nature have their*
> *minds set on what that nature desires; but those who live*
> *in accordance with the Spirit have their minds set on what*
> *the Spirit desires. The mind of sinful man is death, but*
> *the mind controlled by the Spirit is life and peace"*
> (ROMANS 8:5-6).

A. Key Verse to Memorize

The inspiring lyrics from Mandisa's hit single "My Deliverer" gave glory to God for helping her find freedom from food addiction. Since her national debut on *American Idol*, Mandisa has become a Grammy-nominated Christian recording artist. She stated that the changes in her life extend far beyond a slimmer waistline and slender legs.

"It's more than the physical and more than what I am eating. It's a spiritual change. I've had to not turn to food for comfort and validation anymore, and that is a complete mind change. Because my entire life, that is what I have done."[34]

Tragically, Mandisa traces the roots of her food addiction to being molested as a child and raped at age 16. "I equated being beautiful with being in danger. When I was heavy, men were not looking at me and I felt safe."[35] But, as Mandisa learned to conform to God's pattern for her life rather than to the world's values, she not only lost weight but also gained vitality.

"God is showing me that my value, my dependence, and my satisfaction need to come from Him. Satisfaction doesn't need to come from food. It doesn't need to come from what other people think about me. Finding satisfaction in God is what true freedom is."[36]

Mandisa's joyful outlook on life is manifested in her single hit "Dance, Dance, Dance," which encourages people to praise God in the midst of pain. "The song... shows people that, even though they may not understand all of the things God has done in their lives, they can still praise Him with their dancing. It's like David in the Psalms. I love that!

"This song resonates so much with me because my great God has set me free. I'm going to praise Him with dancing because of all that He has done in my life."[37]

Mandisa's mind-set has changed. She has gone from fear to faith in God, and all that she does is for the glory of God. The Bible says,

> *"Whether you eat or drink or whatever you do,*
> *do it all for the glory of God"*
> (1 CORINTHIANS 10:31).

B. Key Passage to Read and Reread

The choicest meats and wine were set before him and mouth-watering smells wafted through the air, but for Daniel, the royal place setting left nothing but a stench.

Without a doubt, the food that lined Daniel's plate had been offered to a pagan god, and the meat had not been prepared in accordance with Mosaic law. Based on spiritual conviction, Daniel would rather go hungry than defile himself by partaking of royal delicacies from the hand of King Nebuchadnezzar.

Daniel and three other young men from Judah had been brought to Babylon following the king's besieging blow upon their nation. They were selected to one day enter the king's service because they were choice men "without any physical defect, handsome, showing aptitude for every kind of learning, well informed, quick to understand, and qualified to serve in the king's palace" (Daniel 1:4).

So then Daniel and his companions—in the midst of being trained in the literature and language of the Babylonians—found themselves in a defilement dilemma. But Daniel was confident in the provision of his God—the one and only true God—and trusted in His provision. He petitioned a royal guard, "Please test your servants for ten days: Give us nothing but vegetables to eat and water to drink. Then compare our appearance with that of the young men who eat the royal food, and treat your servants in accordance with what you see" (Daniel 1:12-13).

The guard agreed, and the test was on. At the end of ten days, the four men "looked healthier and better nourished than any of the young men who ate the royal food" (Daniel 1:15). And as a testimony to their unwavering commitment to the sovereign God, they continued eating only vegetables. Pleasing God was far more important than pleasing their appetite or the king.

The obedience displayed by Daniel and his companions was richly rewarded, and God blessed them with far more than just great health:

> *"To these four young men God gave knowledge and understanding*
> *of all kinds of literature and learning. And Daniel could*
> *understand visions and dreams of all kinds...*
> *In every matter of wisdom and understanding about which*
> *the king questioned them, he found them ten times better than*
> *all the magicians and enchanters in his whole kingdom"*
> (DANIEL 1:17,20).

OBEDIENCE TO GOD BRINGS PHYSICAL AND SPIRITUAL STRENGTH
Daniel 1:8-21

- Daniel made a commitment to obey God. . . . . verse 8
- God backed up Daniel's resolve with supernatural support. . . . . verse 9
- Daniel requested only vegetables and water for himself and his three companions for their meals for ten days. . . .verse 12
- Daniel trusted in the faithful provision of his God. . . . . .verse 13
- The four men became noticeably healthier and better nourished. . . . . .verse 15
- They continued eating only vegetables as testimony to their unwavering commitment to obey God. . . . . .verse 16
- God blessed Daniel and the other men with great knowledge and understanding. .verse 17
- God further blessed Daniel with the ability to interpret dreams and visions. . . . . .verse 17
- King Nebuchadnezzar considered the four men to be ten times wiser than anyone in his kingdom. . . . . .verse 20

C. How to Decipher the Do's and Don'ts of Wise Weight Loss

Mandisa *doesn't* want to become fixated on reaching a certain weight, but she *does* want to run a 10-minute mile.[38]

While dropping six dress sizes in nine months, Mandisa learned a lot about the do's and don'ts of weight loss. In the past she had been on countless diets that helped her lose weight, but she always put the pounds back on again as soon as she stopped dieting. But after Mandisa progressed from dieting to a dramatic lifestyle change, she realized for herself these basic principles: Don't eat at random. Do measure proper serving sizes. Don't eat large meals. Do eat six mini-meals (three small meals and three snacks) filled with fiber each day.[39]

For anyone willing to incorporate serious exercise into their lifestyle, the general principle is this: Don't exercise only occasionally. Rather, commit to doing a 30- to 45-minute workout three to five days a week.[40]

Mandisa is not obsessed with attaining an ideal weight. Rather, she is focusing on being healthy and fit. And she knows who will help her accomplish all the do's and avoid all the don'ts:

> *"It is God who arms me with strength*
> *and makes my way perfect"*
> (PSALM 18:32).

- *Don't* say, "I am dieting."
  - *Do* say, "I'm eating healthy foods."

- *Don't* start a new eating plan during a crisis, illness, holiday, or high-stress situation.
  - *Do* consult a doctor before beginning any new eating plan.

- *Don't* adopt a plan just because it worked for someone else.
  - *Do* adopt a personalized plan that will work for your individual lifestyle.

- *Don't* fail to set goals.
  - *Do* set realistic, short-term, incremental goals.

- *Don't* weigh yourself every day.
  - *Do* record your weight once a week.

- *Don't* keep unhealthy food around you.
  - *Do* keep healthy food prepared for snacks.

- ***Don't*** shop for groceries on impulse or when you are hungry.
  - ***Do*** shop with a prepared list.

- ***Don't*** buy packaged food without reading the labels.
  - ***Do*** notice the first ingredients listed; these make up the highest percentage of what's in the food.

- ***Don't*** eat fast!
  - ***Do*** chew slowly. It takes 20 minutes for your brain to register "I'm full."

- ***Don't*** keep your new plan a secret.
  - ***Do*** share your plan with your friends and ask for their support.

- ***Don't*** get caught off guard by temptation.
  - ***Do*** have an alternate plan for when temptation comes (call a friend, memorize Scripture, take a walk, enjoy a hobby).

- ***Don't*** reward yourself with food.
  - ***Do*** focus on the rewards of self-control and a new, healthy lifestyle.

Remember:

> *"A prudent man sees danger and takes refuge,*
> *but the simple keep going and suffer for it"*
> (PROVERBS 22:3).

D. How to Think Healthy

Jesus was preoccupied with food—but not the kind that lines cabinets and fills refrigerators. What consumed Him, what filled and satisfied Him far more than the choicest meats and grains, pertained to matters of the kingdom—namely, pleasing His Father above. "'My food,' said Jesus, 'is to do the will of him who sent me and to finish his work'" (John 4:34).

Let's follow Jesus' example and focus on pleasing our heavenly Father, rather than our own desire for overeating. Let's discover God's will for our lives and carry out the work He has called us to do—*to completion*. When these are operating in sync—pleasing our heavenly Father and carrying out the work we're called to do—there is no greater satisfaction on earth! Scripture reminds us of our very special calling:

"We are God's workmanship,
created in Christ Jesus to do good works,
which God prepared in advance for us to do"
(Ephesians 2:10).

Think of yourself as the person God created you to be.

- God has given me a new nature in Jesus Christ.
- God has given me all I need to live a self-controlled life.
- God has given me an escape from ungodly eating desires.

  "He has given us his very great and precious promises, so that
  through them you may participate in the divine nature and
  escape the corruption in the world caused by evil desires"
  (2 Peter 1:4).

Have the correct motive for losing weight.

- I want to take good care of my physical body, the "temple of the Holy Spirit" (1 Corinthians 6:19).
- I want to be free from the bondage of self-indulgence.
- I want to be healthy and live the life God has planned for me.

  "We make it our goal to please him, whether we
  are at home in the body or away from it"
  (2 Corinthians 5:9).

Identify the real reasons you overeat.[41]

- Am I responding to a lack of love because of _____?
- Am I responding to feelings of insignificance because of _____?
- Am I fearful and insecure because of _____?

  "Search me, O God, and know my heart;
  test me and know my anxious thoughts"
  (Psalm 139:23).

Make a personal commitment to obey God.

- Acknowledge your need for change.

- Acknowledge that you are powerless to change.
- Acknowledge God's power in you to change.
- Acknowledge His constant presence within you.

> *"Those who obey his commands live in him, and*
> *he in them. And this is how we know that he lives*
> *in us: We know it by the Spirit he gave us"*
> (1 JOHN 3:24).

Know how to listen to the Lord.

- Listen to God through His written Word.
- Listen for His leading through the Holy Spirit.
- Learn to identify Satan's lies.

> *"I will instruct you and teach you in the way you should go;*
> *I will counsel you and watch over you"*
> (PSALM 32:8).

Develop an exercise plan that will increase your metabolism. Vary the plan.

- Walk or ride a bicycle for 30-45 minutes a day three to five times a week.
- Do aerobics for 30-45 minutes a day three to five days a week.
- Walk up the stairs instead of using an elevator.
- Make a commitment to join in athletic activities with friends.

> *"He who ignores discipline despises himself,*
> *but whoever heeds correction gains understanding"*
> (PROVERBS 15:32).

Eat only when you are hungry, and only foods you should eat.

- Develop a knowledge of good nutrition.
- Choose to eat healthy foods.
- Don't give up if you blow it.

> *"Do not destroy the work of God for the sake of*
> *food. All food is clean, but it is wrong for a man to eat*
> *anything that causes someone else to stumble"*
> (ROMANS 14:20).

Allow for flexibility and include some pleasure foods in your diet.

- Recognize the value of variety and of occasionally having a special treat.
- Realize the legitimate God-given enjoyment of tasty foods.
- Resist the urge to binge.

> *"Delight yourself in the LORD and he will*
> *give you the desires of your heart"*
> (PSALM 37:4).

Let the Holy Spirit direct your plans and provide needed self-control.

- Pray throughout the day that your choices will reflect the self-control of Christ.
- Meditate on specific scriptures (especially those about self-control).
- Ask God to remind you of His protection and power over temptation.

> *"The Counselor, the Holy Spirit, whom the Father will*
> *send in my name, will teach you all things and will*
> *remind you of everything I have said to you"*
> (JOHN 14:26).

Focus to the healthy foods you need to eat.

- Keep a small notebook with you.
- Write down when and what you eat, along with its caloric or fat value.
- Record your thoughts and feelings.
- Choose a scripture to think about and memorize daily or weekly.

> *"A wicked man puts up a bold front, but an*
> *upright man gives thought to his ways"*
> (PROVERBS 21:29).

Have a thankful heart.

- Thank God for His faithfulness to you.
- Thank God for the unique person you are, including your body shape and size.

- Know that God never gives up on you. If you blow it, start again—God is faithful!

> *"Being confident of this, that he who began a good work in you*
> *will carry it on to completion until the day of Christ Jesus"*
> (PHILIPPIANS 1:6).

E. How to Benefit from the Best Beverages

It's been said that nothing quenches the thirst better than a glass of water.

Water is free of calories and additives and has a host of health benefits. It delivers nutrients and oxygen to cells, regulates body temperature, removes toxins from organs, cushions the joints, and maintains moisture in the skin. [42]

The cleansing benefits of water are best illustrated in the ceremonial cleansing of the priestly tribe of Levi, when the Lord tells Moses,

> *"Make them ceremonially clean. To purify them, do this: Sprinkle*
> *the water of cleansing on them; then have them shave their*
> *whole bodies and wash their clothes, and so purify themselves"*
> (NUMBERS 8:6-7).

- **Drink** water, water, water.
  - *Avoid* carbonated beverages that have no nutritional value.
- **Drink** 100 percent natural fruit juices.
  - *Avoid* juices with added sugar and corn syrup. Many healthy juices are made from grapes, oranges, grapefruit, blueberries, and cranberries.
- **Drink** skim or 1 percent milk.
  - *Avoid* whole milk, which is high in fat and is never necessary for adults and teenagers.
- **Drink** vegetable juices.
  - Tomato juice is a source of nutrients, including vitamin C, folate, and potassium. Tomato juice and other tomato products contain large amounts of lycopene. [43]
  - Carrot juice is an "excellent source of antioxidant compounds and the richest vegetable source of the pro-vitamin A carotenes." [44]
  - Beet juice contains "powerful nutrient compounds that help

protect against heart disease, birth defects, and certain cancers, especially colon cancer."[45]

When it comes to our spiritual needs, the only thing that will truly satisfy is "living water" (John 4:10). Jesus communicated this truth to a lonely Samaritan woman who came to draw water at a well. He offered her the gift of salvation—*Himself*—and said the water He provides quenches thirst not just temporarily, but also for eternity. Read Jesus' words:

> *"Everyone who drinks this water will be thirsty again,*
> *but whoever drinks the water I give him will never thirst"*
> (John 4:13-14).

F. How to Find the Healthiest Foods

The current "evil" word in the world of weight loss is *carbs*, something seemingly to be avoided like the plague. Carbohydrates have been blamed for the obesity epidemic and have been targeted as the source of increased health risks and disease. But not all carbs are bad.

According to many health experts, it is vital to incorporate *unprocessed, high-fiber* carbohydrates into a well-balanced diet of whole grains, lean meats, fruits, and vegetables.[46]

God has certainly blessed us with an abundance to choose from:

> *"I give you every seed-bearing plant*
> *on the face of the whole earth*
> *and every tree that has fruit with seed in it.*
> *They will be yours for food"*
> (Genesis 1:29).

The most nutritious foods to eat are found in six categories: fruits, vegetables, nuts, protein, dairy, and grains. Notice the absence of candy, cookies, and cakes! But we also need to realize it is possible to prepare healthy food in an *unhealthy* way. Likewise, some vegetables are healthier to eat than other vegetables.

- **Eat** fresh and/or frozen fruit.
  - *Avoid* canned fruit that contains high fructose corn syrup.

- **Eat** darker vegetables, which have more vitamins than lighter vegetables.
  - *Avoid* iceberg lettuce, which has no nutritional value.

- **Eat** vitamin-rich sweet potatoes.
  - *Avoid* white potatoes.

- **Eat** the skins of food.
  - *Avoid* peeling the skin of potatoes. The skins contain vitamin C, vitamin B6, folic acid, beta carotene, and iron. When preparing mashed potatoes, cook the potatoes with the skin on to add vitamins and fiber.[47]

- **Eat** food with natural sweetness (fruit, sweet potatoes).
  - *Avoid* sugar, fructose, and sucrose.

- **Eat** nuts in their natural form.
  - *Avoid* nuts that are honey roasted or prepared with saturated fat.

- **Eat** broiled or baked meat, poultry, fish, and vegetables.
  - *Avoid* fried foods, which are high in fat.

- **Eat** whole grain bread and English muffins.
  - *Avoid* white bread and items with bleached white flour that remove the beneficial vitamins. (Croissant rolls are very high in fat.)

The Lord created you to need food, to have hunger, and to eat. Your responsibility is to be wise and eat the proper foods at the proper time.

> *"The eyes of all look to you, and you give them their*
> *food at the proper time. You open your hand and*
> *satisfy the desires of every living thing"*
> (PSALM 145:15-16).

G. How to Grab Good Food on the Go

We're all tempted—and too often, we succumb. We're standing in the checkout line at the grocery store, surrounded by racks of candy bars, chips, and many other products dripping with saturated fats and sugar. As the cashier totals up the cost of our asparagus, bananas, and ever-so-lean chicken…*plop*…a big, fattening candy bar winds up in the mix. *How did I let that happen?* we later lament.

Along with planning ahead and predetermining not to give in to unhealthy foods, the following tips will equip you to resist when certain cravings crash upon you outside the home. And when you commit your desires and goals to the Lord, you will find success.

"Commit to the LORD whatever you do,
and your plans will succeed"
(PROVERBS 16:3).

PLANS FOR THE ROAD

- Avoid ordering junk food, which is high in fat and low in nutrition.
- Don't eat at restaurants without planning ahead.
- Eat at restaurants that offer a variety of healthy foods.
- Keep a small cooler in your car so you can carry healthy snacks with you.
- Predetermine the best foods to order when eating out (fish, turkey, chicken, spinach, broccoli, asparagus, etc.).
- Take healthy foods with you when you are away from home (fruit, nuts, low-fat cheese).

As you consider your strategy for eating on the go, remember that both planning and implementing are necessary for success. And remember that you are not alone in making plans—the Lord Himself makes and carries out His plans:

"'I know the plans I have for you,' declares the LORD,
'plans to prosper you and not to harm you,
plans to give you hope and a future'"
(JEREMIAH 29:11).

═══════════════ *Reducing Body Fat* ═══════════════

QUESTION: "Should I eat only once or twice a day in order to lose weight?"

ANSWER: No! You can optimize your body's fat-burning ability by eating five or six times each day: breakfast, morning snack, lunch, afternoon snack, and dinner (with an additional snack if you have an early dinner). Keep portion sizes no larger than your fist. Remember, caloric intake for women will need to be lower than for men of the same height and weight because women have a naturally slower metabolism.

The priests serving God's chosen people were to follow strict instructions concerning the fat of offerings, as recorded in the Bible:

"He shall remove all the fat, just as the fat is
removed from the fellowship offering"
(LEVITICUS 4:31).

H. How to Tailor Multiple Treatment Strategies for Binge Eating

No one approach to overcoming well-established patterns of binge eating can effectively address all the issues involved in this complex disorder. The soul (mind, will, emotions), body, and spirit all work together to create and support eating patterns. Therefore, all these elements need to be engaged and working together toward the same goal of healthy eating if treatment is to be successful. Seek wise counsel as you consider all of your options.

> *"Plans fail for lack of counsel, but with many advisers they succeed"*
> (PROVERBS 15:22).

FOUR OBJECTIVES FOR RESTORING HEALTH[48]

- To progress toward emotional, physical, and spiritual healing and wholeness
- To adopt healthy attitudes toward body and self-image
- To initiate sound eating habits that limit the possibility for binge eating
- To reach and maintain a healthy weight and lifestyle

FOUR AIDS ON YOUR PATH TOWARD HEALTH

As you take steps toward better health, here are some different options for you to consider in your effort to stay on the path to wholeness:

- Professional counseling—Working with a therapist to reveal hidden issues that may have contributed to binge eating or other destructive behavior patterns may help you to make important life changes.
- Medical intervention—You may need to speak with a doctor and nutritionist about options for reaching and maintaining a healthy weight, including diet, exercise, lifestyle changes, and medication.
- Individualized strategy—Evaluate the benefits and weaknesses of beginning a weight loss program, attending a support group, or visiting a health club to determine whether this would help you reach your goals.
- Spiritual dependence—As you consider your options for reaching your goal of a healthy body, you need to include taking the time to cultivate your relationship with Jesus Christ and make sure you remain dependent on His strength to help you in your weakness.

*"But he [the Lord Jesus] said to me, 'My grace is sufficient
for you, for my power is made perfect in weakness.'
Therefore I [Paul] will boast all the more gladly about my
weaknesses, so that Christ's power may rest on me"*
(2 CORINTHIANS 12:9).

Listen and Learn

QUESTION: "What is involved in listening to your body?"

ANSWER: Listening to your body is somewhat like listening to a friend—you listen for what is meant and what is felt, what is needed and what is wanted. Your body is in constant communication with you regarding its needs and desires, its pains and pleasures. Your body knows when it needs to be fed and when it needs to be held. It knows when it needs fuel and when it is full. Listening means knowing when the desire for food means you need nutrition and when it means you need nurturing.

Here are three helpful hints for listening to your body:

- *Eat because you are hungry*, not because you are bored, stressed, or lonely.
  - Eat when your stomach is growling.
  - Eat when you have a headache.
  - Eat when several hours have passed since you last ate.

- *Eat what you want*, not what you dislike.
  - Eat in moderation.
  - Eat appealing, enjoyable foods.
  - Eat what your body both needs and desires.

- *Eat until you are content*, not until you are full or stuffed.
  - Eat while sitting down.
  - Eat slowly and methodically.
  - Eat purposefully, focusing on the tastes, smells, and textures of your foods.

If you listen to your body and love it by responding to what it truly needs, you will find that overeating will become a pattern of the past and healthy eating will become your present pattern.

Remember the words the Lord spoke to the prophet Isaiah as you begin treating your body in a new way:

> *"Forget the former things; do not dwell on the past.*
> *See, I am doing a new thing!*
> *Now it springs up; do you not perceive it?*
> *I am making a way in the desert and streams in the wasteland"*
> (ISAIAH 43:18-19).

I. How to Customize Self-care to Help Conquer Bingeing

Along with taking advantage of therapy options, practicing self-care gives you a greater sense of control over your choices and a sense of personal responsibility for your ultimate success. Since control issues are often related to binge eating, exercising control in a positive, productive way is critical to and compatible with overall good health. By developing a healthy eating plan and persevering with that plan, you can enjoy God's best for your physical body.

> *"So do not throw away your confidence; it will be richly*
> *rewarded. You need to persevere so that when you have done*
> *the will of God, you will receive what he has promised"*
> (HEBREWS 10:35-36).

You can customize your own self-care treatment from these suggestions for conquering binge eating:

SELF-CARE STEPS[49]

- **Don't diet** unless you are supervised by a professional dietitian, nutritionist, and/or medical doctor.
- **Don't eat when bored.** Engage in some other activity that will distract your thoughts away from food.
- **Don't eat just to eat.** Eat foods that contain essential vitamins, minerals, and nutrients.
- **Don't sacrifice your sleep.** Try taking quick power naps and getting a good night's sleep so your body will shed fat faster.
- **Don't withdraw from others.** Instead, reach out and share your specific struggles and strengths with trusted individuals.
- **Don't store food.** Buy only what you need for a specified period of time.

- **Don't skip therapy.** Work your plan and stay accountable to yourself and others.
- **Don't toy with temptation.** Pledge to never shop when you are hungry, upset, frustrated, lonely, or feeling down so that you will make good choices when you do shop.
- **Do exercise** in appropriate ways, for reasonable lengths of time, and with another person.
- **Do test your hunger** to determine whether you are hungry for food or for love.
- **Do love yourself** by not eating whatever you want, but by engaging in activities that are fun, relaxing, and energizing.
- **Do be kind to yourself** by rejecting critical, accusatory, and demeaning self-talk and by clinging to your identity in Christ. Remember, you have been made a child of God and His Spirit is within you, helping you to conform to His character.
- **Do eat breakfast** so that you will not feel the need to consume calories unwisely during the day.
- **Do learn your eating triggers** and develop a plan of action for countering them.
- **Do keep a record** of the times you eat, what and how much you eat, and your emotional state when you eat in order to identify your eating patterns and triggers.
- **Do snack smart** by eating low-fat, low-calorie snacks like fruit or vegetables with a fat-free dip.

Should you engage in emotional eating, quickly accept God's forgiveness, forgive yourself, and then start anew. Learn from experience by identifying what triggered your emotional need to eat and devising a plan for responding differently in the future. Rather than dwelling on your failure, focus on the successes you are having as you replace your unhealthy eating patterns with healthy ones. Thank God for the good work He is doing within you and cooperate with Him by leaning on Him and drawing on His resources.

> *"No temptation has seized you except what is common to
> man. And God is faithful; he will not let you be tempted
> beyond what you can bear. But when you are tempted, he will
> also provide a way out so that you can stand up under it"*
> (1 CORINTHIANS 10:13).

As you customize your self-care program, keep clinging to Jesus, your constant companion, counselor, and comfort—your refuge, strength, and ever-present help in times of trouble.

> *"God is our refuge and strength, an ever-present help in trouble"*
> (PSALM 46:1).

J. How to Understand Why Weight Training Helps Weight Loss

Many people are physically unable to make weight training part of their weight loss program. Others place too much stress on exercise. But most people try to strike a good balance between burning calories through exercise and consuming fewer calories through proper meal planning.

The apostle Paul compared physical training to spiritual training, and his words serve as an encouragement to us all to subdue our bodies through self-discipline, not just for physical reasons but also for spiritual benefit:

> *"Everyone who competes in the games goes into strict training.*
> *They do it to get a crown that will not last; but we do it to get*
> *a crown that will last forever. Therefore I do not run like a*
> *man running aimlessly; I do not fight like a man beating the*
> *air. No, I beat my body and make it my slave so that after I have*
> *preached to others, I myself will not be disqualified for the prize"*
> (1 CORINTHIANS 9:25-27).

Haven't we all watched acrobats or other athletes with lean, powerful muscles perform what seem to many of us to be physically impossible feats? Haven't we found ourselves momentarily envying their immense energy and muscle power, admiring their physical prowess and perfect precision as they perform some rigorous routine? And haven't we all felt a tinge of guilt that we huff and puff after walking up the stairs at work or watering the yard at home?

If you want to turn your envy into positive action, then consider the ways weight training can...

- Improve basal metabolic rate (metabolism)
- Produce strong, sinewy muscles
- Multiply muscle power
- Lessen body fat

You may not be interested in performing hair-raising feats, but you will appreciate having additional muscle power that makes it possible for you to do the maximum amount of work within the shortest amount of time.

You will also want to consider the ways strength training can...

- Improve the strength of your general body structure
- Increase the thickening of your tendons
- Build up the density of your bones
- Lower the possibility of injury

Weight training can also help you maintain good blood pressure, body posture, and general appearance.

The Bible gives these words of exhortation that apply to weight training:

> *"Strengthen your feeble arms and weak knees"*
> (HEBREWS 12:12).

―――――――――― *Excessive Excerise* ――――――――――

QUESTION: "Is it possible for me to exercise too much?"

ANSWER: Yes. Aerobic exercise that exceeds more than one hour in length increases your risk of injury due to fatigue. Increasing the frequency of aerobic activity beyond five times per week does not give your body a chance to fully recover and can even reduce your body's capability to defend itself against illness. Listen to what your body is trying to tell you and heed what Scripture says:

> *"Physical training is of some value, but godliness has value for all things, holding promise for both the present life and the life to come"*
> (1 TIMOTHY 4:8).

K. How to See that Success Is Just a Choice Away

Life and death...blessings and curses...

God placed before His people, the nation of Israel, two distinct paths leading in entirely different directions. They were free to choose the path they would follow, but they also had to be prepared to accept the consequences of their choice.

God longed for the Israelites to choose "life"—loving Him, obeying Him, and thus receiving from Him boundless blessing. But should they choose "death"—forsaking Him and failing to honor His hallowed name—then curses and great disaster would befall them.

You too have two distinct paths before you. You can choose to seek God's help in overcoming your overeating habits and find victory, or you can attempt to stop overeating in your own strength and face defeat after defeat. As with the Israelites, God wants you to choose Him, and you'll soon discover that *success is just a choice away*:

> *"Now choose life, so that you…may live and that you*
> *may love the LORD your God, listen to his voice, and*
> *hold fast to him. For the LORD is your life"*
> (DEUTERONOMY 30:19-20).

My Daily Choices for Change

Decide each day to accept this challenge for change.
Accept the challenge to make these daily choices,
realizing that success is just a choice away.
Life is a series of choices; therefore…

I choose to give control of my life to the Lord Jesus Christ.
I choose to change my eating habits through the power of Christ within me.
I choose to live to please God, not to please my appetite.
I choose to make wise choices when tempted to eat unwisely.
I choose to make right choices when tempted to eat excessively.
I choose to glorify God and reflect Him through my body.
I choose to focus not on food but on faithfulness to the Lord in my life.
I choose to let God be my God—not to let food be my god.

Although I've failed in the past,
with God's help I don't have to fail in the future!

> *"My flesh and my heart may fail,*
> *but God is the strength of my heart*
> *and my portion forever"*
> (Psalm 73:26).

There is only one God.
So if food is your god, then God is not your God.
—June Hunt

"Whether you eat or drink or whatever you do,
do it all for the glory of God"

(1 Corinthians 10:31).

Overeating: Answers in God's Word

QUESTION: "What happens to those who ignore discipline?"

ANSWER: *"He who ignores discipline despises himself, but whoever heeds correction gains understanding"* (Proverbs 15:32).

QUESTION: "Who is like a city whose walls are broken down?"

ANSWER: *"Like a city whose walls are broken down is a man who lacks self-control"* (Proverbs 25:28).

QUESTION: "Should I worry about having food to eat or clothes to wear?"

ANSWER: *"I tell you, do not worry about your life, what you will eat or drink; or about your body, what you will wear. Is not life more important than food, and the body more important than clothes?"* (Matthew 6:25).

QUESTION: "What do those who live according to their sinful nature have their minds set on? What would be a better way to live?"

ANSWER: *"Those who live according to the sinful nature have their minds set on what that nature desires; but those who live in accordance with the Spirit have their minds set on what the Spirit desires"* (Romans 8:5).

QUESTION: "What should my attitude be when I eat or drink?"

ANSWER: *"So whether you eat or drink or whatever you do, do it all for the glory of God"* (1 Corinthians 10:31).

QUESTION: "Is it wrong to eat certain things if it makes me or someone else stumble?"

ANSWER: *"Do not destroy the work of God for the sake of food. All food is clean, but it is wrong for a man to eat anything that causes someone else to stumble"* (Romans 14:20).

QUESTION: "What has God's divine power given us?"

ANSWER: *"His divine power has given us everything we need for life and godliness through our knowledge of him who called us by his own glory and goodness"* (2 Peter 1:3).

QUESTION: "Who gives me strength to do what I need to do?"

ANSWER: *"I can do everything through him [Jesus] who gives me strength"* (Philippians 4:13).

QUESTION: "What can I offer as a spiritual act of worship?"

ANSWER: *"I urge you, brothers, in view of God's mercy, to offer your bodies as living sacrifices, holy and pleasing to God—this is your spiritual act of worship"* (Romans 12:1).

QUESTION: "Everything is permissible for me, but is everything beneficial?"

ANSWER: *"'Everything is permissible for me'—but not everything is beneficial. 'Everything is permissible for me'—but I will not be mastered by anything"* (1 Corinthians 6:12).

THE WORLD OF SEXUAL ADDICTION
The Way Out of the Web

THE WORLD OF SEXUAL ADDICTION:
The Way Out of the Web

It starts with a single thread…and before long, a spider weaves an intricately designed web with only one intention—to capture prey.

It starts with a single picture, a single sexual image that pops onto the computer screen. And before long, you're ensnared, entrapped in a complex, all-consuming web of sexual addiction. You're undeniably stuck—you look around and all you see, all you think about, is sex. You're obsessed with erotic excitement, continually contemplating where and when you'll feed your sexual appetite.

Like an alcoholic who craves alcohol, you crave sex—you must have sexual stimulation. But there's another side to what is called *sexual addiction*: What stimulates also brings *shame*…with *fear* that you'll never find your way out of the web.

God created sexuality and blessed it within the context of marriage. And He can help you break free of the binding web that keeps your mind captive. He can give you the strength to break free from the web, and He can replace harmful passions with healthy ones.

Even if you feel that your mind and heart have been too defiled, remember that God is a Redeemer—a Deliverer! There is no willing soul that He can't make clean.

> *"You, O LORD, have delivered my soul from death, my*
> *eyes from tears, my feet from stumbling, that I may*
> *walk before the LORD in the land of the living"*
> (PSALM 116:8-9).

I. DEFINITIONS OF SEXUAL ADDICTION
Saint by day, sex addict by night.

Mark was fully aware of the dangerous dynamics that accompany a double life. He lived on both sides for more than 30 years—constantly dodging suspicion, continually fearing getting caught. He wrestled constantly with guilt and shame, but *still* he couldn't stop; he couldn't end his insatiable drive for sexual excitement. And that's why, like the alcoholic who craves a drink or the chain smoker who craves a cigarette, Mark craved sex, out-of-control sex, which categorized him with millions of others around the world as a *sex addict*.

By day, Mark served as a pastor and counselor, taught at a Christian college, and volunteered on the local school board. But by night, Mark slipped over to the seedier side of town, losing himself in lust, in the shadows hiding his shame.[1] And Mark would be the first to admit:

> *"Everything in the world—the cravings of sinful man,*
> *the lust of his eyes and the boasting of what he has and does—*
> *comes not from the Father but from the world"*
> (1 JOHN 2:16).

A. What Is the Scope of Sexual Addiction?

The respected titles, the reviling behavior, just didn't add up. Not only was Mark respectfully addressed as Reverend Mark Laaser, he earned a PhD in psychology, tagging him also as *Dr.* Mark Laaser. Mark was supposed to be a model of spiritual discipline, an expert on assessing and controlling human behaviors. But his addiction got the best of him, and it was the demon that drove his life.

Since college, Mark had struggled with excessive "self sex," and in graduate school he started visiting X-rated bookstores and patronizing massage parlors, where he'd have sex with so-called "masseuses." These practices continued while he worked vocationally as a pastor and a counselor, but eventually Mark's nighttime and daytime worlds merged. Hurting, vulnerable women who came to his counseling practice became part of his sexual addiction as Mark initiated affairs with several of them.[2]

The scope of Mark's sexual addiction was staggering. Hiding behind his religious exterior, he was like a lion in cover:

> *"He lies in wait like a lion in cover; he lies in wait to catch the*
> *helpless; he catches the helpless and drags them off in his net"*
> (PSALM 10:9).

Sexual addiction is...

- *Compulsive*. A compulsive dependence on erotic excitement, resulting in detrimental patterns of thinking and behaving

- **Immoral**. The Greek noun *porneia*, translated as "fornication" or "immorality," is an umbrella word that covers all forms of sexual immorality.[3] We are told to "put to death, therefore, whatever belongs to your earthly nature: sexual immorality, impurity, lust, evil desires and greed, which is idolatry" (Colossians 3:5).

- **Enslaving**. The Greek word *douloo* means "to bring under bondage or enslave."[4] The Bible says, "They promise them freedom, while they themselves are slaves of depravity—for a man is a slave to whatever has mastered him" (2 Peter 2:19).

Have you ever wondered whether those who have been caught for years in the snare of sexual addiction can ever be set free? The simple answer is *yes*! God's Word gives absolute assurance that anyone can be set free. The Bible says,

> *"My eyes are ever on the LORD, for only*
> *he will release my feet from the snare"*
> (PSALM 25:15).

Sexual Desire vs. Lust

QUESTION: "At what point does the normal sexual desire turn into lust?"

ANSWER: It is natural to be attracted to someone, but unnatural to *sexualize* a person. When your mind moves from normal attraction to consuming passion to do a sexually-impure act, then you experience lust. The Bible says, "Do not let sin reign in your mortal body so that you obey its evil desires" (Romans 6:12).

B. What Are the Streets into Sexual Addiction?

At age 11, Mark discovered pictures of naked women, pictures today he would describe as soft porn. Mark was fixated. The images imprinted on his mind eventually preoccupied his thoughts. The young son of a preacher next found himself caught up in another vice: stealing *Playboy* magazines from the local drugstore.

"I knew that stealing was bad," Mark recalled. "But I was willing to go ahead with it because the high was so fantastic of what I was experiencing."[5]

For many people sinking in the sands of sexual addiction, their first introduction to pornography came during childhood. The idyllic picture of innocent children building castles in the sand is too often marred by the quicksand of childhood sexual abuse. The Bible says,

> *"If anyone causes one of these little ones who believe in me to sin,*
> *it would be better for him to have a large millstone hung*
> *around his neck and to be drowned in the depths of the sea"*
> (MATTHEW 18:6).

Some seemingly harmless avenues of modern entertainment are actually dangerous back alleys leading to sexual seduction.

- *Advertisements*—provocative lingerie, perfume, billboards, catalogs containing sensual images
- *"Adult"*—bookstores, peep show booths, nightclubs
- *Cards*—pornographic postcards, playing cards, photographs
- *Computers*—sexual games, Internet sites, chat rooms
- *Covert businesses*—escort services, massage parlors
- *Movies*—slasher films, R-rated and X-rated films
- *Music*—sexually explicit lyrics
- *Nudity*—topless bars, nudist camps and beaches
- *Printed literature*—pornographic books, magazines, cartoons, comics
- *Telephone*—900 numbers, phone sex, texting sexual images, and videos on cell phones
- *Television*—cable, soap operas, videos portraying sensuality and adultery

When you find yourself heading down the wrong street, follow this instruction from Proverbs:

> *"Above all else, guard your heart, for it is the wellspring of life.*
> *Put away perversity...Let your eyes look straight ahead,*
> *fix your gaze directly before you. Make level paths for your feet*
> *and take only ways that are firm. Do not swerve to the right*
> *or the left; keep your foot from evil"*
> (PROVERBS 4:23-27).

"Harmless" Porn

QUESTION: "Pornography is harmless, so why should it ever be illegal?"

ANSWER: Pornography is far from being harmless. Everyone who has been caught in the web of sexual addiction has obliterated that myth.

- Pornography is addictive and often leads to abuse of others.

- According to the Federal Bureau of Prisons, 76 percent of those convicted of an Internet-related crime against a child were also guilty of physically abusing children, with an average of 30 child victims each.[6]

- All of us would be wise to share the resolve of King David: "I will set before my eyes no vile thing" (Psalm 101:3).

C. What Is the Springboard into Sexual Quicksand?

But visualizing simply wouldn't suffice...

By high school, Mark took his sexual addiction to the next level, wanting to "act out" his sexual fantasies, wanting *more* sexual excitement. Mark continued to look at magazines, but he also began viewing pornographic videos, and his masturbation habits heightened.

Mark's one great hope—the one person he thought could pull him out of the sexual quicksand—was his high school sweetheart, Debra. Debra knew nothing of Mark's secret life, and Mark, believed marriage would help cure his crazed sexuality. He remembers thinking, *All this crazy stuff in the past—that will be over now. I'm getting married. I'll have a regular sexual partner.*[7]

But old habits die hard, and early into his marriage Mark found himself once again feeding his sexual appetite with pornography. The sexual quicksand eventually swallowed Mark, continuing 15 years into their marriage. Debra indeed would become one of many strong arms who helped to pull Mark out.

If only every addict had heeded the words in the very first book of the Bible: "If you do what is right, will you not be accepted? But if you do not do what is right, sin is crouching at your door; it desires to have you, but you must master it" (Genesis 4:7).

What Is Pornography?

- *Pornography* is the depiction of erotic activity for the purpose of arousing sexual, lustful excitement.[8]

- *Pornography* is from the Greek word *porne*, which means "prostitute or harlot."[9]

- *Pornography* debases sexuality and ridicules Christian values in favor of lust and immorality. The Bible says, "The body is not meant for sexual immorality, but for the Lord, and the Lord for the body" (1 Corinthians 6:13).

===== *Nudity and Porn* =====

QUESTION: "Since God created the human body as sexual, what's wrong with nudity and pornography?"

ANSWER: God ordained human sexuality for intimacy in marriage and for procreation, while pornography and the nudity found in it is designed simply to arouse indiscriminate sexual lust.

Jesus said, "You have heard that it was said, 'Do not commit adultery.' But I tell you that anyone who looks at a woman lustfully has already committed adultery with her in his heart" (Matthew 5:27-28).

What Is Soft-core Porn?[10]

— *Soft-core porn* is the depiction of adult nudity or nonexplicit sexual activity between adults.

— *Soft-core porn* is usually not illegal.

Regardless of what man says is legal, it is always wise to know and obey God's laws and to follow only those who do. Exodus 23:2 says, "Do not follow the crowd in doing wrong."

===== *Objection to Legal Porn* =====

QUESTION: "Since adult bookstores, X-rated movies, and other types of adult pornography are usually legal, why should anyone object to them?"

ANSWER: Sadly, legality is not synonymous with morality.

• Just because something is legal doesn't make it morally right.

• Lawmakers often respond to pressures of lobbyists or the most vocal special interest groups, settling for less than the excellence set by God's moral law. Sadly, many whose business it is to make laws do not realize or believe "we must obey God rather than men!" (Acts 5:29).

===== *Medical Books vs. Porn* =====

QUESTION: "Are all sexually explicit images pornographic?"

ANSWER: No. A medical book containing sexually explicit pictures designed to teach or inform others would not be considered pornographic. A presentation of the human body from an artist's viewpoint may not necessarily be considered pornographic either. Consider Michelangelo's *David*. Proverbs 17:24 says, "A discerning man keeps wisdom in view, but a fool's eyes wander to the ends of the earth."

What Is Hard-core Porn?

- *Hard-core porn* is the depiction of explicit or bizarre sexual activity that is clearly offensive and blatantly degrading to human beings.
- *Hard-core porn* is the street term for *obscene*, which means that it is illegal.[11]
- *Hard-core porn* can include urinating, defecating, or vomiting on another.

> *"Let us behave decently, as in the daytime, not in orgies and drunkenness, not in sexual immorality and debauchery, not in dissension and jealousy. Rather, clothe yourselves with the Lord Jesus Christ, and do not think about how to gratify the desires of the sinful nature"*
> (ROMANS 13:13-14).

PORNOGRAPHIC MATERIAL	GOD'S MANDATE
Heterosexual porn depicts explicit sex acts between males and females, including oral and group sex.	*"Marriage should be honored by all, and the marriage bed kept pure, for God will judge the adulterer and all the sexually immoral"* (HEBREWS 13:4).
Homosexual porn depicts explicit sex acts between members of the same sex.	*"Do not lie with a man as one lies with a woman; that is detestable"* (LEVITICUS 18:22).
Kiddie porn depicts children having sex with adults and with other children. Though illegal to own or produce, child porn is especially used by pedophiles. (Pedophilia is a "sexual perversion in which children are the preferred sexual object."[12])	*"If anyone causes one of these little ones who believe in me to sin, it would be better for him to be thrown into the sea with a large millstone tied around his neck"* (MARK 9:42).

Bestiality porn depicts sexual activity between humans and animals, such as dogs, horses, pigs, or donkeys.

"Cursed is the man who has sexual relations with any animal" (DEUTERONOMY 27:21).

Sexual-devices porn depicts the use of "toys," such as mousetraps, fishhooks, and rings on the sexual anatomy. In bondage sex, devices such as handcuffs, wrist cuffs, ankle cuffs, bedpost straps, passion paddles, and chains are used to depict dominance and submission.

We should line up with King David's conviction: *"Men of perverse heart shall be far from me; I will have nothing to do with evil"* (PSALM 101:4).

Sadomasochistic porn depicts torture of all kinds, including bondage, rape, mutilation, and murder. Slasher films and snuff films are X-rated movies that contain perverted sex acts and extreme violence, and culminate in murder.

"Don't you know that you yourselves are God's temple and that God's Spirit lives in you? If anyone destroys God's temple, God will destroy him; for God's temple is sacred, and you are that temple" (1 CORINTHIANS 3:16-17).

Classification of Illegal Porn

QUESTION: "What determines whether sexual material is classified as illegal pornography?"

ANSWER: Material classified as illegal varies from country to country. However, in most countries, that which is obscene is considered illegal. In the 1973 case *Miller v. California*, the United States Supreme Court established a three-part test to define what is legally obscene.

- **Pornography that is obscene...**[13]
    - Appeals to inordinately lustful appetites as understood by the community
    - Depicts clearly offensive sexual conduct as defined by state law
    - Lacks serious literary, realistic, political, or scientific value

- **Obscenity** appeals to, and even urges, vileness instead of virtue
- **Obscenity** degrades the value of human beings

> *"Among you there must not be even a hint of sexual immorality,*
> *or of any kind of impurity, or of greed, because these are*
> *improper for God's holy people. Nor should there be obscenity,*
> *foolish talk or coarse joking, which are out of place"*
> (EPHESIANS 5:3-4).

Legislating Morality and Porn

QUESTION: "Since we can't legislate morality, why is there so much concern about pornography?"

ANSWER: We can legislate morality, and we do in the sense that most laws deal with morality. Biblical laws, such as those against murder, lying, and stealing, are seen in the laws of every civilized society.

- Laws generally reflect the morality of those who make them (but laws can never legislate morality in the hearts of people).
- Laws help restrain immoral behavior (but they have no power to make people moral). Ultimately, who would desire to live in a society where morality and the legal system were entirely disconnected? No one would feel secure living in a community that provided no legal recourse against robbery or assault. So, why would anyone choose to allow the porn industry to produce sexually exploitive products that are like weapons that assault human dignity and steal minds, hearts, and money?

Every legal code in human history has been undergirded by the (written or unwritten) moral code of the community, and laws reflect society's morals:

> *"You shall not murder... You shall not steal... You shall not*
> *give false testimony against your neighbor"*
> (EXODUS 20:13,15-16).

D. What Is the Difference between Male and Female Sexual Addiction?

Here they come again: vows of "I'm never going to do that again!" But they vanish quickly and repeatedly as the addict plunges once again into a perverted pool of sexual pleasure. Strugglers ultimately come to believe there is no hope. They feel that they are locked into a behavior that will dog them the rest of their lives.

Male and female addicts respond in different ways to their struggle. Female addicts often find coping strategies to manage their despair and shame. For example, they clean compulsively, shop, or pour themselves into family activities. Some turn to the church, serving in a variety of ways, while others will exercise, eat, or drink in excess.[14] Each struggler is looking for something that will at least temporarily break the cycle of sexual addiction.

By contrast, men seem to be able to compartmentalize their lives more easily. They think, *As long as I perform well at my job, then I'm okay.* At least, that's the justification they give.

=========== *Contrast Male and Female Sex Addicts* ===========

MALE ADDICTS	FEMALE ADDICTS
• Men seek sexual passion.	• Women seek closeness and connection.
• Men are less relational—not necessarily involved with others.	• Women are more relational—usually involved with others.
• Men tend to involve spouses.	• Women involve other men—not spouses.
• Men are more apt to seek out prostitutes.	• Women seek out acquaintances.
• Men may "flash" themselves to others.	• Women may flaunt themselves before others.
• Men are more accepted by others.	• Women are more condemned by others.
• Men have many available support groups.	• Women have few available support groups.
• Men are less likely to lose their jobs.	• Women are more likely to lose their jobs.
• Men are called *studs*.	• Women are called *sluts*.
• Men are less likely to trade or sell sex.	• Women are more likely to trade or sell sex.
• Men don't use uncharacteristically foul language.	• Women often explode with foul language when alone or in a recovery group.

HUSBANDS OF FEMALE ADDICTS	WIVES OF MALE ADDICTS
• Husbands are more likely to divorce their wives.	• Wives are more likely to remain married to their husbands.
• Husbands are encouraged to divorce.	• Wives are encouraged to forgive.
• Husbands feel greater shame.	• Wives feel greater guilt.
• Husbands are viewed as victims of their wife's addiction.	• Wives are viewed as the cause of their husband's addiction.
• Husbands are slow to acknowledge their own dysfunction.	• Wives are quick to acknowledge their own dysfunction.
• Husbands are reluctant to seek help.	• Wives are eager to seek help.
• Husbands react more with anger.	• Wives react more with sadness.
• Husbands become controlling.	• Wives become depressed.

Who ultimately is responsible for a spouse's sexual addiction? Who is accountable for any act of sin? The addict is not to blame his or her spouse. The Bible makes it plain: "Each of us will give an account of himself to God" (Romans 14:12).

II. CHARACTERISTICS OF SEXUAL ADDICTION

As a little girl, Marnie Ferree was exposed to an unhealthy, untrue, and unbiblical equation: sex=love.

From age 5 to 20, she was indoctrinated in a skewed sexual code of conduct:[15]

- Significant relationships are supposed to be sexual.

- Sexuality is powerful and should be used to control and manipulate others.

- No one could be counted on to nurture or protect her.

The man who spewed forth these lies wasn't a sexual predator who randomly plucked Marnie off a playground. He was considered a dear family friend, and to Marnie, *a beloved father figure*. It wasn't until Marnie was well into her thirties that she came to understand the diabolical deception behind his corrupt conduct, and it took her just as long to realize that this alternative, nurturing father figure was actually her abuser.[16]

The twisted messages Marnie received about sexuality, her neediness in a dysfunctional family, and her confusing experiences during her formative years all propelled Marnie down a path of sexual addiction that almost dead-ended in suicide. The Bible gives this word of warning:

> *"There is a way that seems right to a man,*
> *but in the end it leads to death"*
> (Proverbs 14:12).

A. What Are the Characteristics of Sexual Addiction?

The unholy equation of sex=love had been firmly planted in Marnie's mind, and during her teen years, she knew multiple sexual partners.

If Marnie wanted to feel loved, *she had to have sex.* If Marnie wanted to feel significant, *she had to have sex.* If Marnie wanted to feel secure, *she had to have sex.* "I was trying to get nonsexual needs met sexually, and that was the only way I knew how to meet those needs," she recalled.

Marnie's first marriage was anything but monogamous and ended in divorce. Her second marriage was on the same track until a diagnosis of cervical cancer caused by a sexually transmitted disease brought her to a screeching halt. Marnie almost died from surgical complications, but as soon as her body healed, her sexual addiction went back into overdrive.

Marnie led the proverbial double life. Some knew her as sensual, but many perceived her as spiritual. Marnie taught in Sunday school, sang in the choir, led a women's Bible study, and published her Christian writings. "I was wracked with shame and tried time and time again to stop," Marnie said painfully. "On the outside, I looked like I had it all together. On the inside, I was a total wreck."

The double life Marnie was leading totally demoralized her, and in suicidal despair, she finally sought help.

What Constitutes a Sexual Addiction?

Not everyone who is sexually immoral is sexually addicted. While many adulterers and all rapists are sex offenders, such offenders are not all sex addicts. (Rape is an act of violence, a power play emanating from anger.) What constitutes a sexual addiction? Within the heart of every addict is a sense of shame—shame because they feel unlovable, unworthy, and unwanted—shame resulting from repeated failure and abandonment. This shame within an addict produces predictable sexual beliefs and behavior. Proverbs 18:3 says that "with shame comes disgrace."

Is your sexual activity...

S—Secretive . . . . not within normal cultural boundaries and filled with guilt and shame (living a double life)?

H—Hollow . . . . not a relationship with a spouse, but a relationship focused on sexual passion (prioritizing sexual passion over people)?

A—Abusive . . . . not uplifting to yourself or to others, but degrading to both (exploiting others and debasing yourself)?

M—Mood-altering . not facing difficult feelings, but seeking an emotional quick fix (using sexual passion for comfort or to avoid working through painful emotions)?

E—Essential . . . . not believing you can live without frequent sex (convincing yourself that sex is the most important thing in life)?

Me? A Sex Addict?

How do you know whether you have a sexual addiction or just a high sex drive? Answer these questions with a check mark (✓) in order to assess whether the word *addict* applies to you.

☐ Do you keep your sexual behavior secret from those closest to you?

☐ Do you feel driven to have sex with people you wouldn't normally choose or in places you wouldn't normally be?

☐ Do you habitually look for anything sexually arousing in newspapers, magazines, and other media?

☐ Do your sexual fantasies inhibit intimate bonding within your closest relationship?

☐ Do you often want to get away from your sex partner after having sex?

☐ Do you frequently feel guilt, shame, or remorse following a sexual encounter?

☐ Do you hate your body and at times avoid touching it?

☐ Does every new relationship end in the same destructive manner as past relationships?

☐ Does your sexual behavior require more variety and increased frequency to bring the same level of excitement you formerly experienced?

☐ Does your sexual behavior ever put you in danger of being arrested?

☐ Does your sexual behavior compromise your spiritual values and growth?

☐ Does your sexual behavior put you at risk for unwanted pregnancy, violence, or sexually transmitted diseases?

☐ Does your sexual behavior ever leave you feeling lonely, isolated, or alienated from others?

☐ Does your sexual behavior cause you to feel helpless, hopeless, and at times suicidal?

If you have a continual obsession with sex that results in compulsive sexual behavior—despite risking loss of marriage, health, employment, or freedom—you are a sex addict. The Bible gives this vivid description of strugglers entrapped in sexual addiction:

> *"God gave them over in the sinful desires of their hearts to sexual impurity for the degrading of their bodies with one another... God gave them over to shameful lusts. Even their women exchanged natural relations for unnatural ones. In the same way the men also abandoned natural relations with women and were inflamed with lust for one another. Men committed indecent acts with other men, and received in themselves the due penalty for their perversion"*
> (ROMANS 1:24,26-27).

B. What Is the Spiral of Sexual Addiction?

Abandonment is woven throughout the spiral of sexual addiction. Every single sex addict, a full 100 percent of cases, has experienced some form of abandonment, whether physical, emotional, sexual, spiritual, or a combination of those factors.

Marnie's abandonment issues began with the death of her mother from colon cancer when she was just three years old. What compounded her sense of abandonment was that her mother was never mentioned or talked about in the family, creating a further disconnect for Marnie.

"I have no category for 'mom,' or even for 'mother,'" Marnie shared. "I had no sense of the person who was my mother, of her likes and dislikes, her hopes and fears, her dreams and disappointments."

Marnie also experienced abandonment from her father, who traveled extensively and was away from home most of the time. Realizing her own craving for connection, Marnie described sexual addiction as "quieting our spirits' ache for perfect connection."

THE DOWNWARD SPIRAL OF SEXUAL ADDICTION

- *Curiosity* is a seemingly harmless temptation to view people as sexual objects. If the sexual temptation is not rejected, but rather continually viewed, then the repeated sexual viewing becomes a habit.

  > *"Each one is tempted when, by his own evil*
  > *desire, he is dragged away and enticed"*
  > (JAMES 1:14).

- *Addiction* is a recurring stimulus in the brain. When a person experiences significant stimulation with highly sexualized images, the hormone epinephrine (or adrenaline) is secreted into the bloodstream by the adrenal gland. Epinephrine stamps emotional memories into the brain. These memories continue to resurface as flashbacks—regardless of the struggler's desire to forget. In addition, powerful, pleasure-producing chemicals are released during the sex act that are highly addictive (the same chemicals that are released during cocaine use!).

  > *"Do not be deceived: God cannot be*
  > *mocked. A man reaps what he sows"*
  > (GALATIANS 6:7).

- *Compulsive masturbation* is a response of sexual self-comfort to relieve the arousal. This act becomes part of a sexual ritual. This compulsion keeps the struggler feeling enslaved to masturbation.

  > *"Jesus replied, 'I tell you the truth,*
  > *everyone who sins is a slave to sin'"*
  > (JOHN 8:34).

- **Escalation** is the need for more explicit or shocking sexuality in order to be sexually stimulated.

  "Having lost all sensitivity, they have given themselves
  over to sensuality so as to indulge in every kind of
  impurity, with a continual lust for more"
  (Ephesians 4:19).

- **Desensitization** is when the shocking sexuality no longer produces the same stimulation; therefore, the level required for stimulation escalates higher and higher.

  "Are they ashamed of their loathsome conduct? No, they have
  no shame at all; they do not even know how to blush"
  (Jeremiah 6:15).

- **Acting out** is a compulsion to do (to enact) what has been seen and imagined. The acting out feels necessary because the visual experience is no longer satisfying in itself.

  "The acts of the sinful nature are obvious: sexual
  immorality, impurity and debauchery"
  (Galatians 5:19).

- **Despair** is the feeling of disgust that comes in response to the sexual behavior, and the struggler feels a sense of utter hopelessness with regard to any possibility of change.

  "I do not understand what I do. For what I want
  to do I do not do, but what I hate I do"
  (Romans 7:15).

Many people assume certain addictions can never be overcome. However, any struggler can be rescued from any addiction. The Bible says,

  "No temptation has seized you except what is common to
  man. And God is faithful; he will not let you be tempted
  beyond what you can bear. But when you are tempted, he will
  also provide a way out so that you can stand up under it"
  (1 Corinthians 10:13).

C. What Are the Stages of Sexual Addiction?

For women, sexual addiction tends to be more relational in nature than for men. Marnie's sexual addiction was manifested in numerous affairs during both of her marriages. She was always searching for that "perfect" connection. Under the umbrella of sexual addiction, women typically have been romance or fantasy addicts, consumed with a real or imagined Prince Charming with whom they can have an ideal relationship.

Technology has many women on a slippery slope when it comes to sexual addiction, and many female sex addicts now find themselves at a further stage: engaging in cybersex to connect with their Prince Charming. Almost 80 percent of women who participate in sexually oriented chat rooms eventually meet their online partners there.[17]

According to Marnie, there often is a double standard associated with sexual addiction. When a man is a sex addict, people will excuse him with a "men will be men" mentality, whereas when a woman is a sex addict, crass and hurtful labels are ascribed to her. The resulting shame for a woman can be enormous, Marnie observed. The Psalms describe this kind of painful shame, of reproach, of derision and disgrace:

> *"My disgrace is before me all day long,*
> *and my face is covered with shame"*
> (PSALM 44:15).

═══════════ *Stages of Sexual Addiction*[18] ═══════════

ACTIVITIES

Stage 1	*Stage 2*	*Stage 3*
• Pornography	• Obscene phone calls	• Child molestation
• Masturbation	• Voyeurism (watching others, being a Peeping Tom)	• Pedophilia
• Promiscuity		• Incest
• Homosexuality		• Rape
• Prostitution	• Exhibitionism	• Sadomasochistic sex
• Cross-dressing	• Sexual harassment	
• Fetishism		
• Sex talk phone lines/ chat rooms		

CONSEQUENCES

Stage 1 Low risk	Stage 2 Moderate risk	Stage 3 High risk
• Some behavior illegal	• Always illegal	• Always illegal
• Occasional job threat	• Possible job loss	• Probable job loss
• Usually considered "victimless"	• Always involves a victim	• Always involves a victim

Do not be deceived. Activities thought harmless by the world's standards can be deadly to the body, soul, and spirit. The Bible says, "Do not deceive yourselves. If any one of you thinks he is wise by the standards of this age, he should become a 'fool' so that he may become wise. For the wisdom of this world is foolishness in God's sight" (1 Corinthians 3:18-19).

D. What Is the Cycle of Sexual Addiction?

The last stop in the cycle of sexual addiction is the same for each and every addict: *self-condemnation*. Those who were once held captive by the power of sexual addiction but who were later set free can identify these three distinct components of their journey: The Setup, The Sequence, and The Solution.

The Setup

No one lives with more shame, isolation, and fear of alienation than the sex addict. Addicts believe that they can't help the way they are. Each time they surrender to sexual temptation, sin's tenacious grip gets a stronger hold on their hearts. Sex addicts believe that the only solution to getting their love needs met is through sexual stimulation. Their minds and bodies are held captive to sexual passion.

> *"What I do is not the good I want to do; no, the evil*
> *I do not want to do—this I keep on doing"*
> (ROMANS 7:19).

- **Worthless Feelings**
  - "I can't control my sexual urges."
  - "I feel like a failure."
  - "I'm not a good person."
- **Withdrawal**
  - "I can't trust people."

- "If they knew what I've done, they would be disgusted."
- "If they knew the real me, they would reject me."

- **Warped Assumptions**
  - "Sex is my greatest need in life."
  - "Sex is the solution to my need for love."
  - "Sex is the solace for all my pain."

- **Wrong Actions**
  - Purchasing explicit pornographic material
  - Pursuing sexual relationships outside of marriage
  - Practicing illicit sex with multiple partners

> *"All a man's ways seem right to him,*
> *but the LORD weighs the heart"*
> (PROVERBS 21:2).

The Sequence

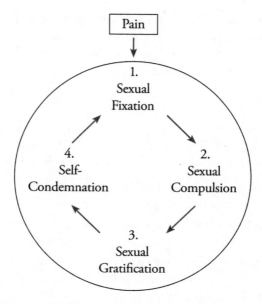

> *"After desire has conceived, it gives birth to sin;*
> *and sin, when it is full-grown, gives birth to death"*
> (JAMES 1:15).

1. Sexual Fixation[19]
The struggler enters into an erotic, trancelike state in which obsessing on sex becomes a sedative for emotional pain.

2. Sexual Compulsion
The struggler engages in compulsive, ritualistic routines that heighten the excitement and intensify sexual arousal (cruising, pornography, stalking).

3. Sexual Gratification
The struggler—feeling a sense of sexual intoxication with a total loss of self-control—now commits the actual sex act.

4. Self-Condemnation
The struggler soon feels engulfed by shame, condemnation, and hopelessness. To find relief from painful self-condemnation and self-contempt, the addict escapes into another fixation on sex, and the sexual cycle perpetuates itself—it starts all over again. The Bible warns of the destruction that is sowed from these kinds of seeds:

> *"The one who sows to please his sinful nature, from that nature will reap destruction; the one who sows to please the Spirit, from the Spirit will reap eternal life"*
> (Galatians 6:8).

The Solution
The last thing sexual strugglers need is rejection, although rejection is usually the first thing that occurs when they are found out. Strugglers who live their lives emotionally isolated because of their fear of discovery need...

- *Emotional connection* with caring people who will offer *unconditional love and emotional support* no matter what
- *Heart-to-heart sharing* with people who are safe enough that a struggler can *tell them anything* without fear of rejection
- *Friend-to-friend commitment* with people who can be counted on in both happy and hard times and who will commit to *lifelong relationships*
- *Spiritual relationships* with people who are mature in the Lord, have an active prayer life, and are willing to *provide spiritual guidance and support*

Because sexual addiction is an obsessive relationship with erotic passion itself, healing comes through secure relationships with loving people. Sexual addiction is an intimacy disorder; therefore, strugglers desperately need healthy intimacy. A safe place for addicts to begin opening up and moving out of their secret addictions is an accountability group of fellow strugglers or friends—ultimately, people who can "hate the sin, but truly love the sinner." The Bible tells us,

> *"There is a friend who sticks closer than a brother"*
> (PROVERBS 18:24).

E. What Are Forms of Female Sexual Addiction?

If you pull back the curtain on female sexual addiction, you will find that it has different faces and plays different roles. This often makes this addiction difficult to identify, and easy to deny. Sexual addiction can range from mild to severe, involve one person or many, be enjoyed or just endured, provide a hideout or an escape. Sexual addiction is about connection, closeness, or comfort by "medicating" emotional pain. But *it is never about sex*!

Sex is merely the means to an end but is never the end. Sex is what is *given* in an attempt to *get* what is lacking. And because sex is not the ultimate end, this addiction often remains unidentified and untreated. After all, how can a person be addicted to sex when it is merely a means of transportation to a desired destination?

For Marnie Ferree—who was totally unaware that she was wrestling with abuse and abandonment issues—the many sexual affairs she pursued were supposed to give her the affirmation and sense of significance she so desperately longed for. But instead of building her up, her sexual addiction tore her down. Instead of feeling significant, Marnie ultimately felt totally insignificant—and eventually, even suicidal. Sex is just as addictive as any drug a person might use in an attempt to escape pain. It produces just as much of a high. In truth, for the sex addict, the "means" becomes the mean master, the terrible tyrant, the diabolical destroyer. Yet most do not have a clue about their real struggle.

> *"The waywardness of the simple will kill them,*
> *and the complacency of fools will destroy them"*
> (PROVERBS 1:32).

FORMS OF FEMALE SEXUAL ADDICTION

- **The Adulteress**
  - Has a "relationship" or "love" addiction

- Has established a precedence of promiscuity
  - Has engaged in numerous affairs
  - Has multiple sequential or simultaneous relationships
- **The Anorexic**
  - Is no longer sexually acting out and is disinterested in sex with her husband to the point that she makes him sex-starved as well
  - Is desirous of engaging in numerous sexual encounters, but never with her spouse
  - Is not interested in acting out sexually with anyone, but instead obsesses over imaginary sex partners or fantasy relationships
  - Is no longer acting out sexually or having imaginary sex, but has transferred her addiction to religion and is becoming more and more rigid
- **The Co-addict**
  - Has an insatiable desire for increased sexual stimulation with other sex addicts
  - Has a continual string of enmeshed relationships with other addicts while denying her own obsession with sex
  - Has explosive relationships with sex partners who actively participate in compulsive, pornographic sex with her
  - Has a continual sexual preoccupation with how her sexually addicted husband acts out with her
- **The Controller**
  - Seeks power by using her body sexually to exercise influence over men
  - Seeks power by attracting affluent men and then attaching herself to them
  - Seeks power by having men "grovel at her feet" or "eat from her hand"
  - Seeks power over all sex partners through her relationship, romance, or fantasy addictions
- **The Cyclist**
  - Has only certain periods of time when she is compulsively acting out

- Has some long periods of time when she doesn't engage in sexually addictive behavior at all
- Has sex sprees called "acting out," during which she binges on sexual activity similar to the binge alcoholic or binge eater
- Has starvation sprees called "acting in," during which she denies herself any sexual activity and may even convince herself she is "cured," until the cycle begins again

- **The Dreamer**
  - Fabricates romantic relationships in her mind and avoids acting out sexually
  - Fabricates the belief that a man who exhibits common courtesy toward her has never-ending love for her
  - Fabricates having a fantasy family with a passing stranger, a new acquaintance, or a neighbor
  - Fabricates a fantasy life to avoid real life and obsesses about it to the point of being addicted to it

- **The Exhibitionist**
  - Uses her body to get an adrenaline rush by sexually arousing others
  - Uses her body to attract attention, acquire accolades, or achieve approval from others
  - Uses her body to show off her titillating attire and sexually seductive maneuvers
  - Uses her body to gain power over others by stimulating sexual desire within them, but not allowing them sexual access to her

- **The Looker**
  - Is generally a young woman immersed in Internet porn, cybersex, or phone sex because of the accessibility, affordability, and the anonymity they offer
  - Is particularly attracted to the relational aspects of Internet pornography (the "crack cocaine" of sex addiction)
  - Is customarily involved in chat rooms, forming powerful relationships with people online and then generally progressing to physically acting out with them in person

  – Is hooked by the power of pornography and any visual stimulus just as much as the average male

- **The Romantic**
  – Is primarily focused on the pursuit and possession of a particular prey
  – Is mesmerized by the feeling of falling in love, rather than the joy of the relationship itself
  – Is enthralled by the intense, seductive cat-and-mouse chase
  – Is disinterested in the relationship once the pursuit is over and the prey is snared

- **The Self-stimulator**
  – Chooses to masturbate within the world of pornography, cyber-sex, sexual fantasy, or without any outside stimulation whatsoever
  – Chooses self-stimulation because of early sexual highs from child abuse or self-exploration
  – Chooses to evade problems, ease pain, or elevate mood through habitual masturbation
  – Chooses self-sex over marital sex to ignite her sexual desire for someone other than her husband, to express anger toward him, or to have leverage over him

- **The Swapper**
  – Trades sexual activity for special favors, such as good grades in school from teachers, promotions at work from employers, or help with parental responsibilities from husbands
  – Trades sexual satisfaction for expensive gifts or money spent on entertainment
  – Trades sex for physical protection in a dangerous neighborhood, community, or country
  – Trades sex regularly for the sense of satisfaction that her body has some value to others

Life is a series of choices. Just as a struggler is free to choose slavery to addiction, that same struggler is free to choose what the Bible calls slavery to righteousness—being compelled to do whatever is right in God's sight. The result of the first choice is death, and the result of the second is clearly life.

God would not tell you to do something you eventually couldn't do. Notice how the Word of God squarely addresses these two distinct choices and their vastly different consequences:

> *"Just as you used to offer the parts of your body in slavery to impurity so now offer them in slavery to righteousness leading to holiness. When you were slaves to sin... What benefit did you reap at that time from the things you are now ashamed of? Those things result in death! But now that you have been set free from sin and have become slaves to God, the benefit you reap leads to holiness, and the result is eternal life"*
> (ROMANS 6:19-21).

F. Could You Be a Female Sex Addict?

Being familiar with the definitions, characteristics, and causes of sexual addiction makes it fairly easy for objective, honest people to identify its presence and pressure in their lives. All addictions leave their prey feeling paralyzed and unable to move away from their pull so that they may gain freedom from their enslavement. To do so requires immense personal effort, immersion in a recovery program, and immeasurable hope in God—hope that banishes fear and shame, hope that brings security and safety.

> *"If you put away the sin that is in your hand and allow no evil to dwell in your tent, then you will lift up your face without shame; you will stand firm and without fear. You will surely forget your trouble, recalling it only as waters gone by. Life will be brighter than noonday, and darkness will become like morning. You will be secure, because there is hope; you will look about you and take your rest in safety"*
> (JOB 11:14-18).

The first step toward becoming healthy is identifying what within us is unhealthy.

SEXUAL ADDICTION SELF-TEST

1. I sometimes wonder if my sex-related thoughts and actions are typical in comparison with other women.
2. I have been unsuccessful in trying to stop or even decrease unacceptable sexual thoughts and actions.
3. I use sex fantasies or sex encounters to ease stress and anxiety or to lessen emotional pain and loneliness.
4. I experience guilt, shame, regret, or sadness after having real or even imagined sexual encounters that do not involve my spouse.
5. I feel more and more compelled to engage in sexual activity either mentally or physically.
6. I cannot have sex with my spouse without its being tainted by my sinful sexual activity.
7. I have to fantasize or think about past sexual encounters to help me experience sexual satisfaction.
8. I find myself becoming mentally or physically involved with one person after another in a quest to find my one true soul mate.
9. I truly believe a special someone exists who will one day satisfy all of my sexual longings, and then I will no longer need other sexual outlets or experiences.
10. I absolutely must have someone in my life to meet my emotional and sexual needs, no matter the cost or the risk.
11. I have put myself and my loved ones in harm's way in my quest for the perfect relationship or sex partner.
12. I have had more trouble focusing on and finishing tasks since my sexual preoccupation has increased.
13. I have suffered unpleasant repercussions and discouragement as a result of my inappropriate sexual activity.
14. I was sexually exploited when I was young.

If you answered only a small number of these questions in the affirmative, you would be wise to get involved in a sex addiction recovery program and to seek help and loving support from both God and trustworthy people.

*"Sin shall not be your master, because you
are not under law, but under grace"*
(ROMANS 6:14).

III. CAUSES OF SEXUAL ADDICTION

She is a woman who has been wounded by the sin of sexual betrayal and has come to understand that it has nothing to do with sex. She is the wife of Dr. Mark Laaser.

Debra Laaser now knows that sexually addictive behaviors—such as viewing pornography or attending strip clubs—are only the tip of the iceberg. And the humongous mass of the proverbial iceberg lodged deeply within the soul of a sexually addicted person is weighed down with pain.

"I know today that Mark's soul was filled with pain before I even met him."[20] Childhood sexual abuse and exposure to erotic material at an early age were contributors to sexual fixation and addiction. If sexuality is awakened in children, then sexual acts are often mistakenly associated with love and nurturing, and a child doesn't have the discernment to distinguish the difference. As adults, sexuality is then equated with a nurturing comfort that helps to deal with the stresses of life.

Key components were in place to "birth" a sexual addiction: childhood sexual abuse, a nonnurturing mother, and overexposure to sensual images.[21]

When it comes to sexual addiction, we've all asked ourselves, *Why did I do that?* The answer is simple: Our beliefs "birth" our behaviors. The messages we received in childhood, especially those regarding our own worth, relationships, and sexuality, formed our beliefs. These beliefs are powerful, for from them come all of our priorities, choices, habits, and, yes, even our addictions.[22]

> *"A simple man believes anything,*
> *but a prudent man gives thought to his steps"*
> (PROVERBS 14:15).

A. What Leads to the Birth of an Addiction?

Everyone has three inner needs: the needs for love, significance, and security.[23] If these God-given needs were not met in childhood, then your beliefs reflect that painful lack of nurturing, and you will attempt to fill the void in some way or another. The *male* sex addict believes that *sexual passion* or *sexual power* is comforting and nurturing, whereas the *female* sex addict believes *sexual connection* is comforting and nurturing. Thus both believe that a sexual experience will meet their needs for love, significance, and security.

Because people have not been dependable, the addict does not risk a relationship with a person, but enters into a *relationship with passion/connection*. People and things are merely the stimuli used. Because the addict desires passion/connection, their relationship is with passion/connection. The Bible says,

> *"At one time we too were foolish, disobedient,*
> *deceived and enslaved by all kinds of passions"*
> (Titus 3:3).

Considering the Need for Love

BASIC BELIEF: "I am unlovable."

- "If you really knew me, you wouldn't love me."
- "I am bad—bad things should happen to me."
  - Feeling that no one really cares
  - Feeling that people care only if they can get something

RESULT: "I must be *powerful* and *in control* to protect myself."

- Enters into a "relationship with sex" not based on love

EXAMPLES:

- A relationship with passion, but using a wife
- A relationship with passion, but using a prostitute
- A relationship with passion/connection, but using a child

Yet, regarding the need for love, God says, "I have loved you with an everlasting love; I have drawn you with loving-kindness" (Jeremiah 31:3).

Considering the Need for Significance

BASIC BELIEF: "I am unworthy."

- "If you really knew me, you wouldn't value me."
- "I have failed; I'm a failure."
  - Feeling insignificant
  - Feeling at fault for everything

RESULT: "I must be in *charge* to protect myself."

- Enters into a "relationship with sex" that can't threaten the addict's significance

EXAMPLES:

- A relationship with passion by being a Peeping Tom
- A relationship with passion by being a flasher
- A relationship with passion by being a rapist

Yet, regarding the need for significance, the Bible says, "He made us accepted in the Beloved" (Ephesians 1:6 NKJV).

Considering the Need for Security

BASIC BELIEF: "I am unwanted."

- "If you really knew me, you would abandon me."
- "I've lost hope in people—I'm hopeless."
  - Can't depend on others to meet my needs
  - Can't risk rejection

RESULT: "I must be *self-sufficient* to protect myself."

- Enters into a "relationship with sex" so that security won't be threatened

EXAMPLES:

- A relationship with passion by looking at pornography
- A relationship with passion by staring at a stripper
- A relationship with passion by watching a peep show

Yet regarding the need for security, the Bible says, "No power in the sky above or in the earth below—indeed, nothing in all creation will ever be able to separate us from the love of God that is revealed in Christ Jesus our Lord" (Romans 8:39 NLT).

B. What Are the Double Delusions of Sexual Addiction?

Debra Laaser has a very clear message she wants to send to every spouse who is a victim of sexual betrayal: *It's not about you.*[24]

The marriage partners who view pornography or have affairs are using sexual behavior as a coping mechanism to deal with painful feelings, and it is a sinful choice. Sex addicts doubly delude themselves into thinking that sinful sexual behavior will provide the comfort and connection they're so desperately seeking. But instead, all they're left with is guilt, shame, and a void that can best be described as a hole in the soul.

Delusions are unrelenting false beliefs about yourself and others. In other words, being delusional means you believe your own lies. The faulty beliefs of sex addicts enable them to manufacture and believe their own elaborate defense systems. This interactive process between beliefs and denials results in seriously impaired thinking, moving them further and further from reality. The Bible says,

"The integrity of the upright guides them,
but the unfaithful are destroyed by their duplicity"
(PROVERBS 11:3).

THE DOUBLE DELUSIONS OF SEXUAL ADDICTION[25]

The addict lives in two worlds: the outward appearance
of normalcy, and the inward state of depravity.

Unbridled Beliefs	*Distorted Defenses*
All people and places, all joys and pains are seen by the addict through sexual lenses.	Addicts must employ an army of defenses in an effort to not lose face when their behavior is attacked by others or by their own conscience.

JUSTIFICATIONS

- Sex is the source of excitement.
- Sex is the balm for abuse.

- "I have to have sex."
- "I was molested as a child."

BLAME SHIFTING

- Sex is the remedy for rejection.
- Sex is the payment for performing well.

- "You're so unresponsive."
- "My boss is too demanding."

EXCUSES

- Sex is the panacea for pain.
- Sex is the salve for stress.

- "I have never felt loved."
- "I have to find ways to relax."

ARGUMENTS

- Sex is the antidote to anger.
- Sex is the light of my life.

- "You're out to get me."
- "She really did want it; she liked it."

RATIONALIZATIONS

- Sex is the treatment for tension.
- Sex is the answer to anxiety.

- "I just have to experience release."
- "I have to relieve the pressure."

DENIALS

- Sex is the basis for being.
- Sex is the key to comfort.

- "I didn't do anything wrong."
- "I didn't hurt anyone."

"How long will you love delusions and seek false gods?"
(PSALM 4:2).

C. What Is the Root Cause of Sexual Addiction?

Debra Laaser and Marnie Ferree both agree that the clinical term *sexual addiction* really is not the best label for compulsive sexual behavior.

They much prefer *intimacy disorder*, with Debra describing it as "a need to connect at a deep emotional and spiritual level with one's spouse and with others but a lack of the skills to do so. The problem, then, is much deeper than sexual impurity itself. It is about a yearning for something more and a determination to find more—even at emotional, spiritual, and relational prices no human being can afford."[26]

Marnie believes intimacy disorder is a more precise clinical term for sex addicts because they are looking for acceptance, approval, and affection. But ultimately, sex is a false substitute for intimacy.[27]

WRONG BELIEF:

"The most important thing in my life is sex. I will do whatever is necessary to get my sexual needs met."

RIGHT BELIEF:

"The most important thing in my life is to be changed by an intimate love relationship with Jesus. My first priority is to love my Lord and then to love others with a pure heart. Jesus loved me enough to die for me, and He now lives in me. Because my body belongs to Him, He promises to meet all of my true needs."

*"The body is not meant for sexual immorality, but for the
Lord, and the Lord for the body…Do you not know that
your body is a temple of the Holy Spirit, who is in you, whom
you have received from God? You are not your own; you were
bought at a price. Therefore honor God with your body"*
(1 CORINTHIANS 6:13,19-20).

IV. STEPS TO SOLUTION

It seems inconceivable, but the strength of spider webs has been likened to that of steel. Dr. Frauke Grater, a German scientist at the Heidelberg Institute for Theoretical Studies, makes the following observation: "Silk fibers exhibit astonishing mechanical properties. They have an ultimate strength comparable to steel, toughness greater than Kevlar (a synthetic fiber), and a density less than cotton or nylon."[28]

And the webs that Mark Laaser and Marnie Ferree found themselves entangled in were just as strong and seemingly unbreakable. They just couldn't break free. Every desperate attempt simply drew them back into their isolated, shame-filled worlds. They were caught in the middle of their webs...and filled with self-contempt.

But there is One stronger than both spider silk and steel, *the Sovereign Lord.* He stands ready to rescue and redeem the ensnared—those willing to cry out to Him, "Free me from the trap that is set for me, for you are my refuge" (Psalm 31:4).

A. Key Verse to Memorize

In the Old Testament, Joseph serves as our role model for fleeing from sexual immorality. When the wife of Potiphar (the captain of Pharaoh's guard) tried to seduce Joseph to sleep with her, there was no pausing or pondering on his part. He simply fled, knowing even a single second could mean the difference between standing or falling with regard to the commands of God. "Though she spoke to Joseph day after day, he refused to go to bed with her or even be with her" (Genesis 39:10).

> *"Flee from sexual immorality.*
> *All other sins a man commits are outside his body,*
> *but he who sins sexually sins against his own body"*
> (1 CORINTHIANS 6:18).

B. Key Passage to Read and Reread

Whatever God tells you to do, He will equip you to do it. When God calls you to avoid sexual immorality, He will enable you to do it. Don't live as a prisoner of past defeat. *Live in light of your high calling!*

When you say *no* to sexual immorality, remember, blessings will abound and the character of Christ will become more deeply ingrained in your spirit. God's decrees and ordinances are not meant to deny us; they're meant to protect and preserve us, enabling us to live holy lives and to heed our heavenly calling. God couldn't have put it more clearly: "Be holy, because I am holy" (1 Peter 1:16).

WHY AVOID IMMORALITY?
1 THESSALONIANS 4:1-8

- You will please God. . . . . .verse 1
- You will prove that you can take instruction from God. . . . verse 1
- You will respond to the authority of God. . . . . .verse 2
- You will be in the will of God. . . . . .verse 3
- You will be sanctified (set apart). .verse 3
- You will control your own body. . . . . .verse 4
- You will do what is honorable and holy. . . . . .verse 4
- You will not display passionate lust. . . . . .verse 5
- You will not be like the heathen. .verse 5
- You will not wrong another person. . . . . .verse 6
- You will not take advantage of another. . . . . .verse 6
- You will not be impure. . . . . .verse 7
- You will live up to your holy calling. . . . . .verse 7
- You will not reject God. . . . . .verse 8

C. How to Open the Door Out of Addiction

For Mark Laaser, the door out of sexual addiction wasn't opened, *it was busted down*. And he doesn't have a single regret that he ultimately walked through it.

After decades of a disturbing and dangerous double life, Mark finally got caught. A colleague at his counseling practice found out about one of his affairs. Mark was immediately fired, and several days later he entered a treatment center for sexual addiction. The following months for Mark were filled with pain as he reflected on childhood memories and experiences, absorbed the impact of the abuse he perpetrated on others, and grieved over the humiliation he brought to his wife and children.

But there was also joy—the renewed hope of healing, the freshness of an honest lifestyle, and restored relationships with his wife, family, and friends. Yet Mark will tell you that perhaps the greatest blessing of all is that he finally found peace, and he "wouldn't trade it for the world."[29]

When you trust Jesus Christ as your Lord and Savior, you are given a new identity. The Bible says you are not just a creation of God, but a child of God. You are "set apart," you are in His family, you receive a new nature, and you are to reflect His character. What an extraordinary privilege! Because sexual sin doesn't reflect Christ accurately, you can be assured that He has already provided a way out for you:

> *"The one who calls you is faithful and he will do it"*
> (1 THESSALONIANS 5:24).

- **Decide** whether you really want to be set free.
  - "Am I ready to take responsibility for my addiction?"
  - "Am I sick and tired of being in this bondage?"
  - "Am I willing to go to war in order to win?"

> *"Prepare your minds for action; be self-controlled"*
> (1 PETER 1:13).

- **Dispel** the myth that you don't need help.
  - "I admit I'm out of control."
  - "I admit my sexual addiction is sin."
  - "I admit I can't change myself."

> *"Create in me a pure heart, O God, and*
> *renew a steadfast spirit within me"*
> (PSALM 51:10).

- **Deal** with the secret of child abuse. (Some experts say that over 80 percent of addicts were sexually abused and over 90 percent were emotionally abused.[30])
  - Talk with a friend—let go of the secret.
  - Talk to a counselor trained to help victims of childhood sexual abuse.
  - Talk to the perpetrator, but only when you and your counselor have worked through a plan for doing so and only when it is safe to do so (it might be best to bring someone with you)—confrontation is biblical.

> *"If your brother sins against you, go and show him his fault, just*
> *between the two of you. If he listens to you, you have won your*
> *brother over. But if he will not listen, take one or two others along"*
> (MATTHEW 18:15-16).

- **Discern** the inner needs you have tried to satisfy through sexual passion.
    - Is it your need for sacrificial love?[31]
    - Is it your need for significance?
    - Is it your need for security?

    > *"Surely you desire truth in the inner parts; you teach me wisdom in the inmost place"*
    > (PSALM 51:6).

- **Determine** to let Jesus meet your needs.
    - Ask Him to forgive you for your willful sin.
    - Ask Him to come into your life as your personal Lord and Savior.
    - Ask Him to meet your deepest inner needs.

    > *"My God will meet all your needs"*
    > (PHILIPPIANS 4:19).

- **Dedicate** your life to the Lord Jesus (see chapter 14).
    - Let His will be your will.
    - Let the Lord be Lord of your life.
    - Let Christ have absolute control.

    > *"If anyone would come after me, he must deny himself and take up his cross daily and follow me. For whoever wants to save his life will lose it, but whoever loses his life for me will save it"*
    > (LUKE 9:23-24).

D. How to Break Free

Marnie Ferree believes the hope of healing for sex addicts is tucked away in Romans 12:2: "Be transformed by the renewing of your mind." It is the only way possible for struggling people to meet the high and holy calling found in Romans 12:1: "Offer your bodies as living sacrifices, holy and pleasing to God."

Breaking free, according to Marnie, occurs through a threefold approach: acquiring knowledge about genuine, healthy intimacy; committing to sexual behavior only in marriage; and coming to the understanding that our most important need is not sex but intimacy in a relationship—acceptance, approval, affection. Changing beliefs and behaviors, Marnie concludes, can truly transform a sex addict.[32]

Imagine that you, as a bank president, receive word that a time bomb placed inside the bank's vault is set to go off at midnight. The combination lock has been electronically jammed. If you don't get rid of the bomb, the bank will be destroyed. You must break the code! Similarly, in every addict's mind, a sexual time bomb threatens to destroy both the body and soul. With the right combination you can break the code. The Bible says,

> *"The man who looks intently into the perfect law that gives*
> *freedom, and continues to do this, not forgetting what he has*
> *heard, but doing it—he will be blessed in what he does"*
> (JAMES 1:25).

Cracking the Code

The mind of every addict is locked by faulty beliefs. Your beliefs are what you think regarding your own value, your relationships, and your sexuality. They determine all of your behavior. If your thinking is faulty, your findings are faulty, and then the way you function will be faulty.

The Bible tells you not only that you *can* change, but also *how* you can change. Romans 12:2 says, "Be transformed by the renewing of your mind." You must reprogram your mind with the right code, with the truth. Every day for the next 12 weeks, read the following life-changing truths. Pray that God will open your heart. Jesus says,

> *"The truth will set you free"*
> (JOHN 8:32).

YOUR NEED FOR LOVE[33]

FALSE BELIEF: "I am unlovable. Sex gives me the feeling of being loved."

TRUE BELIEF: You are loved. God loves you.

- Jesus loved you enough to die on the cross for you. "God so loved the world that he gave his one and only Son, that whoever believes in him shall not perish but have eternal life" (John 3:16).

- Your heavenly Father loved you enough to adopt you into His family. "How great is the love the Father has lavished on us, that we should be called children of God!" (1 John 3:1).

CONCLUSION: While sex should always be an expression of love, sex is not love, and love is not sex—rather, sex is sex. Love is a commitment that seeks the highest good and very best for another person. Since God loves you in this way, He will give you the ability to develop other loving relationships in which sex is not a substitute for love. The Bible says,

"[Love] is not self-seeking"
(1 CORINTHIANS 13:5).

YOUR NEED FOR SIGNIFICANCE

FALSE BELIEF: "I am unworthy. Sex makes me feel significant."

TRUE BELIEF: You already have worth. God has established your worth.

- God created you. Therefore, you have worth. "You created my inmost being; you knit me together in my mother's womb" (Psalm 139:13).

- If you are a Christian, you have worth because Christ lives in you. "To them God has chosen to make known among the Gentiles the glorious riches of this mystery, which is Christ in you, the hope of glory" (Colossians 1:27).

CONCLUSION: Sex does not give you significance. You are significant because you are a new creation in Christ with a new source of power. He is your source of power and significance.

"His divine power has given us everything we need for life and godliness through our knowledge of him who called us by his own glory and goodness"
(2 PETER 1:3).

YOUR NEED FOR SECURITY

FALSE BELIEF: "I am unwanted. Sex numbs the pain of my insecurity."

TRUE BELIEF: You are wanted. The Lord wants you.

- The Lord wants to be your Shepherd throughout life. "The LORD is my shepherd, I shall not be in want" (Psalm 23:1).

- The Lord wants to walk with you through life. "When you pass through the waters, I will be with you; and when you pass through the rivers, they will not sweep over you. When you walk through the fire, you will not be burned; the flames will not set you ablaze" (Isaiah 43:2).

CONCLUSION: Sex does not give you security. Your security is found in a love relationship with the Lord. This true security can never be taken away from you.

> *"The LORD himself goes before you and will be*
> *with you; he will never leave you nor forsake*
> *you. Do not be afraid; do not be discouraged"*
> (DEUTERONOMY 31:8).

Cracking the Code with the Freedom Formula

- Don't focus on the negative "combination."

    Every time you focus on quitting a sexual obsession, you will want it all the more. Living under the "law" never changes you. If you focus only on what you shouldn't do, you will be pulled more powerfully to do it.

    - "I need to quit thinking about sex."
    - "I won't rent X-rated movies."
    - "I have to get over this addiction."
    - "I shouldn't call the sex phone line."
    - "I'll quit cruising next month."

    > *"The power of sin is the law"*
    > (1 CORINTHIANS 15:56).

- **Focus** on the positive "combination."

    - *A new purpose*—"I want to reflect the character of Christ through what I see and do. I am...

    > *'predestined to be conformed to the likeness of his Son'"*
    > (ROMANS 8:29).

    - *A new priority*—"I will do whatever it takes to have a pure heart and a transformed life."

    > *"Do not conform any longer to the pattern of this world,*
    > *but be transformed by the renewing of your mind"*
    > (ROMANS 12:2).

    - *A new plan*—"I will rely on Christ's strength, not on my own."

"I can do everything through him who gives me strength"
(PHILIPPIANS 4:13).

A Transformed Life: God's Gift of Self-control

Commit to…

- Seeing pornography as sin
- Destroying all erotic material
- Purchasing and reading only uplifting material
- Avoiding tempting situations
- Turning quickly to a preplanned project (exercise, hobbies, reading, etc.) when tempted
- Focusing on Philippians 4:8-9 when tempted
- Making needed changes in old routines (driving route, television, reading material, etc.)
- Blocking all X-rated programs from TV, cable, hotels
- Resisting channel surfing on TV
- Being accountable to a friend as frequently as necessary (monthly, weekly, or even daily)
- Memorizing and applying pertinent Scriptures
- Breaking the chain of obsession

The Bible tells us,

"Whatever is true, whatever is noble, whatever is right, whatever is pure, whatever is lovely, whatever is admirable—if anything is excellent or praiseworthy—think about such things"
(PHILIPPIANS 4:8).

E. How to Walk the Pathway to Purity

On the pathway to purity, Dr. Mark Laaser has placed a nonnegotiable stop sign: no sexual activity for at least 90 days. Sex addicts who hope to find healing must first agree to a "celibacy contract," he explains, and that includes those who are married. "This contract reverses a sex addict's core belief and shows that 'sex is *not* my most important need.'"[34]

Dr. Laaser likens sexual addiction to food addiction. Food addicts can't stop eating forever, and most sex addicts are either in marital relationships or one day will be; therefore, it is unlikely that they will stop having sex forever. So the key to victory is learning how to control sexual urges, practice restraint, and operate within boundaries. "Married sex addicts, likewise, will learn that sex with their spouse is appropriate and beautiful when, instead of being a way to avoid intimacy or escape negative feelings, it expresses the intimacy of the marriage."[35]

Does the thought of purity seem impossible to you? Unattainable? Take heart. God would never call you to be pure without giving you all that you need to be pure. So be encouraged. As you yield your life to Him, you have God's guarantee that you can have a pure heart and live a pure life. The Bible says,

> *"God did not call us to be impure, but to live a holy life"*
> (1 Thessalonians 4:7).

Purity

P—Participate in an accountability group dealing with sex addictions.

- Meet regularly and talk specifically each week.
- Set realistic guidelines and goals.
- Admit each time that you slip.

> *"Two are better than one, because they have a good return for their work: If one falls down, his friend can help him up. But pity the man who falls and has no one to help him up!"*
> (Ecclesiastes 4:9-10).

U—Uphold boundary lines that must be off limits.

- With the help of an accountability partner, make a list of times in your daily routine, places in your home, in the community, or on the Internet where you are tempted.
- With your accountability partner, establish ways of breaking routines and setting boundaries (like installing blocking or monitoring software on your computer or changing schedules) to avoid tempting situations.
- Establish a regular pattern of accountability by giving your accountability partner permission to ask you about your behavior and, where necessary, make further changes in your routine to avoid temptation.

> *"The prudent see danger and take refuge,*
> *but the simple keep going and suffer for it"*
> (PROVERBS 27:12).

R—RID yourself, your home, and your work of all sexually addictive items.

- Throw away all pornography.
- Clear away all erotic paraphernalia.
- Discard addresses and calling cards of all sexual contacts.

> *"Wash and make yourselves clean. Take your evil deeds*
> *out of my sight! Stop doing wrong, learn to do right!"*
> (ISAIAH 1:16-17).

I—INCORPORATE the power of Christ daily when temptation overwhelms you.

- "Lord, I'm relying on You to be my Redeemer."
- "Lord, I'm depending on You to be my Deliverer."
- "Lord, in my weakness I need Your strength."

> *"'My [Jesus] grace is sufficient for you, for my power is made perfect*
> *in weakness.' Therefore I [Paul] will boast all the more gladly*
> *about my weaknesses, so that Christ's power may rest on me"*
> (2 CORINTHIANS 12:9).

T—TAKE on positive habits of discipline, such as exercise, sports, regular sleep, and new hobbies.

- Make a to-do list of healthy activities you enjoy.
- Do one item from the list when you are tempted.
- Write a letter, call a friend, or help someone in need.

> *"He who heeds discipline shows the way to life, but*
> *whoever ignores correction leads others astray"*
> (PROVERBS 10:17).

Y—YIELD your mind to meditating on and memorizing Scripture.

- Read a chapter from the New Testament each day.
- Read Romans chapter 6 once a week.
- Read Colossians 3:1-5 each day and memorize Philippians 4:8-9.

"Get rid of all moral filth and the evil that is so prevalent and humbly accept the word planted in you, which can save you" (JAMES 1:21).

Jim—the Secret Struggle

When I asked Jim Cress (to whom this book is dedicated)—my friend and co-host on *Hope in the Night*—if he would share his story in this book, I felt doubly blessed when he said *yes*.

⌒

When I was four, an older boy in my neighborhood convinced me to perform a sexual act with him. To this day, I vividly remember my surroundings—the sounds, the smells, and the sight of several other boys watching my every move. I admired and trusted this older boy and sincerely believed, *Since he suggested it, this must be the right thing to do.*

From that point onward throughout early adolescence, my life was filled with sexual experimentation. As a young boy, I developed an insatiable desire to connect with neighborhood girls, often encouraging them to sneak away so we could kiss, sexually fondle each other, or even attempt what we thought was actually "sex." During many a sleepover at friends' homes, kissing and sexually touching the girls would be the grand finale of the night.

A healthy physical connection with another person was painfully absent in my home, which fueled my desperate search. Born fifth in a family of six children, my parents had little to give emotionally. Affection and affirmation were almost nonexistent as my parents grappled with the daily dramas of raising a family. I have no enjoyable memories of my father during those years—no recollection of his trying to build a relationship with me. Although our family attended church three times a week, my father never talked with me about sexuality, the Christian life, God, or anything else of substance.

Not only did my home life lack healthy forms of touch, but there were also times when my father would angrily whip me with a belt. And my undiagnosed ADHD—Attention Deficit Hyperactivity Disorder—only compounded my ever-deepening feelings of loneliness, shame, rejection, and confusion.

When I was 12, an older boy began talking to me about masturbation. Prior to that, I had developed serious misgivings about it, having heard it could give me acne or cause me to go blind. My worldly-wise friend, however, quickly dismissed these myths and showed me how to masturbate, adding that if I wanted to really enhance the experience, I should look at racy pictures of women.

I carefully noted his instructions, even though the part about looking at pictures of women made no sense to me. Even so, a few weeks later, when I tried it for myself, I looked at a department store catalog. My friend knew what he was talking about—I was instantly hooked.

Thus began my secret habit, which, over time, developed into an addiction to pornography and masturbation. During those years I couldn't find actual pornography, but my mom had several catalogs in the house—"poor man's pornography"—which laid the foundation for an "arousal template." Pictures of women in lingerie became my favorite type of visual stimulation.

Throughout my teen years I participated actively in church and was, in fact, growing spiritually. I earnestly believed that if I prayed enough, did church activities enough, and dated good Christians enough, I would finally win the war with lust. My plan did not work.

In my twenties, I sincerely believed that if I attended a Christian college and surrendered my life to full-time Christian ministry, I would find the solution to my problem. I was sincere, but sincerely wrong.

Still, I convinced myself that if I could just marry a beautiful Christian woman, I would certainly find the solution. My plan worked—until, as a newly married man, I found myself one night unable to get my way sexually. To my deep dismay, my old, dark habit came roaring back. Even as I was earning a master's degree from seminary—actively involved in ministry—my secret struggle continued.

My wife's discovery of my addiction seemed, at first, to be the worst thing that could have happened. As it turned out, it was one of the best. My secret had been exposed, and I was held accountable. Understandably, Jessica felt devastated. In fact, she and I experienced a several-year period of celibacy as each of us dealt with our emotional wounds. Although I didn't enthusiastically embrace it at the time, I now see that this period afforded me valuable time to rid my brain and body of the toxic grip of a lifetime of sexual addiction.

Through years of individual, marital, and group counseling, I came to realize that sex was not my greatest need. I learned that sex addicts are highly likely to have experienced damage to their self-worth as children—trauma that damages their ability to bond with and trust others. I faced my issues of childhood abandonment and gained understanding of how my sexual fantasy was a futile attempt to escape the reality of my painful past. I forgave my "four-year-old self" for naïvely participating in my own sexual abuse. And I came to realize that no amount of sex could fill the hole in my heart—a spot reserved for God alone.

During my recovery, I also experienced a rich healing in my relationship with my father. Dad and I shared many tender moments and deep, honest conversations about life, our relationship with each other, and God. When my father died, we were at peace.

God continues to redeem the tragedies of my past, using my abuse, abandonment, and pain to give me empathy and compassion so I can offer help and hope to others. Today I minister as a licensed professional counselor, certified sex addiction therapist, and a national radio talk show cohost on two programs that allow me to help others who are trapped in the bondage of sexual addiction.

The search for sexual gratification is no longer my master—Jesus Christ is my Master. Through His grace, I have experienced the truth of Genesis 50:20: What others meant for harm to me, God meant for good.

F. How to Sever the "Soul Ties" and Strongholds

Severing "soul ties" and strongholds begins with a strong sense of *powerlessness*. "Like many other biblical principles," according to Marnie, "this one involves a great paradox. It's only through surrender that there can be salvation. Only through admitting defeat can victory be gained."[36]

Sex addicts must seek God's help and surrender their will and life to God. For Marnie, that didn't come easily. Five months into therapy, Marnie still wasn't sexually sober. Then all of a sudden she found herself at a watershed moment. Whose will would she obey—her own, or God's? Would self or the Sovereign One be on the throne of her life?

Making the Choice

A 2:00 a.m. phone call to a friend in recovery jolted Marnie into finally making the decision that would determine the course of her life. Her friend told her, "Marnie, this is really pretty simple. Either you believe God's in control and you submit to that—or you don't. There aren't any other choices."[37]

The black-and-white words ultimately delivered Marnie from her gray world of compromise, rationalizations, and justifications. She got down on her knees and surrendered her will to God, and as a recovering sex addict, *it's something she must do on a daily basis.*

When two people engage in a sexual relationship, a soul tie is established between them. Fantasizing about an illicit relationship with another person can also create an unholy bond with that person in your mind and heart. All sexual relationships outside of marriage need to be broken, even if they occurred in the past and are over. Begin by praying along these lines:

> God, thank You for loving me in spite of my wrong choices. I confess each sexually immoral relationship as sin. Lord Jesus, through Your supernatural power, I ask You to break all unholy sexual bonds that exist between me and anyone else. I pray that the soul ties with (names) be broken. [Pray this sentence naming each person with whom you have been sexually and/or emotionally involved.] Lord Jesus, from this moment on, I will rely on Your power and live in Your strength.

> *"Do you not know that he who unites himself with a prostitute is one with her in body? For it is said, 'The two will become one flesh.' But he who unites himself with the Lord is one with him in spirit"*
> (1 Corinthians 6:16-17).

Severing the Stronghold

When a series of sexually impure relationships occur, a sexual stronghold is formed. Until God demolishes the stronghold, you will continue in the sexually impure patterns of the past. Pray that the sexual stronghold be demolished.

> Lord Jesus, I affirm that sex is not my master. Rather, You are my Master. Through the supernatural power of Christ, I pray that You destroy every stronghold—physical, mental, emotional, and sexual—in my life. Keep me from justifying impure thoughts. May I see sin as You see it and hate sin as You hate it. Lord, I give You control of my life.

> *"Though we live in the world, we do not wage war as the world does. The weapons we fight with are not the weapons of the world. On the contrary, they have divine power to demolish*

> *strongholds. We demolish arguments and every pretension*
> *that sets itself up against the knowledge of God, and we*
> *take captive every thought to make it obedient to Christ"*
> (2 CORINTHIANS 10:3-5).

G. How to Answer Key Questions

Debra Laaser refers to it as the million-dollar question asked by sexually betrayed wives: "Will I ever be able to trust my husband again?"

Rebuilding trust is a process, according to Debra, and countless women struggle more with the lies than with the sexual betrayal. Their mind-set goes something like this: If he's lied about having affairs, what else has he lied about?

True healing and restored trust will occur between a husband and wife only when full disclosure takes place. The unfaithful spouse must "put all the cards on the table" so that both know precisely what they're dealing with. "Knowing the whole truth is foundational to building a new life together because the new structure must be built on honesty and openness. And it doesn't require *you* to uncover all the facts."[38]

===== *Sex Talk Lines* =====

QUESTION: "How can I stop calling sex talk lines, which give me an incredible high? Day after day, my mind feels intoxicated with sex."

ANSWER: Everyone has a God-given need to feel significant, but phone sex with a stranger gives a false sense of significance. To be set free from this sexual addiction, you need to replace that which is false with that which is true.

- The truth is that you are so significant that Jesus not only died on the cross for you, but also designed a wonderful plan for your life.
- The truth is that phone sex will never give you lasting significance.
- The truth is that your significance comes by realizing you were created in the image of God.

You will feel no greater sense of significance than when you are being conformed to the character of Christ. Pray, "Thank You, God, for planning to conform me to the character of Christ."

> *"Those God foreknew he also predestined to be*
> *conformed to the likeness of his Son"*
> (ROMANS 8:29).

=== *Lustful Fantasies* ===

QUESTION: "How can I control my lustful fantasies? I simply can't stop fantasizing."

ANSWER: God would never tell you to stop lusting without giving you the power to stop. Centuries ago, Martin Luther painted a graphic picture of this principle by quoting an even older proverb: "You can't keep the birds from flying over your head, but you can keep them from making a nest in your hair." The starting point for victory is realizing that when a sexual thought flashes through your mind:

- *You must redirect* that sexual thought or replace it. You are the only one who controls how long you will entertain a thought—how long you will dwell on it.

- *Make a covenant* with your mind that you will not allow an immoral thought to reside there.

- *Make a commitment* with your eyes that you will not maintain a gaze that leads to an immoral thought. Follow Job's example:

> *"I made a covenant with my eyes not to look lustfully at a girl"*
> (JOB 31:1).

=== *Mentally Sexualizing Others* ===

QUESTION: "How can I stop mentally undressing every attractive woman I see?"

ANSWER: The moment you find yourself in the midst of sexual temptation, you must immediately...

- *Turn your eyes* away without delay. Say in your heart, "I refuse to dwell on that thought. I refuse to let my eyes lead me into sexual sin."

- *Turn your mind* toward integrity. Declare out loud, "I'm determined to be a man of moral integrity."

- *Turn in prayer* to God. "Lord, I'm committing myself to be pure in both my mind and my body. I'm turning away from impurity and turning to You for purity. I'm yielding my thoughts and desires to Your power to make me pure." The Bible says,

> *"Everyone who confesses the name of the Lord*
> *must turn away from wickedness"*
> (2 TIMOTHY 2:19).

Masturbation

QUESTION: "I am not married, and I struggle with masturbation, a habit I developed as a teenager. I am a Christian, and the guilt is overwhelming. How can I overcome this sexual addiction?"

ANSWER: Masturbation is not mentioned in Scripture, but it is a perversion of what God intended just by the fact that it is self-focused and self-gratifying. God designed sex to bond a husband and wife together, to be mutually gratifying and other-focused. A biblical principle is applicable here: "'Everything is permissible for me'—but not everything is beneficial. 'Everything is permissible for me'—but I will not be mastered by anything" (1 Corinthians 6:12).

The implication is that anything that has mastery over you is sin because Christ should be your Master. A major step toward gaining mastery over guilt-producing habits is to take immediate control of your thoughts at the first urge.

- *Pray for God's highest purpose* for your life. "Lord, I'll do whatever it takes to be conformed to Your character" (see Romans 8:29).
- *Say to yourself*, "My body belongs to God. I will only do what is pleasing to Him" (see 2 Corinthians 5:9).
- *Distract yourself* from this compulsive desire by doing a positive physical activity such as cleaning a closet, sorting books on a shelf, engaging in exercise, or taking the traditional "cold shower."
- *Do something positive*: sing a song, pray a prayer, phone a friend, write a letter, read the Word, or repeat this truth five times: "I can do all things through Christ who strengthens me" (Philippians 4:13 NKJV).

As a Christian, you have Christ living in you, empowering you to live a godly life.

> *"Thanks be to God that, though you used to be slaves to sin...*
> *You have been set free from sin and have become slaves to*
> *righteousness...Just as you used to offer the parts of your body*
> *in slavery to impurity and to ever-increasing wickedness, so*
> *now offer them in slavery to righteousness leading to holiness"*
> (ROMANS 6:17-19).

Teen Addicted to Internet Porn

QUESTION: "My teenage son is addicted to pornography on the Internet—he refuses to stop accessing it no matter what I say. What can I do?"

The World of Sexual Addiction   335

Answer: While an Internet filter should certainly be installed, many Internet surfers eventually learn how to circumvent the system. Nevertheless, you need to communicate and maintain your convictions and boundaries about pornography.

- Tell your son that because you love him, you will do whatever it takes to help him become a young man of moral character.

- Remove the computer from his room and move it to an open family area. (If it's already in an open location, then tell him someone must be in the room with him when he uses it.)

- No matter how much he says he needs a computer for school, accessing pornography was his choice. Therefore, he has chosen his own consequence.

- Explain why you are being so firm:

"Son, I love you and want you to have increased freedom. But I also know pornography has such a strong pull that many people become addicted to it. That is just one reason we are prohibiting you from accessing porn sites. There are other reasons:

- Pornography poisons your mind and, at the same time, pollutes our home.

- Pornography not only violates our values, but it also offends the heart of God—it debases the very human beings whom He made in His image.

"Because you're having such difficulty with self-control, you've left us with no choice but to revoke all computer privileges when you are alone. After a month, we can talk about how you can regain our trust."

Scripture addresses the seriousness of sin: "If your right eye causes you to sin, gouge it out and throw it away. It is better for you to lose one part of your body than for your whole body to be thrown into hell. And if your right hand causes you to sin, cut it off and throw it away" (Matthew 5:29-30).

====== *Pornography Affects the Marriage Relationship* ======

Question: "Doesn't pornography enhance a couple's sex life?"

Answer: Pornography is addictive and often leads to abuse of others. Pornography debases sexuality and ridicules Christian values in favor of lust and immorality. God ordained human sexuality for intimacy in marriage and for procreation. To the contrary, pornography is designed simply to arouse indiscriminate sexual lust.

Pornography introduces perversion into your marriage and home life—a perversion that diverts from the true intent of something or turns something to a wrong end or use.[39] By attempting to enhance your sex life through pornography, you risk corrupting the beauty God intended for you to experience in your sexual union with your mate.

Pornography typically leads addicts to…

- Devalue their mates. Love turns to lust for the "ideal" sexual mate.
- Force their mates to perform perverted acts. The beauty of the sexual union turns to unnatural acts seen in pornographic materials.
- Commit adultery. Pornography encourages indiscriminate sex.
- Pass on the addiction to children, who then also become addicted. They are often used and abused.

Just as pornography is progressive, all sexual addiction, if not stopped, progresses into more blatant and risky behavior. What was once sexually stimulating becomes ineffective. More explicit acts are required to create the same level of sensual excitement previously experienced.

> *"You will bear the consequences of your lewdness*
> *and your detestable practices,' declares the L*ORD*"*
> (EZEKIEL 16:58).

H. How to Find the Way Out of the Web

Stop the rituals, stop the fantasies, says Dr. Mark Laaser.

Many sex addicts don't realize they go through rituals before sexually acting out. Discerning those rituals is the first step toward exercising discipline over them. For example, a sex addict may be stimulated by something he or she sees on TV. Then he gets in the car, goes to an ATM machine to get money, and then winds up at a massage parlor. Healthy boundaries must be put in place to halt ritualistic behavior, and in this case, that would mean avoiding all sexually graphic material on television.

Fantasy is a symptom of the spiritual and emotional condition of sex addicts, distracting them from painful feelings.[40] Fantasy is also one of the greatest hurdles to cross over on the road to recovery because sex addicts have countless images and memories emblazoned in their minds. Victory can come through examining the *whys* behind the fantasies, addressing the painful feelings, and discussing them with a trusted friend, pastor, or counselor.

Many who have become addicted to pornography on the Internet promise themselves or others they will stop, only to keep coming back for more. Even finding ways to get around the Internet filters, blockers, and controls on their computers can become an exciting adventure. Realistically, aside from canceling or totally blocking Internet access, there are no 100 percent guarantees that can keep addicts from accessing sexually enticing materials. There are, however, creative ways to help addicts become free or gain control of their addictive behavior. Freedom begins with a commitment to the Lord to do whatever He wants you to do in order to be sexually pure. Based on that decisive commitment, the next step is to strategically plan for success. The following suggestions will help you follow through with your decision.[41]

- Use a Christian Internet service provider (ISP) that filters the Internet at the server side and requires a password before you can change the controls. (Allow your wife or trusted friend to keep you accountable by password-protecting the filter!)

- In many cases, canceling all Internet access for a period of time is necessary to help break the cycle of sexual addiction.

- If you struggle with late-night Internet pornography, use a filter that blocks late-night access. Several Internet guardian programs allow the password holder to limit access to the Internet at certain hours.

- Be sure to find a guardian filter that is guaranteed to work with your Internet browser. Several Christian Internet filters do not block Internet access if someone uses the AOL browser.

- Find an ISP or an Internet filter that allows the password holder to access a protected file that tracks all Internet activity. This serves as a major reminder that all Internet activity will be monitored, and it prohibits the user from erasing the history of Internet sites that were visited.

- Monitoring software provides a helpful alternative to blocking software. Trusted friends are e-mailed all the sites you visit each month, with questionable sites flagged, enabling them to hold you accountable for the material you view on the Internet.

- Because e-mails that invite access to a porn site are so common, be sure your filter either sifts out pornographic e-mail or stops you from being linked to a pornographic site.

- Place your computer in a part of the house where there is heavy traffic and where the computer screen can be easily seen. Avoid places where computer use can be secretive or hidden.

> *"Nothing in all creation is hidden from God's sight.*
> *Everything is uncovered and laid bare before the eyes of him*
> *to whom we must give account"*
> (HEBREWS 4:13).

I. How to Help with Accountability Questions

Many who have known success in their struggles with temptation say, "I couldn't have made it without someone holding me accountable. God knew that's what I needed!"

But at times having an accountability partner isn't effective. Why? Realize that many strugglers hope no one will ask them *specifically* how they are doing sexually. Asking specific questions is a key component of effective accountability. Strugglers need to know that they are going to be asked targeted questions. They also need to know they will have someone *trustworthy* to hold them accountable. The Bible says, "If someone is caught in a sin, you who are spiritual should restore him gently. But watch yourself, or you also may be tempted" (Galatians 6:1).

ACCOUNTABILITY QUESTIONS

Since we last spoke:

1. Have you thought about someone in a lustful way?
2. Have you been exposed to pornography, whether intentionally or unintentionally? If so, what, and how many times?
3. Have you looked at anything else sexually stimulating such as magazines, movies, videos, TV, advertisements, Internet sites, even if by accident? How did you respond?
4. Have you listened to anything sexually arousing, such as radio/phone sex?
5. Have you "objectified" someone—that is, looked at a person as a sex object?
6. Did you flirt with someone or use sexual humor?

7. Have you contributed to the sexual temptation of someone else?

8. Have you attempted to attract the inappropriate attention of others? Have you used provocative behavior or any form of exhibitionism?

9. Have you used the fantasy stored in your memory to act out sexually?

10. Have you had any thoughts about having an affair? If so, with whom? Have you done anything to move toward acting on this affair?

11. Have you acted out sexually in any way? Does your mate know? Who else knows?

12. Have you just twisted the truth or lied to me?

> *"He who conceals his sins does not prosper,*
> *but whoever confesses and renounces them finds mercy"*
> (PROVERBS 28:13).

Note to Mentors: Any of these questions can be traded out for other questions. During the first session together, ask those who want victory to select three or four questions most appropriate for their struggle:

- Ask, "Are there specific areas in which you know you need to be held accountable?"
- Then after several sessions, ask, "How is this accountability working for you?"
- "If our positions were reversed, what would you do differently if you were me?"

Remember, Christ is shaping and maturing both of you through this time of accountability, and you want the struggler to be set free!

> *"As iron sharpens iron, so one man sharpens another"*
> (PROVERBS 27:17).

J. How to Tell the Truth to Your Mate

If you want a *full recovery* from your sexual addiction, then you must make a *full disclosure* of your sexual addiction. If you want the hope of *full healing* for your marriage, then you must make a *full disclosure* to your marriage partner.

You may try to fight taking this step, especially if you are thinking, *But God forgives and forgets!* While that is true of God, we are called to be accountable to others for our failures. Because of all the lies, deception, and cover-ups inherent in addictive behavior, disclosing the absolute truth is necessary for three reasons: (1) to become a person of integrity, (2) to learn to speak the truth, and (3) to seek to rebuild trust.

Invite God to teach you to be trustworthy with the truth:

> *"Guide me in your truth and teach me, for you are God*
> *my Savior, and my hope is in you all day long"*
> (Psalm 25:5).

Write a Full Disclosure

To ensure you say what needs to be said, write out your disclosure first.

- Pray for the courage to write an honest account of your history of sexual acting out. "God, I ask for Your moral courage to tell the complete truth."
- Make a chronological time line from your earliest inappropriate sexual experiences to the present.
- Do not hide anything concerning how you have acted out your sexual addiction, with whom, how many times, and where. But do not share unnecessary details (such as the duration of each sex act) or any titillating descriptions.

Making the Disclosure

A *onetime* full disclosure to your spouse is necessary and nonnegotiable. (Ideally, the disclosure would take place in the presence of a counselor trained in addiction recovery—one who can mediate the disclosure.)

- First, share your sexual history with the counselor, who can make helpful suggestions.
- Then, when you and your spouse are prepared to meet together with the counselor, plan to arrive in separate vehicles, as it may be too difficult for your spouse to share a ride home following the session. Likewise, you could arrange for a place to stay for the night, in case your spouse needs time and space to be alone. Do not push your marriage partner for reconciliation or intimacy.
- When you begin sharing your disclosure, take full responsibility for all of your actions.

- Never disclose your addiction by eking out information little by little, bit by bit. Instead, no matter how difficult, *tell the truth and nothing but the truth!*

The Word of God gives this crucial counsel:

> *"He who conceals his sins does not prosper,*
> *but whoever confesses and renounces them finds mercy"*
> (PROVERBS 28:13).

K. How to Write an Inventory of Your Life and Addiction

To speed up the recovery process, be specific when you write out your sexual history. Be thorough, honest, and prayerful. Ask God to bring to your mind every sexual encounter.

> *"I acknowledged my sin to you and did not cover up my iniquity.*
> *I said, 'I will confess my transgressions to the LORD'"*
> (PSALM 32:5).

- **Experience:** Make a list of all of your sexual experiences, beginning with your very first. How old were you, who was present, and what do you remember about that experience?
- **Lies:** Make a list of all the ways you have lied and been dishonest in your addiction.
- **Excuses:** Make a list of all the excuses you have made or used to justify your actions. ("I can't help it.")
- **Rationales:** Make a list of all the rationales you have made for your addiction. ("No one will ever know.")
- **People hurt:** Make a list of all the people you have hurt, including loved ones you have "stolen" time from when you were acting out.
- **Employment:** Make a list of all the times you acted out or were lost in fantasy while at work.
- **Costs:** Make a list of all the "costs" of your addictions. Make a tally, "billing yourself" at your hourly pay rate for all the time you have spent in fantasy and acting out. This can give you a unique perspective as to just one "cost" of your addiction.

> *"If [an addict] turns away from the wickedness [addictive behavior]*
> *he has committed and does what is just and right, he will save*

his life. Because he considers all the offenses he has committed
and turns away from them, he will surely live; he will not die"
(EZEKIEL 18:27-28).

L. What Are Sexually Transmitted Diseases?

An STD (sexually transmitted disease) is an infection transmitted by an infected person to another person through sexual activity, whether through vaginal, anal, or oral sex, or through intimate skin-to-skin contact.

- **Bacterial STDs** can be cured with antibiotics.
- **Viral STDs** can never be cured. Symptoms, such as sores or warts, can be treated, but the virus remains in the body, causing the symptoms to flare up again and again.

History: In the sixteenth century, *syphilis* was the only identified venereal disease (VD). Then, in the nineteenth century, *gonorrhea* joined syphilis as a cause of infertility. Both were classified as incurable until the discovery of penicillin in 1943, which eradicated VD as a major public health issue.

However, the unrestrained sexual revolution of the 1960s became a breeding ground for a myriad of STDs (the new label), including Chlamydia and HPV in 1976 and HIV/AIDS in the early 1980s. Today there are more than 25 STDs (see charts on pages 343-44.)

CURABLE SEXUALLY TRANSMITTED DISEASES[42] (MOST PREVALENT)

Disease	Classification/ Transmission	Symptoms	Harmful Effects
Chlamydia *(most common bacterial STD)*	**Bacteria**—produces pus *Vaginal, anal, and oral sex* *Mother to child*	**Males and Females:** Asymptomatic or: **Males:** Discharge from penis **Females:** May experience discharge and pain when urinating	**Females:** Pelvic Inflammatory Disease (PID), sterility, risk of contracting HIV/AIDS increased
Gonorrhea *(second most common bacterial STD)*	**Bacteria**—highly infectious *Vaginal, anal, and oral sex* *Mother to child*	**Males and Females:** Asymptomatic or: **Males:** Pus from urethra, burning during urination **Females:** Painless sore, rash, fever, fatigue, pus-like discharge	**Males:** Sterility, scarring of urethra, and urinary tract problems **Females:** Pelvic Inflammatory Disease (PID), sterility damage to heart and brain
Syphilis *(oldest known STD)*	**Bacteria**—produces highly infectious sores or patches on the genitals or mouth *Vaginal, anal, and oral sex* *Mother to child*	**Males:** Swollen, nonpainful ulcers on genitalia, fever, enlarged lymph nodes **Females:** Discharge, burning during urination, venereal-type warts	**Males:** Damage to heart and brain, blindness **Females:** Damage to heart, brain, and nervous system; can cause birth defects or death in newborns **Males and Females:** Death Risk of contracting HIV/AIDS increased
Trichomonas	**Parasite**—causes genital infection *Vaginal and anal sex* *Mother to child*	**Males and Females:** Asymptomatic or: **Males:** Discharge from the penis and burning during urination **Females:** Foul-smelling vaginal discharge and genital pain, vaginal bleeding, swelling, and irritation of the genitals, painful urination	**Males and Females:** Risk of contracting HIV/AIDS increased **Females:** Premature rupture of membranes that protect unborn babies

Incurable Sexually Transmitted Diseases (Most Prevalent)

Disease	Classification/ Transmission	Symptoms	Harmful Effects
Genital Herpes *(herpes simplex virus) HSV-1 associated with the mouth; HSV-2 associated with the genitals*	**Virus**—infects skin and mucous membrane *Vaginal, anal, and oral sex / Congenital*	**Males and Females:** Asymptomatic or painful blisters or sores on the genitals, buttocks, thighs, or mouth	**Males and Females:** Genital ulcers, higher risk of HIV
Hepatitis B	**Virus**—common blood-borne infection *Vaginal, anal, and oral sex / Congenital and needles*	**Males and Females:** Asymptomatic or yellow skin/eyes, fatigue, nausea	**Males and Females:** Liver damage, cancer, ultimately death
HPV *(human papillomavirus or "genital warts")*	**Virus**—infects skin and mucous membrane *Intimate skin-to-skin Vaginal, anal, and oral sex*	**Males:** Wart-like genital growths **Females:** Asymptomatic (may be detected by a pap smear)	**Males:** Cancer of the penis and anus **Females:** Causes 99 percent of cervical cancer, genital warts
HIV/AIDS *(Human immunodeficiency virus)/ (Acquired Immune Deficiency Syndrome)*	**Virus**—invades immune system destroying it over time *Vaginal, anal, and oral sex / Needles*	**Males and Females:** Asymptomatic or flu-like symptoms (fatigue, fever, aches) initially *Later:* Skin and oral lesions, diarrhea, difficulty breathing (pulmonary infections), difficulty thinking (meningitis)	**Males and Females:** Intestinal infections and candida mouth infections, immune system failure, TB, cancer, and death

Epilogue

Mark Laaser and Marnie Ferree have been set free!

- *Every single one* of their sexual sins has been forgiven—they are clean before God.
- They have been redeemed from the pit, freed from the web of sexual addiction.
- They have received the Lord's unconditional love and ceaseless compassion.
- They have been given the comfort of Psalm 103:2-4: "Praise the LORD, O my soul, and forget not all his benefits—who forgives all your sins…who redeems your life from the pit and crowns you with love and compassion."

Indeed, Mark and Marnie's lives have not only been redeemed for eternity, they've been redeemed for a purpose in the here and now. Mark and his wife, Debra, founded Faithful and True Ministries, a Christian recovery ministry for people struggling to overcome sexual addiction. Dr. Mark Laaser has gone on to become one of the foremost experts on sexual addiction in both the Christian and secular communities.

And Marnie became a licensed marriage and family therapist and founded Bethesda Workshop Ministry, which provides intensive clinical workshops for sex addicts, their spouses, and sexually addicted couples. In 1997 she founded a treatment program, which was the first of its kind in the country, for female sex addicts.

If God can rescue Mark and Marnie, *He can rescue you*—no matter the length of your addiction or the strength of the web. Both of them testify to the Lord's life-changing work in their lives, for "then they cried to the LORD in their trouble, and he saved them from their distress. He brought them out of darkness and the deepest gloom and broke away their chains" (Psalm 107:13-14).

Make a commitment to Christ
not to dwell on an impure thought.
Make a covenant with Christ
to live with purity in your heart.

—JUNE HUNT

SEXUAL ADDICTION: ANSWERS IN GOD'S WORD

QUESTION: "Does God care if I have impure thoughts?"

ANSWER: *"God did not call us to be impure, but to live a holy life"* (1 Thessalonians 4:7).

QUESTION: "Why should I keep my eyes focused on the Lord?"

ANSWER: *"My eyes are ever on the LORD, for only he will release my feet from the snare"* (Psalm 25:15).

QUESTION: "Can I make a covenant with my eyes to not look with lust?"

ANSWER: *"I made a covenant with my eyes not to look lustfully at a girl"* (Job 31:1).

QUESTION: "What happens if I am tempted beyond what I can bear?"

ANSWER: *"No temptation has seized you except what is common to man. And God is faithful; he will not let you be tempted beyond what you can bear. But when you are tempted, he will also provide a way out so that you can stand up under it"* (1 Corinthians 10:13).

QUESTION: "How is it possible to have only true and pure thoughts?"

ANSWER: *"Whatever is true, whatever is noble, whatever is right, whatever is pure, whatever is lovely, whatever is admirable—if anything is excellent or praiseworthy—think about such things"* (Philippians 4:8).

QUESTION: "Why is it important to avoid sexual immorality?"

ANSWER: *"It is God's will that you should be sanctified: that you should avoid sexual immorality"* (1 Thessalonians 4:3).

QUESTION: "Is it possible to commit adultery in my heart?"

ANSWER: *"Anyone who looks at a woman lustfully has already committed adultery with her in his heart"* (Matthew 5:28).

QUESTION: "How should I handle my earthly nature?"

ANSWER: *"Put to death...whatever belongs to your earthly nature: sexual immorality, impurity, lust, evil desires and greed, which is idolatry"* (Colossians 3:5).

QUESTION: "What is the harm in sowing to my fleshly desires?"

ANSWER: *"Do not be deceived: God cannot be mocked. A man reaps what he sows. The one who sows to please his sinful nature, from that nature will reap destruction; the one who sows to please the Spirit, from the Spirit will reap eternal life"* (Galatians 6:7-8).

QUESTION: "Is is possible to not conform to the pattern of this world?"

ANSWER: *"Do not conform any longer to the pattern of this world, but be transformed by the renewing of your mind. Then you will be able to test and approve what God's will is—his good, pleasing and perfect will"* (Romans 12:2).

Part 2:

LEAVING THE WORLD OF ADDICTIONS

LEAVING THE
WORLD OF ADDICTIONS

The addicted live in a world of pain—pain mixed with pleasure. But as time goes on, the pain increases to the extent of compromising their character, harming their health, and wrecking their relationships.

Those who haven't struggled with an addiction—whether it be alcohol or drug abuse, anorexia or bulimia, sexual addiction, compulsive eating, gambling or spending—might logically think, *Why don't they just stop?*

What keeps strugglers buried under a landslide of pain?

The truth is, the addicted struggler longs to be free. No one delights in being addicted; no one wants to be held in bondage. No one's first choice is to stay in bondage. So why do those who are addicted continually repeat the behaviors that produce pain?

The key word here is *pain*. The struggler assumes, "I can't stop. It would be too painful—much more painful than what I'm experiencing now." The pain these people have known is familiar and it's laced with pleasure. But these strugglers feel a deep dread about the pain awaiting them should they begin the ascent from their familiar world of addiction.

What I say to addicted strugglers is this: Either way you go, you're going to have pain. If you stay as you are, you're going to have pain. If you leave the world of addiction, you're going to have pain. But making the courageous decision to break free of the addiction is the only way you will ultimately experience freedom.

Make no mistake about it—going through rehab can be grueling. Sticking with a 12-step program is strenuous. Finding your "new normal" doesn't come fast and easy. A person struggling to break free of an addiction will experience pain—you can count on it. But don't underestimate the devastating pain and perhaps irreversible consequences of staying pinned by the gravitational pull of addiction.

Pain can be your *ally* or your *enemy*. Pain is our *ally* when it serves as the catalyst for a life-changing move. Pain is our *enemy* when it draws us into the world of addiction and entraps us. I tell strugglers on *Hope in the Night* (our live call-in, counseling radio program), "It's going to hurt either way. You can either endure the pain now...or later." One pain is *destructive*, the other, *constructive*.

Those leaving the World of Addiction ultimately realize...there's much *more* pain than pleasure in staying! They cautiously, but bravely, step away from their wildly spinning world and onto the road to recovery, not knowing all the positive life changes that await them but hanging on to hope that a better life...a better world is ahead. If that first step is never taken, renewed self-worth...restored relationships...revitalized health...will never be realized.

It's a new world, indeed...and one worth discovering at all costs. For where there is now pain, there can be peace. Where there is now hurt, there can be healing. A world spiraling out of control can one day be set on a positive course leading to freedom and a life lived to fully please God.

The decision to leave the World of Addiction can be bolstered by the following biblical account. Remember the prodigal son...who requested his share of his father's inheritance early...who spent every penny of it on wild living...who became addicted to whatever brought him pleasure? Well, it didn't take long for *pain* to overtake *pleasure* in his life. He not only ended up feeding pigs to make a living, he longed to eat their food!

But one day he made a bold and brave decision...he would make a *painful* admission before his father...he would walk that humbling, difficult, and *painful* road back home...in hopes of a better life. He confessed to his father that he had squandered his inheritance and hoped he would find *limited freedom* in his household, as a slave.

But the painful road to recovery...led to *full freedom*...as his father compassionately embraced him, still fully recognized him as his son, and even hosted a celebration!

The father figure in the story represents God, who longs to restore *you*, to help *you*, to grant *you* full freedom from whatever has you in bondage! Like the prodigal, exchange your pain and anxiety...for peace and joy!

"It is for freedom that Christ has set us free"
(GALATIANS 5:1).

THE POWERFUL WORLD OF PRAYER:

How to Pray When You Don't Know What to Say

A fter reading about Frank's struggle with addiction and then Karen's (see chapter 1), I was in awe. Just a few days prior, the thought of sharing their stories—particularly in this book—was nonexistent. What had transpired was completely unplanned (but clearly planned by God). Of course, this should have been no surprise because the Lord says, "I know the plans I have for you...plans to give you hope and a future" (Jeremiah 29:11).

And there's more! As Karen and I talked deep into the night, she shared about her tenuous walk out of addiction. She was seriously scared. How would she handle those first days, weeks, months...and yes, even years? With a solid ten-year binge (minus two days) as her background, where exactly would she begin?

Praying for Perseverance

Initially Karen found herself in the greatest struggle of her life. After beginning her walk out of bondage, she couldn't afford to lose control—she couldn't allow the addiction to win. Karen had to keep her focus on the Lord. She knew her victory would come only through Him.

Because of her desperate desire to stay sober, Karen prayed often—*simply for herself.* In the morning, throughout the day, and in the evening she kept herself continually grounded in prayer, asking for God's amazing grace. The following prayers reflect what she prayed (which can also be prayed by any struggler).

1. *"Forgive Me"—My Morning Prayer (Didn't Make It Through the Night)*

Breaking an addiction is never charted as a straight, upward line on a graph.

When a single step backward happens, strugglers fear a downward plunge isn't far away. And when a few steps backward happen, then it becomes extremely hard not to give up—not to assume failure is inevitable. Strugglers want to hope but are afraid to hope because of so many past failed attempts. They need assurance that a sober life is within reach—that it is indeed possible!

> O Father, have mercy on me. *I can't do this!* I'm afraid to hope…I'm afraid to try. I keep messing up! I've failed again—and that hurts so much.
>
> Father God, I'm so sorry. I don't want to be this way, this kind of person. I have no clue how to be okay with myself.
>
> Once again, Father, forgive me. Please have mercy on me. I know You're not surprised by what I did last night, but I am. I'm scared—I'm scared to hope, scared to think that a life of freedom could be possible. Please, please give me the strength to hope. Build in me the desire to want to change.
>
> God, I know I can't do this, but I know *You can*! Please…today! Lord, please continue the change You have begun in me, even if I can't see it or feel it. Thank You, Father, for Your compassion. Thank You for not giving up on me. Precious Lord, thank You.

> *"LORD, forgive my iniquity, though it is great…Have mercy on me, O God, according to your unfailing love; according to your great compassion blot out my transgressions. Wash away all my iniquity and cleanse me from my sin"*
> (PSALM 25:11; 51:1-2).

2. *"Strengthen Me"—My Morning Prayer (Made It Through the Night)*

After a night of abstaining, strugglers still know they are but one step away from relapse—after all, they've failed so many times before. They need continual strength and prayer to persevere—strength beyond themselves.

> Father God, thank You! I praise You for allowing me victory last night, but I need Your strength—now! You have given me Your promise that "I can do all things through Christ who strengthens me" (Philippians 4:13 NKJV). Enable me to cling to that promise. O God, wrap Your thoughts around my thoughts. Take control of my mind. Give me a guarded mind.
>
> Father, please, *please* guard me from choosing my old habits— my old life of bondage—and give me strength to make new choices,

to choose the new life of freedom. Take this addiction. Once again, I give it to You today. Fill my weakness with Your strength. I need the freedom You have planned for me.

Precious Lord, I know who is doing this through me. I know it's You. Thank You!

> *"My soul is weary with sorrow; strengthen me*
> *according to your word. Keep me from deceitful*
> *ways; be gracious to me through your law"*
> (PSALM 119:28-29).

3. *"Restore Me"—My Midday Prayer (Need to Make It Through the Day)*

Afternoon to evening is the prime time to pray because it is also the prime time for the enemy to begin his work on the mind of the struggler. Whatever feelings the struggler may have in the morning hours tend to recede by midday as thoughts turn to making specific plans for the evening. Once an after-work routine is decided on and put in place, the mental and emotional shift is immediate and strong. Without the power of prayer, personal weakness—coupled with attacks from the enemy—almost guarantee a relapse. A key initiative also is to focus on the ultimate goal—restoration. This involves a restored heart, restored health, and restored hope.

> O Father, heal me. Restore me. I want the life You want for me. I so want You! Build my trust in You. Replace these thoughts that are consuming me. *I cannot do this*—but I know You can. And I know You want freedom for me.
>
> *Restore my heart* so that I want what You want for me. Create in me a pure heart, O God. Keep me close to You. I want to trust You; I need to trust You. Help me to trust You.
>
> *Restore my health.* Grant me a willing spirit to do what's best for my body—make me willing to be willing! I want to be willing to do what is right. Loving Lord, replace anything that is impure with only what is pure.
>
> *Restore my hope*—hope for the life You've promised me, the life You've created for me from the beginning of time, even knowing how I would mess up so much of it. Thank You for not leaving me. Help me, Lord Jesus. Open my eyes to see You today, to trust You, to see Your hand at work restoring my life. Precious Lord, thank You.

> *"Create in me a pure heart, O God, and renew a steadfast*
> *spirit within me...Restore to me the joy of your salvation*
> *and grant me a willing spirit, to sustain me"*
> (PSALM 51:10,12).

4. *"Protect Me"—My Evening Prayer (Help Me Make It Through the Night)*

At the close of the workday, when a recovering person's responsibilities are concluded, the darkness seems to usher in a weakening of the will—a weakening of resolve and desire. An open schedule poses a great danger. It feels as if all of the enemy's forces intensify and attack as the structured obligations of the workday are replaced by the person's self-imposed structure—or lack of it—for the evening.

> O Father, precious God, surround me! I need Your protection. I need Your power. I need You. I cannot fight the temptation alone. Please take it. Please *do* it!
>
> You promise to go ahead of me and to come behind me. You promise to come alongside me and protect me. Father, I need Your protection now. Keep me close to You tonight. Wrap me in the shelter of Your wing. Hide my weakness in Your strength. Thank You that You will strengthen me.
>
> Lord, I want to live a life of total integrity, but I can't do it without You. Precious Lord, protect me tonight. Thank You.

> *"Guard my life and rescue me; let me not be put to shame,*
> *for I take refuge in you. May integrity and uprightness*
> *protect me, because my hope is in you... You are my*
> *hiding place; you will protect me from trouble"*
> (PSALM 25:20-21; 32:7).

5. *"Rescue Me"—My Refuge Prayer (When I Need a Refuge—Day or Night)*

> Father, precious God, You are my Refuge, my Rock, my Deliverer. I cannot fight this battle by myself. I need Your strength. I need You! Victorious God, I need You—I need Your victory in my life.
>
> Precious God, I do want the life You want for me. I so want to be the person You created me to be. I yield my will to Your will.
>
> You are my Rescuer, You are my Refuge, You are my Rock! Thank You, precious Lord, thank You! In Your strong name I pray.

*"Turn your ear to me, come quickly to my rescue; be my rock of
refuge, a strong fortress to save me. Since you are my rock and
my fortress, for the sake of your name lead and guide me. Free
me from the trap that is set for me, for you are my refuge"*
(Psalm 31:2-4).

6. *"Preserve Me"—My Daily Prayer*

Every day, strugglers need to focus their hearts and minds on what will preserve their lives.

O God, preserve my life. Please, precious Father, don't let it be wasted. Thank You for the hope of this new life. Father, allow me today to live the life You have planned for me. Turn my thoughts from worthless things. Focus my mind on Your things—on Your will for me, Your Word for me, Your way for me.

Father God, focus my heart on Your heart. You are my *focus*. You *are* my life.

Think through me, love through me, live through me today. Precious God, preserve me. I'm so human. The things I'm drawn to are such a waste of time, a waste of life, so incredibly worthless.

Father God, continue to guide me in Your way. Hold me close—don't let me slip. Preserve me, fill me, strengthen me. Precious Lord, thank You. Thank You for grace!

*"Turn my eyes away from worthless things;
preserve my life according to your word...
I have suffered much; preserve my life, O Lord"*
(Psalm 119:37,107).

7. *"Shield Me"—Destroy the Stronghold*

For seeking God's supernatural support during the spiritual battle:

How I thank You, Father, for accepting me into Your family, for adopting me as Your child—what a great gift! And, thank You that Christ, who is in me, is greater than any enemy who could defeat me. I know I've been bought with a price. My body isn't my own anymore—it belongs to Christ.

Lord God, I acknowledge that the enemy is already defeated and has no authority over me. I refuse all thoughts that are not from You, and I resist the enemy's power. As I stand in the full armor of God, I ask You to destroy any stronghold in my life.

Just as You put a hedge of protection around Job, I ask You to put a hedge of protection completely around me. Station Your strong and sturdy angels around me today that they may guard me. Please, please, please protect me.

In the strong name of Jesus I pray.

> *"The LORD is my rock, my fortress and my deliverer; my God is my rock, in whom I take refuge. He is my shield and the horn of my salvation, my stronghold... You are my refuge and my shield; I have put my hope in your word"*
> (PSALM 18:2; 119:114).

Praying the Scriptures

The Lord, who is our Shepherd, cares about His sheep. He wants all His sheep to return to Him, to be under His care. Although we've all wandered far from home, far from the truth, He loves His wanderers and wants His best for each one.

At times Karen would pray the Scriptures for her brother, putting Frank's name in the verses. At other times she would pray the verses for herself as a reminder of the truth that "the LORD is my shepherd" (Psalm 23:1).

The Psalms express many sensitive prayers to God—sometimes pleading, sometimes thankful—prayers that ask for God's intervention. Many of these prayers express fear, doubt, and despair. Others convey strength, hope, and freedom. And they were all written with a heart seeking after God's own heart.

"Free Me" Scripture Prayer

"My eyes are ever on the LORD, for only he will release my feet from the snare... The troubles of my heart have multiplied; free me from my anguish...In my anguish I cried to the LORD, and he answered by setting me free" (Psalm 25:15,17; 118:5).

"Guard Me" Scripture Prayer

"Hear, O LORD, and answer me, for I am poor and needy. Guard my life, for I am devoted to you. You are my God; save your servant who trusts in you...Set a guard over my mouth, O LORD; keep watch over the door of my lips" (Psalm 86:1-2; Psalm 141:3).

"Teach Me" Scripture Prayer

"Have mercy on me, O LORD, for I call to you all day long... Teach me your way,

O LORD, *and I will walk in your truth; give me an undivided heart, that I may* [*honor*] *your name"* (Psalm 86:3,11).

"Deliver Me" Scripture Prayer

"I love the LORD, *for he heard my voice; he heard my cry for mercy. Because he turned his ear to me, I will call on him as long as I live…For you, O* LORD, *have delivered my soul from death, my eyes from tears, my feet from stumbling, that I may walk before the* LORD *in the land of the living"* (Psalm 116:1-2,8-9).

Praying for Strugglers

Prayer is talking with God. It is inviting Him to intervene in our situation. Prayer is bringing all He is into our situation.

Because strugglers experience so many failed attempts at dealing with their addictions, friends and family sometimes find it hard to stay closely connected. They experience frustration and despair as the struggler, inconceivably to them, falls yet another time. It may take decades of prayer and a thousand false starts, but we are to continue to pray for our strugglers—no matter what they do or don't do. The Bible says, "As for me, far be it from me that I should sin against the LORD by failing to pray for you" (1 Samuel 12:23).

My friend Karen shared these poignant words with me:

> Loving our strugglers can be agony for us because we want so badly to "fix" them—*which we cannot do.* But in the process, *we learn we can trust Him*—which seems to take way too long. Yet in that "way-too-long" time, we come to meet God, and know Him more deeply, through prayer.
>
> In reality, the most valuable part of our prayers is not merely an effort to get what we want but rather an effort *to get what He wants.* Through prayer, God allows us to know Him better—the true image of Him, not the punishing image I'd carried for so many years.
>
> Realize that the Lord begins His work inside the struggler—*to hate the sin* and *to desire change*—long before it is evident on the outside. We are helpless to bring someone into clean and sober living.

"Set the Captive Free" Scripture Prayer

While the needs of strugglers are different, there are ways we can lift them up to the Lord that will speak specifically to what they are experiencing during different times of the day. Karen prayed for her brother all through his recovery, and continues to pray for him.

Thank You, Father, for (<u>name</u>). Thank You for allowing him another day. God, surround him and allow him to feel Your love—touch him today in a real way and let him feel Your presence, Your hope, Your promise. Open his eyes and heart to You, Lord. You've promised to give freedom to the captive and bind up the brokenhearted. Oh Father, free him from his darkness. Release him from his prison of addiction. I claim these promises for (<u>name</u>) today. God, he needs all of this and more.

"[Jesus] has sent me to bind up the brokenhearted, to proclaim freedom for the captives and release from darkness for the prisoners"
(Isaiah 61:1).

"On the Wrong Road" Scripture Prayer

Frank prays often for the people God brings into his life. Some are not yet prepared to address their addiction and walk toward freedom, while others have bravely determined to step out on the new path toward the life God has prepared for them. The following two prayers reveal how, as a recovery pastor and friend, Frank lifted up a struggler named "Jake" during his journey down two different paths.

Heavenly Father, thank You for putting (<u>name</u>) in my life and for Your plans for him. I lift him up to You. May he allow You to move in his heart and to prepare him for total change. Lord, please protect him from himself as he continues down this road.

May he develop a desire for something better for his life. Take away the pleasure that comes from this addiction and replace it with an emptiness that only You can fill. Bring him to the point where he realizes there is no joy in his dependency.

Lord, use whatever means necessary to bring him to his knees, to have a willing heart to answer to Your call, to have a change of mind that leads him to seek Your help.

And, Lord, help me to be willing and able to respond when he is ready. Thank You for Your many mercies toward me.

Show (<u>name</u>) the right path, O Lord; point out the road for him to follow. Lead him by Your truth and teach him for You are the God who saves (from Psalm 25:4-5).

"On the Right Road" Scripture Prayer

As Jake became willing to take that step and ask for help, Frank was on hand to surround him with practical support, a sense of community, and sincere prayer. Even though Jake was no longer on the wrong path, he still needed prayer as much as ever. All strugglers need to know someone is faithfully lifting them up in prayer and asking that they will find strength to stay on the right path.

> Heavenly Father, thank You for the mercy You've given me and the mercy You have shown (<u>name</u>) in allowing him the strength and courage to fight this battle with addiction. Lord, I pray he would know that in every temptation, You provide a way of escape. And I pray he would realize that no temptation is greater than he can handle if he continues to look to You for strength.
>
> Father, make Your presence felt in his heart, and each day touch him and draw him closer to You. Help him to see You as his strong and loving Father who waits for him with open arms, wanting nothing more than a restored fellowship with him.
>
> Thank You for putting him on this path toward hope and healing. In Your merciful name I pray.

How natural, then, for Frank to share with Jake 1 Corinthians 10:13: "No temptation has seized you except what is common to man. And God is faithful; he will not let you be tempted beyond what you can bear. But when you are tempted, he will also provide a way out so that you can stand up under it."

As Frank ministers to all of the "Jakes" in his life, he sees how his mess has become his ministry. God has made his personal test become his testimony. And it's absolutely been proven true countless times that *what the enemy meant for evil, God has used for good.*

THE VITAL WORLD OF CRISIS INTERVENTION:
How to Confront...Because You Care

One of the most powerful acts on behalf of someone struggling with addiction is a *crisis intervention*[1]—a carefully orchestrated meeting that brings together family, friends, coworkers, and other caring individuals in an effort to persuade the struggler to voluntarily engage in treatment. During the meeting, group members recount specific ways in which the struggler's addictive behavior has become a major detriment.

This "tough love" method of intervention is effective 80 percent of the time in motivating strugglers to receive the critical help they so desperately need. And the most powerful aspect of a crisis intervention is the group dynamic—it's true that there is power in numbers! Typically, when just one family member seeks to stop an addict's behavior, the appeal will fall on deaf ears. And as others state their concern privately one by one, each plea is dismissed.

While as individuals they are powerless to persuade the struggler to get help, as a group, they are powerful. In fact, a group can be empowered by God to move the immovable. God's Word lays out the blueprint for such an intervention:

> *"If your brother sins against you, go and show him his*
> *fault, just between the two of you. If he listens to you, you*
> *have won your brother over. But if he will not listen, take*
> *one or two others along, so that every matter may be*
> *established by the testimony of two or three witnesses"*
> (MATTHEW 18:15-16).

Steps to a Successful Crisis Intervention
- **Pray for wisdom** and understanding from the Lord.

"The LORD gives wisdom, and from his mouth
come knowledge and understanding"
(PROVERBS 2:6).

- **Educate yourself regarding crisis intervention programs.** Read materials on intervention and visit treatment facilities.

    "The heart of the discerning acquires knowledge;
    the ears of the wise seek it out"
    (PROVERBS 18:15).

- **Call a counseling office** and request a referral to a Christian leader who is trained in intervention procedures.

    "Plans fail for lack of counsel,
    but with many advisers they succeed"
    (PROVERBS 15:22).

- **Meet with a trained leader** (usually referred to as an *interventionist*) to plan the intervention. Learn how an intervention works and discuss treatment program options, preadmission plans, procedures, insurance, and the impact of treatment on the struggler's employment.

    "Listen to advice and accept instruction,
    and in the end you will be wise"
    (PROVERBS 19:20).

- **Enlist the participation of key people** affected by the struggler's harmful behavior who are willing to confront him or her (caring family members, friends, coworkers, doctor, employer, spiritual leader).

    "A truthful witness saves lives"
    (PROVERBS 14:25).

- **Hold a first meeting** (*in absolute confidentiality* and *without the struggler present*) to give everyone a chance to get to know each other, to share the impact the struggler's behavior has had on each person's life, and to receive complete details on how the intervention will happen.

    "A truthful witness gives honest testimony"
    (PROVERBS 12:17).

- **Hold a second meeting** (*in absolute confidentiality* and *without the struggler present*) during which key people rehearse (with the interventionist) *what* they will say, *how* they will say it, and *the order* in which they will confront. They will also all determine and agree upon the consequences if the struggler declines their help.

  > *"Better is open rebuke than hidden love.*
  > *Wounds from a friend can be trusted"*
  > (PROVERBS 27:5-6).

- **Hold a third meeting** (*with the struggler present*) and have each person communicate his or her genuine care for the struggler and share the rehearsed confrontations. (Examples are found in "The Six Ps of an Appeal" in the next section.)

  > *"The tongue that brings healing is a tree of life,*
  > *but a deceitful tongue crushes the spirit"*
  > (PROVERBS 15:4).

- **After everyone has shared**, the interventionist conveys the courage it took for everyone involved to be there and their willingness to support the struggler throughout the treatment period. The interventionist clearly details the negative consequences of the addiction if treatment is refused. The struggler is then given reasons why immediate, urgent care is necessary and is told that a room has been reserved at a treatment facility.

  > *"Who is wise? He will realize these things. Who is discerning?*
  > *He will understand them. The ways of the LORD are right; the*
  > *righteous walk in them, but the rebellious stumble in them"*
  > (HOSEA 14:9).

- **This third meeting should conclude** with the struggler either immediately entering a treatment program or experiencing the repercussions for refusing treatment previously agreed on by the group.

  > *"He who rebukes a man will in the end gain more*
  > *favor than he who has a flattering tongue"*
  > (PROVERBS 28:23).

Those who participate in crisis interventions experience deep anguish at the suffering of different loved ones and can readily relate to these words:

> *"I will not keep silent;*
> *I will speak out in the anguish of my spirit"*
> (Job 7:11).

The Six Ps of an Appeal[2]

1. *The Personal*

Affirm rather than attack.

- "I want you to know how much I care about you—that's why I'm here."

- "I sincerely love you, and I'm terribly concerned about you."

> *"Do not let any unwholesome talk come out of your mouths,*
> *but only what is helpful for building others up according*
> *to their needs, that it may benefit those who listen"*
> (Ephesians 4:29).

2. *The Past*

Give a recent, specific example describing the struggler's negative behavior and the personal impact it has had on you. Be brief, keeping examples to three or four sentences.

- "Dad, last night I felt so embarrassed when you were obviously (insert behavior) and slurring your speech in front of my friends."

- "Mom, you 'forgot' my last three school programs. I don't feel like you really love me."

> *"A man of knowledge uses words with restraint,*
> *and a man of understanding is even-tempered"*
> (Proverbs 17:27).

3. *The Pain*

Emphasize the painful impact the struggler's behavior has had on you. Use "I" statements.

- "I've felt so humiliated at being yelled at in front of our friends. I can't begin to describe the pain!"

- "As your best friend, I feel cut out of your life. That hurts me so much!"

> *"A wise man's heart guides his mouth,*
> *and his lips promote instruction"*
> (Proverbs 16:23).

4. *The Plea*

Make a personal plea for your struggler to receive treatment.

– "I plead with you to get the help you need to overcome your addiction."

– "If you're willing, you'll have my help and my deepest respect."

"The tongue has the power of life and death"
(PROVERBS 18:21).

5. *The Plan*

Be prepared to implement an immediate plan if treatment is agreed on.

– "Your bags have been packed."

– "You have been accepted into the treatment program at _____."

*"Rescue those being led away to death; hold back those
staggering toward slaughter. If you say, 'But we knew nothing
about this,' does not he who weighs the heart perceive
it? Does not he who guards your life know it? Will he not
repay each person according to what he has done?"*
(PROVERBS 24:11-12).

6. *The Price*

If the plan for treatment is refused, detail the repercussions.

– "We cannot allow you to come home or to be with our family until after you've been through the treatment program."

– "You must be addiction-free for (name a specific period of time)."

*"Stern discipline awaits him who leaves the
path; he who hates correction will die"*
(PROVERBS 15:10).

The Don'ts of Dialogue[3]

We can be on the side of *right*, yet our actions can still be *wrong*. However, many times we can influence a person to want to change not by what we say but by how we say it. The Bible says, "If someone is caught in a sin, you who are spiritual should restore him gently" (Galatians 6:1).

• ***Don't* get involved in name-calling,** preaching, or being judgmental. Instead, focus on the struggler's behavior.

– "Last night, I felt belittled when you called me those vile names."

> *"A man who lacks judgment derides his neighbor,*
> *but a man of understanding holds his tongue"*
> (PROVERBS 11:12).

- ***Don't* come to the defense** of the struggler when others are confronting him or her. Instead, affirm the feelings of the confronter.
  – "It's understandable that his (the struggler's) actions were extremely hurtful to you."

> *"There is a...time to be silent and a time to speak"*
> (ECCLESIASTES 3:1,7).

- ***Don't* argue** if your facts are disputed.
  – "I'm hearing you say your words weren't cutting. We'll just agree to disagree."

> *"The Lord's servant must not quarrel"*
> (2 TIMOTHY 2:24).

- ***Don't* overreact.** Instead, keep your emotions under control.
  – If you are verbally attacked, calmly state your position. If opposed again, calmly repeat the same words again...and again. "This is in your best interest."

> *"Everyone should be quick to listen, slow to speak*
> *and slow to become angry, for man's anger does not*
> *bring about the righteous life that God desires"*
> (JAMES 1:19-20).

- ***Don't* give ultimatums** unless you are prepared to follow through with them. Hold your ground.
  – If your struggler hasn't followed through and finished what was promised and then says, "Let me come back home. I've learned my lesson! I promise not to do it again," you should say, "No, you cannot come back until you have completed the program."

> *"Let your 'Yes' be yes, and your 'No,' no"*
> (JAMES 5:12).

- ***Don't* shield your loved one from facing the consequences of addiction.** Instead, maintain your integrity.

  – "I will not lie to your boss again."

  > *"A man reaps what he sows"*
  > (Galatians 6:7).

- ***Don't* accept promises with no commitment** for immediate action. Instead, realize that words without actions are worthless.

  – If the response is, "I can't go now, but I promise to go next month," your role as the boundary setter is to convey the repercussions for delay.

  > *"A simple man believes anything,*
  > *but a prudent man gives thought to his steps"*
  > (Proverbs 14:15).

To some, the idea of participating in a crisis intervention could seem like a conspiracy against the struggler. And other would-be participants could fear that they will offend or jeopardize the relationship with the struggler. Rather than viewing intervention as a conspiracy, however, think of it as a collaboration—a caring group of loving, committed supporters willing to temporarily forego the understanding and approval of a struggler in exchange for the possibility of a greater long-term good. Take heart in knowing that one day your struggler will most likely see your role of courageous compassion through God's eyes, and thank you, realizing that "wounds from a sincere friend are better than many kisses from an enemy."[4]

A Few Words from Frank

As a recovery pastor, I've participated in many crisis interventions. One of the most memorable confrontations was conducted by the family of a very close friend.

"Steve" had become so consumed by his addiction that he no longer viewed his actions as right or wrong. He was able to rationalize and excuse almost any wrong behavior so long as it helped him meet his "needs." And his greatest need was the next high.

As Steve's heroin addiction mushroomed, so did his need to find ways to finance it. For years prior to the intervention, he had borrowed money, stolen possessions, cheated, and lied to virtually every family member, friend, and acquaintance he had. He told me later his motivation wasn't as much about seeking pleasure as it was about numbing the pain. Yet the consequences of his actions were catastrophic.

At the despairing depth of his addiction, being sober was synonymous with experiencing extreme pain—the pain of withdrawal, failed relationships, financial crises, and hopelessness. Steve's drug of choice had long since stopped providing any pleasure. Instead, it had become his only means of escaping his tortured existence.

Steve's family conducted the intervention beautifully, with each participant compassionately pouring out love, concern, and a desire to be there for him throughout his recovery—should he choose that path. At first, Steve steadfastly resisted their strong show of support. He was desperately afraid of facing a sober life. His poor choices had created such a mountain of consequences that he had lost all hope for change. (It's hard to communicate the confusing chasm we face at the end of our addiction. We cannot stand the thought of living one more day under its influence, but we are even more fearful of being deprived of its effect.)

Eventually Steve found the courage and motivation to enter rehab. Though he's had a couple of slips along the way—quite common for those attempting to break free from addiction—he now has logged over a year of sobriety. I believe—as does Steve—that if it were not for the remarkable support of his loving family and their willingness to intervene on his behalf, Steve would not be alive today.

THE HEALING WORLD OF REHAB:

How to Know the Ins and Outs

M y friend Frank admitted that he couldn't have conquered his decades of
addiction had it not been for rehab. In a forthright manner, he reflected
on the role of rehab in his recovery.

> As someone who's gone through rehab, I found that a residential set-
> ting away from my own home provided the *enforced break* from my
> addiction that I so desperately needed. The rehab experience gave
> me time to "come to my senses."
>
> Residential rehab may not be possible in every situation due to
> budget or unchangeable responsibilities, but for a long-term user
> like me, it was invaluable. I needed this type of structured program
> because on my own, I had tried—and failed—so many times. I just
> couldn't muster the willpower to try again. I needed professional
> help—and a lot of it.
>
> For me, a male-only program was important. Coed centers can
> have additional distractions that detract from one's progress dur-
> ing treatment.
>
> At the rehab center, I was offered the option of either a tradi-
> tional track (a secular 12-step program) or a Christian track (which
> ties the 12 steps to Christian principles). Both options can be very
> effective depending on the individual. No matter the approach, I
> needed a fresh lens through which to view my problem.
>
> After participating in a monthlong residential program, I moved
> to a transitional living environment known as a "sober living house."
> This arrangement provided increased freedom while maintaining a
> high level of supervision and support. Most rehab centers offer this

transitional option to patients because it helps you learn to live without being dependent.

As an alcoholic, I relied on chemicals for so long I had very little ability to cope with the daily stresses and strains that are a normal part of life. My chronic abuse, as a coping tool, short-circuited my emotional development. As a result, I needed as much time as possible to develop and recalibrate my emotional responses.

A residential rehab isn't the only effective treatment method. A day care rehab program or intensive outpatient program (IOP) is another strong solution. These programs offer the same basic content as a residential treatment facility, but allow strugglers to maintain their jobs and return home at night. While it takes longer to receive the same amount of counseling, the end result is the same. Professional input is needed to help you decide whether this option is a good one for you.

Realize that a lack of knowledge or willpower rarely keeps a person from sobriety. Rather, it's their unresolved issues (fear, resentment, guilt) that typically perpetuate the addiction. For this reason, if the day treatment option is chosen, it's essential for strugglers to return each evening to a loving, supportive home environment.

I thank God for beginning my healing at rehab and I cannot overstate its importance in my life. For me, it proved to be pivotal in my recovery.

Addiction, by definition, is chronic. Addicted strugglers cannot "just say no," end their addiction, and be cured. Though God can—and sometimes does—miraculously intervene by delivering a person "overnight," the vast majority of sufferers require long-term help or repeated periods of care to recover.

Chronic addiction damages every aspect of a person's being: physical, psychological, social, and spiritual. As a result, treatment is not simple.

Is a Rehabilitation Program Necessary?

For strugglers like Frank who cannot stop on their own, a treatment program can help manage the withdrawals and teach valuable skills for sober living. Such programs, commonly called "rehabs," are geared toward helping...

- Stop addiction
- Maintain a healthy and addiction-free lifestyle
- Function productively within a family, at work, and in society

How to Choose a Rehabilitation Program[1]

Ask these questions:

1. Does the program accept health insurance? If not, will they work with the struggler and family to create an affordable payment plan?
2. Is the program run by trained professionals who are state-accredited/licensed?
3. Is the facility clean, organized, and well-run?
4. Does the program offer treatment for a full range of needs?
5. Does it address disabilities and provide age, gender, and culturally appropriate treatment services?
6. Is the struggler's treatment plan continuously assessed to ensure it meets changing needs?
7. Is medication, if appropriate, part of the treatment?
8. Is long-term aftercare encouraged or provided?
9. Are strategies in place to engage and keep the struggler in longer-term treatment so as to have a greater opportunity for success?
10. Is there ongoing monitoring after the struggler is released to help prevent a relapse?
11. Are there services or referrals offered to family members to ensure they understand the process and support the struggler in the course of recovery?
12. Are counseling and other behavioral therapies provided to help the struggler function within the family and community?

What Does Rehabilitation Involve?[2]

Certain key elements are common to nearly all effective rehabilitation programs. These include:

- **Initial assessment.** If the assessment reveals that urgent medical attention is needed, the struggler will be referred to a health care provider to oversee this process. (See "Detoxification" below.)
- **Plan development.** A counselor or case manager will be assigned to create a detailed treatment plan to be executed by a team of trained individuals. And just as the struggler needs support, education, and counseling, so does the family. That's because an addiction negatively

impacts how the family functions. Program providers should engage the family in treatment as early as possible.

- **Therapy.** Rehabilitation typically involves individual and group counseling. In addition, comprehensive programs will include individual-growth assignments, addiction education, life-skills training, relapse-prevention training, spiritual care, nutrition, participation in physical activities, and pain management, if necessary.

- **Discharge and aftercare.** Upon discharge, strugglers receive an aftercare plan that should be followed carefully. Aftercare is designed to provide coping skills for everyday living and be a safeguard against relapses. Aftercare plans often include a recommendation to attend some type of group counseling, such as a 12-step program (see pages 377-85), and regular meetings with a therapist. Christian programs stress the importance of active church involvement.

What Is Detoxification?

In cases involving physical addiction, many substance abusers will need to go through detoxification (often referred to as *detox*) before starting treatment.

- **Detoxification** refers to the clearing of toxins from the system of an alcohol- or drug-dependent person. It is part of a medically managed process designed to alleviate the short-term symptoms of withdrawal from alcohol and drug dependence.[3]

- **Detoxification** is the process of weaning the body from chemical dependence. It is arduous at best, and should be undertaken with a doctor's supervision. The risk for the most serious withdrawal symptoms (such as seizure, heart failure, and hallucination) is generally confined to a three-week period, but other signs of withdrawal (like anxiety or difficulty in sleeping) could remain for an entire year of sobriety. A doctor will often prescribe medications to lessen the most severe withdrawal symptoms and to help remove the struggler's dependence on drugs or alcohol.

Anyone who is chemically dependent should consult their doctor for help with withdrawal and recovery. Physical, emotional, and spiritual care is needed to break the chains of addiction. For many, this will mean entering a clinic or rehabilitation facility, but others may be able to visit doctors, counselors, and therapists while recovering at home.

What Are the Primary Types of Rehabilitation Programs?

Rehabilitation may take place in a variety of settings. Most programs offer similar therapies, but the duration and the level of medical care may vary. The most common types of rehabilitation programs are:

- **Hospital- or medical clinic-based.** Inpatient stays in specialized rehab units are less common than they used to be, primarily because of changes in insurance coverage.

- **Residential treatment facilities.** Living in a residential facility while recovering from addiction can be especially helpful to strugglers who have little social support or who need isolation from destructive influences.

- **Partial hospitalization (day treatment).** These strugglers live at home while taking part in day treatment. This treatment works best for strugglers with supportive families and stable home environments.

- **Outpatient programs.** These types of programs are offered at hospitals, health and mental health clinics, counseling offices, and residential facilities with outpatient clinics. Many operate in the evenings and on weekends, allowing participants to continue working as they seek treatment.

- **Intensive outpatient programs.** These are more effective for people who are motivated to participate and who have supportive families and friends.

Which Should You Choose?

The selection of a rehabilitation program depends on the struggler's individual circumstances. A doctor can also help determine which type of program is best.

Information on various option plans is easily obtainable; therefore, careful research will help ensure an apples-to-apples comparison. Discuss expectations, program features, costs, insurance details, and related questions with program staff.

What Are Rehab Success Rates?

No treatment program can categorically guarantee that a struggler will not relapse. Rehab "success" rates are notoriously difficult to quantify.

It is not uncommon for strugglers to relapse. Most studies indicate that between 50 to 90 percent of those who recover from addiction revert back following their initial recovery.[4]

Key factors that contribute to relapsing back into addictive behavior include external pressures, emotional distress, mental illness, or an arrogant attitude. Similarly, major factors that reduce the risk of relapse are abstaining from the addiction, being treated by a medical professional, and becoming part of a 12-step program like Alcoholics Anonymous, Narcotics Anonymous, Gamblers Anonymous, or Overeaters Anonymous.[5]

Addictions have the power to control the lives of so many strugglers. But that power is nothing compared with the power of Christ to free strugglers from their strongholds. The Bible says, "The weapons we fight with are not the weapons of the world. On the contrary, they have divine power to demolish strongholds" (2 Corinthians 10:4).

THE 12-STEP WORLD OF RECOVERY:
How to Walk Toward Freedom

C an strugglers with addictions find lasting freedom? Yes, of course—millions have! But often the march to freedom is marked by "two steps forward, one step back." In the final analysis, what makes the difference between success and failure? For the majority of strugglers it is some type of 12-step program. My friend Frank explained it this way:

> For those recovering from alcohol and drug abuse, it would be hard to overemphasize the importance of participating in a 12-step program. The program I followed provided me with a step-by-step process for resurrendering my life to God and cleansing myself of the damaging debris I'd collected during the years of my addiction.
>
> Following these steps not only led me to sobriety, but also to a restored relationship with Christ. As I worked my way through the program, my attitude progressed—from despair to hope, and finally to happiness and gratitude. It's truly amazing what these 12 biblically based principles can do, and how they continue to transform the lives of people who practice them.
>
> The first three steps provide the necessary foundation not only for recovery, but also for a life dedicated to Christ. I like to sum up these steps as "I can't. He can. I'll let Him."
>
> Without acknowledging these first three foundational steps, there is no power for overcoming an addiction. I have known countless people who are unable to be set free because their pride would not allow them to admit they were powerless and they needed God's help. We have a saying in the program: "My own best thinking got

me here." Simply stated, as long as we maintain control of our lives, we are doomed to fail.

For me, steps 4 through 6 provided the path to begin honestly identifying the anger, resentment, fear, and guilt that was poisoning my life. At the beginning of my journey, my head much preferred getting on these well-worn mental trails. However, they turned out to be the quickest route back to my addiction. When I'm faithful to identify and confess these issues to God—and to another person— I'm freed from their bondage and able to enjoy my life in Christ. I like to tell newcomers to the 12-step program that steps 4 through 6 put the "smile in sobriety."

Steps 7 through 9 build on the previous six steps by prompting me to make things right with others to the extent that I am able. At first, I was anxious about step 9—making amends. But I was surprised at how gracious and forgiving most people were as I began to apologize, ask forgiveness, and offer to make restitution. I often hear step 9 referred to as "taking out the trash"—the final cleaning out of our temple for the Holy Spirit, who resides in us.

The last three steps are maintenance steps. We must...

Step 10—Continue dealing with our resentment
and fear as they arise

Step 11—Seek to strengthen our relationship with God

Step 12—Pass on to others this wonderful gift of real
hope for sobriety that we've been given

Helping others keeps us from dwelling on our own circumstances and constantly reinforces an "attitude of gratitude" for our new life.

As a recovery pastor, I regularly see three groups of people: Those who are not recovering, those who are recovering, and those who are grateful for their recovery. Continuously working the 12 steps is what differentiates the second group of people from the third. Those in the last group have done the work to bring a cleansing and healing from their past. Those in the second group are some of the unhappiest people I know. They are sober but they haven't released the resentment, guilt, and fear that is poisoning their lives. Ironically, they are often unhappier than those still abusing substances because they no longer have their addiction as a crutch.

As I work with people in each group, I encourage them to join me on this 12-step journey to experience a new freedom they never dreamed possible. I invite them to experience a fulfilling life beyond their wildest dreams.

My friend Frank has been living out the original plan created by a doctor and an investor, both highly successful but deeply broken individuals, who began meeting together in 1935 to help each other overcome their dependence on alcohol. Their partnership gave birth to the famous 12 steps of Alcoholics Anonymous.[1] In the years since, more than two million people have experienced recovery due, in part, to following the principles prescribed by Alcoholics Anonymous.[2] In time, others adapted the principles from AA to aid in recovery from addictions such as gambling, overeating, drugs, and sex.

While AA embraces spirituality, it is not an explicitly Christian organization. It is focused solely on the problem and process of overcoming substance abuse. Although not everyone involved with or benefiting from AA is a follower of Christ, the principles that provide support for the well-known and effective 12 steps represent timeless truths found in the Bible. Although Frank benefited from the "secular" 12 steps, his journey to recovery was influenced by his Christian faith. As you journey into recovery or help others do so, be certain to take a distinctively Christian approach:

The 12-Step Program: A Christian's Guide[3]

1. **Admit you are powerless** over your dependency.

   "I am unable to manage my life; I cannot control my life."

   - *Accept* your dependent condition and your vulnerability to addiction.
   - *Acknowledge* your inability to manage your life and to overcome your addiction and dependency.
   - *Articulate* to God your total inadequacy and your desperate need of His power in your life.

   "In our hearts we felt the sentence of death. But this happened that we might not rely on ourselves but on God, who raises the dead"
   (2 Corinthians 1:9).

2. **Realize that the God who made you** and saved you has the power to restore you.

   "I am asking Christ to be my Redeemer, to restore every area of my life."

— *Accept* the Lordship of Christ Jesus in your life as your Master, Ruler, and Owner.

— *Acknowledge* your need for God to comfort you and to restore you to wholeness.

— *Articulate* your gratitude to God for His saving power operating within your mind, will, and emotions, and thank Him for what He plans to do in and through your life.

> *"Though you have made me see troubles, many and bitter, you will restore my life again; from the depths of the earth you will again bring me up. You will increase my honor and comfort me once again"*
> (PSALM 71:20-21).

3. **Yield your will** to the will of the Lord.

"I am asking Christ to take control of my life."

— *Accept* the fact that your sinful nature died on the cross with Jesus and that sin (your addiction) is no longer to rule your life.

— *Acknowledge* the devastation that has resulted from your self-willed living in the past.

— *Articulate* your determination to stop your self-willed living and your decision to yield your will to the Lord.

> *"Trust in the LORD with all your heart and lean not on your own understanding; in all your ways acknowledge him, and he will make your paths straight"*
> (PROVERBS 3:5-6).

4. **Face reality**—face your true self.

"I will look honestly at my life, asking God to uncover my sins and character flaws."

— *Accept* the truth that you have deceived yourself about your dependency and your desperate need for help.

— *Acknowledge* your previous reluctance to face the truth about your wrong choices and patterns.

— *Articulate* to God and to others your willingness to know the truth about yourself and your commitment to honestly evaluating your life, your strengths, and your weaknesses.

> *"Search me, O God, and know my heart; test me and*
> *know my anxious thoughts. See if there is any offensive*
> *way in me, and lead me in the way everlasting"*
> (PSALM 139:23-24).

5. **Admit your struggle with sin**, both to God and to someone else.

"May I see my sin as God sees it and hate my sin as God hates it."

- *Accept* the depth and the duration of your struggle with addiction.
- *Acknowledge* to a supportive person the power that your dependency has had over you. Confirm your present commitment to freedom.
- *Articulate* to both God and a friend your desire to overcome your dependency and to live in the victory Jesus secured for you.

> *"If we claim to be without sin, we deceive*
> *ourselves and the truth is not in us"*
> (1 JOHN 1:8).

6. **Humbly accept God's help** to change your patterns of the past.

"I will commit my life into the care of Christ."

- *Accept* your limitations and your need for help in changing your unhealthy patterns of dealing with life.
- *Acknowledge* your frailty and the feebleness of your willpower and self-effort to effect change.
- *Articulate* to God your helplessness and your pledge to cooperate with Him as He changes you from the inside out.

> *"Humble yourselves, therefore, under God's mighty*
> *hand, that he may lift you up in due time. Cast all*
> *your anxiety on him because he cares for you"*
> (1 PETER 5:6-7).

7. **Confess your defects** and daily failings.

"I'm willing to see myself as God sees me."

- *Accept* that you are not perfect and that you will fail at times despite your good intentions.

- *Acknowledge* your failures immediately and confess them to God and to those you have offended. Then correct your course.

- *Articulate* any sins and shortcomings to God on a daily basis, and claim His forgiveness and cleansing.

> *"Create in me a pure heart, O God, and renew a steadfast*
> *spirit within me. Do not cast me from your presence or*
> *take your Holy Spirit from me. Restore to me the joy of your*
> *salvation and grant me a willing spirit, to sustain me"*
> (Psalm 51:10-12).

8. **Ask forgiveness** of those you have offended.

"I will find those whom I've hurt and from my heart ask for forgiveness."

- *Accept* your need to ask forgiveness of anyone you have offended, even though you may have been offended yourself.

- *Acknowledge* your great need of God's mercy and grace and your resolve to extend mercy and grace to others.

- *Articulate* your grief and regret to both God and to those you have offended, and your resolve to change the things you need to change.

> *"If you are offering your gift at the altar and there remember*
> *that your brother has something against you, leave your*
> *gift there in front of the altar. First go and be reconciled*
> *to your brother; then come and offer your gift"*
> (Matthew 5:23-24).

9. **Make restitution** to those you have wronged.

"I will go and make amends where possible with the help of God."

- *Accept* your obligation to do whatever is within your power in order to right your wrongs.

- *Acknowledge* to God and to those whom you have wronged your desire to make amends in any way possible.

- *Articulate* your responsibility to make restitution and your commitment to repay whatever debt you owe, whether repaying money or labor, correcting a lie, showing respect, or extending love.

> *"If he gives back what he took in pledge for a loan, returns what he has stolen, follows the decrees that give life, and does no evil, he will surely live; he will not die. None of the sins he has committed will be remembered against him. He has done what is just and right; he will surely live"*
> (EZEKIEL 33:15-16).

10. **Keep a clean slate** when you realize you have been wrong.

"Each day I will take responsibility for my irresponsibility."

- *Accept* your charge to keep a clean slate before God and every person.

- *Acknowledge* each and every failure in order to live as God would have you to live.

- *Articulate* each failure to God on a moment-by-moment basis, making no excuses, but recommitting yourself to living a self-controlled, Spirit-empowered life.

> *"The grace of God that brings salvation has appeared to all men. It teaches us to say 'No' to ungodliness and worldly passions, and to live self-controlled, upright and godly lives"*
> (TITUS 2:11-12).

11. **Pray to know God's path** for your life.

"I want to be led by the Lord and to walk only on His path."

- *Accept* your new dependence on God and your vital need to communicate with Him on a daily basis through Bible study and prayer.

- *Acknowledge* your need to have the prayer support of others to know God's truths and His ways.

- *Articulate* to God your desire to be what He wants you to be and to do what He wants you to do.

"Show me your ways, O LORD, teach me your paths;
guide me in your truth and teach me, for you are God
my Savior, and my hope is in you all day long"
(PSALM 25:4-5).

12. **Reach out to others** with your hand and your heart.

"I will care for those who need care and will help with a heart of compassion."

  – *Accept* your need of others and their need of you.

  – *Acknowledge* your giftedness from God and His mandate to use your God-given gifts to serve others in tangible, practical ways.

  – *Articulate* ways God may be leading you to minister to others and ask for His confirmation and for the guidance of mature Christians who can help you reach out to others.

"Carry each other's burdens, and in this way
you will fulfill the law of Christ"
(GALATIANS 6:2).

The simple yet powerful prayer below, crafted during World War II, has become world-renowned. Every day, countless numbers of people around the globe pray these words. They are looking to God for the grace, courage, and wisdom to walk though each day totally surrendered to the only One who has overcome the world—and the very One who enables us to be overcomers in this world.

THE SERENITY PRAYER[4]

God, give us grace to accept with serenity the things that
   cannot be changed,
Courage to change the things which should be changed,
and the wisdom to distinguish the one from the other.
Living one day at a time, enjoying one moment at a time,
Accepting hardship as a pathway to peace, taking, as Jesus did,
This sinful world as it is, not as I would have it,
Trusting that You will make all things right, if I surrender
   to Your will,
So that I may be reasonably happy in this life,
and supremely happy with You forever in the next. Amen.

—REINHOLD NIEBUHR (1892–1971)

Jesus imparts to us this comforting promise:

> *"In this world you will have trouble.*
> *But take heart! I have overcome the world"*
> (JOHN 16:33).

Victory Is Possible

Life for the recovering struggler is lived just as *every* life should be lived: one day—and often one moment—at a time. Yes, there are those instances when God miraculously removes the vice grip and a captive is immediately set free. But that is the rarest of exceptions. In most cases, addiction recovery is incremental and relapses are the rule, not the exception.

Do not lose hope when you or a loved one find yourselves farther back on the road than you'd hoped to be. Complete victory is possible—not only in the perfection we'll know in heaven, but right here in our fallen, imperfect world. This victory comes to us through the limitless power of Christ. The apostle Peter said, "His divine power has given us everything we need for life and godliness through our knowledge of him who called us by his own glory and goodness" (2 Peter 1:3).

12

THE BREAKTHROUGH WORLD OF BRAIN IMAGING:

How Seeing Is Believing!

What is one of the most loving things you can do for loved ones with addictions? Show them a brain scan! And that's exactly what I did.

Although I knew this was something my nephew wouldn't want to see, I showed it to him anyway. My words were simple. "You know I love you, don't you?" (*Yes.*) "Well, if I say I love you, then I *have to* show this to you. If I don't, I would be acting as if I don't care about you or your future."

He understood. Although he had an extraordinarily high IQ, he barely graduated from high school because of his addiction. How could I *not* share the scans with him...and his parents?

Did the scans have any impact? Of course they did! What a gift they are to the world of addiction today, both to those who are addicted and to those who love them. They provide an opportunity for them to see the danger that's present and take refuge. "A prudent man sees danger and takes refuge, but the simple keep going and suffer for it" (Proverbs 22:3).

What the Scans Show

For some, the pictures are sobering. For others they are startling, even downright shocking. A three-dimensional image of the top of a healthy brain shows a slightly dimpled yet smooth surface, indicating normal blood flow and function within the brain. But the images of brains affected by addictions are anything but normal. They serve as a jolting wake-up call, vividly displaying indisputable evidence of the destructive effects of addiction on the brain.

- *Sizeable holes resembling small craters* cover the surfaces of brains damaged by sustained use of alcohol, methamphetamine, heroin, and marijuana.

- *Gaping holes* cover the surface of a brain affected by three years of using inhalants, and resemble the brain of Alzheimer patients.

The three-dimensional images of brain scans are invaluable for diagnosis and treatment of brain dysfunction and are obtained with the help of a special camera and an injected substance called a tracer. A SPECT scan (Single-Photon Emission Computerized Tomography)…

- Measures the brain's blood flow and shows how the brain is functioning—which areas are working well and which are overactive or underactive
- Provides visual evidence of medical conditions that frequently contribute to addiction, such as brain injuries or depression
- Enables those already in recovery to have a physical representation of their illnesses
- Helps reveal any brain malfunction that could contribute to relapses (for example, if damage occurs to the prefrontal cortex, which is located behind the forehead and is the part of the brain involved in logic and decision making, recovery efforts can be delayed)

An informed understanding that brain differences or abnormalities can contribute to susceptibility to addictions can help lessen the shame, stigma, and self-loathing that often accompany addiction and abuse. Although poor choices certainly played a role, self-forgiveness is an important step for recovery as strugglers grab onto hope for true and lasting change—armed with the promise that God "gives strength to the weary and increases the power of the weak."[1]

SPECT scans also serve to…

- Graphically show how certain treatments affect brain function
- Encourage strugglers to stick with a treatment program by showing that addiction is a treatable brain illness
- Prevent doctors from inadvertently prescribing treatments that could hurt a patient, such as stimulants for an already overactive part of the brain or, conversely, depressants that could slow an already underactive area[2]

Seeing Is Believing

Like the disciple Thomas, who refused to acknowledge Jesus' resurrection until he could see the nail marks for himself,[3] for those in denial—or unaware of the dangerous effects of addiction—seeing the actual damage to their own brains can be a key motivator for lasting change.

Fortunately, as these scans illustrate, human brains can heal, and SPECT scans can track the healing process. In some cases, prescribed medications are also in order. Regardless, sustained abstinence, nutritious foods, adequate sleep, regular exercise, biblical meditation, group support, persistent prayer, and a host of other wholesome practices are all potent building blocks that can help a person regain the vitality God masterfully engineered into the human brain.

As King David said, "I praise you because I am fearfully and wonderfully made; your works are wonderful, I know that full well" (Psalm 139:14).

In the following SPECT scans,* areas in the brain of those with addictions look like holes, indicating regions of decreased blood flow and function. (Brain SPECT images courtesy of The Clements Clinic, Plano, Texas.)

HEALTHY SPECT IMAGE—SURFACE VIEW, TOP OF BRAIN

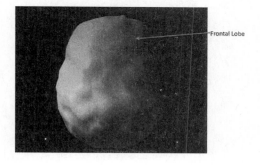

Frontal Lobe

ALCOHOLIC—37-YR.-OLD MALE HEAVY DRINKER

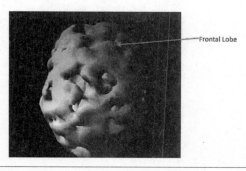

Frontal Lobe

* To view brain scan images in color, please visit www.hopefortheheart.org/habits.

METHAMPHETAMINE 22-YR.-OLD MALE—5 YEARS OF BINGE USING

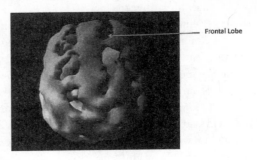

Frontal Lobe

HEROIN—7 YEARS OF SPORADIC AND BINGE USAGE

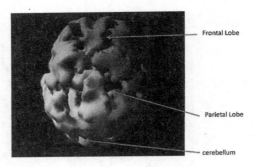

Frontal Lobe

Parietal Lobe

cerebellum

INHALANTS—3 YEARS OF HEAVY USAGE

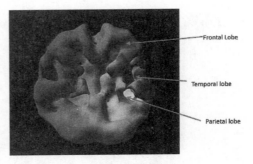

Frontal Lobe

Temporal lobe

Parietal lobe

MARIJUANA—26-YEAR-OLD DAILY USER

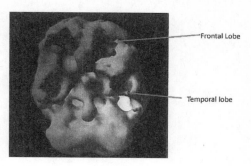

18-YR.-OLD DAILY MARIJUANA AND ALCOHOL USER WITH 30 DAYS OF SOBRIETY

18-YR.-OLD DAILY MARIJUANA AND ALCOHOL USER WITH 2 YEARS OF SOBRIETY (SIGNIFICANT BRAIN HEALING HAS TAKEN PLACE)

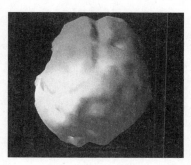

13

THE CRIPPLING WORLD OF CODEPENDENCY:

How Your Help Can Actually Hurt

Since 1996, countless callers have talked with me on *Hope In The Night* (our live two-hour call-in counseling program), ardently attempting to help an addicted loved one. Too often, however, I find these well-intentioned "helpers" need as much healing as their addicted strugglers. In reality, too many have come to the point where *their help isn't helpful*. And the cause for this is called *codependency*.

Codependent people ignore, deny, justify, defend, excuse, and sometimes even protect strugglers from being exposed. They have become too dependent on pleasing their addicted loved ones. Instead, they need to see their folly and forsake their self-destructive patterns of depending on someone other than God to meet their deep inner needs.

> *"My salvation and my honor depend on God;*
> *he is my mighty rock, my refuge"*
> (PSALM 62:7).

What Is Codependency?

The term *codependency* is often associated with addictions because of the dysfunctional relationships between addicted strugglers and the "people pleasers" around them.

- *Codependent* was a word first used in the 1970s to describe a family member living with someone *dependent* on alcohol or who had another addictive behavior. The prefix *co* means "with" or "one associated with the action of another."[1]

- *Codependency* became a term used to describe the dysfunctional behavior of family members or significant others who sought to adapt to the struggler's negative behavior. The dynamic of codependency is similar to that of having an elephant in your living room that no one talks about but everyone maneuvers around and tries to avoid upsetting. Everyone maneuvers in such a way to minimize the negative impact of the addiction.

- *Codependent people* or *enablers* enable the struggler to continue on with the addiction without drawing and maintaining boundaries.

- *Codependency* is a *relationship addiction*. Just as a struggler is dependent on his or her addiction, the codependent is overly dependent on the relationship with the struggler.

- *Codependent* today refers to anyone who is dependent on another to the point of being controlled or manipulated by that person.

- *Co-addict* refers to someone who is not in recovery for his or her own relationship dysfunction.

Those who are codependent fail to confront or to hold strugglers accountable for their actions. They are desperately trying to please the struggler. However, they would be wise to ask themselves,

> *"Am I now trying to win the approval of men, or of God?*
> *Or am I trying to please men? If I were still trying to*
> *please men, I would not be a servant of Christ"*
> (GALATIANS 1:10).

Who Are Enablers?

Every addiction recovery program includes support groups for those involved in the lives of strugglers, whether the addiction is to alcohol, drugs, food, gambling, or sex. These "victims" of the addict's behavior need to be encouraged and equipped to help their loved ones. They need help to stop being enablers. But how?

Enablers have gone beyond healthy dependency into unhealthy codependency. Enablers keep giving strugglers what they want—or what they demand—but to their detriment, and often their demise. While loving codependents think they're exhibiting unconditional love and doing what is "right," Scripture reminds us:

> *"There is a way that seems right...but in the end it leads to death"*
> (PROVERBS 16:25).

Typically, enablers are so tightly enmeshed in the life of a struggler that their own lives are swallowed up in perpetual chaos and frustration. They...

- Have a pattern of unhealthy dependencies in relationships and live unbalanced lives
- Have low self-esteem and feel inferior to and less important than others
- Have their identity in an unhealthy person whose happiness is always their highest priority
- Feel a sense of value only after receiving appreciation from others
- Have difficulty identifying personal feelings but are acutely attuned to the feelings of others
- Will violate their personal values and convictions to prevent being rejected
- Engage in extreme behaviors to try to control the thoughts, feelings, and actions of others to satisfy personal emotional needs

Codependent people often unwittingly enable strugglers to continue in their addictions, all the while complaining about their destructive behavior. They resign themselves to being victims. They feel they need to be "fixers" (to fix people), and they use that role to feel significant and meet their own inner needs. However, the Bible says our God is to be our Need-meeter:

> *"God will meet all your needs according to*
> *his glorious riches in Christ Jesus"*
> (Philippians 4:19).

=== *Being an Enabler* ===

Question: "How can I know whether I am being an enabler?"

Answer: You are an enabler if you perpetuate another's addictive behavior by protecting that person from experiencing painful consequences that could actually serve as motivation for change. Ask yourself, *How many lies have I told to protect the one I love from suffering negative repercussions from unwise choices?* The Bible has strong words about those who protect the guilty:

> *"Whoever says to the guilty, 'You are innocent'—peoples will curse him"*
> (Proverbs 24:24).

How to Stop Being a Codependent

Many people are stuck in an addictive habit that must be broken if they are ever going to become healthy. But how can you stop enabling them once they are dependent on your help? Realizing that you *must* stop is a vital first step. Making excuses for and shielding your addicted struggler from the painful consequences of destructive choices actually perpetuates the behavior you hope to prevent. Adopting a new way of relating is one of the most loving things you can do. But it will take courage and firm resolve because enabling them has become *your norm*, and being rescued has become *their norm*. To create a new normal, you need to...

- **Educate yourself about personal boundaries** and begin putting them into place.

  – Read a book or listen to recordings about codependency and enabling.[2]

  – Consider joining a related support group. Codependents Anonymous groups exist worldwide. Many churches host such support groups.

  – Enlist an accountability partner to help you maintain your resolve and boundaries.

  > *"Let the wise listen and add to their learning,*
  > *and let the discerning get guidance"*
  > (PROVERBS 1:5).

- **Determine when your help isn't helpful.** Galatians 6:2 tells us to "carry each other's burdens, and in this way you will fulfill the law of Christ." However, Galatians 6:5 says, "Each one should carry his own load."

  – At first glance, these commands seem contradictory. However, careful analysis will show they are both true.

  – In verse 2, the Greek word translated "burden" is *baros*, which means "weight," implying a load or something that is pressing heavily.[3] When you help carry what is too heavy for someone else to bear alone, your assistance fulfills the law of Christ.

  – In verse 5, the Greek word translated "load" is *phortion*, which means "something carried."[4] Clearly, when you carry what others should carry, you are not wise.

We are not called by God to relieve others of their rightful responsibilities, nor are we to expect or demand that others take on our God-given responsibilities. Codependent people try to get their needs met by *carrying loads that others should be carrying*. To move out of a codependent relationship, both individuals need to quit trying to be the other person's "all in all" and should instead encourage each other to take responsibility for their own lives and to live dependently on the strength of God.

- **Admit your codependency** to your loved one and state that your behavior has been preventing both of you from being your own person.
    - Apologize for being an enabler and announce plans to stop, beginning now.
    - Explain specific behaviors that you will change.
    - Describe the boundaries you will establish.

        > *"As iron sharpens iron, so one man sharpens another"*
        > (Proverbs 27:17).

- **Allow repercussions** to be experienced when behavior is out of line (and it will happen).
    - Do this each and every time inappropriate behavior occurs.
    - Resolutely resist the urge to rescue your loved one.
    - Consistently maintain your boundaries.

        > *"Do not be deceived...A man reaps what he sows"*
        > (Galatians 6:7).

- **Stop providing support** for inappropriate behavior. For example...
    - *For a child still in the home,* if you've been acting as a "helicopter parent" who hovers over a child's every move, step back and allow room for him to succeed—or fail—and to take responsibility for his own actions. If he's gambling with money you have given to him, stop giving him money. If he's caught participating in a crime, don't help him evade the law's penalties. If you need to be protected from him, don't hesitate to involve the police.
    - *For an adult child,* if you've been paying bills for an addictive daughter who has been irresponsibly spending money—whether on classy clothes or cosmetics, trips or trinkets, drinking

or drugs—it's time to let her face the consequences of her poor choices.

If the only time your daughter contacts you is when she needs something from you, realize this isn't a good relationship and explain that you would like to have a relationship with her but you will no longer be bailing her out because of her irresponsible lifestyle.

— *For a spouse*, if you have been lying to cover up your mate's poor behavior—such as calling the boss to say, "I'm so sorry but my husband has the flu" when instead he has a hangover—make it clear that you will no longer lie to protect him.

— If you've allowed yourself to be treated disrespectfully, calmly insist that you and other family members be treated with the dignity and respect everyone deserves.

> *"The wise in heart are called discerning,*
> *and pleasant words promote instruction"*
> (PROVERBS 16:21).

- **Expect resistance**. You will likely be accused of being unloving, uncaring, and un-Christian.

  — Stand firm—consistency is critical. As you change your ways, you will find the family dynamics changing too.

  — Realize that even if the struggler doesn't change, your changes will garner the self-respect and peace of mind that comes from knowing you're behaving in a way that genuinely is in his best interest and is pleasing to God.

  — Enlist the support of your accountability partner and a close group of prayer partners to help you hold your ground and even to speak tough truths to you through the inevitable difficult moments.

> *"Wounds from a friend can be trusted,*
> *but an enemy multiplies kisses"*
> (PROVERBS 27:6).

How to Set Beneficial Boundaries with the Struggler

Too many times I've talked with codependent parents who have continued to "fund" their children's drug habit, wives who have funded their husbands' gambling addiction, husbands who have funded their wives' compulsive spending, friends who have funded their friends' compulsive eating. In doing so, they've only encouraged the addiction.

Boundaries are barriers that work like fences. They protect people from external harm and guard them against internal harm. Those involved with addicted strugglers need to learn how to set appropriate limits on what they do for their loved ones. These boundaries will help prevent them from taking on responsibilities that belong to their loved ones and that God intends to use to develop Christlike character within them.

Boundaries serve to keep the *struggler's* problem from becoming *your* problem.

> *"Above all else, guard your heart,*
> *for it is the wellspring of life"*
> (PROVERBS 4:23).

As a rule, those who struggle with addictions require a tough, hard-hitting approach to help them break their dependencies—they need clear, nonnegotiable boundaries. They need the emotional support of those who will consistently reinforce responsible choices and enforce repercussions for irresponsible actions—thus providing the strugglers with opportunities for making positive changes.

Be aware that you could be "loving your loved one to death." As the Bible says,

> *"There is a way that seems right to a man,*
> *but in the end it leads to death"*
> (PROVERBS 14:12).

In your role as both a boundary-setter and boundary-keeper...

- **Give up all expectations** of the struggler and put your hope in God alone to give you peace.

    > *"Find rest, O my soul, in God alone; my hope comes from him"*
    > (PSALM 62:5).

- **Learn to detach** from the struggler's problem and take control of your own life.

    > *"My eyes are ever on the LORD, for only he*
    > *will release my feet from the snare"*
    > (PSALM 25:15).

- **Shift your focus** from the struggler's behavior to your responses.

  "Let us examine our ways and test them,
  and let us return to the LORD"
  (LAMENTATIONS 3:40).

- **Ask yourself**, "What is my role in this problem? Am I making it easy or difficult for the dependence to continue?"

  "Wisdom is supreme; therefore get wisdom.
  Though it cost all you have, get understanding"
  (PROVERBS 4:7).

- **Learn all you can** about addictions.

  "Hold on to instruction, do not let it go;
  guard it well, for it is your life"
  (PROVERBS 4:13).

- **Stop enabling actions** (making excuses, protecting) and hold your loved one accountable.

  "If one falls down, his friend can help him up.
  But pity the man who falls and has no one to help him up!"
  (ECCLESIASTES 4:10).

- **Determine to be a positive influence** and plan ways to do that effectively.

  "Be diligent in these matters; give yourself wholly to
  them, so that everyone may see your progress"
  (1 TIMOTHY 4:15).

- **Let the struggler know** the negative effects of their behavior on you and on others.

  "Each of you must put off falsehood and speak truthfully"
  (EPHESIANS 4:25).

- **Write out** specific destructive events resulting from the dependency. Include everything!

  "A prudent man sees danger and takes refuge,
  but the simple keep going and suffer for it"
  (PROVERBS 22:3).

- **Say to your struggler:** "I have seen how your behaviors have negatively impacted your life—it's not right for me to keep enabling you in this behavior. Tell me now that you *will* or you *will not* be committed to doing whatever is necessary to bring about change."

> *"The wisdom of the prudent is to give thought to*
> *their ways, but the folly of fools is deception"*
> (PROVERBS 14:8).

- **Pray for and expect God** to bring consequences into the struggler's life.

> *"A man's ways are in full view of the LORD,*
> *and he examines all his paths"*
> (PROVERBS 5:21).

God has worked miracles in the lives of so many who have had misplaced dependencies on others, turning frustration and futility into lives of peace and fulfillment—lives of loving others, but with healthy boundaries. But they all had to face the truth that they were wrong, that their lives were too enmeshed with, too dependent on, too controlled by another person. They needed to face the truth that through the strength of Christ, they could change. And when they acted on the truth, the truth set them free. As Jesus said,

> *"Then you will know the truth, and the truth will set you free...*
> *So if the Son sets you free, you will be free indeed"*
> (JOHN 8:32,36).

14

THE LIFE-CHANGING
WORLD OF SALVATION:
How to Receive Spiritual Healing

No one is "born" a bulimic, no one starts life a sex addict, no one comes into this world an alcoholic or a compulsive gambler, eater, or spender. Yet somehow along life's tumultuous journey, we can become hooked on harmful, addictive habits—horribly hooked.

So how does this "somehow" happen? Consider what our greatest need is as humans. Some say food, clothing, or shelter—focusing primarily on our outer needs. Others say love, significance, or security—prioritizing our inner needs. And while all these are vitally important to our lives, addressing these needs will not fulfill the deepest part of our inner being. Many have longed for an inner healing that has eluded them for years—a true healing for painful brokenness.

From God's perspective, then, what is our greatest need? The Bible tells us that every person who has ever lived has thought thoughts, said words, and done deeds that fall short of God's perfect standard (what the Bible calls sin). And the punishment for sin is spiritual death (meaning an eternity separated from God).

Typically, people won't want to be separated for all eternity from God. That being the case, our greatest need *is to have our sins forgiven*. That is, to not have our sins counted against us. Only then can we receive true spiritual healing.

In truth, because of God's great love for us, God doesn't want us separated from Him. He has provided a way for our sins to be forgiven so that we can become all He created us to be *today* and live with Him *forever*.

This is the *why* of Jesus. Although we can't change the fact that we've sinned, Jesus doesn't want us separated from Him either.

Realize that the all-powerful Trinity is comprised of God the Father, God the Son, and God the Holy Spirit. And Jesus, who is God the Son, chose to leave heaven and come to earth for the purpose of dying on the cross for our sins. Understand that He wasn't a victim of the cruelty of His crucifiers. Jesus said about His own life, "No one takes it from me, but I lay it down of my own accord" (John 10:18).

Spiritual healing begins with a personal belief in what happened at Calvary almost 2000 years ago—Jesus Christ died in our place for our sins. By entrusting our lives to Christ—giving Him control of our lives—we gain forgiveness for our sins and therefore the free gift of eternal life! The Bible makes it clear that spiritual healing, or salvation, comes only through Jesus Christ. And while religious activities (like attending church, reading the Bible, giving offerings) can be forms of worship, they have no power to bring spiritual healing.

Complete *emotional healing* from destructive addictions can take several years, but that's not the case with *spiritual healing*. At the moment of belief (when someone places their entire dependence solely upon Jesus as Lord and Savior), spiritual healing occurs—*instantaneously*. Every sin—past, present, and future—is cleansed.

So while you're seeking God's help for overcoming your harmful habits, you can allow the Four Points of God's Plan (given below) to lead you into a personal relationship with Jesus Christ. He will meet your greatest need, the one that counts for all eternity!

Listen to this plea found in the Bible:

> *"Heal me, O LORD, and I will be healed;*
> *save me and I will be saved, for you are the one I praise"*
> (JEREMIAH 17:14).

Four Points of God's Plan

1. *God's Purpose for You…Is* Salvation

- What was God's motivation in sending Jesus Christ to earth?

    - To express His love for you by saving you! The Bible says…

        > *"God so loved the world that he gave his one and only Son,*
        > *that whoever believes in him shall not perish but have*
        > *eternal life. For God did not send his Son into the world to*
        > *condemn the world, but to save the world through him"*
        > (JOHN 3:16-17).

- What was Jesus' purpose in coming to earth?

    - To forgive your sins, to empower you to have victory over sin, and to enable you to live a fulfilled life. Jesus said,

        > *"I have come that they may have life, and that*
        > *they may have it more abundantly"*
        > (JOHN 10:10 NKJV).

2. *Your Problem...Is* Sin

- What exactly is sin?

  - Sin is living independently of God's standard—knowing what is right, but choosing what is wrong. The Bible says,

    > *"Anyone, then, who knows the good he ought*
    > *to do and doesn't do it, sins"*
    > (JAMES 4:17).

- What is the major consequence of sin?

  - Spiritual death, or eternal separation from God. Scripture states,

    > *"Your iniquities [sins] have separated you from*
    > *your God...The wages of sin is death, but the gift*
    > *of God is eternal life in Christ Jesus our Lord"*
    > (ISAIAH 59:2; ROMANS 6:23).

3. *God's Provision for You...Is the* Savior

- Can anything remove the penalty for sin?

  - Yes! Jesus died on the cross to personally pay the penalty for your sins. The Bible says,

    > *"God demonstrates his own love for us in this:*
    > *While we were still sinners, Christ died for us"*
    > (ROMANS 5:8).

- What is the solution to being separated from God?

  - Believe in (entrust your life to) Jesus Christ as the only way to God the Father. Jesus says,

    > *"I am the way and the truth and the life.*
    > *No one comes to the Father except through me...*
    > *Believe in the Lord Jesus, and you will be saved"*
    > (JOHN 14:6; ACTS 16:31).

4. *Your Part...Is* Surrender

- Give Christ control of your life by entrusting yourself to Him.

  > *"Jesus said to his disciples, 'If anyone would come after me, he*
  > *must deny himself and take up his cross [die to your own self-*
  > *rule] and follow me. For whoever wants to save his life will lose*

> *it, but whoever loses his life for me will find it. What good will it*
> *be for a man if he gains the whole world, yet forfeits his soul?'"*
> (MATTHEW 16:24-26).

— Place your faith in (rely on) Jesus Christ as your personal Lord and Savior and reject your good works as a means of earning God's approval.

> *"It is by grace you have been saved, through faith—*
> *and this not from yourselves, it is the gift of God—*
> *not by works, so that no one can boast"*
> (EPHESIANS 2:8-9).

The moment you choose to receive Jesus as your Lord and Savior—and entrust your life to Him—He comes to live inside you. Then He gives you His power so you can live the fulfilled life God has planned for you. If you want to be fully forgiven by God and become the person God created you to be, you can tell Him in a simple, heartfelt prayer like this:

Prayer of Salvation

> *"God, I want a real relationship with You.*
> *I admit that many times I've chosen to go my own way*
> *instead of Your way. Please forgive me for my sins.*
> *Jesus, thank You for dying on the cross to pay the penalty*
> *for my sins. Come into my life to be my Lord and my Savior.*
> *Change me from the inside out and make me the person*
> *You created me to be. In Your holy name I pray. Amen."*

What Can You Now Expect?

With this spiritual healing and the Lord in your life, you can know that never again will you struggle alone with a harmfully addictive habit. Realize that God's supernatural power can break the most powerful stronghold. He longs to be your Helper, your Hope, and your Hand of Protection.

When you feel weak, lean on His unsurpassed strength. Allow Him to help you break free from your bondage and start walking in freedom. And take comfort in these compassionate words from Jesus:

> *"My grace is sufficient for you, for my power*
> *is made perfect in weakness"*
> (2 CORINTHIANS 12:9).

THE MOUNTAIN CLIMBER

Have you ever faced a mountain and thought, *It's just too high*? Have you ever gazed at steep, rocky crags and said to yourself, *It's just too hard*? Anyone who knows anything about mountain climbing would be quick to affirm that the hike to the top is anything *but* easy.

In many ways, conquering a mountain is the same as conquering an addiction: Both take planning, preparation…and *perseverance*.

In my early experience of hiking the Colorado Rockies, I learned several techniques for increasing stamina and *perseverance*.

- You make it to the top not by sprinting, but by *pacing your steps evenly*, by setting a hiking stride. This may sound simplistic, but it works. You put one foot in front of the other at a steady, even pace. You try not to break the rhythm, but maintain it. This will *enable you to persevere*.

- You make it to the top not by focusing on the top, but by *focusing on short-range goals*. As I hiked, my focus was to make it to the next fir tree…to the next small bush…to the next huge rock. All along the way I spotted small, achievable goals. As a result, one step after another, one goal after another, I was *able to persevere*.

- You make it to the top not by refusing to stop, but by *planning needed stops*. I needed to bandage a blister, tend to a cut finger, and rest my aching muscles. I also needed to stop to take in the right kind of refreshment—water and food for nourishment. When hiking, oranges were my favorite food item because they serve as a fast source of energy. When you are on the climb, you need to stop… pause…then *continue to persevere*.

- You make it to the top not by refusing to fall down, but by *knowing that slipping and falling does not mean defeat*. Each time I slipped or a rock gave way and I fell, I struggled back onto my feet. And each time you slip and fall, you need to make the *choice* to struggle to your feet. Those first critical steps are necessary for survival. Each forward step thereafter becomes a tiny victory that echoes the resolve that truly "I can do all things through Christ who strengthens me" (Philippians 4:13 NKJV). That is why, whenever you fall, *you must get up and persevere*.

Attaining victory over any addiction is like climbing a mountain. And that mountain is not insurmountable—victory is yours for the taking! That's why the climb is worth the effort. The Bible says, "You need to persevere so that when you have done the will of God, you will receive what he has promised" (Hebrews 10:36).

The climb becomes harder after you've ascended above the foothills, for you've still got a long ways to go to reach the peak. From that point onward, it's not realistic to expect you can continue your ascent upward in a straight path. Rather, you have to zigzag, move laterally, and even backtrack to eventually make it to the top. That's where strategy, training, and equipment come in, along with the necessary commitment and courage—the very same "gear" needed to conquer the craggy world of addictions.

Without these tools, many an ill-equipped climber has bottomed out—discouraged, disoriented, defeated—and not just once, but over and over again. Fortunately, that climber need not be *you*. Not any longer. You, my friend, now possess the specialized tools to traverse this tough terrain, and the spiritual toughness to triumph.

Let's survey your newly acquired "climbing gear":

- *An atlas of knowledge* filled with Definitions, Characteristics, Causes, and Solutions that will help you find freedom from harmful habits and addictions
- *A spiritual compass*, direction from the Word of God, which can point you in the right way and provide you with time-tested understanding and wisdom
- *Travel advisories* from others who have gone before and can provide you with firsthand testimonies, including warnings about rockslides, switchbacks, and trail conditions
- *Location maps* for finding established routes and back trails, refuge from bad weather, and refreshment (mountain streams) along the way

With these four travel tools, you have in hand the ironclad assurance that the trek up and out of the world of addictions is not only possible, but worth every painful, hard-fought step. For when you make it to the top, you will experience an unparalleled victory and an irrepressible spiritual high.

And don't be surprised if, in His timing, God equips *you* to become a guide to help a friend make it up the mountain—to the summit of freedom. With the four travel tools you now possess, you'll be a guide with the right gear!

Now, if you find yourself still stuck at the base camp, there'll never be a better time than *this very moment* for you to step up and out in faith. Keep putting one foot in front of the other. Eventually you *will* make it to the top.

Whether you travel now as the guide or the guided, one thing is certain: You need not travel alone. God is with you, for you, and ready to guide you. He has prepared a path just for you. Let this be your prayer:

> *"Show me your ways, O LORD, teach me your paths;*
> *guide me in your truth and teach me, for you are God my Savior,*
> *and my hope is in you all day long"*
> (PSALM 25:4-5).

Imagine for a moment stepping upon the peak of the mountain and silently surveying the breathtaking panorama all around you. Imagine gazing down in awe at the low place where you once lived and seeing incredible opportunities all around.

As you raise your arms in exhausted yet exalted victory, you realize they are in a posture of praise. You find yourself praising the merciful God who gave you His grace and the strength to survive. And not just survive, but overcome. So now, at last, you stand free! Totally free...victoriously free...forever free!

NOTES

Acknowledgments

1. Psalm 119:105.
2. Habakkuk 3:19 (NLT).

Chapter 2—The World of Habits and Addictions

1. Registered trademark of ABC Sports with the United States Patent Office registration number: 1074755.
2. Random House, *Random House Webster's Unabridged Dictionary,* 2d ed. (New York: Random House, 2001), s.v. "biathlon."
3. Ed Grabianowski, "How Biathlon Works" (Silver Spring, MD: Discovery Communications, n.d.), http://adventure.howstuffworks.com/outdoor-activities/snow-sports/biathlon5.htm.
4. W.E. Vine, Merrill F. Unger, and William White, *Vine's Expository Dictionary of Biblical Words* (Nashville: Thomas Nelson, 1985), s.v. "learn."
5. Vine, Unger, and White, *Vine's Expository Dictionary of Biblical Words*, s.v. "way."
6. Vine, Unger, and White, *Vine's Expository Dictionary of Biblical Words*, s.v. "way."
7. Vine, Unger, and White, *Vine's Expository Dictionary of Biblical Words*, s.v. "life."
8. James M. Citrin, *The Dynamic Path: Access the Secrets of Champions to Achieve Greatness* (Emmaus, PA: Rodale, 2007), 56.
9. *Merriam-Webster's Dictionary of Basic English*, s.v. "impulse."
10. *Merriam-Webster's Dictionary of Basic English*, s.v. "habit."
11. *Merriam-Webster's Dictionary of Basic English*, s.v. "obsession."
12. *Merriam-Webster's Dictionary of Basic English*, s.v. "compulsion."
13. *Merriam-Webster's Dictionary of Basic English*, s.v. "addiction."
14. *China Daily*, "Magnar Solberg," http://www.chinadaily.com.cn/olympics/2007-07/26/content_6002457.htm.
15. *CBS News*, "Michael Vick: 'I Blame Me'" (August 16, 2009), http://www.cbsnews.com/stories/2009/08/10/60minutes/main5231257.shtml?tag=contentMain;contentBody.
16. *CBS News*, "Michael Vick: 'I Blame Me.'"
17. United Youth Football and Cheer, "NFL Player/Professional Advisory Council," http://www.unitedyfl.com/advisorycouncil.html.
18. United States District Court for the Eastern District of Virginia Richmond Division, "United States of America v. Purnell A. Peace, Quanis L. Phillips, Tony Taylor, Michael Vick—Indictment" (Richmond, VA: US District Court, July 2007), http://assets.espn.go.com/media/pdf/070717/vick_indictment.pdf.
19. Timothy Morral, "History of the Pit Bull," http://www.pitbull411.com/history.html.

20. Juliet Macur, "Vick Receives 23 Months and a Lecture," *The New York Times* (December 11, 2007), http://www.nytimes.com/2007/12/11/sports/football/11vick.html?pagewanted=1.

21. *CBS News*, "Michael Vick: 'I Blame Me.'"

22. David Chaikin and Jason Campbell Sharman, *Corruption and Money Laundering: A Symbiotic Relationship* (United Kingdom: Palgrave Macmillan, 2009), 160.

23. Lance Morrow, "Essay: The Shoes of Imelda Marcos," TIME.com (March 31, 1986).

24. "Imelda Marcos Acquitted, Again," NYTimes.com (March 11, 2008).

25. Philippines Travel Guide, "Coconut Palace Manila, Come and Judge for Yourself!" (n.p.: 2004), http://www.philippines-travel-guide.com/coconut-palace-manila.html.

26. Art Stricklin, "Michael Vick Shares First-Ever Testimony" *Baptist Press* (February 8, 2010), http://www.bpnews.net/bpnews.asp?id=32239.

27. Associated Press, "Michael Vick Receives Ed Block Courage Award," *The Times—Picayune* (March 9, 2010), http://www.nola.com/saints/index.ssf/2010/03/michael_vick_receives_ed_block.html.

28. For the following list see Gary R. Collins, *Christian Counseling—A Comprehensive Guide,* rev. ed. (Nashville: Thomas Nelson, 1988), 507-8.

29. Stricklin, "Michael Vick Shares First-Ever Testimony."

30. Associated Press, "Jones Pleads Guilty, Admits Lying About Steroids" (October 5, 2007), http://nbc-sports.msnbc.com/id/21138883//.

31. Associated Press, "Jones Pleads Guilty, Admits Lying About Steroids."

32. Associated Press, "Jones Pleads Guilty, Admits Lying About Steroids."

33. On the three God-given inner needs, see Lawrence J. Crabb, Jr., *Understanding People: Deep Longings for Relationship* (Grand Rapids: Zondervan, 1987), 15-16; Robert S. McGee, *The Search for Significance,* 2d ed. (Houston, TX: Rapha, 1990), 27-30.

34. Associated Press, "Jones Pleads Guilty, Admits Lying About Steroids."

35. Associated Press, "Jones Pleads Guilty, Admits Lying About Steroids."

36. CBS Studios Inc., "One-Armed Surfer Turns Pro," *Inside Edition* (March 31, 2009), http://www.insideedition.com/news.aspx?storyID=2786.

37. Bethany Hamilton, "Biography," http://bethanyhamilton.com/about/bio/.

38. Mark Moring, "A Surfer with Soul," *Christianity Today* (April 5, 2011), http://www.christianitytoday.com/ct/movies/interviews/2011/surferwithsoul.html.

39. Moring, "A Surfer with Soul."

40. Bethany Hamilton, Sheryl Burk, and Rick Bundschuh, *Soul Surfer* (Kindle ed.) (New York: Simon and Schuster, 2004), n.p.

41. Hamilton, Burk, and Bundschuh, *Soul Surfer.*

42. Soul Surfer Wave, "Meet the Hamiltons" (TriStar Pictures, Inc., 2011), http://www.soulsurferwave.com/meetthehamiltons.

43. See also Neil T. Anderson, *A Way of Escape* (Eugene, OR: Harvest House, 1994), 117-33.

44. See also Erwin Lutzer, *How to Say "No" to a Stubborn Habit: Even When You Feel Like Saying Yes* (Wheaton, IL: Victor, 1986), 76-78.

45. See also Lutzer, *How to Say "No" to a Stubborn Habit,* 131-40.

46. Sandra Simpson LeSourd, *The Compulsive Woman* (Tappan, NJ: Fleming H. Revell, 1996), 53.

47. Sandra Simpson LeSourd, *The Compulsive Woman,* 177.

48. Sandra Simpson LeSourd, *The Compulsive Woman,* 82.

49. Sandra Simpson LeSourd, *The Compulsive Woman,* 91.

50. Sandra Simpson LeSourd, *The Compulsive Woman,* 91.

51. Sandra Simpson LeSourd, *The Compulsive Woman,* 94.

52. Sandra Simpson LeSourd, *The Compulsive Woman*, 100.

53. Sandra Simpson LeSourd, *The Compulsive Woman*, 100.

54. Sandra Simpson LeSourd, *The Compulsive Woman*, 184.

55. Sandra Simpson LeSourd, *The Compulsive Woman*, 132.

56. Hamilton, Burk, and Bundschuh, *Soul Surfer*.

57. For Bethany Hamilton's workout regimen, see Jen Murphy, "A Surfer and Phenom At Her Very Core," *The Wall Street Journal* (April 12, 2011), http://online.wsj.com/article/SB1000142405274870 3712504576244631924797232.html.

58. TRX Training, "Soul Surfer Bethany Hamilton's Amazing Comeback" (April 8, 2011), http://www. trxtraining.com/connect/blog/2011/04/08/soul-surfer-bethany-hamiltons-amazing-comeback/.

59. Hamilton, Burk, and Bundschuh, *Soul Surfer*.

60. See also Lutzer, *How to Say "No" to a Stubborn Habit,* 57-58, 76-84.

61. For the following section see *The World's Best Anatomical Charts: Diseases and Disorders* (Skokie, IL: Anatomical Chart Company, 2000), 29.

62. For this section see Well Being of Wyoming, "Smokeless Tobacco—Newsletter" (Casper, WY: Wyoming Department of Health, August 2008), http://www.wellbeingofwyoming.org/newsletter.htm.

63. American Academy of Otolaryngology—Head and Neck Surgery, "What Is Spit Tobacco?" (Alexandria, VA: American Academy of Otolaryngology, n.d.), http://www.entassociates.net/html/spit_tobacco_-_it_s_no_game.html.

64. See Ruth Engs, "How Can I Manage Compulsive Shopping and Spending Addiction (Shopaholism)" (Bloomington, IN: Indiana University, 2006), http://www.indiana.edu/~engs/hints/shop.html; Spenders Anonymous, "Abstinence in Spending" (Minneapolis-St. Paul, MN: Twin Cities Minnesota Intergroup of Spenders Anonymous, 2006), http://www.spenders.org/abstinence.html.

65. Hamilton, Burk, and Bundschuh, *Soul Surfer*.

66. Hamilton, Burk, and Bundschuh, *Soul Surfer*.

67. Hamilton, Burk, and Bundschuh, *Soul Surfer*.

Chapter 3—The World of Alcohol and Drug Abuse

1. Information on Mickey Mantle is from Merlyn Mantle, et al., with Mickey Herskowitz, *A Hero All His Life: A Memoir by the Mantle Family* (New York: HarperCollins, 1996); Ed Cheek, *Mickey Mantle: His Final Inning* (Garland, TX: ATS, n.d.).

2. Mantle, et al., *Hero All His Life,* 5.

3. Mantle, et al., *Hero All His Life,* 16.

4. Mantle, et al., *Hero All His Life,* 98.

5. Mantle, et al., *Hero All His Life,* 26.

6. Mantle, et al., *Hero All His Life,* 34.

7. For this section see Jeff VanVonderen, *Good News for the Chemically Dependent and Those Who Love Them,* rev. ed. (Nashville: Thomas Nelson, 1991), 21-22.

8. Mantle, et al., *Hero All His Life,* 19.

9. For this section see James R. Beck, "Substance-Use Disorders," in *Baker Encyclopedia of Psychology,* ed. David G. Benner (Grand Rapids: Baker, 1985), 1128-29.

10. For the following sections on intoxication, abuse, addiction, and withdrawal see American Psychiatric Association, *Diagnostic and Statistical Manual of Mental Disorders: DSM-IV-TR,* 4th ed. (Washington, DC: American Psychiatric Association, 2000), 191-95, 198-99.

11. Elizabeth J. Taylor, ed., *Dorland's Illustrated Medical Dictionary,* 27th ed. (Philadelphia, PA: W.B. Saunders, 1988), 848.

12. See http://mlb.mlb.com/team/player.jsp?player_id=285078.

13. Evan Grant, "Faith Brings Texas' Rangers Hamilton Back from the Brink," *The Dallas Morning News* (January 27, 2008), electronic ed., n.p.

14. For this section see Ronald Rogers and Chandler Scott McMillin, *Under Your Own Power: A Guide to Recovery for Nonbelievers…and the Ones Who Love Them* (New York: G.P. Putnam's Sons, 1992), 140-43.

15. Albert Chen, "The Super Natural," SportsIllustrated.com (May 27, 2008).

16. I Am Second, "Josh Hamilton video" (Plano, TX: I Am Second, n.d.), http://www.iamsecond.com/.

17. I Am Second, "Josh Hamilton video."

18. Chen, "The Super Natural."

19. Evan Grant, "Faith Brings Texas Rangers' Hamilton Back from the Brink."

20. I Am Second, "Josh Hamilton video."

21. Timothy S. Naimi, Robert D. Brewer, Ali Mokdad, Clark Denny, Mary K. Serdula, and James S. Marks, "Binge Drinking Among US Adults," *Journal of the American Medical Association*, vol. 289, no. 1 (Chicago: American Medical Association, January 2003), 71.

22. Naimi, Brewer, et al., "Binge Drinking Among US Adults," 72.

23. Centers for Disease Control and Prevention, "Alcohol and Public Health—Fact Sheets: Caffeinated Alcoholic Beverages," http://www.cdc.gov/alcohol/fact-sheets/cab.htm.

24. Centers for Disease Control and Prevention, "Alcohol and Public Health—Fact Sheets: Excessive Alcohol Use and Risks to Women's Health," http://www.cdc.gov/alcohol/fact-sheets/womens-health.htm.

25. National Institute on Alcohol Abuse and Alcoholism, "NIAAA Council Approves Definition of Binge Drinking," NIAAA Newsletter, no. 3 (Bethesda, MD: National Institutes of Health, Winter 2004), 3, http://pubs.niaaa.nih.gov/publications/Newsletter/winter2004/Newsletter_Number3.pdf.

26. Centers for Disease Control and Prevention, "Alcohol and Public Health—Fact Sheets: Binge Drinking," http://www.cdc.gov/alcohol/fact-sheets/binge-drinking.htm.

27. Centers for Disease Control and Prevention, "Alcohol and Public Health—Fact Sheets: Binge Drinking."

28. Centers for Disease Control and Prevention, "Alcohol and Public Health—Fact Sheets: Caffeinated Alcoholic Beverages."

29. Centers for Disease Control and Prevention, "Alcohol and Public Health—Fact Sheets: Binge Drinking."

30. Gerard J. Connors, Dennis M. Donovan, and Carlo C. Diclemente, *Substance Abuse Treatment and the Stages of Change: Selecting and Planning Interventions* (New York: Guilford Press, 2004), 174.

31. Centers for Disease Control and Prevention, "Alcohol and Public Health—Fact Sheets: Excessive Alcohol Use and Risks to Women's Health."

32. Centers for Disease Control and Prevention, "Alcohol and Public Health—Fact Sheets: Excessive Alcohol Use and Risks to Men's Health," http://www.cdc.gov/alcohol/fact-sheets/mens-health.htm.

33. Centers for Disease Control and Prevention, "Alcohol and Public Health—Fact Sheets: Excessive Alcohol Use and Risks to Men's Health"; Centers for Disease Control and Prevention, "Alcohol and Public Health—Fact Sheets: Excessive Alcohol Use and Risks to Women's Health"; New York City Department of Health and Mental Hygiene, "Chemical Dependency: Women, Alcohol and Health," http://home.nyc.gov/html/doh/html/basas/walc.shtml.

34. Alcohol dehydrogenase.

35. Evan Grant, "Faith Brings Texas Rangers' Hamilton Back from the Brink."

36. Evan Grant, "Faith Brings Texas Rangers' Hamilton Back from the Brink."

37. Evan Grant, "Faith Brings Texas Rangers' Hamilton Back from the Brink."

38. Marc Galanter, ed., *Recent Developments in Alcoholism*, vol. 13, Alcohol and Violence (New York: Plenum Press, 1997), 10.

39. Mandy Stahre and Michele Simon, "Alcohol-Related Deaths and Hospitalizations by Race, Gender, and Age in California," Open Epidemiology Journal (3) 2010 (Oak Park, IL: Bentham Science Publishers, 2010), 3.

40. National Institute on Alcohol Abuse and Alcoholism, "Traffic Crashes, Traffic Crash Fatalities, and Alcohol-Related Traffic Crash Fatalities, United States, 1982–2004" (Bethesda, MD: National Institutes of Health, 2006), http://www.niaaa.nih.gov/Resources/DatabaseResources/QuickFacts/TrafficCrashes/Pages/crash01.aspx.

41. Galanter, ed., *Recent Developments in Alcoholism,* 9.

42. Evan Grant, "Faith Brings Texas Rangers' Hamilton Back from the Brink."

43. American Psychiatric Association, DSM-IV-TR, 221.

44. American Psychiatric Association, DSM-IV-TR, 219.

45. See Jarmes R. Milam and Katherine Ketcham, *Under the Influence* (New York: Bantam, 1983), 34-37, quoted in Andre Bustanoby, *When Your Child Is on Drugs or Alcohol* (San Bernardino, CA: Here's Hope, 1986), 19.

46. See American Heritage Electronic Dictionary (New York: Houghton Mifflin, 1992), s.v. "disease."

47. For this section see also Jeffrey VanVonderen, *Good News for the Chemically Dependent and Those Who Love Them* (Minneapolis: Bethany House, 1995), 31-32.

48. Grant, "Faith Brings Texas Rangers' Hamilton Back from the Brink."

49. I Am Second, "Josh Hamilton video."

50. Norm Miller with H.K. Hosier, *Beyond the Norm* (Nashville, TN: Thomas Nelson, 1996), p. 43.

51. Miller with Hosier, *Beyond the Norm,* p. 18.

52. Miller with Hosier, *Beyond the Norm,* p. 31.

53. Norm Miller, "Norm Miller: Personal Testimony" (Dallas, TX: Interstate Battery System International, 2011), http://corporate.interstatebatteries.com/norm_miller/testimony/.

54. Norm Miller with H.K. Hosier, *Beyond the Norm,* p. 42.

55. Miller, "Norm Miller: Personal Testimony."

56. Miller, "Norm Miller: Personal Testimony."

57. Miller, "Norm Miller: Personal Testimony."

58. Miller, "Norm Miller: Personal Testimony."

59. Chen, "The Super Natural."

60. S.C. Gwynne, "Josh Hamilton Finds Strength After Misstep in Recovery from Addiction," *The Dallas Morning News* (October 4, 2010), http://www.dallasnews.com/incoming/20101003-Josh-Hamilton-finds-strength-after-misstep-1474.ece.

61. Chen, "The Super Natural."

62. Chen, "The Super Natural."

63. For this section see Robert S. McGee, Pat Springle, and Susan Joiner, *Rapha's Twelve-Step Program for Overcoming Chemical Dependency: With Support Materials from The Search for Significance,* 2d ed. (Houston, TX: Rapha, 1990); Stephen Van Cleave, Walter Byrd, and Kathy Revell, *Counseling for Substance Abuse and Addiction* (Dallas: W Pub Group, 1988), 103-10.

64. David Falkner, "The Last Days of Mickey Mantle," *Dallas Observer* (December 14, 1995), http://www.dallasobserver.com/1995-12-14/news/the-last-days-of-mickey-mantle/.

65. Mantle, et al., *Hero All His Life,* 153.

66. For this section see Van Cleave, Byrd, and Revell, *Counseling for Substance Abuse and Addiction,* 116-17.

67. Falkner, "The Last Days of Mickey Mantle."

68. Mantle, et al., *Hero All His Life,* 8.

69. For this section see Van Cleave, Byrd, and Revell, *Counseling for Substance Abuse and Addiction*, 116-17.

70. Cheek, *Mickey Mantle: His Final Inning*.

71. Cheek, *Mickey Mantle: His Final Inning*.

72. Richard Durrett, "Josh Hamilton Avoided Alcohol Showers," ESPNDallas.com (September 27, 2010).

73. Cheek, *Mickey Mantle: His Final Inning*.

74. John 5:24.

75. Falkner, "The Last Days of Mickey Mantle."

Chapter 4—The World of Anorexia and Bulimia

1. Anonymous, "Dying to be Thin: A Pro-Ana Blog" (January 4, 2009), http://anaregzig.blogspot.com/.

2. Anonymous, "Dying to be Thin: A Pro-Ana Blog."

3. For information concerning Karen Carpenter see Richard Carpenter, "Introducing Carpenters," http://www.richardandkarencarpenter.com/biography.htm.

4. Richard Carpenter, "At a Cost," http://www.richardandkarencarpenter.com/biography-8.htm.

5. Carpenter, "Enter Karen, the Singer," http://www.richardandkarencarpenter.com/biography-3.htm.

6. Carpenter, "At a Cost."

7. American Psychiatric Association, *Diagnostic and Statistical Manual of Mental Disorders: DSM-IV-TR*, 4th ed. (Washington, DC: American Psychiatric Association, 2002), 583-84.

8. New Oxford Dictionary of English, electronic ed. (n.p.: Oxford University Press, 1998).

9. American Psychiatric Association, *Diagnostic and Statistical Manual of Mental Disorders*, 583.

10. American Psychiatric Association, *Diagnostic and Statistical Manual of Mental Disorders*, 583-84.

11. Carpenter, "At a Cost."

12. See American Psychiatric Association, *Diagnostic and Statistical Manual of Mental Disorders*, 583.

13. See American Psychiatric Association, *Diagnostic and Statistical Manual of Mental Disorders*, 583.

14. American Psychiatric Association, *Diagnostic and Statistical Manual of Mental Disorders*, 585.

15. See "Anorexia Athletica" at Eating DisordersOnline.com, http://www.eatingdisordersonline.com/explain/anorathletica.php.

16. See "Anorexia Athletica" at Eating DisordersOnline.com.

17. See also Peggy Claude-Pierre, *The Secret Language of Eating Disorders: The Revolutionary New Approach to Understanding and Curing Anorexia and Bulimia* (New York: Times, 1997), 98.

18. *Merriam-Webster's Collegiate Dictionary*, electronic ed., s.v. "bulimia."

19. See Frank Minirth, Paul Meier, Robert Hemfelt, Sharon Sneed, and Don Hawkins, *Love Hunger* (Nashville: Thomas Nelson, 1990), 13.

20. Mayo Clinic, "Rumination Syndrome" (Rochester, MN: Mayo Foundation for Medical Education and Research, 2010), http://www.mayoclinic.org/rumination-syndrome/.

21. Carpenter, "At a Cost."

22. Finding Balance, "What Is Orthorexia?" http://www.findingbalance.com/articles/disorders/orthorexia.asp.

23. Finding Balance, "What is Orthorexia?"

24. American Psychiatric Association, *Diagnostic and Statistical Manual of Mental Disorders*, 594.

25. For this section see American Psychiatric Association, *Diagnostic and Statistical Manual of Mental Disorders*, 594.

26. For body dysmorphic disorder see American Psychiatric Association, *Diagnostic and Statistical Manual of Mental Disorders,* 507-11.

27. Carpenter, "Last Performance, Continued Success," http://www.richardandkarencarpenter.com/biography-10.htm.

28. Carpenter, "Last Performance, Continued Success."

29. *The New Shorter Oxford Dictionary of English* (Oxford: Clarendon Press, 1993), s.v. "compulsion."

30. Robert Hilburn, "Elton's Exorcism: On the Eve of His First U.S. Tour in Three Years, Elton John Talks about His Battle with the Demons of Drugs, Alcohol, and Despair," *The Los Angeles Times* (August 23, 1992), http://articles.latimes.com/1992-08-23/entertainment/ca-7209_1_elton-john.

31. Hilburn, "Elton's Exorcism."

32. Hilburn, "Elton's Exorcism."

33. Hilburn, "Elton's Exorcism."

34. Sandra G. Boodman, "Eating Disorders: Not Just for Women," *Washington Post* (March 13, 2007), http://www.washingtonpost.com/wp-dyn/content/article/2007/03/09/AR2007030901870.html.

35. The Renfrew Center Foundation for Eating Disorders, "Eating Disorders 101 Guide: A Summary of Issues, Statistics, and Resources" (October 2003), 3.

36. Nicole Lampert, "Anorexics Find Posh a Thinspiration," *Daily Mail* (June 28, 2006), http://www.dailymail.co.uk/tvshowbiz/article-392841/Anorexics-Posh-thinspiration.html.

37. Ellen Teal personal testimony, unpublished letter (Plano, TX: Hope for the Heart, n.d.), 2.

38. Ellen Teal personal testimony, 2.

39. Ellen Teal personal testimony, 3.

40. Ellen Teal personal testimony, 3.

41. Ellen Teal personal testimony, 3.

42. Lampert, "Anorexics Find Posh a Thinspiration."

43. Angela Wagner, Howard Aizenstein, Vijay K. Venkatraman, Julie Fudge, J. Christopher Bay, Laura Mazurkewicz, Guido K. Frank, Ursula F. Bailey, Lorie Fischer, Van Nguyen, Cameron Carter, Karen Putnam, and Walter H. Kaye, "Altered Reward Processing in Women Recovered from Anorexia Nervosa," *American Journal of Psychiatry,* 164 (12) (Arlington, VA: American Psychiatric Association, 2007), 1842, 1849.

44. For this section see Jose Luis Barbosa-Saldivar, and Theodore B. Van Itallie, "Semistarvation: An Overview of an Old Problem," Bulletin of the New York Academy of Medicine, vol. 55 (8) (Bethesda, MD: National Center for Biotechnology Information, 1979), 774-76, 786.

45. For this section see Barbosa-Saldivar and Van Itallie, "Semistarvation: An Overview of an Old Problem," 774-76.

46. Martin Bashir, "Diana's 1995 BBC interview," Frontline Online (Boston: WGBH Educational Foundation, 1997), http://www.pbs.org/wgbh/pages/frontline/shows/royals/interviews/bbc.html.

47. Bashir, "Diana's 1995 BBC interview."

48. Bashir, "Diana's 1995 BBC interview."

49. Bashir, "Diana's 1995 BBC interview."

50. Bashir, "Diana's 1995 BBC interview."

51. Bashir, "Diana's 1995 BBC interview."

52. See also Lynn Ponton, "Coping with Denial in Eating Disorders" (Newburyport, MA: Psych Central, 2006), http://psychcentral.com/lib/2006/coping-with-denial-in-eating-disorders/.

53. Bashir, "Diana's 1995 BBC interview."

54. Bashir, "Diana's 1995 BBC interview."

55. Bashir, "Diana's 1995 BBC interview."

56. Bashir, "Diana's 1995 BBC interview."

57. Bashir, "Diana's 1995 BBC interview."

58. American Psychiatric Association, *Diagnostic and Statistical Manual of Mental Disorders,* 594.

59. Diana, Princess of Wales, "Speech on Eating Disorders" (April, 27, 1993), http://www.settelen.com/diana_eating_disorders.htm.

60. Diana, Princess of Wales, "Speech on Eating Disorders."

61. Diana, Princess of Wales, "Speech on Eating Disorders."

62. Diana, Princess of Wales, "Speech on Eating Disorders."

63. Diana, Princess of Wales, "Speech on Eating Disorders."

64. Bashir, "Diana's 1995 BBC interview."

65. Bashir, "Diana's 1995 BBC interview."

66. Bashir, "Diana's 1995 BBC interview."

67. Bashir, "Diana's 1995 BBC interview."

68. Sam Lister, "Diana Effect Is Credited with Decline in Bulimia" (San Antonio: HealthyPlace.com, February 26, 2007), http://www.healthyplace.com/eating-disorders/articles/diana-effect-is-credited-with-decline-in-bulimia/menu-id-58/.

69. See Vredevelt, Newman, Beverly, and Minirth, *The Thin Disguise: Understanding and Overcoming Anorexia and Bulimia,* 236.

70. David B. Morris, *Illness and Culture in the Postmodern Age* (Berkeley, CA: University of California Press, 2000), 150-51.

71. See Morris, *Illness and Culture in the Postmodern Age,* 150.

72. Morris, *Illness and Culture in the Postmodern Age,* 151.

73. Morris, *Illness and Culture in the Postmodern Age,* 151.

74. Morris, *Illness and Culture in the Postmodern Age,* 151.

75. Morris, *Illness and Culture in the Postmodern Age,* 154.

76. Morris, *Illness and Culture in the Postmodern Age,* 151-52.

77. Morris, *Illness and Culture in the Postmodern Age,* 152.

78. Jena Morrow, *Hollow: An Unpolished Tale* (Chicago: Moody, 2010), 13.

79. Morrow, *Hollow,* 20.

80. Morrow, *Hollow,* 20.

81. Morrow, *Hollow,* 20.

82. Morrow, *Hollow,* 30-32.

83. Morrow, *Hollow,* 32.

84. Morrow, *Hollow,* 33.

85. Morrow, *Hollow,* 53-54.

86. Morrow, *Hollow,* 69.

87. Morrow, *Hollow,* 46.

88. Morrow, *Hollow,* 46.

89. Morrow, *Hollow,* 87.

90. Morrow, *Hollow,* 97-98.

91. Morrow, *Hollow,* 99-100.

92. Morrow, *Hollow,* 103.

93. Morrow, *Hollow,* 176-77.

94. Quotations in this paragraph from Morrow, *Hollow: An Unpolished Tale,* 14.

95. Morrow, *Hollow,* 15.

96. Hebrews 4:12.

97. See Raymond Lemberg, ed. with Leigh Cohn, *Eating Disorders: A Reference Sourcebook* (Phoenix: Oryx Press, 1999), 166.

98. Cherry Boone O'Neill, *Starving for Attention* (New York: Continuum Publishing, 1982), 110.

99. O'Neill, *Starving for Attention*, 135-36.

100. O'Neill, *Starving for Attention*, 150.

101. O'Neill, *Starving for Attention*, 150.

102. O'Neill, *Starving for Attention*, 150.

103. Karen Way, *Anorexia Nervosa and Recovery: A Hunger for Meaning* (Binghamton, NY: Haworth Press, 1993), 37.

104. Erica Goode, "Study Finds TV Alters Fiji Girls' View of Body" *New York Times* (New York: The New York Times Company, May 20, 1999), http://www.nytimes.com/1999/05/20/world/study-finds-tv-alters-fiji-girls-view-of-body.html?src=pm.

105. O'Neill, *Starving for Attention*, 95.

106. O'Neill, *Starving for Attention*, 173.

107. Sari Fine Shepphird, *100 Questions & Answers About Anorexia Nervosa* (Sudbury, MA: Jones and Bartlett, 2001), 219.

108. See also Pam Vredevelt and Joyce Whitman, *Walking a Thin Line: Anorexia and Bulimia, the Battle Can Be Won* (Portland, OR: Multnomah , 1985), 208-14; Vredevelt, Newman, Beverly, and Minirth, *The Thin Disguise: Understanding and Overcoming Anorexia and Bulimia*, 230-36.

109. O'Neill, *Starving for Attention*, 171.

Chapter 5—The World of Gambling

1. Net Industries, "Pete Rose—Awards and Accomplishments," http://sports.jrank.org/pages/4065/Rose-Pete-Awards-Accomplishments.html.

2. Pete Rose, *My Prison Without Bars* (New York: Rodale Books, 2004), x.

3. Pete Rose, *My Prison Without Bars*, xi.

4. See Madalina Diaconu, *International Trade in Gambling Services* (Frederick, MD: Aspen Publishers, 2010), 14.

5. *Merriam-Webster's Dictionary of Basic English*, s.v. "pari-mutuel."

6. R. Laird Harris, Robert Laird Harris, Gleason Leonard Archer, and Bruce K. Waltke, *Theological Wordbook of the Old Testament*, electronic ed. (Chicago: Moody Press, 1999), 294.

7. *Merriam-Webster's Dictionary of Basic English*, s.v. "greed."

8. Gerhard Kittel, Geoffrey William Bromiley, and Gerhard Friedrich, *Theological Dictionary of the New Testament*, vol. 6, electronic ed. (Grand Rapids: Eerdmans, 1976), 271.

9. Pete Rose, *My Prison Without Bars*, xi.

10. Pete Rose, *My Prison Without Bars*, xi.

11. Henry R. Lesieur and Robert L. Custer, "Pathological Gambling: Roots, Phases, and Treatment," *Annals of the American Academy of Political and Social Science*, vol. 474 (July 1984), 146-56.

12. For this section see American Psychiatric Association, *Diagnostic and Statistical Manual of Mental Disorders: DSM-IV-TR*, 4th ed. (Washington, DC: American Psychiatric Association, 2002), 673-74.

13. The American Psychiatric Association does not discuss a separate category of "compulsive" gambling but includes characteristics listed here as compulsive under "pathological" gambling.

14. Cesar Brioso and Peter Barzilai, "The Rose Scandal," *USA Today* (January 5, 2004), http://www.usa-today.com/sports/baseball/2004-01-05-rose-timeline_x.htm.

15. Murray Chass, "The Pete Rose Inquiry: Rose Incurred Debts of $400,000 in 3 Months, Betting Report Says," *The New York Times* (June 27, 1989), http://www.nytimes.com/1989/06/27/sports/pete-rose-inquiry-rose-incurred-debts-400000-3-months-betting-report-says.html.

16. Joe Sexton, "Baseball: Rose Remains Defiant Over Report," *The New York Times* (July 2, 1989), http://www.nytimes.com/1989/07/02/sports/baseball-rose-remains-defiant-over-report.html.

17. Brioso and Barzilai, "The Rose Scandal."

18. Sexton, "Baseball: Rose Remains Defiant Over Report."

19. Sexton, "Baseball: Rose Remains Defiant Over Report."

20. See also Sabrina D. Black, "Gambling Addiction," *Counseling for Seemingly Impossible Problems,* eds. Lee N. June, Sabrina D. Black (Grand Rapids: Zondervan, 2002), 21-23.

21. Massachusetts Council on Compulsive Gambling, "Signs of Problem Gambling" (Boston, MA: Massachusetts Council on Compulsive Gambling, n.d.), http://www.masscompulsivegambling.org/paths/help_signs.php.

22. Dan Horn, "Gambling Problems Underestimated," *The Cincinnati Enquirer* (January 6, 2004), http://reds.enquirer.com/2004/01/06/red1e.html.

23. American Psychiatric Association, *Diagnostic and Statistical Manual of Mental Disorders: DSM-IV-TR,* 4th ed. (Washington, DC: American Psychiatric Association, 2000), 674.

24. Committee on the Social and Economic Impact of Pathological Gambling, *Pathological Gambling: A Critical Review* (Washington, DC: National Academy Press, 1999), 115.

25. Black, "Gambling Addiction," *Counseling for Seemingly Impossible Problems,* eds. Lee N. June and Sabrina D. Black (Grand Rapids: Zondervan, 2002), 19.

26. See Black, "Gambling Addiction," *Counseling for Seemingly Impossible Problems,* 19.

27. Harold J. Wynne, "Female Problem Gamblers in Alberta: A Secondary Analysis of the Gambling and Problem Gambling in Alberta Study" (Alberta: Alberta Alcohol and Drug Abuse Commission, 1994), 10.

28. Stephanie Covington, "Helping Women Recover: Creating Gender-Responsive Treatment," *The Handbook of Addiction Treatment for Women: Theory and Practice,* eds. S.L.A. Straussner and S. Brown (San Francisco: Jossey-Bass, 2002), 2-3.

29. John Erardi, "Sobbing Pete Rose Repents for Betting on Baseball," *The Cincinnati Enquirer* (September 12, 2010), http://news.cincinnati.com/article/20100911/SPT04/9120366/Sobbing-Pete-Rose-repents-betting-baseball.

30. Howard Wilkinson, "Review: 'My Prison Without Bars,'" *The Cincinnati Enquirer* (January 8, 2004), http://reds.enquirer.com/2004/01/08/rosereview.html.

31. Committee on the Social and Economic Impact of Pathological Gambling, *Pathological Gambling: A Critical Review,* 124-26.

32. Wilkinson, "Review: 'My Prison Without Bars.'"

33. Pete Rose, *My Prison Without Bars,* xii.

34. Pete Rose, *My Prison Without Bars,* 10.

35. On the three God-given inner needs, see Lawrence J. Crabb, Jr., *Understanding People: Deep Longings for Relationship* (Grand Rapids: Zondervan, 1987), 15-16; Robert S. McGee, *The Search for Significance,* 2d ed. (Houston, TX: Rapha, 1990), 27-30.

36. "Gambling: Why Pick on Pete Rose?" *Time* (July 10, 1989), http://www.time.com/time/magazine/article/0,9171,958108,00.html.

37. "Pete Rose Timeline," *The Cincinnati Enquirer* (January 6, 2004), http://reds.enquirer.com/2004/01/06/red1timeline.html.

38. See Wilkinson, "Review: 'My Prison Without Bars.'"

39. Wilkinson, "Review: 'My Prison Without Bars.'"

40. Wilkinson, "Review: 'My Prison Without Bars.'"

41. See Joseph Shapiro, "America's Gambling Fever," U.S. News and World Report (January 15, 1996), 58, http://www.probe.org/site/c.fdKEIMNsEoG/b.4219137/k.C8BD/Gambling.htm#text13.

42. Diane Dew, "What Does the Bible Say About Gambling?" http://nolotto.faithweb.com/gambling1.html.

43. Focus on the Family Issue Analysis, "Cause for Concern (Gambling)" (Colorado Springs: Focus on the Family, 2008), http://www.focusonthefamily.com/socialissues/gambling/gambling/cause-for-concern.aspx.

44. W. Thompson and D. Rickman, "The Social Cost of Gambling in Wisconsin," *Wisconsin Policy Research Institute Report*, vol. 9, 144.

45. Chad Hills, "Gambling and Crime," *Citizen Link* (Colorado Springs: Focus on the Family, June 11, 2010), http://www.citizenlink.com/2010/06/11/gambling-and-crime/.

46. Chad Hills, "National Gambling Impact Study Commission Report (Summary, Part 1)," *Citizen Link* (Colorado Springs: Focus on the Family, June 14, 2010), http://www.citizenlink.com/2010/06/14/ngisc-report-summary-part-1/.

47. Focus on the Family Issue Analysis, "Cause for Concern (Gambling)."

48. Focus on the Family Issue Analysis, "Cause for Concern (Gambling)."

49. R. Gupta and J.L. Derevensky, "Familial and Social Influences on Juvenile Gambling Behavior," *Journal of Gambling Studies*, vol. 13, no. 3, 179-92.

50. National Problem Gambling Awareness Week, "Problem Gambling Information: Facts and Figures" (Washington, D.C.: National Council on Problem Gambling, 2011), http://www.npgaw.org/problemgamblinginformation/factsfigures.asp.

51. Focus on the Family Issue Analysis, "Cause for Concern (Gambling)."

52. National Problem Gambling Awareness Week, "Problem Gambling Information: Facts and Figures."

53. Focus on the Family Issue Analysis, "Cause for Concern (Gambling)."

54. Focus on the Family Issue Analysis, "Cause for Concern (Gambling)."

55. Focus on the Family Issue Analysis, "Cause for Concern (Gambling)."

56. Focus on the Family Issue Analysis, "Cause for Concern (Gambling)."

57. Focus on the Family Issue Analysis, "Cause for Concern (Gambling)."

58. John Warren Kindt and Anne E.C. Brynn, "Government-Sanctioned Gambling as Encouraging Transboundary Economic Raiding and Destabilizing National and International Economies," *Research of the Program in Arms Control, Disarmament, and International Security* (Urbana, IL: University of Urbana-Champaign, 2005), 4 (https://www.ideals.illinois.edu/bitstream/handle/2142/41/Kindt_and_BrynnOP.pdf?sequence=1).

59. Kerby Anderson, "Gambling" (Plano, TX: Probe, 2005), http://www.probe.org/site/c.fdKEIMNsEoG/b.4219137/k.C8BD/Gambling.htm.

60. Anderson, "Gambling."

61. Anderson, "Gambling."

62. Bessie Ng, "The New Ways of Mahjong in Hong Kong," *Hong Kong Stories* (Hong Kong: University of Hong Kong, 2009), http://jmsc.hku.hk/hkstories/content/view/781/7065/1/0/.

63. Bessie Ng, "The New Ways of Mahjong in Hong Kong."

64. HFTH Testimony from Jasmine, name changed to protect her identity.

65. HFTH Testimony from Jasmine, name changed to protect her identity.

Chapter 6—The World of Overeating

1. See David A. Kessler, *The End of Overeating: Taking Control of the Insatiable American Appetite* (New York: Rodale, 2009), 5, 128.

2. See *Merriam-Webster's Online Dictionary*, s.v. "overeat."

3. Raymond E. Vath, *Counseling Those with Eating Disorders, Resources for Christian Counseling*, ed. Gary R. Collins, vol. 4 (Waco, TX: Word, 1986), 58.

4. Manuel Uribe, Associated Press, "700-pound Man's Birthday Wish? Marriage," http://www.msnbc.msn.com/id/25085766/.

5. Associated Press, "700-pound Man's Birthday Wish? Marriage."

6. *New Oxford Dictionary of English*, electronic ed. (New York: Oxford University Press, 1998), s.v. "compulsive."

7. Susan Nolen-Hoeksema, *Eating, Drinking, Overthinking: The Toxic Triangle of Food, Alcohol, and Depression—and How Women Can Break Free* (New York: Henry Holt, 2006), 23.

8. See *Merriam-Webster's Online Dictionary*, s.v. "binge."

9. For Night Eating Disorder, see Eating Disorders Online, "Night Eating," http://www.eatingdisordersonline.com/explain/nighteating.php.

10. World Health Organization, "Global Strategy on Diet, Physical Activity and Health: Obesity and Overweight" (Geneva, Switzerland: World Health Organization, 2011), http://www.who.int/diet-physicalactivity/publications/facts/obesity/en/.

11. World Health Organization, "Global Strategy on Diet, Physical Activity and Health: Obesity and Overweight."

12. Also spelled Renaud.

13. See Sergio Boffa, *Warfare in Medieval Brabant* (Rochester, NY: Boydell Press, 2004), 15-17.

14. Thomas Costain, *The Three Edwards: A History of the Plantagenets* (New York: Doubleday, 1962), 166-67.

15. Costain, *The Three Edwards*, 167.

16. John 6:35.

17. For this checklist see Bill Perkins, *Fatal Attractions: Overcoming Our Secret Addictions* (Eugene, OR: Harvest House, 1991), 48-49.

18. Judy Lightstone, "Understanding Compulsive Overeating" (n.p.: Eating Disorder Referral and Information Center, n.d.), http://www.edreferral.com/compulsive_overeating.htm.

19. For this section see National Eating Disorders Association, "Laxative Abuse: Some Basic Facts" (New York: NEDA, 2005), http://www.nationaleatingdisorders.org/nedaDir/files/documents/handouts/Laxative.pdf.

20. Laurie Cunningham, "Behold: The World's 10 Fattest Countries," *Globalpost* (November 25, 2009), http://www.globalpost.com/dispatch/commerce/091125/obesity-epidemic-fattest-countries?page=0,0.

21. Cunningham, "Behold: The World's 10 Fattest Countries."

22. For the three God-given inner needs, see Lawrence J. Crabb, Jr., *Understanding People* (Colorado Springs: NavPress, 1992), 15-16; McGee, *The Search for Significance* , 2d ed. (Houston, TX: Rapha, 1990), 27-30.

23. *Today*, "Biggest Loser's Abby: 'Happiness is a Choice,'" http://today.msnbc.msn.com/id/33590392/ns/today-biggest_loser_on_today/.

24. Access Hollywood, " 'Biggest Loser' Abby Rike Overcoming Tragedy," http://www.hulu.com/watch/91701/access-hollywood-biggest-loser-abby-rike-overcoming-tragedy.

25. Jenny Schafer, "The Biggest Loser's Abby Rike: From Family Tragedy to Personal Triumph," *Life and Style* (October 30, 2009), http://www.lifeandstylemag.com/2009/10/.

26. *Today*, "Biggest Loser's Abby: 'Happiness is a Choice.'"

27. *Today*, "Biggest Loser's Abby: 'Happiness is a Choice.'"

28. *Today*, "Biggest Loser's Abby: 'Happiness is a Choice.'"

29. Philippians 4:11,13 NKJV.

30. For the three God-given inner needs, see Crabb, *Understanding People*, 15-16; McGee, *The Search for Significance,* 27-30.

31. See Crabb, *Understanding People,* 15-16; McGee, *The Search for Significance,* 27-30.

32. Steve Almasy, "Whatever Happened to American Idol's Mandisa?" http://articles.cnn.com/2009-03-11/entertainment/mandisa_1_cruise-ship-christian-pop-deliverer?_s=PM:SHOWBIZ.

33. Almasy, "Whatever Happened to American Idol's Mandisa?"

34. Almasy, "Whatever Happened to American Idol's Mandisa?"

35. See "Mandisa Weight Loss," http://ifitandhealthy.com/mandisa-weight-loss/.

36. Andrew Funderburks, "Mandisa Celebrates Her New Freedom," http://www.newreleasetuesday.com/article.php?article_id=201.

37. Funderburks, "Mandisa Celebrates Her New Freedom."

38. See "Mandisa Weight Loss."

39. See "Mandisa Weight Loss."

40. See "Mandisa Weight Loss."

41. For the three God-given inner needs, see Crabb, *Understanding People*, 15-16; McGee, *The Search for Significance*, 27-30.

42. Leslie Beck, "To Quench Your Thirst, Plain Old Water Is Best," http://www.theglobeandmail.com/life/health/to-quench-your-thirst-plain-old-water-is-best/article1597469/.

43. Thunder Bay Regional Health Sciences Centre, "You Say Tomato, I Say Healthy," http://www.tbrhsc.com/patient_information/nutrition_articles/tomato.asp.

44. The World's Healthiest Foods, "Carrots," http://www.whfoods.org/genpage.php?tname=foodspice&dbid=21.

45. The World's Healthiest Foods, "Beets," http://www.whfoods.org/genpage.php?tname=foodspice&dbid=49.

46. See M. Warren Peary, *The 10 Biggest Diet Myths & Greatest Health Secrets Revealed* (Santa Fe, NM: The American Institute for Abundant Living, 2005), 53.

47. Geoffrey Harris, "Dr. Harris Finally Writes About a Potato," http://www.superfoodsrx.com/nutrition/nutritional-research/dr.-harris-finally-writes-about-a-potato.html.

48. Mayo Clinic, "Binge Eating Disorder—Treatment and Drugs," http://www.mayoclinic.com/health/binge-eating-disorder/DS00608/DSECTION=treatments-and-drugs.

49. Mayo Clinic, "Binge Eating Disorder—Lifestyle and Home Remedies."

Chapter 7—The World of Sexual Addiction

1. Mark Laaser, *Faithful & True: Sexual Integrity in a Fallen World* (Grand Rapids: Zondervan, 1996), 13.

2. Mark Laaser, *Faithful & True: Sexual Integrity in a Fallen World*, 14.

3. See J.P. Louw and Eugene A. Nida, *Greek-English Lexicon of the New Testament: Based on Semantic Domains,* 2d ed. (New York: United Bible Societies, 1989), 1:771.

4. W. E. Vine, Merrill F. Unger, and William White, Jr., *Vine's Complete Expository Dictionary of Biblical Words,* electronic ed. (Nashville: Thomas Nelson, 1996).

5. Keith Morrison, *Battling Sexual Addiction,* NBC News (February 24, 2004).

6. Candice Kim, "From Fantasy to Reality: The Link Between Viewing Child Pornography and Molesting Children," Child Sexual Exploitation Update, vol. 1, no. 3 (Alexandria, VA: American Prosecutor's Research Institute, 2004), http://www.ndaa.org/publications/newsletters/child_sexual_exploitation_update_volume_1_number_3_2004.html.

7. Keith Morrison, *Battling Sexual Addiction.*

8. *Merriam-Webster's Collegiate Dictionary* (2001), http://www.m-w.com.

9. Spiros Zodhiates, *The Complete Word Study Dictionary: New Testament,* electronic ed. (Chattanooga, TN: AMG Publishers, 2000), #4204.

10. For this section see Jerry R. Kirk, *A Winnable War: How to Fight Pornography in Your Community* (Pomona, CA: Focus on the Family, 1989), 6.

11. Kirk, *A Winnable War,* 6.

12. *Merriam-Webster's Online Dictionary,* s.v. "pedophilia."

13. See Marguerite S. Shaffer, ed., *Public Culture: Diversity, Democracy, and Community in the United States* (Philadelphia: University of Pennsylvania Press, 2008), 342.

14. Marnie C. Ferree, *No Stones: Women Redeemed from Sexual Shame* (Downers Grove, IL:InterVarsity, 2010), 84.

15. Marnie C. Ferree, L.I.F.E. Guide for Women (Xulon Press, n.d.), 13.

16. Marnie C. Ferree, *No Stones: Women Redeemed from Sexual Shame,* 127.

17. Marnie C. Ferree, *No Stones: Women Redeemed from Sexual Shame,* 65.

18. See also Patrick Carnes, *Out of the Shadows: Understanding Sexual Addiction* (Minneapolis, MN: CompCare, 1983), 54-55.

19. For this section see Carnes, *Out of the Shadows,* 9.

20. Debra Laaser, *Shattered Vows: Hope and Healing for Women Who Have Been Sexually Betrayed* (Grand Rapids: Zondervan, 2000), 93.

21. Debra Laaser, *Shattered Vows: Hope and Healing for Women Who Have Been Sexually Betrayed,* 93.

22. For basic beliefs that lead to addictions see also Carnes, *Out of the Shadows,* 77-85.

23. On the three God-given inner needs, see Lawrence J. Crabb, Jr., *Understanding People: Deep Longings for Relationship* (Grand Rapids: Zondervan, 1987), 15-16; Robert S. McGee, *The Search for Significance,* 2d ed. (Houston, TX: Rapha, 1990), 27-30.

24. Debra Laaser, *Shattered Vows: Hope and Healing for Women Who Have Been Sexually Betrayed,* 98.

25. For this section see also Carnes, *Out of the Shadows,* 7.

26. Debra Laaser, *Shattered Vows: Hope and Healing for Women Who Have Been Sexually Betrayed,* 94.

27. Marnie Ferree, "Female Sexual Addiction, Part 1" (New York: Vimeo, 2011), http://www.vimeo.com/3345157.

28. Science Daily, "Scientists Seek to Explain Why Spider Web Silk is so Strong" (n.p.: SciNews, 2011), http://scinewsblog.blogspot.com/2011/03/scientists-seek-to-explain-why-spider.html28. Science Daily, "Scientists Seek to Explain Why Spider Web Silk is so Strong" (n.p.: SciNews, 2011), http://scinewsblog.blogspot.com/2011/03/scientists-seek-to-explain-why-spider.html.

29. Mark Laaser, *Faithful & True: Sexual Integrity in a Fallen World,* 14.

30. See Carnes, *Out of the Shadows,* 98-99.

31. On the three God-given inner needs, see Crabb, *Understanding People,* 15-16; McGee, *The Search for Significance,* 27-30.

32. Ferree, "Female Sexual Addiction, Part 1."

33. See Crabb, *Understanding People,* 15-16; McGee, *The Search for Significance,* 27-30.

34. Mark Laaser, *Faithful & True: Sexual Integrity in a Fallen World,* 147.

35. Mark Laaser, *Faithful & True: Sexual Integrity in a Fallen World,* 147.

36. Marnie C. Ferree, *No Stones: Women Redeemed from Sexual Shame,* 157.

37. Marnie C. Ferree, *No Stones: Women Redeemed from Sexual Shame,* 159.

38. Debra Laaser, *Shattered Vows: Hope and Healing for Women Who Have Been Sexually Betrayed,* 177.

39. *Webster's Revised Unabridged Dictionary,* electronic ed. (Plainfield, NJ: MICRA, 1998).

40. Mark Laaser, *Faithful & True: Sexual Integrity in a Fallen World,* 153.

41. For the following suggestions see also Henry J. Rogers, *The Silent War: Ministering to Those Trapped in the Deception of Pornography* (Green Forest, AR: New Leaf, 2000), 142-46.

42. For further information see KidsHealth for Parents, "What Are STDs?" (Wilmington, DE: Nemours Foundation, n.d.), http://kidshealth.org/PageManager.jsp?dn=KidsHealth&lic=1&article_set=23006&cat_id=20046&&ps=106; Aim for Success, Staff Development and Community Leadership Manual (Dallas: Aim for Success, 2004), 17; *Is Sex Safe? A Look at: Sexually Transmitted Diseases (STDs)* (Boise, ID: Grapevine, 1997); The Medical Institute for Sexual Health, "Sexually Transmitted Diseases"; The Medical Institute for Sexual Health, http://www.medinstitute.org/content.php?name=FactsAboutCondoms; Ngozi A. Osondu, ed., "Your Guide to Sexually Transmitted Diseases" (WebMD Medical Reference), http://my.webmd.com/content/article/10/2953_51

1?z=3074_00000_1069_00_07; American Social Health Association, "Facts and Answers About STDs," http://www.ashastd.org/stdfaqs/index.html; Hepatitis B Foundation, "Statistics," http://www.hepb.org/hepb/.

Chapter 9—The Vital World of Crisis Intervention

1. For this section see StephenVan Cleave, Walter Byrd, and Kathy Revell, *Counseling for Substance Abuse and Addiction* (Dallas: W Pub Group, 1995) 83-6; Carolyn Johnson, *Understanding Alcoholism* (Grand Rapids: Zondervan, 1991), 145-50; Christina B. Parker, *When Someone You Love Drinks Too Much: A Christian Guide to Addiction, Codependence, & Recovery* (New York: Harper & Row, 1990), 55-56.
2. For this section see Van Cleave, Byrd, and Revell, *Counseling for Substance Abuse and Addiction,* 87.
3. For this section see Van Cleave, Byrd, and Revell, *Counseling for Substance Abuse and Addiction,* 86-87; Parker, *When Someone You Love Drinks Too Much,* 54-55.
4. Proverbs 27:6 (NLT).

Chapter 10—The Healing World of Rehab

1. These questions are from the Substance Abuse and Mental Health Services Administration (SAMHSA) and can be found at "Network of Care, a Quick Guide to Finding Effective Alcohol and Drug Addiction Treatment" (San Rafael, CA: Trinity Integrated Resources, 2011), http://ventura.networkofcare.org/veterans/library/detail.cfm?id=2302&cat=447.
2. Center for Substance Abuse Treatment, "Treatment Improvement Protocols" (Rockville, MD: Substance Abuse and Mental Health Services Administration, 1993), http://www.ncbi.nlm.nih.gov/books/NBK26171/.
3. Center for Substance Abuse Treatment, "Treatment Improvement Protocols."
4. See Caron Treatment Centers, "Current Statistics" (Wernersville, PA: Caron Pennsylvania, n.d.), http://www.caron.org/current-statistics.html.
5. See Caron Treatment Centers, "Current Statistics," http://www.caron.org/current-statistics.html.

Chapter 11—The 12-step World of Recovery

1. Alcoholics Anonymous World Services, *Twelve Steps and Twelve Traditions* (New York: Alcoholics Anonymous World Services, 2005), 16-17.
2. Alcoholics Anonymous World Services, *Twelve Steps and Twelve Traditions*, 15.
3. These steps are inspired by Alcoholics Anonymous World Services, *Twelve Steps and Twelve Traditions.*
4. The best-known version of the prayer is a shortened form adapted by Alcoholics Anonymous. Several other variants exist with only slight differences in pronoun usage.

Chapter 12—The Breakthrough World of Brain Imaging

1. Isaiah 40:29.
2. This section from Dr. Todd Clements, The Clements Clinic, Plano, TX.
3. John 20:25-28.

Chapter 13—The Crippling World of Codependency

1. *Merriam-Webster's Online Dictionary,* s.v. "co-."
2. Recommended Biblical Counseling Keys: *Anger, Codependency, Conflict Resolution, Depression, Dysfunctional Family, Fear, Guilt, Hope, Identity, Manipulation, Marriage, Rejection, Self-worth* (Dallas: Hope For The Heart, 1986–2011).
3. W.E. Vine, Merrill F. Unger, and William White, Jr., *Vine's Expository Dictionary of Biblical Words* (Nashville: Thomas Nelson, 1985), s.v. "burden, burdened, burdensome."
4. Vine, Unger, and White, *Vine's Expository Dictionary of Biblical Words,* s.v. "burden, burdened, burdensome."

SELECTED BIBLIOGRAPHY

Aim for Success. *Staff Development and Community Leadership Manual.* Dallas: Aim for Success, 2004.

American Psychiatric Association. *Diagnostic and Statistical Manual of Mental Disorders.* DSM-IV-TR 4th ed. Washington, DC: American Psychiatric Association, 2000.

Anderson, Neil T., and Dave Park. *Purity Under Pressure.* Eugene, OR: Harvest House, 1995.

Beck, James R. "Substance-Use Disorders." In *Baker Encyclopedia of Psychology.* Ed. David G. Benner, 1128-30. Grand Rapids: Baker, 1985.

Bustanoby, Andre. *When Your Child Is on Drugs or Alcohol.* San Bernardino, CA: Here's Hope, 1986.

Carnes, Patrick. *Out of the Shadows: Understanding Sexual Addiction.* Minneapolis, MN: CompCare, 1983.

Cheek, Ed. *Mickey Mantle: His Final Inning.* Garland, TX: ATS, n.d.

Coyle, Neva, and Marie Chapian. *The All-New Free to Be Thin.* rev. ed. Minneapolis, MN: Bethany House, 1993.

Crabb, Lawrence J., Jr. *Understanding People: Deep Longings for Relationship.* Grand Rapids: Zondervan, 1987.

Jantz, Gregory L., *Hope, Help & Healing for Eating Disorders: A New Approach to Treating Anorexia, Bulimia, & Overeating.* Wheaton, IL: Harold Shaw, 1995.

Hall, Laurie. *An Affair of the Mind: One Woman's Courageous Battle to Salvage Her Family from the Devastation of Pornography.* Colorado Springs: Focus on the Family, 1996.

Hall, Laurie Sharlene. *The Cleavers Don't Live Here Anymore: Bringing Hope and Radical Forgiveness to the Bewilderment, Betrayal, and Bitterness of Real Family Life.* Ann Arbor, MI: Vine, 2000.

Hunt, June. *Bonding with Your Teen through Boundaries.* Wheaton, IL: Crossway, 2010.

Hunt, June. *Counseling Through Your Bible Handbook.* Eugene, OR: Harvest House, 2008.

Hunt, June. *Hope for Your Heart: Finding Strength in Life's Storms.* Wheaton, IL: Crossway, 2011.

Hunt, June. *How to Forgive...When You Don't Feel Like It.* Eugene, OR: Harvest House, 2007.

Hunt, June. *How to Handle Your Emotions.* Eugene, OR: Harvest House, 2008.

Hunt, June. *How to Rise Above Abuse,* Eugene, OR: Harvest House, 2010.

Hunt, June. *Keeping Your Cool...When Your Anger Is Hot!* Eugene, OR: Harvest House, 2009.

Hunt, June. *Seeing Yourself Through God's Eyes.* Eugene, OR: Harvest House, 2008.

Institute for Health Policy, Brandeis University. "Substance Abuse: The Nation's Number One Health Problem; Key Indicators for Policy." October 1993. The Robert Wood Johnson Foundation. http://said.dol.gov/htree13.

Is Sex Safe? A Look at: Sexually Transmitted Diseases (STDs). Boise, ID: Grapevine, 1997.

Johnson, Carolyn. *Understanding Alcoholism.* Grand Rapids: Zondervan, 1991.

Kirk, Jerry R. *A Winnable War: How to Fight Pornography in Your Community.* Pomona, CA: Focus on the Family, 1989.

Mantle, Merlyn, et al., with Mickey Herskowitz. *A Hero All His Life: A Memoir by the Mantle Family*. New York: HarperCollins, 1996.

McGee, Robert S. *The Search for Significance*. 2nd ed. Houston, TX: Rapha, 1990.

McGee, Robert S., Pat Springle, and Susan Joiner. *Rapha's Twelve-Step Program for Overcoming Chemical Dependency: with Support Materials from The Search for Significance*. 2d ed. Houston, TX: Rapha, 1990.

Milam, Jarmes R., and Katherine Ketcham. *Under the Influence*. New York: Bantam, 1983.

Minirth, Frank, Paul Meier, Robert Hemfelt, Sharon Sneed, and Don Hawkins. *Love Hunger*. Nashville: Thomas Nelson, 1990.

Morris, Marilyn. *ABC's of the Birds and Bees for Parents of Toddlers to Teens*. 2d ed. Dallas: Charles River, 2000.

Morris, Marilyn. *Choices that Lead to Lifelong Success*. Dallas: Charles River, 1998.

Morris, Marilyn. *Teens, Sex and Choices*. 3d ed. Dallas: Charles River, 2004.

Parker, Christina B. *When Someone You Love Drinks Too Much: A Christian Guide to Addiction, Codependence, & Recovery*. New York: Harper & Row, 1990.

Perkins, Bill. *Fatal Attractions: Overcoming Our Secret Addictions*. Eugene, OR: Harvest House, 1991.

Rogers, Henry J. *The Silent War: Ministering to Those Trapped in the Deception of Pornography*. Green Forest, AR: New Leaf, 1999.

Rogers, Ronald, and Chandler Scott McMillin. *Under Your Own Power: A Guide to Recovery for Nonbelievers…and the Ones Who Love Them*. New York: G.P. Putnam's Sons, 1992.

Ross, George R. *Treating Adolescent Substance Abuse: Understanding the Fundamental Elements*. Boston: Allyn and Bacon, 1993.

Schaumburg, Harry W. *False Intimacy: Understanding the Struggle of Sexual Addiction*. Colorado Springs: NavPress, 1992.

Shaughnessy, Collette. *Reachout. Q & A Columns*. March 1999. Lowe Family Foundation. http://www.lowefamily.org/reachout/mar99.html (accessed October 22, 2003).

Substance Abuse and Mental Health Services Administration. "Summary of Findings from the 2000 National Household Survey on Drug Abuse (NHSDA Series: H-13, DHHS Publication No. SMA 01-3549)." 2001. US Department of Health and Human Services. http://www.samhsa.gov/oas/2k2/suicide/suicide.pdf.

Taylor, Elizabeth J., ed. *Dorland's Illustrated Medical Dictionary*. 27th ed. Philadelphia, PA: W.B. Saunders, 1988.

US Department of Transportation, National Highway Traffic Safety Administration. "Traffic Safety Facts 2001: A Compilation of Motor Vehicle Crash Data from the Fatality Analysis Reporting System and the General Estimates System." 2001. http://www-nrd.nhtsa.dot.gov/pdf/nrd-30/NCSA/TSFAnn/TSF2001.pdf.

Van Cleave, Stephen, Walter Byrd, and Kathy Revell. *Counseling for Substance Abuse and Addiction*. Resources for Christian Counseling, ed. Gary R. Collins, vol. 12. Dallas: Word, 1987.

Van Pelt, Nancy. "Straight Talk About Sexual Purity." Hope for the Family. http://www.lovetakestime.com/art-straighttalk.html.

VanVonderen, Jeff. *Good News for the Chemically Dependent and Those Who Love Them*, rev. ed. Nashville: Thomas Nelson, 1991.

Vath, Raymond E. *Counseling Those with Eating Disorders*. Resources for Christian Counseling, ed. Gary R. Collins, vol. 4. Waco, TX: Word, 1986.

White, John. *Eros Redeemed: Breaking the Stranglehold of Sexual Sin*. Downers Grove, IL: InterVarsity, 1993.

The World's Best Anatomical Charts: Diseases and Disorders. Skokie, IL: Anatomical Chart Company, 2000.

Other Harvest House Books by June Hunt

Counseling Through Your Bible Handbook
The Bible is richly relevant when it comes to the difficult dilemmas of life. Here are 50 chapters of spiritual wisdom and compassionate counsel on issues such as anger, adultery, depression, fear, guilt, grief, rejection, and self-worth.

How to Rise Above Abuse
Compassionate, practical, hands-on guidance for the toughest issues to talk about—childhood sexual abuse, spiritual abuse, verbal and emotional abuse, victimization, and wife abuse. Filled with the hope and healing only Christ can give.

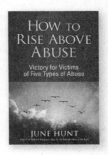

How to Handle Your Emotions
In Scripture, God gives counsel that helps us process our full range of emotions in a healthy way. Learn how to better navigate your emotions by understanding their definitions, characteristics, and causes, as well as the solutions that lead to emotional growth.

How to Forgive...When You Don't Feel Like It
Though we know God has called us to forgive, we find ourselves asking hard questions: What if it hurts too much to forgive? What if the other person isn't sorry? How can I let the other person off the hook for doing something so wrong? June Hunt speaks from experience as she offers biblical answers, hope, and true freedom through forgiveness.

Keeping Your Cool... When Your Anger Is Hot

This book explores the causes and kinds of anger and the biblical steps toward resolution. You will learn how to identify the triggers of anger, ways of dealing with past angers, what the Bible says about righteous and unrighteous anger, and how to bring about real and lasting change.

Seeing Yourself Through God's Eyes

How you view yourself can have a profound effect on your everyday living. The key is to see yourself through God's eyes. Discover the great riches of your identity in Christ in the 31 devotions in this book.

About the Author

ne Hunt is founder and CEO of **Hope For The Heart** (www.HopeForTheHeart .org) and is a rnamic Christian leader who has yielded landmark contributions to the field of Christian coun- ling. Hope For The Heart provides biblically based counsel in 24 languages and has worked in 60 untries on six continents. June, who celebrated 25 years of ministry in 2011, is also an author, eaker, musician, and has served as guest professor to a variety of colleges and seminaries.

arly family pain shaped June's heart of compassion. Her bizarre family background left her feel- g hopeless and caused June to contemplate "drastic solutions." But when June entered into a life- anging relationship with Jesus Christ, the trajectory of her life was forever altered. As a result, she ew passionate about helping people face life's tough circumstances.

s a youth director, June became aware of the need for real answers to real questions. Her personal periences with pain and her practical experience with youth and parents led June into a lifelong ommitment to *Providing God's Truth for Today's Problems*. She earned a master's in counseling at riswell College in 2007 and has been presented with two honorary doctorates.

etween 1989 and 1992, June Hunt developed and taught *Counseling Through the Bible*, a scrip- urally based counseling course addressing 100 topics in categories such as marriage and family, motional entrapments and cults, as well as addictions, abuse, and apologetics. Since then, the oursework has been continuously augmented and refined, forming the basis for the *Biblical Coun- ling Library*. Her *Biblical Counseling Keys* became the foundation of the ministry's expansion, cluding the 2002 creation of the *Hope Biblical Counseling Institute* (BCI) initiated by Criswell College to equip spiritual leaders, counselors, and people with hearts to help others with practical olutions for life's most pressing problems.

he *Biblical Counseling Keys* provide a foundation for the ministry's two daily radio programs, *Hope or The Heart* and *Hope In The Night*, both hosted by June. *Hope For The Heart* is a half-hour of inter- ctive teaching heard on over 100 radio outlets across America, and *Hope In The Night* is June's live wo-hour call-in counseling program. Together, both programs air domestically and internationally n more than 1000 stations. In 1986, the National Religious Broadcasters (NRB) honored *Hope For he Heart* as "Best New Radio Program" and awarded it Radio Program of the Year in 1989. Women n Christian Media presented June Hunt with an Excellence in Communications award in 2008. The inistry received NRB's Media Award for International Strategic Partnerships in 2010.

As an accomplished musician, June has been a guest on numerous national TV and radio programs, ncluding NBC's *Today*. She has toured overseas with the USO and has been a guest soloist at Billy Graham Crusades. June communicates her message of hope on five music recordings: *The Whisper f My Heart*, *Hymns of Hope*, *Songs of Surrender*, *Shelter Under His Wings*, and *The Hope of Christmas*.

June Hunt's numerous books include *Seeing Yourself Through God's Eyes*, *How to Forgive... When You Don't Feel Like It*, *Counseling Through Your Bible Handbook*, *How to Handle Your Emotions*, *How to Rise Above Abuse*, *Bonding with Your Teen through Boundaries*, *Keeping Your Cool... When Your Anger Is Hot*, *Caring for a Loved One with Cancer* (June is a cancer survivor), and *Hope for Your Heart: Finding Strength in Life's Storms*. She is also a contributor to the *Soul Care Bible* and the *Women's Devotional Bible*.

June Hunt resides in Dallas, Texas, home of the international headquarters of Hope For The Heart.